Barnsley Libraries

...ET LAW

... Wild, Mr Stuart Weinstein
...nd Mr Neil MacEwan

OLD BAILEY PRESS

OLD BAILEY PRESS
at Holborn College, Woolwich Road,
Charlton, London, SE7 8LN

First published 2005

© Dr Charles Wild, Mr Stuart Weinstein and Mr Neil MacEwan 2005.

ISBN 1 85836 573 2

British Library Cataloguing-in-Publication.

A CIP Catalogue record for this book is available from the British
Library.

Printed and bound in Great Britain.

Contents

e-Crime

Preface

This book is the first to combine the formerly disparate aspects of what we have termed 'Internet Law'. Consequently, it brings together, in one text, the law relating to Internet contracts, e-Finance, Private International Law, Intellectual Property, Encryption, Data Protection and e-Crime. The evolution of the Internet charts a transition from a restricted, academic and predominantly theoretical concept to an open-access, commercially driven, global medium. Its growth has brought concomitant legal concerns which have required responses from both national and international law. This book will appeal to undergraduate and postgraduate students who seek a critical introduction to this important, ever-growing legal arena. The authors would like to thank the staff at Old Bailey Press for their continued encouragement, support and patience during the writing and editorial processes of this book.

Charles Wild
Stuart Weinstein
Neil MacEwan

July 2005

Table of Cases

Table of Statutes and Other Materials

e-Commerce

1 Domain Names, Trademarks and Passing Off

1.1 Domain Names

1.2 Trademarks

1.3 Passing Off

Increasingly, we live in a world of 'singular brands'. By this, we mean that if you were to visit China, you would see many of the brands that are common to the high street in England. For instance, a trip to China would find you looking at advertised products featuring the football player, David Beckham, soft drinks products such as Coca Cola®, computer software manufactured by Microsoft®, and cigarette brands such as Dunhill® and Marlboro®.

The Internet, in fact, is not very different. If you were to surf the Net, you would find the very same brands that you see on television, in the newspapers and on the street. The question raised by this is very simple: how does a brand protect its goodwill and reputation on the Internet? The answer to this question can be found in a discussion of domain names, trademarks and passing off.

1.1 Domain Names

The Domain Name System (DNS) helps users find their way around the Internet. Every computer on the Internet has a unique address called its 'IP address' (Internet Protocol address). Because IP addresses (which are strings of numbers) are hard to remember, the DNS allows a familiar string of letters (the 'domain name') to be used instead. So rather than typing '192.0.34.65,' you can type 'www.icann.org'.[1]

Within the DNS, the Internet Corporation for Assigned Names and Numbers (ICANN) – an internationally organized, non-profit corporation – has responsibility for IP address space allocation, protocol identifier assignment, generic (gTLD) and country code (ccTLD) Top-Level Domain name system management, and root server system management functions. ICANN performs these functions, formerly performed under United States Government contract, by the Internet Assigned Numbers Authority (IANA) and other entities. ICANN now performs the IANA function.[2] ICANN is responsible for coordinating the management of the technical elements of the DNS to ensure universal resolvability so that all users of the Internet can find all valid addresses.[3] It does this by overseeing the distribution of unique technical identifiers

---

[1] This illustration and the information that relates can be found at: http://www.icann.org/general/.
[2] Ibid.
[3] Ibid.

used in the Internet's operations, and delegating Top-Level Domain names (such as .com, .info, etc).[4]

In the UK, Nominet UK (Nominet) is the Government recognised registry for United Kingdom Internet names.[5] Nominet's website[6] points out that the United Kingdom country code is separated into sub-categories, called Second Level Domains (SLDs) in which individuals and entities may register a domain name within the SLD that corresponds to their type of activity. SLDs managed by Nominet include:

*   .co.uk for commercial enterprises (the largest SLD in the UK);

*   .me.uk for personal domains;

*   .org.uk for non-commercial organisations;

*   .ltd and .plc for registered company names only;

*   .net.uk for Internet Service Providers; and

*   .sch.uk for schools.[7]

However, some United Kingdom SLDs are not managed by Nominet and are managed by other companies and organisations. They are:

*   .ac.uk for academic establishments;

*   .gov.uk for government bodies;

*   .nhs.uk for NHS organisations;

*   .police.uk for United Kingdom police forces; and

*   .mod.uk for United Kingdom Ministry of Defence entities.[8]

The general requirement for a domain name is, first, that it must be unique. A domain name similar to another is inherently problematic. While there are no set rules for what makes for a successful domain name, essentially it is one that precisely identifies the host, sets forth its general purpose/function (eg, a business, academic establishment, not for profit organisation or governmental agency) and specifies whether it is international or domestic in scope (should the business be registered as '.com' as opposed to '.co.uk'?).

It should be noted that domain names are not necessarily trademarks: however, they are considered in many ways similar to trademarks as they perform the same function on the Internet – identifying the maker of the particular goods or the provider of certain services.

Just because an entity has a registered trademark, this does not automatically entitle such entity to the right to use that mark as its domain name.[9] Similarly, because the

---

[4] Ibid.
[5] See http://www.nic.uk for more information.
[6] Ibid.
[7] Ibid.
[8] Ibid.
[9] http://www.patent.gov.uk/tm/whatis/domain.htm.

same mark may be registered by different proprietors for different goods or services, someone else may also have legitimately registered the mark as their domain name.[10] Conversely, if an entity has a registered domain name, it does not automatically entitle that entity to a trademark in the same name.[11]

The United Kingdom Patent Office (UKPO) points out that even if a domain name has been properly registered, a similar trademark may not satisfy the basic requirements for trademark registration, or it may be confusingly similar with someone else's earlier mark.[12] If someone else has registered a domain that an entity believes should belong to it, the UKPO suggests that such entity seek legal advice and pursue dispute resolution procedures such as those operated, for example, by the World Intellectual Property Organization (WIPO).[13]

Both ICANN and Nominet employ dispute resolution procedures to avoid being dragged into court in the event of a dispute over a particular domain name. For instance, with respect to ICANN, all registrars in the .biz, .com, .info, .name, .net, and .org top-level domains follow the Uniform Domain Name Dispute-Resolution Policy[14] (often referred to as the 'UDRP').[15] Under the UDRP, most types of trademark-based domain name disputes must be resolved by agreement, court action, or arbitration before a registrar will cancel, suspend, or transfer a domain name.[16] Disputes alleged to arise from abusive registrations of domain names (for example, cybersquatting) may be addressed by expedited administrative proceedings that the holder of trademark rights initiates by filing a complaint with an approved dispute-resolution service provider.[17] To invoke the policy, a trademark owner should either file a complaint in a court of proper jurisdiction against the domain name holder (or where appropriate an in-rem action concerning the domain name), or in cases of abusive registration submit a complaint to an approved dispute-resolution service provider.[18]

Nominet operates its own dispute resolution service (DRS) for the very small proportion of disputes that occur with respect to TLD registrations in the United Kingdom. Nominet estimates that this figure is approximately 0.05 per cent of all registrations.[19] However, a dispute may arise when one party feels they have a greater right to use a domain name. The DRS does not replace the role of the courts: however, the decision is binding on the parties involved.[20] As a result of a DRS decision, Nominet does have the power to transfer, cancel or suspend the domain name registration.[21] If either party is dissatisfied with the outcome of the Nominet DRS, they

---

[10] Ibid.
[11] Ibid.
[12] Ibid.
[13] http://www.arbiter.wipo.int.
[14] http://www.icann.org/udrp/udrp.htm.
[15] Ibid.
[16] Ibid.
[17] Ibid.
[18] Ibid.
[19] http://www.nic.uk/DisputeResolution/AboutTheDrs/.
[20] Ibid.
[21] Ibid.

may appeal within five working days of the decision being made.[22] The appeal will be heard by a panel of three members selected by Nominet.[23]

The UKPO issues some specific guidelines in its work manual for staff[24] which they are to use when examining a proposed mark incorporating a domain name. Chapter 6, section 28 of the work manual, entitled 'Domain Names and Section 3(1) [Trademarks Act 1994]', offers the following guidance:

'A domain name is a written representation of an Internet electronic address, eg www.patent.gov.uk, which is the [UK Patent] Office's website. It is common-place for goods and services to be sold in the UK under such a name, ie, the domain name is being used as a trade name or trademark, and the Registrar will, subject to the usual criteria of the Act, permit domain names to be registered as trademarks.

Elements of the domain name such as ".com" or ".co.uk" are to be considered totally non-distinctive, much in the same way as "Ltd" or "Plc". As a general rule, one should consider whether the remainder of the mark is descriptive or non-descriptive; if so, there is likely to be an objection under s3(1)(b) of the Act.

There may be exceptions. For example, TWIST AND SEAL would be liable to an objection for storage jars on the basis that it describes a characteristic of the goods, whereas the addition of ".COM" gives the sign as a whole trademark character.'[25]

And, of course, if all else fails, the holder of a register trademark may have legal remedies against someone who has registered the domain name simply for the purpose of profiting by its sale to the rightful trademark owner.[26] An overview of trademarks and the legal remedies available when a trademark is infringed follows.

1.2 Trademarks

A trademark identifies the maker of a particular product or the provider of a particular service and acts as the customer's kite mark that the product or service he or she is purchasing is of a certain standard or quality. One need only conjure up the associations in one's head with the trademark Rolls Royce® to appreciate the value of such a trademark for a brand.

Trademarks allow the owner of a mark to register them on the Register of Trademarks – a publicly-accessible roll of marks – upon proof of qualification. Once this is done, a greater level of protection can be expected. This property right is not granted without reciprocal responsibilities; ie, the continuing obligation to exploit and use the trademark. Registration is essential for a trademark to be granted. This is quite different from copyright in which the creation of a copyrighted work, by itself, conveys rights under law. A trademark is valid as long as it is being used in commercial activity. In addition to disuse, a trademark can become worthless if it takes on a generic meaning that no longer distinguishes one product from all others.

---

[22] Ibid.
[23] Ibid.
[24] Available at: http://www.patent.gov.uk/tm/reference/workman/chapt6/chaptersix.pdf.
[25] Ibid.
[26] Op cit at footnote 9.

Under s1 Trademarks Act (TMA) 1994[27] as amended[28], an undertaking[29] may register '… any sign capable of being represented graphically which is capable of distinguishing goods or services of one undertaking from those of other undertakings'.

Anything that can be used to identify a business – an 'identifier' – to distinguish one product from another or one service from another can be trademarked. This is subject to the proviso that the general public will recognise the identifier as a precise way to differentiate the business from another.

Under the TMA 1994, any or all of the following may constitute a trademark:

- words (including personal names);
- designs;
- letters;
- numerals;
- the shape of goods or their packaging;
- colours;
- musical tones; and
- smells.[30]

The main qualification for a trademark is that it distinguishes the goods and/or services of one undertaking from those of another. In order for goods or services to be registered, a trademark must:

- be capable of graphical representation;
- be distinctive;
- not be descriptive; and
- not be excluded under TMA 1994 (eg, excluded for public policy).

Section 3 of the TMA 1994 sets forth both the absolute and relative grounds for refusal of registration.

Absolute grounds for refusal of a trademark include an application for a mark that:

- fails to satisfy the requirements of the TMA 1994, s1(1);
- is devoid of distinctive character;

---

[27] The Trademarks Act 1994 was passed in order that the UK be in compliance with Directive 89/104/EC, OJ 2989 L 40/1 (the European Trademark Directive).

[28] Trademarks Act 1994 as amended by: the Trademarks (EC Measures Relating to Counterfeit Goods) Regulations 1995 (SI 1995/1444) (1 July 1995); s13 of the Olympic Symbol, etc (Protection) Act 1995 (21 September 1995); Part IV of the Patents and Trademarks (World Trade Organisation) Regulations 1999 (SI 1999/1899) (29 July 1999); s6 of the Copyright, etc and Trademarks (Offences and Enforcement) Act 2002 (20 November 2002); and the Trademarks (Proof of Use, etc) Regulations 2004 (SI 2004/946) (5 May 2004).

[29] An 'undertaking' is the term of art used in the TMA 1994 to identify a trademark holder.

[30] TMA 1994, s1(1) et seq.

- consists exclusively of descriptive elements;
- consists exclusively of terms that are customary in the specific trade in which the trademark is sought;
- is of a shape purely functional in nature; or
- is contrary to public policy.[31]

Relative grounds exist (s5 TMA 1994) for refusal of an application for registration of a trademark. This is a situation where both the trademark and the services or goods they identify are not in their own right unique enough to distinguish them from other trademarks, goods or services. Relative grounds exist in relation to other trademarks, goods or services. They include:

- when the proposed trademark is identical to an earlier trademark and the goods or service for which the trademark is applied for are identical to those for which the earlier trademark protects;
- when the proposed trademark is identical or similar to an earlier trademark and the goods or services for which the trademark is applied for are similar goods or services; or
- when the proposed trademark is similar to the earlier trademark and is to be used for identical goods or service.[32]

Two primary trademark infringement situations arise where:

- an identical or similar mark is used in respect of goods or services which are identical or similar to those forming the subject of the trademark and where there is a consequential likelihood of confusion on the part of the public; or
- the identical or similar mark is used but the goods or services are not identical or similar to those forming the subject of the trademark.[33]

In the latter instance, the applicant is in essence 'piggy backing' on the reputation of the established trademark to bolster its market. Section 10(3) of the TMA 1994 protects against the dilution of the distinctive nature of the trademark. Thus, where 'the trademark has a reputation in the United Kingdom and where its reproduction takes unfair advantage of, or is detrimental to the distinctive character or repute of the trademark'.[34] Additionally, if a trademark application is made in bad faith, it will not be registered or, if it has already been registered, its registration will be stricken from the trademark.[35] Use of a competitor's trademark in the context of honest comparative advertising is permitted pursuant to s10(6).

---

[31] TMA 1994, s3.
[32] TMA 1994, s9.
[33] TMA 1994, s10.
[34] Ibid.
[35] *Road Tech Computer Systems Ltd* v *Unison Software (UK) Ltd* [1996] FSR 805 discusses 'bad faith' for TMA 1994 purposes. *Gromax Plasticulture Ltd* v *Don & Low Nonwovens Ltd* [1999] RPC 367 expands on this concept.

Once registration in the United Kingdom is awarded, the holder of the trademark has the right to use the trademark pursuant to s9 TMA 1994. The types of acts that may infringe are set forth in s10 TMA 1994. An examination of these infringing acts reveals that they are similar to the relative grounds set forth in s3 TMA 1994.

Exceptions to infringements are contained in s11 TMA 1994:

• use by a person of his own name or address;

• use of indications of the kind, quality, quantity, intended purpose, value, geographical origin, the time of production of goods or rendering of services, or other characteristics of goods or services;

• use, where necessary, to indicate where necessary, the intended purpose of a product or service, in particular, as accessories or spare parts; or

• use of an earlier right in a particular locality.

Section 11 TMA 1994 provides that when two trademarks are legitimately registered in different classes, there is in principle no infringement.

Registration of a trademark lasts for ten years and the renewal period is also for ten years.[36] However, there is no upper limit to the duration of a trademark, which can be renewed perpetually, so long as the mark has not been dormant for a period of five or more years.[37]

A European Community trademark[38] may be registered which will be valid in all EU Member States with only one central application being submitted to the Office for Harmonisation in the Internal Market (Trademarks and Designs) based in Alicante, Spain. The Community trademark operates simultaneously with the national systems in place in Member States.

At the international level, the Madrid Protocol[39] provides for a system of international recognition of trademarks in that recognition in one signatory country will generally be recognised in another. The system is organised by the World Intellectual Property Organisation (WIPO) and offers a trademark owner the possibility to have his trademark protected in several countries by simply filing one application directly with his own national or regional trademark office.[40] An international mark so registered is equivalent to an application or a registration of the same mark effected directly in each of the countries designated by the applicant.[41] If the trademark office of a designated country does not refuse protection within a specified period, the protection of the mark is the same as if it had been registered by that particular office.[42] The

---

[36] TMA 1994, s42.
[37] TMA 1994, s43.
[38] TMA 1994, s51 indicates that a 'Community trademark' has the meaning given by art 1(1) of the Community Trademark Regulation (Council Regulation (EC) No 40/94 of 20 December 1993) on the Community trademark.
[39] TMA 1994, s53, the 'Madrid Protocol' means the Protocol relating to the Madrid Agreement Concerning the International Registration of Marks, adopted at Madrid on 27 June 1989. For the full text and other information about the Madrid Protocol see: http://www.wipo.int/madrid/en.
[40] http://www.wipo.int/madrid/en.
[41] Ibid.
[42] Ibid.

Madrid system also simplifies greatly the subsequent management of the mark, since it is possible to record subsequent changes or to renew the registration through a single procedural step.[43] Further countries may be designated subsequently in addition to the 77 members that are signatories to the Madrid Protocol.[44]

There are 45 international classes of goods and services that can attract protection.[45] Each class requires a separate registration unless the registrant proceeds with a multi-class registration. It is possible for the same trademark to be registered in different classes or for the same trademark to cohabit in several different classes. The fees charged by the UKPO are dependant upon how many different classes an applicant chooses to put the mark in.

In order for a web-based infringement of a UK registered trademark to occur, the offending mark must be displayed on a website that is actively involved in soliciting commerce from the UK.[46] Mere registration of a trademark is not sufficient to provide an adequate basis for bringing an infringement claim; rather, the mark which is offended must actively pursue commerce in the territory where it has legal effect.[47]

In *800 FLOWERS Inc* v *Phonenames Ltd* [2002] FSR 12, the Court of Appeal upheld the ruling of Jacob J in *800 FLOWERS Trade Mark* [2000] FSR 697. Jacob J concluded that in the absence of UK commercial activity, an American company could not be truly said to be using the trademark '800 FLOWERS' which it had registered in the UK in order to provide others in the future the opportunity to develop a toll-free service to receive consumer orders for flowers for forwarding to a network of participating florists. Buxton LJ wrote in the Court of Appeal opinion:

'... the very idea of "use" within a certain area would seem to require some active step in that area on the part of the user that goes beyond providing facilities that enable others to bring the mark into the area.'[48]

Sometimes the Internet gives rise to infringing uses of a trademark that are technically based and, for the most part, remain largely invisible to the general public. One such circumstance involves the use of meta-tags in constructing a webpage in HTML:

'In addition to analyzing the displayed text, the titles and the addresses of Web pages, search engines make particular use of meta-tag keywords. Meta-tag keywords consist of text coding which is hidden from normal view and located within a specially designated portion of the HTML code which generates the Web page. Web page designers use this hidden HTML code to designate keywords which are communicated to search engine software. This is an important associational tool for the Web page designer since search engines are often unable to properly index a particular Web page based on the text of the page. In its cooperation with a search engine, a meta-tag keyword may be thought of as a "pre-hyperlink" since a hyperlink is often created by a search engine in a search results phase when a user performs a search using that keyword. Unfortunately, uses of trademarks

---

[43] Ibid.
[44] http://www.wipo.int/madrid/members.
[45] TMA 1994, s34.
[46] *800 FLOWERS Inc* v *Phonenames Ltd* [2002] FSR 12.
[47] Ibid.
[48] [2002] FSR 12 at 15. See Scottish case *Bonnier Media Ltd* v *Greg Lloyd Smith and Kestrel Trading Corp* (unreported) 1 July 2002.

in ways which cause search engines to improperly associate Web pages with those trademarks have created allegations of intellectual property violations.'[49]

In *Reed Executive plc* v *Reed Business Information Ltd* [2003] RPC 12, this very issue came up. The employment agency, Reed, had registered its name 'REED' as a trademark for employment agency services. The defendant, a business using the name Reed as well, started its own employment agency/recruitment website known as totaljobs.com and employed the name 'REED' as one of its meta-tags. Was this invisible use of the trademark Reed in a meta-tag a sufficient use for infringement purposes? The court, namely Mr Justice Pumfrey, concluded that it was. If the invisible use diverts potential clients from the trademark proprietor's site, then this commercial effect is real and damaging to the trademark holder.[50] Given that the use of the trademark was without the trademark holder's permission and that the trade involved was the very same type of business as that of the trademark holder, it is not surprising that the invisible meta-tags gave rise to such a trademark infringement claim here.

Most recently, a court in France ruled in *Societe des Hotels Meridien* v *SARL Google France* (judgment of 16 December 2004, Nanterre Court (TGI)) that the Google French subsidiary infringed the trademarks of Le Meridien by allowing competitors to bid on these marks as keywords and have advertisements appear prominently in search results.[51] The court singled out the Google AdWords Keyword Tool because it suggests keywords that an advertiser can purchase after the advertiser inputs terms of interest. The problem is that the list of suggested words includes trademarks. This case is similar, in reasoning, to the UK *Reed* case.

The interrelation between the Internet and trademark law comes into play in the context of 'cybersquatting'. Cybersquatting was a practice consisting of registering well-known names as domain names to benefit from the 'first come, first serve' rule that characterised the domain name registration system of the Internet's early days.

A corollary to the problem of 'first come, first serve' was the fact that domain name registries did not ask for, nor seek proof of, the right of a proposed registrant to legitimately use the name he or she was seeking to register. As a result, many businesses found themselves in the unfortunate situation of having to pay 'good money' to 'cybersquatters' to acquire the right to use their own brand names as Internet domain names.

1.3 Passing Off

The trademark registration system provides rights holders with a greater level of

---

[49] Jeffrey R Juester, Peter A Nieves, 'Hyperlinks, Frames and Meta-tags: An Intellectual Property Analysis' (1998) JL & Tech 243, 247.
[50] [2003] RPC 12 at 17. Mr Justice Pumfrey rejected the defendant's claim that they were entitled to rely on TMA 1994, s11(2) in that they were using their own name, Reed, to promote their own business. Here, it was thought that the invisible use by the defendants of the name 'Reed' as a meta-tag was not actual use of the same name to promote the defendant's own business, but rather, a sophisticated way to divert search engines from the trademark holder's website to theirs.
[51] Available at: http://www.juriscom.net/jpt/visu.php?ID=631.

protection than afforded by common law actions, such as 'passing off'. A 'passing off' action is one designed to prevent one party from 'passing off' his or her goods or services as those of another. The TMA 1994 as amended[52] still preserves the right of trademark owners to bring a common law 'passing off' action. This common law action is in addition to a trademark infringement claim that may be brought pursuant to the TMA 1994. It is particularly useful if one has, for instance, a brand name that is too common for it to be trademarked, eg, McDonalds or Sainsbury. A claim of 'passing off' involves a misrepresentation made by a business entity in the course of its business to a potential customer that is designed to injure (or is reasonably foreseeable to injure) the business or goodwill of a competitor resulting in damage (or likely damage) to such a competitor.[53]

In *Marks & Spencer plc* v *One in a Million Ltd* [1998] FSR 265, some of the largest retail outfits in the UK brought action against an Internet domain name dealer. The Internet domain name dealer had registered the names of companies such as British Telecom, Marks & Spencer and Sainsbury and then had the cheek to sell the domain names back to them. The claimants, justifiably upset that they were asked 'to pony up' millions of pounds to buy back the inherent goodwill in their own business names from a clever interloper, went to court seeking injunctive relief. The injunctive relief sought an order that the defendant transfer to each appropriate company the domain name registration belonging to their name. The injunction was granted. The defendant's appeal was dismissed on the grounds that the trial court had jurisdiction to grant the relief sought. Where 'blocking registrations' were involved and made for the purpose of obtaining money from rightful owners of the goodwill attached to the registered names, in order to prevent fraud, a court has the power to invoke the 'passing off' doctrine to prevent injustice.[54] In sum, these court decisions and others illustrate the established rule that UK 'passing off' law will not allow clever persons to 'cybersquat' domain names to make them in essence an instrument of fraud. When this is combined with the Nominet dispute resolution policy[55] which can bind those who participate in Nominet proceedings, the end result is to eliminate 'cybersquatting' in the UK.[56]

A second vexing situation in which the UK courts have dealt with is what happens when two or more entities make concurrent use of a single name. Given that there

---

[52] Trademarks Act 1994, as amended by the Trademarks (EC Measures Relating to Counterfeit Goods) Regulations 1995 (SI 1995/1444) (1 July 1995); s13 of the Olympic Symbol etc (Protection) Act 1995 (21 September 1995); Part IV of the Patents and Trademarks (World Trade Organisation) Regulations 1999 (SI 1999/1899) (29 July 1999); s6 of the Copyright, etc and Trademarks (Offences and Enforcement) Act 2002 (20 November 2002); and the Trademarks (Proof of Use, etc) Regulations 2004 (SI 2004/946) (5 May 2004).

[53] *Erven Warnink Besloten Vennotschap* v *Townend & Sons (Hull) Ltd* [1979] AC 731. The case here involved defendants making an inferior 'knock-off' version of claimant's famed advocaat liqueur with the effect of capturing the claimant's UK market share for its product.

[54] *British Telecommunications plc* v *One in a Million Ltd* [1999] RPC 1. See also *EasyJet Airline Co Ltd* v *Dainty (T/A easyRealestate)* [2002] FSR 6, summary judgment granted to claimants where it was clear that the defendant sought to take unfair advantage of the goodwill of the claimants to build up its own website.

[55] The UK has not adopted the ICANN Uniform Name Dispute Resolution Policy but follows Nominet's policy on the same.

[56] This is not to say that in all cases there may not be legitimate domain name disputes where entities actually share the same name but may be operating in different jurisdictions, etc.

are 45 categories for goods and services that the UKPO will issue a trademark for, it is not surprising that two legitimate entities may make use of the same trademark or name for different categories of goods and services.

In the context of domain names, the case of *Pitman Training Ltd* v *Nominet UK*[57] is instructive. In this case, there were two companies which applied to Nominet UK to register the names 'pitman.co.uk' and 'pitman.com'. First, Pitman – the publishing entity in operation since 1849 and now acquired by Pearson – applied in February 1996 to Nominet UK for the right to use the two domain names and was granted these rights. Second, in March 1996, a second entity, Pitman Training, applied to Nominet UK for the right to use 'pitman.co.uk'. By some mishap, Pitman Training's application to Nominet UK was approved and it was granted the right to use the domain name 'pitman.co.uk'. The mistake was discovered and Nominet applied the 'first come, first serve rule' and awarded the right to use 'pitman.co.uk' to the publishing outfit as opposed to the training company. Pitman, the trainer, brought an action in court seeking an injunction preventing Nominet UK from assigning the domain name to the publishing outfit. The injunction was not sustained. Primarily, Pitman Training alleged that Pitman publishing was 'passing off' itself as the training entity. The court rejected this argument.

---

[57] [1997] FSR 797.

2 Data Protection, Privacy, Marketing and Libel Over the Internet

2.1 Data Protection and Privacy

2.2 Marketing Over the Internet

2.3 Libel and the Internet

In this chapter, we discuss the implications of data protection, privacy and marketing over the Internet. Much has been made of the fact that very sensitive information about individuals, their families and their financial situation can end up being transmitted over the Internet. As the Internet is often the primary marketing tool for many businesses, an understanding of the interrelatedness between marketing and data protection is critical for website operators. Similarly, scrupulous attention to legal requirements must be followed by a website operator to make sure that they do not fall foul of either standard consumer advertising rules or special consumer advertising rules that deal solely with marketing over the Internet (or web advertising).

2.1 Data Protection and Privacy

In the context of data protection and the Internet, the primary sources of law in this area are:

- the Data Protection Act 1998; and

- the Privacy and Electronic Communications (EC Directive) Regulations 2003 (the 'E-Privacy Regulations').

Guidance is available on-line from the Information Commissioner's Office on how to interpret the Data Protection Act 1998 and the E-Privacy Regulations.[1] For instance, the Information Commissioner has promulgated Guidance on the E-Privacy Regulations issued by the Information Commissioner's Office (E-Privacy Guidance). The E-Privacy Guidance is updated from time to time. Similarly, the Information Commissioner's Office has issued guidance on other subjects, such as the Court of Appeal's decision in *Michael John Durant* v *Financial Services Authority* [2003] EWCA Civ 1746.[2] Durant clarified a number of important issues of law concerning the right of access to personal data. In particular, the case addresses what makes data 'personal' within the meaning of the Data Protection Act 1998. The case also considers what is meant by a 'relevant filing system' for the purposes of the same Act. The Information

---

[1] http://www.informationcommissioner.gov.uk.

[2] http://www.informationcommissioner.gov.uk/eventual.aspx?pg=SRcID&=5152. In addition, the Information Commissioner makes available publications such as a factsheet entitled 'What is the Data Protection Act?' available at: http://www.informationcommissioner.gov.uk/cms/DocumentUploads/Data%20Protection%20Act%20Fact%20V2.pdf.

Commissioner is an independent official appointed by the Crown to oversee the Data Protection Act 1998 and the Freedom of Information Act 2000. The Commissioner reports annually to Parliament. The Commissioner's decisions are subject to the supervision of the courts and the Information Tribunal.

Under the Data Protection Act 1998, if a person is an information controller[3] he or she must comply with eight principles to make sure that the information is handled properly. The data must be:

- fairly and lawfully processed;

- processed for limited purposes;

- adequate, relevant and not excessive;

- accurate;

- not kept for longer than is necessary;

- processed in line with your rights;

- secure; and

- not transferred to countries without adequate protection.[4]

If the data contains information that may be considered personal data[5] which is data that related to a living individual who can be identified (1) from such data or (2) from such data and other information which is in the possession of, or is likely to come into the possession of, the data controller, then such data controller must comply with six relevant conditions in order for such information to be considered fairly processed.[6] These are:

1. the data subject has given his consent to the processing;

2. the processing is necessary (a) for the performance of a contract to which the data subject is a party, or (b) for the taking of steps at the request of the data subject with a view to entering into a contract;

3. the processing is necessary for compliance with any legal obligation to which the data controller is subject, other than an obligation imposed by contract;

4. the processing is necessary in order to protect the vital interests of the data subject;

5. the processing is necessary for the administration of justice or exercise of state functions; and

6. the processing is necessary for the purposes of legitimate interests pursued by the data controller or by the third party or parties to whom the data are disclosed, except where the processing is unwarranted in any particular case by reason of prejudice to the rights and freedoms or legitimate interests of the data subject.

---

[3] Data Protection Act 1998, s1(1).
[4] Data Protection Act 1998, s4.
[5] Data Protection Act 1998, s1(1).
[6] Data Protection Act 1998, Sch 2.

Where the information concerned involves sensitive personal data[7] as defined specifically in the Data Protection Act 1998, one of several extra conditions must be met. These conditions include:

- having the explicit consent of the individual;

- being required by law to process the information for employment purposes;

- needing to process the information in order to protect the vital interests of the individual or another person; and

- dealing with the administration of justice or legal proceedings.[8]

Sensitive personal data means personal data consisting of information as to: (1) the racial or ethnic origin of the data subject; (2) his political opinions; (3) his religious beliefs or other beliefs of a similar nature; (4) whether he is a member of a trade union (within the meaning of the Trade Union and Labour Relations (Consolidation) Act 1992); (5) his physical or mental health or condition; (6) his sexual life; (7) the commission or alleged commission by him of any offence; or (8) any proceedings for any offence committed or alleged to have been committed by him, the disposal of such proceedings or the sentence of any court in such proceedings.[9]

In the context of the Internet, the use of such personal data usually comes up in the context of marketing. Therefore, the remainder of this discussion on data protection law will focus specifically on the data protection law implications of marketing on the Internet. In order to consider these issues, there are a host of regulations, directives, codes, guidance and opinions (other than the ones mentioned already) that need to be considered. The following list is not meant to be exhaustive:

- the Electronic Commerce (EC Directive) Regulations 2002 (the 'E-Commerce Regulations');

- the Consumer Protection (Distance Selling) Regulations 2000 (the 'Distance Selling Regulations');

- the British Code of Advertising, Sales Promotion and Direct Marketing (BCASP Codes); and

- the Direct Marketing Association (DMA) Code of Practice (DMA Code).

One should always consult the following websites as well when considering the implications of marketing over the Internet in the United Kingdom:

- the Office of the Information Commissioner available at: http://www.information commissioner.gov.uk/eventual.aspx;

- the Advertising Standards Authority which regulates the the BCASP Codes and can refer offenders to the Office of Fair Trading available at: http://www.asa. org.uk/asa/;

---

[7] Data Protection Act 1998, s2.
[8] Ibid.
[9] Ibid.

- the DMA, an industry watchdog with its own e-commerce standards of ethical conduct available at: http://www.dma.org.uk/content/home.asp;

- the Federation of European Directive and Interactive Marketing is the single voice of the European direct marketing industry available at: http://www.fedma. org/code/page.cfm?id_page=1;

- the Committee on Advertising Practice (CAP) charged with enforcing the BCASP Codes. CAP can be found at: http://www.cap.org.uk/cap/about/.

2.2 Marketing Over the Internet

Primarily, there are four types of online advertising available on today's market.

- A webpage or web page is a 'page' of the World Wide Web, usually in HTML/XHTML format (the file extensions are typically htm or html) and with hypertext links to enable navigation from one page or section to another.[10]

- A web banner or banner ad is a form of advertising on the World Wide Web. This form of online advertising entails embedding an advertisement into a web page. It is intended to attract traffic to a website by linking them to the website of the advertiser. The advertisement is constructed from an image (GIF, JPEG), JavaScript programme or multimedia object employing technologies such as Java, Shockwave or Flash, often employing animation or sound to maximise presence. Images are usually in a high-aspect ratio shape. That is to say, either wide and short, or tall and narrow, hence the reference to banners. These images are usually placed on web pages that have interesting content, such as a newspaper article or an opinion piece.[11]

- Pop-up ads are a form of online advertising on the World Wide Web intended to increase web traffic or capture e-mail addresses. It works when certain websites open a new web browser window to display advertisements. The pop-up window containing an advertisement is usually generated by JavaScript, but can be generated by other means as well. A less intrusive variation on the pop-up window is the pop-under advertisement. This opens a new browser window, but in the background, so as not to interrupt the user's page view.[12]

- Spamming is the use of any electronic communications medium to send unsolicited messages in bulk. In the popular eye, the most common form of spam is that delivered in e-mail as a form of commercial advertising.[13]

The UK and EU have strict laws and a self-regulated enforcement scheme applicable both to traditional advertising and web advertising. As we have seen elsewhere, the

---

[10] Source: article on 'webpage' available at: http://en.wikipedia.org/wiki/Web_page.
[11] Source: article on 'banner ad' available at: http://en.wikipedia.org/wiki/Banner_advertising.
[12] Source: article on 'pop-up ads' available at: http://en.wikipedia.org/wiki/Pop_up_ad.
[13] Source: article on 'spamming' available at: http://en.wikipedia.org/wiki/Spamming.

problem of the borderless nature of the Internet – jurisdiction and choice of law issues – creates special problems in enforcement.[14]

Now in its 10th edition, the BCASP Codes are a comprehensive set of rules for advertisements, sales, promotions and direct marketing. Basic principles are that advertisements must be (1) legal, decent, honest and truthful; (2) prepared with a sense of responsibility to consumers and to society; and (3) in line with the principles of fair competition generally accepted in business. Specific rules exist regarding alcohol and advertising directed at children. There are also rules related to distance selling which are similar in content to the distance selling regulations. In addition, the BCASP Codes contain specific rules with regards to the use of personal details for direct marketing purposes.

CAP is a collective of advertisers, agencies, service suppliers and media owners which writes the BCASP Codes and undertakes some enforcement. The BCASP Codes are the responsibility of two industries CAP (broadcast) and CAP (non-broadcast) and are independently administered by the Advertising Standards Authority (ASA). The ASA regulates the BCASP Codes and online advertisements in paid for space ('pop-up' and 'pop-under' ads), excluding any generic product information on an advertiser's home pages and sales promotions anywhere online. The ASA only deals with complaints under the BCASP Codes. If the complaint is not upheld, no further action is taken; upheld complaints may result in an ad being withdrawn or amended. Persistent or deliberate offenders can be referred to the Office of Fair Trading (OFT).

The OFT is charged with investigating and deterring all forms of anti-competitive behaviour, including cartels and the abuse of market power. In particular, the OFT investigates allegations of breaches of the Competition Act 1998, subject to administrative priorities. The OFT refers some matters to the Competition Commission mergers where it believes that there is or may be expected to be a substantial lessening of competition in a UK market. The OFT also lead other enforcers in robust application of the rules that protect consumers against unfair trading, taking court action where necessary. The OFT will also take practical steps to encourage self-regulation, such as codes of practice. The OFT has power to enforce the rules pursuant to the Control of Misleading Advertisements Regulations 1988 (amended in 2000). As ASA adjudications are published, the threat of bad publicity is a heavy tool to enforce compliance with the BCASP Codes.

The Interactive Advertising Bureau UK[15] (IABUK) is a trade association for interactive advertising, electronic commerce and online marketing that develops and supports standards and guidelines to ease the process of doing business and to increase consumer confidence in the Internet. IABUK is a member of CAP and may require its members to comply with the BCASP Codes. IABUK, however, cannot enforce adjudications of the ASA.

---

[14] See Wild, Weinstein and Riefa, 'Council Regulation (EC) 44/2001 and Internet Consumer Contracts: Some Thoughts on Article 15 and the Futility of Applying "In the Box" Conflict of Law Rule to "Out of the Box" Borderless World', BILETA Conference Paper, 24–25 March 2004, available at: www.bileta.ac.uk.
[15] Available at: http://www.iabuk.net/index.php.

Admark is a 'safe harbour' scheme that lets consumers know that a particular online advertiser has pledged to follow the advertising rules developed by CAP. CAP, as mentioned above, is the advertising trade body that writes and enforces the BCASP Code. Admark is an 'opt-in' scheme that allows member advertisers and publishers to promote their support for legal, decent, honest and truthful advertising by displaying the Admark icon on their 'paid for' ads and by providing information about the scheme on their websites. Admark, however, does not cover advertisers' own claims on their websites apart from sales promotions.

The DMA is a UK direct marketing industry watchdog. It has a code of practice, the DMA Code, for electronic commerce that sets out the standards of ethical conduct and best practices for e-commerce that their members must follow. The DMA Code champions best practice and self-regulation to ensure that its members create an atmosphere of consumer confidence and trust: this section outlines the levels of consumer protection available.

There are a number of statutory controls that are specific to web advertising. For instance, the Data Protection Act 1998 requires e-mail marketers to give written notice to its customers stating that if they do not want their details to be used for the purpose of marketing, they can 'opt out' of receiving unsolicited e-mails. Section 11 of the Data Protection Act 1998 provides individuals with the right to 'opt out' of direct marketing schemes:

'(1) An individual is entitled at any time by notice in writing to a data controller to require the data controller at the end of such period as is reasonable in the circumstances to cease, or not to begin, processing for the purposes of direct marketing personal data in respect of which he is the data subject ...

(3) In this section "direct marketing" means the communication (by whatever means) of any advertising or marketing material which is directed to particular individuals.'

For advertisers that purchase or use publicly available lists of personal data instead of collecting their own data, individuals should additionally be given the opportunity to opt out of receiving further unsolicited e-mails at the first point of contact. The best practice in this area is to have the list 'cleaned' before any unsolicited e-mails are sent by sending the list to Preference Service[16] which removes the details of all individuals who have registered with them that they do not wish to receive (further) unsolicited marketing e-mails. If an individual has registered with an e-mail preference service or has notified a company that it does not wish to receive further unsolicited marketing e-mails, for these to continue constitutes the unfair processing of personal data. Pursuant to s11(2) of the Data Protection Act 1998, a consumer may obtain a court order forcing a data controller to comply with the consumer's request to remove his or her name from the e-mail marketing list.

Under the Consumer Protection (Distance Selling) Regulations 2000 (DSRs) which came into force on 31 October 2000, organisations that sell to consumers over the

---

[16] See http://preference.the-dma.org/products/empssubscription.shtml for more information about the DMA Preference Service.

Internet must comply with these Regulations. However, certain contracts even if entered into by the use of the Internet are not covered by the DSRs. These include contracts:

1. for the sale or other disposition of an interest in land;

2. for the construction of a building where the contract also provides for a sale or other disposition of an interest in land on which the building is constructed, except for a rental agreement;

3. relating to financial services;

4. concluded by means of an automated vending machine or automated commercial premises;

5. concluded with a telecommunications operator through the use of a public pay-phone; and

6. concluded at an auction.[17]

All of these contracts mentioned above in reg 5(1) of the DSRs are covered by other regulatory schemes. Therefore, they are exempted from enforcement by the DSRs.

Regulation 7 of the DSRs provides that the consumer must be informed of the following when he or she is purchasing the product through a distance selling arrangement:

'(i) the identity of the supplier and, where the contract requires payment in advance, the supplier's address;

(ii) a description of the main characteristics of the goods or services;

(iii) the price of the goods or services including all taxes;

(iv) delivery costs where appropriate;

(v) the arrangements for payment, delivery or performance;

(vi) the existence of a right of cancellation except in the cases referred to in reg 13;

(vii) the cost of using the means of distance communication where it is calculated other than at the basic rate;

(viii) the period for which the offer or the price remains valid; and

(ix) where appropriate, the minimum duration of the contract, in the case of contracts for the supply of goods or services to be performed permanently or recurrently.'[18]

These are applicable to Internet sales agreements as well. Regulation 8 of the DSRs requires this information to be provided to the consumer in writing as well, among other requirements.[19]

The Electronic Commerce (EC Directive) Regulations 2002[20] (the 'E-Commerce

---

17 Regulation 5(1) Consumer Protection (Distance Selling) Regulations 2000.
18 Regulation 7(a) Consumer Protection (Distance Selling) Regulations 2000.
19 Regulation 8 Consumer Protection (Distance Selling) Regulations 2000.
20 The Electronic Commerce (EC Directive) Regulations 2002 (SI 2002/2013).

Regulations') implement the E-Commerce Directive[21] The E-Commerce Regulations apply to 'information society services' meaning 'any service normally provided for remuneration, at a distance, by means of electronic equipment for the processing (including digital compression) and storage of data, and at the individual request of a recipient of a service'.[22] 'Information society services' are further qualified to the extent that the E-Commerce Regulations apply only to 'commercial communications' defined as:

'... a communication, in any form, designed to promote, directly or indirectly, the goods, services or image of any person pursuing a commercial, industrial or craft activity or exercising a regulated profession, other than a communication –

(a) consisting only of information allowing direct access to the activity of that person including a geographic address, a domain name or an electronic mail address; or

(b) relating to the goods, services or image of that person provided that the communication has been prepared independently of the person making it (and for this purpose, a communication prepared without financial consideration is to be taken to have been prepared independently unless the contrary is shown).'[23]

These requirements concerning e-mails generally affect spam and all e-mails as well. All e-mails must give the name, geographic address, e-mail address of sender and the details of any 'supervisory authority' to which it belongs, so that recipients can readily take action to avoid receiving such communications in the future. All unsolicited marketing e-mails must be identifiable as such and must identify the person on whose behalf it was sent. All unsolicited marketing e-mails must be clearly identifiable as such as soon as they are received so that they can be deleted without having to read them; and senders of unsolicited marketing e-mail must consult regularly and respect any opt out registers. Spam designed to promote economic activity must be identified as a 'commercial communication' and identify on whose behalf they have been sent. If the spam contains information about a game, the terms and conditions relevant to that offer or game must be easily accessible and clearly and unambiguously presented.

In addition to the Codes, Directives and Regulations identified above, some thought should be given to pre-Internet age statutory and common law bases for regulating web advertising. For instance, the Trade Descriptions Act 1968 makes it an offence to apply a false trade description to any goods or services. This includes an indication of quantity or size, method of manufacture, descriptions for purpose or place or date of manufacture, or any other history of the goods and/or services. A trade description can only be false if it is false to a material degree; minor or inconsequential misdescription of goods may not be unlawful. The offence is one of strict liability and the advertiser may not rely on a disclaimer.

Other bases for claims may be made under the Trademarks Act 1994 in that a trademark is a sign that distinguishes goods or services of one business from those of

---

[21] Directive 2000/31/EC of the European Parliament and of the Council of 8 June 2000 on certain legal aspects of information society services, in particular electronic commerce, in the Internal Market (Directive on Electronic Commerce), OJ L178, 17 July 2000, went into effect on 21 August 2002.
[22] Regulation 2(1) Electronic Commerce (EC Directive) Regulations 2002 (SI 2002/2013).
[23] Ibid.

another. Marketing or advertising goods can require the consent of the trademark owner if, for example, the logo, name or shape of the product is a trademark. Use of a competitor's trademark online is permissible for the true comparison of products and services. A victim of trademark infringement has several remedies: injunction, damages, seizure and destruction of offending goods or brochures. Hand-in-hand with a claim under the Trademarks Act 1994 could be a claim under the common law doctrine of passing off. Passing off aims to prevent people being misled as to the nature, quality or origin of advertised goods and services, eg claiming a connection with another well-established business, imputing the authority or consent of the holder of that goodwill, or using the name or mark of another. Defamation may also be another cause of action as it is a common law and statutorily based doctrine that aims to prevent companies or individuals from making false derogatory remarks about others. Statements in an advertisement must be true and capable of being proved to be true.

The Control of Misleading Advertisements (Amendment) Regulations 2000 (SI 2000/914) allow an advertiser to compare his products with those of a competitor provided the advertiser compares like with like, which means that the advertisement must compare goods or services meeting the same need or intended for the same purpose. An advertisement must objectively compare one or more material, relevant, verifiable and representative features of the goods and services (which may include price) and the advertisement must not discredit or denigrate the trademarks of the competitor.

Consumers may have a claim under the Consumer Protection Act 1987 (1987, cl 43) which states that misleading consumers as to the price of goods or services is unlawful.[24] It is also an offence if the price indication contained in advertisements becomes misleading and the advertiser does not take reasonable steps to prevent consumers from relying on the price indication.[25]

Netiquette is the unofficial code of practice for online users. Sending unsolicited advertisements or marketing material will be considered unacceptable by many recipients and may lead to complaints or direct action from users or Internet Service Providers. Proper netiquette requires: targeted advertisements for products which actually meet a need of the recipient instead of generic material sent out on a blanket basis; do not unnecessarily upset, offend or anger people by the content of the advertisement; do not send out unsolicited e-mails or marketing messages; and include a prominent unsubscribe mechanism.

Spam is unsolicited bulk e-mail including a variety of electronic communications (or short message service (SMS)) (up to 160 characters in length). 'Electronic mail' means 'any text, voice, sound or image message sent over a public communications network which can be stored in the network or in the recipient's terminal equipment until it is collected by the recipient'.[26] Recital 40 of the E-Privacy Directive specifically states that

---

[24] Consumer Protection Act 1987, ss20–21 et seq.
[25] Ibid.
[26] E-Privacy Directive, art 2(h).

this definition includes SMS messages. However, distinguishing between unsolicited commercial e-mail (identified spam) and illegitimate (or 'semi-legitimate') spam is something that the E-Privacy Directive[27] and the E-Privacy Regulations do not do. Equally concerning is the fact that neither the E-Privacy Directive not the E-Privacy Regulations impose restrictions on sending unsolicited e-mails to corporate subscribers in contrast to private individuals. One newsletter points out the following:

'Businesses around the world will lose up to $50 billion in combating spam this year, according to a new report issued by consultancy Ferris Research. Firms in the US will lose $17 billion, while spam will cost UK firms almost $2.5 billion (£1.3 billion).

In terms of cost per head of population, spam costs US business $59 per person, while in Japan the cost is $41, in Germany $55 and in the UK $42 (about £22).

Much of the cost is in lost employee productivity, according to the report. Not included in the figures are immeasurable items, such as the missed "opportunity cost" of a new customer order that's incorrectly discarded as spam.'[28]

Paragraphs (2) and (3) of reg 22 E-Privacy Regulations characterises the new approach to unsolicited e-mails. Regulation 22 allows a 'soft opt in' for existing customers to promote only products that are 'similar' to those previously sold to existing customers. The statutory language more specifically states:

'(2) Except in the circumstances referred to in paragraph (3) … a person shall neither transmit … unsolicited communications for the purposes of direct marketing by means of electronic mail unless the recipient of the electronic mail has previously notified the sender that he consents for the time being to such communications being sent by … the sender.

(3) A person may send or instigate the sending of electronic mail for the purposes of direct marketing where –

(a) that person has obtained the contact details of the recipient of that electronic mail in the course of the sale or negotiations for the sale of a product or service to that recipient;

(b) the direct marketing is in respect of that person's similar products and services only; and

(c) the recipient has been given a simple means of refusing (free of charge except for the costs of the transmission of the refusal) the use of his contact details for the purposes of such direct marketing, at the time that the details were initially collected, and, where he did not initially refuse the use of the details, at the time of each subsequent communication.'

If you receive an e-mail from a store where you have purchased books online offering you other books on 'special offer', this sort of spam is permissible even though no explicit consent was ever obtained from this store to send you such unsolicited e-mails. Regulation 22(3)(a) and (b) would suggest as such. This is all fine and good with communications from reputable and identifiable organisations. Yet, what about those e-mails that emanate from dubious sources. Regulation 23 addresses those which can be pornographic, offensive, misleading and fraudulent:

---

[27] Directive 2002/58/EC of the European Parliament and of the Council of 12 July 2002 concerning the processing of personal data and the protection of privacy in the electronic communications sector (Directive on privacy and electronics communications), OJ L201/37 (31/07/02).
[28] Out-Law.Com, 'Spam costs $50 billion worldwide', 11/03/05, available at: http://www.out-law.com/php/page.php?page_id=spamcostsbilli1110551732&area=news.

'23. A person shall neither transmit, nor instigate the transmission of, a communication for the purposes of direct marketing by means of electronic mail –

(a) where the identity of the person on whose behalf the communication has been sent has been disguised or concealed; or

(b) where a valid address to which the recipient of the communication may send a request that such communications cease has not been provided.'

Unfortunately, it is precisely this kind of spam – the 'spam nasties' – that the E-Privacy Regulations is weakest to stop. First, a large portion of spam originates outside the UK in jurisdictions not subject to the E-Privacy Regulations. Second, by the time a spam address has been identified, the spammer behind it has moved on to another address:

'Spam used to be a nuisance now it is considered as a serious, international, cross-sectoral problem. It has reached worrying numbers. Despite variations in statistics, it is generally estimated that more than 50 per cent of global e-mail traffic is spam. The rate of growth is even more worrying; in 2001, spam was estimated to be "only" 7 per cent of global e-mail traffic. It was estimated at 29 per cent in 2002. And the projections for 2003 show an estimated 51 per cent to be spam.

Efforts to combat the problem are on the rise on the legislative, legal and technological fronts. Spam threatens to erode consumer confidence online, which in turn would undermine the digital economy and the open character of the Internet. The world community plans to take appropriate action to deal with spam at national and international levels. Bill Gates is determined to crack spam by 2006.'[29]

In some ways, the E-Privacy Directive goes further than the E-Privacy Regulations in limiting when legitimate businesses may use spam for marketing purposes. Article 13 (1) allows the use of use of e-mail for the purposes of direct marketing only in respect of subscribers who have given their prior consent. The onus is on the business to obtain the consent of the subscriber. Yet, the exception to the consent requirement, art 13(2), is allowed only where the e-mail address has been obtained 'in the context of the sale of a product or a service'.[30] The E-Privacy Regulations allow an e-mail address to be used if obtained 'in the context of the sale or negotiations for the sale of a product'.[31] One commentator has noted that 'the DTI has taken a liberal approach by allowing the sending of e-mail when the details of the recipient have been obtained not only in the course of the sale of a product or service but also in the course of negotiations for the sale of a product or service'.[32]

In addition to the remedies provided for in the E-Privacy Regulations, there may be other more traditional remedies against spam in the UK. Spamming may constitute trespass or unlawful interference with goods in the possession of another in violation of s1 Torts (Interference With Goods) Act 1977. It may also violate the Computer Misuse Act 1990 as it is in some ways similar to a hacking. Finally, a spam e-mail using someone's e-mail may constitute a trademark violation and an attempt at passing off.

Interestingly, with respect to criminal penalties, the United States has adopted the

---

[29] Abu Bakar Munir, 'Unsolicited Commercial E-Mail: Implementing the E-Mail Directive', CTLR 2004, 10(5), 105–110, 105.
[30] E-Privacy Directive, art 13(2).
[31] E-Privacy Regulations, reg 21(3)(a).
[32] Munir, op cit, p107.

Controlling the Assault of Non-Solicited Pornography and Marketing Act of 2003 (the Can-Spam Act) to regulate interstate commerce by imposing limitations and penalties on the transmission of unsolicited commercial electronic mail via the Internet.[33] The Can-Spam Act provides severe criminal and civil penalties for illegitimate spammers.

2.3 Libel and the Internet

The Internet presents many opportunities for individuals to publish statements that may be libellous in nature on websites, in e-mails, in online archives and on talk boards or blogs. The Internet blog is the latest trend in the World Wide Web for people to post statements that may give rise to liability for libel:

'A weblog, web log or simply a blog, is a web application which contains periodic time-stamped posts on a common webpage. These posts are often but not necessarily in reverse chronological order. Such a website would typically be accessible to any Internet user. The term "blog" came into common use as a way of avoiding confusion with the term server log.

Blogs run from individual diaries to arms of political campaigns, media programs and corporations, and from one occasional author to having large communities of writers. Many weblogs enable visitors to leave public comments, which can lead to a community of readers centered around the blog; others are non-interactive. The totality of weblogs or blog-related websites is usually called the blogosphere. When a large amount of activity, information and opinion erupts around a particular subject or controversy in the blogosphere, it is commonly called a blogstorm or blog swarm.'[34]

The Faulks Committee on defamation[35] has defined defamation as:

'... the publication to a third party of a matter which in all the circumstances would be likely to affect a person adversely in the estimation of reasonable people generally.'

The following principles have been identified as essential for any claim alleging defamation:

'1. the statement which is alleged to be defamatory must be made to someone other than the claimant;

2. the statement must be in a form of words which tends to:

a) lower the claimant in the estimation of normal right thinking people; or

b) expose the claimant to hatred, contempt or ridicule; or

c) cause the claimant to be shunned or avoided.'[36]

In the area of the Internet, the law is focused with the form of defamation known as libel. Libel is defamation in a permanent form (writing); a person who brings a libel action does not have to prove that he has suffered any loss or injury as a result of the

---

[33] The full text of this Act can be found at: http://www.spamlaws.com/federal/108s877enrolled.pdf #search='can%20spam%20act'.

[34] Source: Article on 'blog' from Wikipedia at: http://en.wikipedia.org/wiki/Blog.

[35] Cmnd 5909 (1975).

[36] Peter Carey and Jo Sanders, 'Media Law', 3rd ed, Sweet and Maxwell, London, 2004, p39.

statement, as the statement is actionable per se and damage is presumed to have occurred.[37]

To succeed in an action for defamation the plaintiff must prove three things of the statement made: that it is defamatory; that it may be reasonably understood to refer to the plaintiff; and that it was published. Each of these three elements presents difficulties of proof but in recent years the addition of the Internet as a communications network has presented difficulties of law. Publication means that the statement be communicated to at least one person other than the subject. A letter or e-mail to a third party will suffice, as would posting a comment on a public noticeboard: *Slipper* v *BBC* [1990] 1 All ER 165.

Each time a defamatory statement is published, a fresh cause of action arises on each publication of the defamatory statement. In other jurisdictions, for example the United States, there is a 'single publication rule'.[38] This means that only the first publication gives rise to a cause of action. Subsequent publications may be taken into account when assessing damages but no further right of action will accrue. This has implications for limitation periods. In the United States, the limitation on action runs from the date of the first publication only. By contrast, in the UK, the limitation starts afresh with each and every fresh publication: *Loutchansky* v *Times Newspapers Ltd* [2002] QB 783. In *Berezovsky* v *Forbes* [2001] EMLR 45, the House of Lords considered the issue of whether the publication of an article worldwide should gives rise to a single global publication rule, namely, that the date of the publication is fixed from the date the libellous material was first published anywhere, as opposed to each time it was published in the UK. This argument was rejected.

Article 5(3) of the Brussels Convention, incorporated in the Civil Jurisdiction and Judgments Act 1982, has given rise to the likelihood that a claimant, if faced with a choice of EU states in which to bring an action, may elect to consolidate the entire action in the state in which he is domiciled or he may elect to bring actions in each state where his reputation was harmed. This often means that persons libelled on the continent and in the UK will sue in the UK because of its more favourable libel laws. This was the case in *Shevill* v *Press Alliance SA*.[39] Nonetheless, a court may decline jurisdiction on the basis of forum non conveniens: see *Spiliada Maritime Corporation* v *Cansulex (The Spiliada)* [1987] 1 AC 460. The decision in *Gutnick* v *Dow Jones* [2002] HCA 2002, an Australian Court of Appeal case (where the *Wall Street Journal* was held liable for defamation in Australia even though the defamatory remarks were published only in New Jersey) indicates that Internet publishers can be hauled into court in any jurisdiction where their comments might be downloaded. This viewpoint was affirmed indirectly in the 'boxingtalk' case where Don King was allowed to proceed to suit in the UK against a US online publisher and its author even though all parties were based in the US. The English court believed there to be a sufficient

---

[37] Ibid, p40.
[38] *New York Times* v *Sullivan*, 376 US 254 (1964).
[39] [1996] AC 959.

nexus to England such as to allow the case to be heard here: *King* v *Lewis* [2004] EWHC 168.

The Defamation Act 1996 provides a limited defence for ISPs that innocently publish libellous statements. The Defamation Act 1996 was enacted in an attempt to update the law relating to defamation. It followed a study conducted by the Law Commission which recommended the introduction of a new defence of innocent dissemination:

'1(1) In defamation proceedings a person has a defence if he shows that –

(a) he was not the author, editor or publisher of the statement complained of;

(b) he took reasonable care in relation to its publication; and

(c) he did not know, and had no reason to believe, that what he did caused or contributed to the publication of a defamatory statement.

It is further provided that, still in s1(5):

In determining for the purposes of this section whether a person took reasonable care, or had reason to believe that what he did caused or contributed to the publication of a defamatory statement, regard shall be had to –

(a) the extent of his responsibility for the content of the statement or the decision to publish it;

(b) the nature or circumstances of the publication; and

(c) the previous conduct or character of the author, editor or publisher.'[40]

The section proceeds to define the terms 'author', 'editor' and 'publisher':

'(3) A person shall not be considered the author, editor or publisher of a statement if he is only involved (e) as the operator of or provider of access to a communications system by means of which the statement is transmitted, or made available, by a person over whom he has no effective control.'[41]

It is important to note that these definitions apply only for the purposes of the section.

Courts have indicated that the operator of, or provider of, access to a communications system by means of which the statement is transmitted, or made available, by a person over whom he has no effective control is not a publisher: *Totalise plc* v *Motley Fool Ltd* [2003] 2 All ER 872, confirms such expectation that the website operator was not responsible for publication in contempt of court because there was no editorial content. See also *Godfrey* v *Demon Internet* [1999] 4 All ER 342, where Demon Internet did not exercise reasonable control over the information published and thus could not avoid liability. In this case, Demon was not to be considered as acting as a publisher in respect of the postings and therefore it satisfied the first requirement of the defence. However, Demon failed to demonstrate that they had taken reasonable care to remove a defamatory comment from its service as soon as it was reasonably possible after notification that such comment was posted on their service. In *Venables and Thompson* v *News Group Newspapers and Others* [2001] 1 All ER 908, the High

---

[40] Defamation Act 1996, ss1(1), 1(5).
[41] Defamation Act 1996, s1(3)(e).

Court emphasized that the failure of an ISP to take all reasonable steps to prevent publication of enjoined materials would give rise to liability.

In accord with the Defamation Act 1996 defence and the *Totalise* and *Godfrey* decisions, art 12 of the E-Commerce Directive and Regulation 17 of the Electronic Commerce (EC Directive) Regulations 2002 provides the mere conduit defence in the context of ISPs providing services online, namely, that:

'17(1) Where an information society service is provided which consists of the transmission in a communication network of information provided by a recipient of the service or the provision of access to a communication network, the service provider (if he otherwise would) shall not be liable for damages or for any other pecuniary remedy or for any criminal sanction as a result of that transmission where the service provider –

(a) did not initiate the transmission;

(b) did not select the receiver of the transmission; and

(c) did not select or modify the information contained in the transmission.

(2) The acts of transmission and of provision of access referred to in paragraph (1) include the automatic, intermediate and transient storage of the information transmitted where:

(a) this takes place for the sole purpose of carrying out the transmission in the communication network; and

(b) the information is not stored for any period longer than is reasonably necessary for the transmission.'

Article 15 of the E-Commerce Directive and Regulation 22 of the Electronic Commerce (EC Directive) Regulations 2002 provide further that Member States shall not impose a general obligation on providers, when providing the services covered by arts 12 to 14, to monitor the information which they transmit or store. Nor does it impose a general obligation to actively seek facts or circumstances indicating illegal activity.

As more and more companies make use of e-mail as a method of communication between staff, so there will be increasing exposure to actions on the basis of vicarious liability in respect of the use or misuse of the communications network. In 1997, the Norwich Union company reached a settlement in a libel action brought by a health insurance company, Western Provident Association. Under the terms of the agreement Norwich Union agreed to pay £450,000 in damages and costs relating to libellous messages concerning the Association's financial stability, which had been contained in e-mail messages exchanged between Norwich Union's staff (*The Times*, 18 July 1997). Monitoring of e-mail communications within the workplace may therefore be necesary. The Interception of Communications Act 1985 will govern the interception of e-mail messages passing through a public telecommunications network: this statute does not apply to private networks but see the Regulation of Investigatory Powers Act (RIPA) 2000 and *Halford* v *UK* [1997] IRLR 471. As to the issue of whether commercial speech rises to the same level of protection as non-commercial speech, see Colin R Munro, 'The Value of Commercial Speech', *Cambridge Law Journal*, 62(1), March 2003, pp134–158.

3 Copyright, Patents and the Internet

In the last chapter, we introduced concepts such as the statutorily-based trademark and the common law of passing off as they relate to the Internet. In particular, we paid special attention to the implications involved with domain names. In this chapter, we will introduce the concept of copyright as it relates to the Internet.

3.1 Copyright Generally

Copyright is a statutory right[1] that exists with respect to certain types of broadly creative works. A copyright is a property right[2] that gives the owner exclusive rights to do certain acts with respect to the work, such as making copies or it or adapting it to other mediums.[3] The fundamental idea is to prevent others from taking advantage of a person's creative efforts. The types of work that attract copyright are music, plays, novels, paintings and sculptures, although it also covers less obviously creative works such as computer programmes.[4] Sometimes, copyright has been described as a partial monopoly in that there will be a number of exceptions where a work can be copied without infringing an author's rights. Closely related to the idea of copyright is the concept of 'moral rights'. Moral rights[5] refer to a loose category of rights which protect the author's interests in the desire to be associated with their creations and to object to alterations to their works. Computer programmes and computer-generated work are parts of the exception to the rule requiring the identification of the moral rights.[6]

The rationale for copyright protection is that authors should be able to enjoy the benefits of their original work.[7] Copyright and more generally intellectual property rights were developed as, otherwise, very few people would want to create works if they could not benefit financially from their creation. Copyright law protects the product of a person's skills, labour and artistry. That means that the protection granted is on the form in which the person expresses him or herself but not on the idea that lies

---

[1] The Copyright, Design and Patents Act (CDPA) 1988 is the primary statute of interest here.
[2] CDPA 1988, s1(1).
[3] CDPA 1988, s2(1).
[4] CDPA 1988, s1(1)(a), (b) and (c) identify the following descriptions of work: (a) original literary, dramatic, musical or artistic works, (b) sound recordings, films, broadcasts or cable programmes, and (c) the typographical arrangements of published editions.
[6] CDPA 1988, ss77–87.
[6] CDPA 1988, s79.
[7] See US Constitution, art I, s8, for instance.

behind it: *Green* v *New Zealand Broadcasting Corporation* [1989] RPC 469. The right appears automatically as soon as the work is created and subsists for the prescribed period.[8] There is no need for registration of the work (contrast with trademarks, for example).[9]

As the Internet is truly international in scope, an understanding of the impact that international law has on copyright is essential. Copyright, after all, is more than a product of common law.[10] It is a product of international convention, treaty and European directive. The Berne Convention (1886–1971)[11] has more than 130 signatories and sets out minimum standards in respect of copyright that all members must follow. Some of these provisions include the obligation of 'national treatment', moral rights of authors and the lack of formality requirements for protection for copyrighted status to be effective. The 1971 text of the Berne Convention is incorporated in the TRIPS Agreement 1994.[12]

The TRIPS Agreement 1994 is one of the mandatory agreements that members of the World Trade Organisation (WTO)[13] must abide by as a condition of their membership. The TRIPS Agreement grants members of the WTO those economic rights (but not moral rights) provided for under the Berne Convention.[14] The TRIPS Agreement also introduces the 'most favoured nation rule' (the 'MFN Rule'). The MFN Rule requires that any benefit or advantage granted by any WTO member to another WTO member shall be accorded immediately and unconditionally to all other WTO members.[15] The TRIPS Agreement requires that WTO members shall ensure that enforcement procedures are available under their law so as to permit effective action against any act of infringement of intellectual property rights covered by the TRIPS Agreement.[16]

The Universal Copyright Convention (UCC) 1952–1971[17] is a convention that is of lesser significance than it was in the past because of the fact that its main proponent, the United States, is now a signatory to the Berne Convention. The primary contribution of the UCC to the international copyright regime is the implementation of the copyright symbol ©, accompanied by the name of the copyright proprietor and the year of the first publication placed in such manner and location as to give reasonable notice of the claim of copyright.[18]

---

[8] CDPA 1988, ss2(1) and 3(2).
[9] CDPA 1988, s153 et seq sets forth the specific qualifications for when a copyright is protected.
[10] Ronan Deazley, 'The Myth of Copyright at Common Law', Cambridge Law Journal, 62(1), March 2003, pp106–133.
[11] Berne Convention for the Protection of Literary and Artistic Works of 9 September 1886, completed at Paris on 4 May 1896, revise at Berlin on 13 November 1908, completed at Berne on 20 March 1914, revised at Rome on 2 June 1928, at Brussels on 26 June 1948, at Stockholm on 14 July 1967, and at Paris on 24 July 1971, and amended on 28 September 1979.
[12] Agreement on Trade-related Aspects of Intellectual Property Rights 1994.
[13] The WTO deals with the rules of trade between nations at a global or near-global level with approximately 146 nations as members. For more information on the WTO, see http://www.wto.org.
[14] TRIPS Agreement, art 9, cl 1.
[15] TRIPS Agreement, art 4.
[16] TRIPS Agreement, art 41.
[17] UCC, as revised at Paris on 24 July 1971.
[18] UCC, art III, cl 1.

More recently, the World Intellectual Property Organization Copyright Treaty 1996 (WIPO Copyright Treaty) introduced many of the international copyright law reforms most relevant to the Internet law field including:

- the right of distribution (art 6);
- the right of rental (art 7);
- the right of communication to the public (art 8);
- obligations concerning technological measures (art 11);
- obligations concerning rights management information (art 12); and
- provisions on enforcement of rights (art 14).[19]

Certain copyright conventions and agreements deal with what are called 'related rights'. Related rights are those rights which can be found in, inter alia, the Berne Convention that authors of copyrighted works enjoy that are neither economic rights nor moral rights. These include the right of authors to limit, for instance, the authorisation of cinematic adaptations of their works of literature[20] or 'droit de suite' in works of art and manuscripts.[21] For the most part, related rights are heavily proscribed under UK law. International treaties (other than the TRIPS Agreement) that deal with related rights include the Rome Convention 1961[22], the Phonograms Convention 1971[23] and the WIPO Performances and Phonograms Treaty 1996.[24]

The law of copyright rests on a very clear principle that anyone who by his or her own skill and labour creates an original work of whatever character shall, for a limited period, enjoy an exclusive right to copy that work. Lord Bingham wrote in a speech in 2001 that the essence of copyright is that: 'No one else may for a season reap what the copyright owner has sown'.[25] Yet, what do we mean by original? The notion of originality is not defined in the CDPA 1988. Case law, however, does define it. Copyright law does not protect a mere idea so the work must be recorded. It is the form in which the idea is expressed which must be original. Originality is the result of the author's own skill, effort and capital. See *Walter* v *Lane* [1900] AC 539 which held that a speech that is transcribed can produce two separate copyrights: one, being the copyright of the speaker; and, two, the other being that of the newspaper journalist who wrote it down.

---

[19] WIPO Copyright Treaty adopted by the Diplomatic Conference on 20 December 1996. Many of the WIPO Copyright Treaty provisions have found themselves incorporated into the CDPA 1988 through the implementation of the Copyright Directive in the UK.
[20] Berne Convention, art 14, cl 1.
[21] Berne Convention, art 14.
[22] International Convention for the Protection of Performers, Producers of Phonograms and Broadcasting Organisations (Rome Convention) of 26 October 1961.
[23] Geneva Convention for the Protection of Producers of Phonograms against Unauthorised Duplication of Their Phonograms (Geneva Convention) of 29 October 1971.
[24] WIPO Performances and Phonograms Treaty adopted by the Diplomatic Conference on 20 December 1996.
[25] *Designers Guild* v *Williams* [2001] FSR 11.

In *University of London Press* v *University Tutorial Press* [1916] 2 Ch 601, some thought has been given to the concept of originality as meant for UK copyright law:

> '... the word "original" does not in this connection mean that the work must be the expression of inventive or original thought ... but that it should originate from the author.'

Subsequent to *University of London Press*, another case confirmed the viewpoint that even a compilation can suffice for being sufficiently original provided the compiler exercised the requisite labour, skill and capital in putting his or her compilation together.[26] Here Lord Atkinson noted that originality 'must depend on the facts of the case and must in each case be very much a question of degree'.[27]

While the threshold for 'originality' may be low, there is still a de minimis standard for copyright protection. By this we mean that a single word, even an invented name such as 'Exxon', does not attract copyright protection as a literary work: see *Exxon Corporation* v *Exxon Insurance* [1982] RPC 69. In *Shetland Times* v *Dr Jonathan Wills* [1997] FSR 604, it was arguable that copyright could consist in a newspaper headline of about eight or so words.

There are three types of work that are protected by the CDPA 1988.[28] If a work does not fall into one of these three categories, it will not be protected. Section 3 of the CDPA 1988 sets forth descriptions of work for literary, dramatic and musical works. Interestingly, in addition to a dramatic or musical work, which is written, spoken or sung, a literary work includes: (1) a table or compilation other than a database, (2) a computer program[29], (3) preparatory design material for a computer programme, and (4) a database.'[30] Even though a literary work includes a computer programme, this term is not defined in the CDPA 1988. Preparatory materials for computer programmes are also protected under paragraph (c) of s1(1) of CDPA 1988. Protection of such materials is increasingly important due to the increasing production of multimedia materials and digital works that are based on computer programmes and the preparatory materials used to make such programmes. A website as a whole could come under this category. So can each element of a website.

A 'dramatic work' is defined to include a work of dance or mime.[31] A 'musical work' is defined as a 'work consisting of music, exclusive of any words or action intended to be sung, spoken or performed with the music'. An 'artistic work' means: (1) graphic work, photograph, sculpture or collage, irrespective of artistic quality, (2) a work of architecture being a building or a model for a building, or (3) a work of artistic craftsmanship.[32] The section which defines 'artistic work' also sets forth more specific definitions for 'building', 'graphic work', 'photograph' and 'sculpture'.[33]

---

[26] *Macmillan* v *Cooper* (1923) 93 LJPC 113.
[27] Ibid.
[28] CDPA 1988, s1(1).
[29] Consider an expansive definition of computer programme. In this context, a computer programme may include digital sampling, filmmaking and photography. Might copyright protection be available as a computer programme in addition to being a sound recording, film or photograph?
[30] CDPA 1988, s3(1)(a), (b), (c) and (d).
[31] CDPA 1988, s3(1).
[32] CDPA 1988, s4(1).
[33] Ibid.

With respect to sound recordings, films, broadcasts or cable programmes, it should be noted that these are derivative works in that they involve reproductions of other copyrighted works. For example, a film will be based upon a screenplay (known as the underlying work). Any of the items listed below can constitute a vital element of a website, so it is important to know the importance of these definitions in the event a website is developed that allows access to sound recordings, films, broadcasts or cable programming.

- Sound recordings – these include cassettes, CDs and mini discs. The copyright in a sound recording is different from the copyright in the underlying musical work and also separate from the physical item holding the recording. Digital sampling may cause problems for the protection of copyright. 'Sound recording' is defined in s5A CDPA 1988.

- Films – s5B CDPA 1988 defines a film as meaning 'a recording on any medium from which a moving image may by any means be produced'. The sound track accompanying a film shall be treated as part of the film for copyright purposes.[34]

- Broadcast – s6(1) CDPA 1988 defines a broadcast as a 'transmission by wireless telegraphy of visual images, sounds or other information which (a) is capable of being lawfully received by members of the public, or (b) is transmitted for presentation to the public'.

- Cable programme – s7 CDPA 1988 defines a 'cable programme' as 'any item included in a cable programme service'.

The issue of whether an Internet website falls within the category of 'broadcast' (s6(1) CDPA 1988) has largely been resolved: see UK Patents Office Copyright Directorate, *Consultation on UK Implementation Directive 2001/29/EC: An Analysis of Responses and Government Conclusions* (available at: http://www.patent.gov.uk/about/consultations/responses/copydirect/introduction.htm).

Under s8 CDPA 1988, typographical arrangements of a published edition, or any part thereof, is a protected category of copyrighted work. This is designed to protect the publisher's investment in the publishing process. Thus, photocopying a book would potentially infringe the typographical arrangement right (as well as the author's literary underlying copyright). Newspaper pages are also protected under typographical arrangements.

Section 9 CDPA 1988 defines an 'author' in relation to a work. An author is in essence 'the person who creates it'. It should be noted that authorship and ownership do not necessarily coincide. Section 11(1) CDPA 1988 defines the author of the work as the first owner of copyright. In the context of a literary, dramatic, musical or artistic work, or a film made by an employee in the course of his employment, the employer – not the employee – is the first owner of any copyright in the work.[35] This remains subject to any agreement to the contrary.[36]

---

[34] CDPA 1988, s5B(2).
[35] CDPA 1988, s11(2).
[36] Ibid.

The duration of copyright is set forth in ss12, 13, 14 and 15 CDPA 1988.[37] The chart below identifies the various differences between types of works and their copyright duration.

Copyright work	Authorship	Lifetime of Author	Duration
Literary, dramatic, musical, artistic work	Creator of the work	70 years	70-year remainder term starts end of calendar year of the death of author
Computer generated works	Person by whom the arrangements necessary for the creation are undertaken	50 years	End of calendar year in which the work is produced
Sound recording	Producer	50 years	End of calendar year in which made[38]
Film	Producer and principal director	50 years	End of calendar year of the death of (last to die): a) principal director; b) author of screenplay; c) author of dialogue; d) composer of music specially created for the film
Broadcast	Broadcaster	50 years	End of calendar year broadcast made
Cable programme	Cable programme provider	50 years	End of calendar year programme included in service
Published edition	Publisher	25 years	End of calendar year edition was first published

The owner of the copyright can part with it. Therefore, for example, the author of the work can pass on the rights to the person who commissioned the website. This occurs via assignment or licensing. An assignment is a transfer of ownership. A licence

---

[37] After expiration of the copyright, the work becomes public property and can be freely copied.

[38] Or, if during that period it is released, 50 years from the end of the calendar year in which it is released.

is merely an arrangement between the parties for the use of copyrighted material for a certain period of time. Assignment is a property right; a licence is a contractual right. The requirements for an assignment of a copyright are set forth in s90 CDPA 1988: it must be in writing signed by the assignor. An assignment of a copyright may be partial in that it is limited in scope (whether it covers all the things the copyright owner has the exclusive right to do) or duration (whether it covers the entire period for which the copyright is to subsist).[39] Each element of the copyright can be assigned separately. Rights in a book, for example, can be assigned to create a film adaptation whilst retaining the right to produce a computer game based on the book.

A licence consists of allowing the exploitation of a copyright work in a specified manner. It is only a contractual right and cannot be passed by the licensee to a third party. There is no formal requirement for the validity of licences (oral or in writing; can even be implied from the relationship between the parties). An exclusive licence must be in writing.[40] A licence gives the licensee a right to sue others for infringement of copyright (similar to assignment in that respect).[41] A licensor cannot grant any additional licences of the same right.[42] A non-exclusive license is a contractual right with no powers to sue for infringement. So a licensee will need the licensor's promise to take action against potential infringers. The licensor has the right to grant additional licences in the same right.

The CDPA 1988 sets forth a list of acts that are restricted by copyright.[43] A copyright owner is granted the exclusive right to do the following acts in the UK:

1.   to copy the work;

2.   to issue copies of the work to the public;

3.   to rent or lend the work to the public;

4.   to perform, show or play the work in public;

5.   to broadcast the work or include it in a cable programme service;

6.   to make an adaptation of the work or do any of the above in relation to an adaptation.[44]

Copyright in a work is infringed by a person who, without the licence of the copyright owner does, or authorises another to do, any of the acts restricted by the copyright.[45] In the context of the Internet, a restricted act may include the storing of any work in any electronic medium.[46] Thus, by downloading a page from the Internet, an individual may

---

[39] CDPA 1988, s90(2)(a) and (b).
[40] CPDA 1988, s92.
[41] CPDA 1988, s92(2).
[42] CDPA 1988, s91(3).
[43] CDPA 1988, s16.
[44] Ibid.
[45] Ibid.
[46] CDPA 1988, s17(2). Note, however, that the Copyright and Related Rights Regulations 2003 (SI 2003/2498) which implement Directive 2001/29/EC on the harmonization of certain aspects of copyright and related rights in the information society ([2001] OJ L 167/10) has addressed some of the copyright law shortcomings that have arisen due to the rise of digital technology and the Internet.

unknowingly be making a copy of the page. The delivery of content over the Internet by definition involves both reproduction of the original content and its distribution to others.

In addition to the prohibited acts described above, the CDPA 1988 provides for a number of specific instances in which reproduction of a copyrighted work will not be an infringement thereof. If the reproduction falls within one of the permitted acts enumerated in ss28–76 CDPA 1988, or the public interest exception provided by s171 CDPA 1988, then no infringement has occurred. A full discussion of the fair dealing exceptions provided for in ss29–30 CDPA 1988 and how courts interpret them is beyond the scope of this chapter. However, students should note that fair dealing may be asserted where a work is being copied for the purposes of research and private study,[47] criticism and review[48] or reporting of current events (excluding the use of photographs).[49] Do not confuse the UK fair dealing exceptions (which are narrowly drawn and construed) with the wide-ranging US copyright law concept of fair use.[50]

3.2 Copyright in the Internet Context

In the context of the Internet, all of the following are potentially copyright infringements:

- downloading a web page or software into a computer's memory;

- automatic web page caching[51] – a standard feature of practically all browser software;

- printing of a web page;

- reproducing material downloaded from a website;

- web linking (hyper linking, deep-linking);

- web casting; and

- spamdexing.[52]

The CDPA 1988 distinguishes between two types of infringement: primary infringement and secondary infringement.[53] A primary infringement occurs when a person engages in a restricted act without the copyright holder's permission. Infringement occurs whether or not the person had knowledge of the copyright (strict

---

[47] CDPA 1988, s29. This section has been changed to implement the Copyright Directive and it appears to severely curtail the ability of commercial enterprises to use copyrighted material whilst undertaking research for commercial purposes.
[48] CDPA 1988, s30.
[49] CDPA 1988, s31.
[50] For more on the US concept of fair use, see Lawrence Lessig, 'Free Culture', New York, The Penguin Press, 2004, pp141–143.
[51] This is the making of copies of materials that originate on another local area network machine avoiding transmission through the Internet.
[52] 'This involves repeatedly using certain keywords – registered trademarks, brand names or famous names – in one's web page. Doing this can make a website move to the top of a search engine list, drawing higher traffic to that site, even if the site has nothing to do with the search request: see: http://www.wordspy.com/words/ spamdexing.asp.
[53] CDPA 1988, ss17–22.

liability). A secondary infringement occurs when a person commits a restricted act knowing or having reason to believe that this act is infringing the owner's copyright. An infringement takes place when a restricted act is done on the whole or a substantial part of the copyright without the consent of the copyright owner. The question whether a defendant has copied a substantial part depends much more on the quality than the quantity of what he has taken.[54] This viewpoint was originally enumerated in *University of London Press Ltd* v *University Tutorial Press Ltd* [1916] 2 Ch 601 where it was stated 'what is worth copying is worth protecting'.

The Copyright and Related Rights Regulations 2003 (SI 2000/2498) implement into UK copyright law many of the new 'digital agenda' concepts that arise from the WIPO[55] Copyright Treaty (adopted by the Diplomatic Conference on 20 December 1996), the WIPO Performances and Phonograms Treaty (adopted by the Diplomatic Conference on 20 December 1996) and the Copyright Directive.[56] These changes in international and European copyright law impact directly on Internet website operation and are worth examining, particularly those involved in making available to the public right and transient copies. The Copyright Directive is an attempt to harmonise copyright and related rights across the European Union in response to the growth of the digital economy. In addition to giving authors the exclusive right to authorise or prohibit the reproduction of their works, the Copyright Directive provides similar rights to film and television producers as well as broadcasters. Finally, the Copyright Directive gives new rights to copyright holders and manufacturers of technological protection mechanisms to prevent circumvention of such mechanisms or the removal of electronic rights management information installed in such products to prevent unauthorised copying, etc.[57] An example of such technological protection mechanisms is digital watermarking. Digital watermarking is a technique which allows copyright owners to add hidden copyright notices or other verification messages to digital audio, video, or image signals and documents.[58] While the addition of the hidden message to the signal does not restrict that signal's use, it provides a mechanism to track the signal to the original owner.[59]

An owner of copyright has the exclusive right in the UK to 'communicate the work to the public'.[60] The act of communication to the public becomes one of the acts restricted by copyright in (1) literary, dramatic, musical or artistic work; (2) sound recording or films; or (3) a broadcast.[61] It contains two mutually exclusive types of communication: broadcasting of a work, on the one hand,[62] and the making available

---

[54] Quoting Lord Reid in *Ladbroke (Football) Ltd* v *William Hill (Football)* [1964] 1 WLR 273.
[55] World Intellectual Property Organisation.
[56] Directive 2001/29/EC of the European Parliament and of the Council of 22 May 2001 on the harmonisation of certain aspects of copyright and related rights in the information society.
[57] Sections 296 and 296ZA–ZF of the CDPA 1988.
[58] Source: article on 'Digital Watermarking' from wikipedia available at: http://en.wikipedia.org/wiki/Digital_watermarking.
[59] Ibid.
[60] CDPA 1988, s20.
[61] Ibid.
[62] CDPA 1988, s6.

right to the public on an interactive basis. The difference between broadcast and making available is that making available requires, first, that fixation takes place (initial upload). If transmission is interactive, then it cannot be broadcast. This making available right is in effect the right to place a copyright work on a website or other electronic destination in such a way that members of the public may access the work when they choose.[63]

The Copyright Directive provides for a number of exemptions from infringement which Member States may allow. Only one of those exemptions is mandatory: the exemption for transient copies. Article 5(1) of the Copyright Directive excludes liability from copies of work made on networks as files which are exchanged through the Internet, and where that temporary copying has no economic significance. This relates to the automatic temporary copying that is carried out by computers automatically in the course of online access, such as internet browsing. This has been adopted into law in the UK through the Copyright and Related Rights Regulations 2003 and creates a new s28A of the CDPA 1988:[64]

> 'Copyright in a literary work, other than a computer programme or a database or in a dramatic, musical or artistic work, the typographical arrangement of a published edition, a sound recording or a film, is not infringed by the making of a temporary copy which is transient or incidental which is an integral and essential part of a technical process and the sole purpose of which is to enable:
>
> a) a transmission of the work in a network between third parties by an intermediary; or
>
> b) a lawful use of the work; and which has no independence significance.'

This goes further than the Electronic Commerce (EC Directive) Regulations 2002[65] that implemented into UK law the E-Commerce Directive (published 17 July 2000 in the Official Journal).[66] While the E-Commerce Directive provided an innocent defence to infringement, the Copyright Directive 'deems the reproduction not to be an infringement, irrespective of questions of knowledge'.[67] The Copyright and Related Rights Regulations 2003 also create a legal framework whereby the owners of copyright may more easily secure an injunction against a 'service provider' whose services are used by a third party to infringe a copyright or related right.[68] This can be found in s97A CDPA 1988, which provides for an injunction against service providers. The definition of 'service provider' can be found in the Electronic Commerce (EC Directive) Regulations 2002.[69]

The E-Commerce Directive as implemented by Electronic Commerce (EC

---

[63] Article 3(1) of the Copyright Directive provides that: 'Member States shall provide authors with the exclusive right to authorise or prohibit any communication to the public of their works, by wire or wireless means, including the making available to the public of their works in such a way that members of the public may access them from a place and at a time individually chosen by them'.
[64] The full text of these Regulations are available at: http://www.legislation.hmso.gov.uk/si/si2003/20032498.htm.
[65] SI 2002/2013.
[66] Directive 2000/31/EC on certain legal aspects of information society services, in particular electronic commerce in the Internal Market.
[67] Trevor Cook, 'New copyright regulations – UK', Computer Law & Security Report, Vol 20, No 1, 2004, 17–21.
[68] Ibid at 20.
[69] Regulation 2 of the Electronic Commerce (EC Directive) Regulations 2002.

Directive) Regulations 2002[70] addresses three online liability issues for Internet service providers (ISPs). This covers three main special defences available to ISPs: mere conduit (art 12 of the E-Commerce Directive); caching (art 13 of the E-Commerce Directive); and hosting (art 14 of the E-Commerce Directive). Article 12 (see reg 17 of the Electronic Commerce (EC Directive) Regulations 2002) provides the mere conduit defence, namely that:

'17(1) Where an information society service is provided which consists of the transmission in a communication network of information provided by a recipient of the service or the provision of access to a communication network, the service provider (if he otherwise would) shall not be liable for damages or for any other pecuniary remedy or for any criminal sanction as a result of that transmission where the service provider –

(a) did not initiate the transmission;

(b) did not select the receiver of the transmission; and

(c) did not select or modify the information contained in the transmission.

(2) The acts of transmission and of provision of access referred to in paragraph (1) include the automatic, intermediate and transient storage of the information transmitted where:

(a) this takes place for the sole purpose of carrying out the transmission in the communication network, and

(b) the information is not stored for any period longer than is reasonably necessary for the transmission.'

Article 15 (see reg 22 of the Electronic Commerce (EC Directive) Regulations 2002) provides further that Member States shall not impose a general obligation on providers, when providing the services covered by arts 12 to 14, to monitor the information which they transmit or store. Nor does it impose a general obligation to actively seek facts or circumstances indicating illegal activity.

Caching occurs when an ISP places information into temporary storage in order to increase the efficiency of the system by allowing immediate re-display of a page without the need to retrieve it from the original source. This avoids the technical problem that occurs when information, requested by a computer, takes too long to arrive from the applicable memory source (whether it is the computer's own memory or that of another computer over the Internet). A cache memory is more proximate to the party requesting the information. It holds only that information recently or frequently requested so that this frequently used information is readily available and can be accessed quickly again and again. An Internet cache sits between the web server computer and the computers making requests such as HTML pages, images, files, etc. Some of this information may be stored in a server cache so that next time the information is requested it can be provided quickly. Caching also occurs on the end user's computer. Client caching occurs where the end user's browser copies to its cache memory, recently downloaded images, say, for quick retrieval, rather than having to access the Internet again. Article 13 of the E-Commerce Directive[71] states that the service provider is not liable where the service consists of the transmission in a

---

[70] SI 2002/2013.
[71] Regulation 22 of the Electronic Commerce (EC Directive) Regulations 2002.

communications network of information provided by a recipient of the service where the information is the subject of automatic, intermediate and temporary storage for the sole purpose of making more efficient the onward transmission of the information to other recipients of the service upon their request.

Regulation 18 of the Electronic Commerce (EC Directive) Regulations 2002 sets forth the caching regulations:

'18. Where an information society service is provided which consists of the transmission in a communication network of information provided by a recipient of the service, the service provider (if he otherwise would) shall not be liable for damages or for any other pecuniary remedy or for any criminal sanction as a result of that transmission where – (a) the information is the subject of automatic, intermediate and temporary storage where that storage is for the sole purpose of making more efficient onward transmission of the information to other recipients of the service upon their request, and (b) the service provider – (i) does not modify the information; (ii) complies with conditions on access to the information; (iii) complies with any rules regarding the updating of the information, specified in a manner widely recognised and used by industry; (iv) does not interfere with the lawful use of technology, widely recognised and used by industry, to obtain data on the use of the information; and (v) acts expeditiously to remove or to disable access to the information he has stored upon obtaining actual knowledge of the fact that the information at the initial source of the transmission has been removed from the network, or access to it has been disabled, or that a court or an administrative authority has ordered such removal or disablement.'

Hosting involves the ISP storing information for the recipient of the service, such as the storage of e-mails for subsequent user access. Under art 14 of the Electronic Commerce Directive, a service provider is not liable in respect of storage if the service provider does not have actual knowledge of illegal activity or information and, where a claim for damages is made, is not aware of the facts or circumstances from which the illegal activity or information would have been apparent or, upon obtaining such knowledge or awareness, the service provider acts expeditiously to remove or disable access to the information. The defence does not apply if the recipient of the service (that is, the recipient who provided the information in question) was acting under the authority or control of the service provider. The provisions for determining whether a service provider has actual notice are the same as those that apply to caching, under reg 22 of the Electronic Commerce (EC Directive) Regulations 2002.

The applicable provisions of the Electronic Commerce (EC Directive) Regulations 2002 are set forth in reg 19:

'19. Where an information society service is provided which consists of the storage of information provided by a recipient of the service, the service provider (if he otherwise would) shall not be liable for damages or for any other pecuniary remedy or for any criminal sanction as a result of that storage where – (a) the service provider – (i) does not have actual knowledge of unlawful activity or information and, where a claim for damages is made, is not aware of facts or circumstances from which it would have been apparent to the service provider that the activity or information was unlawful; or (ii) upon obtaining such knowledge or awareness, acts expeditiously to remove or to disable access to the information, and (b) the recipient of the service was not acting under the authority or the control of the service provider.'

3.3 The Database Right

From 1 January 1998, a new form of intellectual property right was established in UK law with relevance to copyright and the Internet. The Database Directive[72] was implemented in UK law by the Copyright and Rights in Databases Regulations 1997 (SI 1997/3032). SI 1997/3032, reg 6, amended the CDPA 1988[73] creating a new sui generis right effective against the extraction and/or re-utilisation of a substantial part of the contents of a database. This right may subsist concurrently to copyright items that constitute the database.

As a whole, a website can also be a database if it fulfils the following definitional requirements:

'3A. – (1) In this Part "database" means a collection of independent works, data or other materials which – (a) are arranged in a systematic or methodical way, and (b) are individually accessible by electronic or other means. (2) For the purposes of this Part a literary work consisting of a database is original if, and only if, by reason of the selection or arrangement of the contents of the database the database constitutes the author's own intellectual creation.'[74]

Traditionally, one of the basic requirements for a functional database has been that its contents are stored in accordance with a predetermined structure. This emphasis of a predetermined structure as a prerequisite for database protection has been rejected by Mr Justice Laddie:

'Nothing in the [Database] Directive supports the second part [the] submission relating to "database-ness" which runs together two entirely distinct concepts, namely the feature of form which have to exist before a database will be recognized as existing and the features of content or investment which are protected once a database is held to exist. Thus a database consists of a collection of data brought together in a systematic or methodical way so as to be individually accessible by electronic or other means ... On the contrary, what has to be protected is not primarily the form but the investment which into "obtaining, verifying or presenting the contents" of the database as made clear ... [I]t is for this reason that substantial investment in verification still qualifies for database right ...'[75]

More problematic issues will arise where the retrieval software is separate from the data being searched, as is the case with information accessed through the World Wide Web. In other words the list of materials identified by a search engine as meeting the user's request will itself constitute a database. Further problems arise if the items which constitute the data are not themselves copyright, either as individual items or as a non-copyrightable collection.

A new database right will arise when there has been a substantial investment in obtaining, verifying or presenting the contents of the database. The maker of the database will be the first owner of the database right except in the case where the work is created by an employee, in which event the employer will own the right (regs 13 and 14, SI 1997/3032).

---

[72] Directive 96/9/EC.
[73] Section 3A(2) CDPA 1988.
[74] Section 3A(1) and (2) CDPA 1988.
[75] *British Horseracing Board Ltd, the Jockey Club and the Weatherbys Group Ltd* v *William Hill Organization Ltd* [2001] 2 CMLR 232 at 234.

The database right will come into existence when a database is made available to the public and will subsist for a period of 15 years. It is provided in reg 17, SI 1997/3032, however, that:

> 'Any substantial change to the contents of a database, including a substantial change resulting from the accumulation of successive additions, deletions or alterations, which would result in the database being considered to be a substantial new investment shall qualify the database resulting from that investment for its own term of protection.'

The application of this provision should be non-problematic where databases (perhaps a telephone directory) are issued on an annual basis.

3.4 Patent Protection and the Internet

A discussion of the implications of patent law protection for Internet application is beyond the scope of this book. However, some basics are worth noting. First, s1(2)(c) Patents Act (PA) 1977 (see also art 52(2)(c) of the European Patent Convention (the 'EPC')) states that patents are not to be awarded for computer programmes. Despite this, however, both the PA 1977 and the EPC add language to the effect: 'but the foregoing provision shall prevent anything being treated as an invention for the purposes of this Act only to the extent that a patent or an application for a patent relates to that thing as such'.[76] Given this, may a software-related invention be patented? The answer appears to be yes, in the UK and under the EPC, if the patent application applies to something more than just a computer programme.[77] The decision of the European Patent Office Technical Board of Appeal in Vicom/Computer-Related Inventions (July 1986)[78] affirmed the patentability of software-related inventions under the EPC. *Merrill Lynch's Application*[79] does the same for software-related inventions under the PA 1977. For later treatment of the same doctrines and its applicability under the EPC and its interrelation with the TRIPS Agreement 1994, see the February 1999 European Patent Convention Board of Appeal decision in the *Application of IBM*.[80] The TRIPS Agreement (binding on the UK and EU) provides in art 27 that patents should be available for 'any inventions, whether products or processes, in all fields of technology' including software.

At this point the EU is considering changing the current European patent regime with respect to exclusion of software patents.[81] The present exclusion of software from patent protection may be coming to an end: 'After years of debate, the law seems set to get off the ground. EU industry ministers this week broke a 10-month stalemate and voted in favour of the new legislation. But the issue must still go back to the European

---

[76] PA 1977, s1(2); and EPC, art 52(3).
[77] The Community Patent Convention (the Luxembourg Convention) (CPC) was entered into in 1975 with a subsequent agreement being concluded in 1989 (the Luxembourg Agreement). Yet, as of today, the CPC has never entered into force.
[78] *Vicom System's Inc's Application* [1987] 2 EPOR 74.
[79] *Merrill Lynch's Application* [1989] RPC 561, reported at first instance at [1988] RPC 1.
[80] Case T0935/97 [1999] RPC 861.
[81] See proposed Software Patent Directive to the Directive on the Enforcement of Intellectual Property Rights (2004/48/EC, 29 April 2004).

parliament, which has four months to back the law, reject it or table the amendment.'[82] The proposed Software Patents Directive would allow software developers to patent software that makes a technical contribution: 'critics warn that such a definition is far too generous and could open a backdoor route to more general software patents'.[83] They said 'it could prevent developers from building on widely used lines of code'.[84]

The debate on software patents is symptomatic of a larger problem in Europe; it is not so easy to gain patent protection against the EU:

'Pierre-André Dubois, IP partner at Kirkland & Ellis, the Chicago based law firm, believes the failure to create a single, centrally enforceable EU patent is the biggest issue for companies looking to protect their ideas across Europe. He says: "I spoke to a sophisticated US client recently and he thought we could just file a single action in the EU. He was surprised when I told him it would probably take five or six actions in different countries".'[85]

In sum, there is widespread dissatisfaction with the existing community patent system arising from the European Patent Convention. Whether this dissatisfaction with the present system of handling 'bundles of separate national patents administered through the European Patent Office' with litigation over the same in respective national courts will survive another decade remains to be seen. Nonetheless, it highlights just one of the many complexities involved with intellectual property rights arising out of software, a key component of the digital revolution produced through the Internet.

---

[82] Bob Sherwood and Nikki Tait, 'Europe Lacks Vision on Innovation', *Financial Times*, 10 March 2005, p19.
[83] Ibid.
[84] Ibid.
[85] Ibid.

4   Contractual Aspects, Choice of Law and the Internet

4.1   Contractual Aspects of E-Commerce

4.2   Taxation

4.3   Jurisdiction and the Internet

In this chapter, we consider some of the basic contractual aspects involved with the Internet. For instance, suppose a business wishes to hire a consultant to set up an Internet website. Who owns the copyright to the work product that is created? What choice of law aspects must be considered when entering into a contract over the Internet? Jurisdiction creates some very knotty problems for courts to consider in the event that there is a dispute between individuals and companies in different countries. Whose law governs? These and other questions are considered here.

4.1 Contractual Aspects of E-Commerce

E-commerce is generally about the making of contracts using the Internet. It does not form any special branch of English law and is to be dealt with by the normal rules of the law of contract.[1] Some academics and practitioners have questioned whether English law as it stands is capable of coping with this new phenomenon because of the special attributes of online contracting. Online contracts are no different to paper contracts; what is unique is the contracting process.

Contracts are formed in the world of the Internet as easily as they are off line. Under English law for a contract to be valid several conditions must be satisfied:

- offer;

- acceptance;

- consideration;

- intention to create legal relations.

These conditions remain whether the contract is an e-contract or a straightforward online contract.

In the e-contract scenario, often it is the case that the parties do not meet and use distance-selling methods to enter into an agreement. This may not be so unique. After all, this happens frequently in the world of non-e-commerce contracts as well. Similarly, in the case of a contract enabling e-commerce, for instance, a contract for the creation of a website, the contract may be formed by the parties meeting one another or not. The e-contract will relate to the object of the contract rather than its form.

---

[1] For instance, *Obligations: Contract Law Textbook*, D G Cracknell, Old Bailey Press (2005).

For example, a hosting contract enabling a website to be hosted by a professional and made available for customers to access over the Internet.

Offer

An offer is the clear indication of the party to be bound by the terms of the offer. This can be communicated in a number of ways, including electronic communications. An invitation to treat is not intended to be legally binding but unfortunately might be construed by the customer as such. Hence, the cyber-trader will need to ensure that his online communications are set out and framed in such a way so as not to cause uncertainty. He or she must also ensure that the communications are not construed as unilateral offers; *Carlill* v *Carbolic Smoke Ball Co* [1893] 1 QB 256.

It is necessary to distinguish an offer from what the law classifies as an invitation to treat. The intention of the parties is important. The law has laid down various general rules covering standard commercial situations, such as display of goods in a shop (*Fisher* v *Bell* [1961] 1 QB 394; *Pharmaceutical Society of GB* v *Boots* [1953] 1 QB 401) and advertisements of goods and services for sale (*Partridge* v *Crittenden* [1968] 2 All ER 421). It is not yet settled how these general rules, which can be excluded by the contrary intention of the parties, will apply to common e-contract situations.

Consider for instance the following facts:

'A telly for under a fiver? You'd have to be either insane or just back from the updated Argos website, where a Sony TV was on sale for a mere £3.00. The price has now been changed, but the company says it has received a number of multiple orders from online customers. Argos has just updated its site for the autumn season. Over 500 new products – including the bargain TV were added to the site yesterday. The official line is that there was a "transcription error" somewhere between Argos and the company that maintains its website. However, the exact source of the error has yet to be tracked down. Those who spotted the mistake and ordered the Sony television will be disappointed, as Argos has no plans to actually sell the TVs for £3.00. Until money has changed hands, Argos has no contract with its customers, and is under no obligation to fulfil the orders. Which is just as well, since the people who spotted the bargain, put in orders for ten or 15 TVs. The television is now advertised at the correct price of £299.99. A spokeswoman for Argos commented: "We cannot fulfil the orders we have received – even as a gesture of goodwill. It would simply be too expensive." She was not sure how many orders had been received, but assured The Register that it was a significant number. Expect some disgruntled would-be buyers to sue. The courts maybe take a different view on consumer contracts than Argos.'[2]

Withdrawing an offer

Generally, an offer can be withdrawn before a valid acceptance is made. However, a revocation must be received before it is effective. An offer can also be terminated by a counteroffer (see *Hyde* v *Wrench* (1840) 3 Beav 334). In *Hyde*, the defendant's offer to sell his farm for £1,000 was in effect rescinded by the plaintiff's counteroffer for £950. Consider also the problem with the battle of the forms (see *Butler Machine Tool Co* v *Ex-Cell-O Co* [1979] 1 All ER 965). In *Butler*, the buyer accepted the offer

---

[2] Lucy Sheriff, 'Argos welshes on three quid TV Net "offer" ', The Register, 7 September 1999, available at: http://www.theregister.co.uk/1999/09/07/argos_welshes_on_three_quid/.

of the seller but substituted its own terms and conditions instead of using those furnished by the seller. Where the seller had accepted the differing terms, it was bound by such terms and not the original offer.

Acceptance

Acceptance is to be distinguished from a counteroffer (*Hyde* v *Wrench* (1840) 3 Beav 334). Commercial parties usually prefer to deal on their own 'standard terms'. Where two business are negotiating with each other, each insisting that the contract be on its own set of terms, this can result in the so-called 'battle of the forms' (*Butler Machine Tool Co* v *Ex-Cell-O Co* [1979] 1 All ER 965): each side responding to the other by issuing its own standard terms appears to be making a counteroffer.

Communicating acceptance

Acceptance has to be communicated in order to be effective. Acceptance in online transactions has the potential to be extremely controversial. Usually the acceptance is communicated to a machine (the computer) or is made by a machine. This raises the question as to whether English law recognises a computer as a proper contracting party. In general, the law will attribute acts and omissions of a machine to the person who executes it. In *Thornton* v *Shoe Lane Parking* [1971] 2 QB 163, the court had to consider the contractual implications in the use of an automated car park. Denning LJ (as he then was) held that the customer was committed at the very moment when he put his money into the machine:

> 'The contract was thus concluded at that time. It can be translated into offer and acceptance in this way: the offer is made when the proprietor of the machine holds it out as being ready to receive the money. The acceptance takes place when the customer puts his money into the slot.'[3]

The owner or person in control of the computer is bound by the legal communications made by the computer if such communications had been programmed into the computer by the owner or person in control. It would therefore appear that English law would treat a web server as a mere agent of the cyber-trader or cyber-consumer and can make contracts on their behalf provided the relevant communications were pre-programmed by the natural or legal persons concerned.

Unless specifically stipulated, the method of acceptance can be made by any communication method that is reasonable. According to the E-Commerce Directive[4] (as implemented by Electronic Commerce (EC Directive) Regulations 2002[5]) in the case of consumer contracts concluded over the Internet the service provider will need to specify clearly, comprehensibly and unambiguously and prior to the order being placed by the recipient of the service:

---

[3] [1971] 2 QB 163, at 169.
[4] Directive 2000/31/EC of the European Parliament and of the Council of 8 June 2000 on certain legal aspects of information society services, in particular electronic commerce, in the Internal Market (Directive on electronic commerce), OJ L178, 17.7.2000, came into effect on 21 August 2002.
[5] The Electronic Commerce (EC Directive) Regulations 2002 (SI 2002/2013).

- the different technical steps to follow to conclude the contract;

- whether or not the concluded contract will be filed by the service provider and whether it will be accessible;

- the technical means for identifying and correcting input errors prior to the placing of the order; and

- the languages offered for the conclusion of the contract.[6]

Member States must ensure that the service provider indicates any relevant codes of conduct to which he subscribes and the information on how those codes can be consulted electronically.[7] It is also incumbent on the trader to ensure that the terms displayed online can be downloaded and saved for reproduction by the customer.[8] It should be noted that these provisions do not apply where the contract is made exclusively by the exchange of e-mails or equivalent individual communications.[9] They only apply to contracts made over the Internet (usually by a click-wrap method). A click-wrap agreement is one whereby a customer enters into a binding contract by agreeing online via the click of a mouse to be bound by the terms of the contract.[10]

E-mails are to be treated differently[11] because they are not 'real-time' communications in that they are not instantaneous. They must be accessed by the receiver from the 'mail-box'. An Internet web click-wrap contract on the other hand is received and processed almost instantaneously by the receiver's computer.[12] This raises other implications under English law. It would appear that the postal rule[13] will apply to e-mail acceptances but not click-wrap acceptances. Click-wrap acceptances will be treated as an instantaneous communication,[14] and will be treated as effective only when it is received. On the other hand, an e-mail acceptance will probably be treated as effective once it is posted, regardless of whether it has been received or read (*Adams* v *Lindsell* (1818) 1 B & Ald 681; *Byrne* v *Van Tienhoven* (1880) 5 CPD 344).

Verification of authenticity of contracting party: electronic signatures

As will be seen later in the section on e-finance, the fact that the parties may never meet presents unique problems. First, there is the risk from the consumer's point of

---

[6] E-Commerce Directive, art 10(1)(a)–(d).
[7] E-Commerce Directive, art 10(2).
[8] E-Commerce Directive, art 10(3).
[9] E-Commerce Directive, art 10(4).
[10] See David Callan, 'How click-wrap contracts benefit over shrink-wrap contracts', (2004), available online at: http://www.akamarketing.com/click-wrap-shrink-wrap-contracts.html and Martin Samson, 'Internet Law – Click Wrap Agreement', 10 June 2004, available online at: http://www.phillipsnizer.com/library/topics/click_wrap.cfm.
[11] See *Brinkibon Ltd* v *Stahag Stahl und Stahlwarenhandel GmbH* [1982] 1 All ER 293 where the House of Lords dealt with the analogous technological issue of acceptance by telex machine.
[12] See E-Commerce Directive, art 11, which concerns the placing of an order over the Internet. Once again, we are not referring to transactions entered into by e-mail but rather Internet 'click-wrap' agreements.
[13] Where acceptance by post has been requested (or where it is an appropriate and reasonable means of communication between the parties), then acceptance is complete immediately upon posting of the acceptance letter: *Household Fire and Carriage Insurance Co* v *Grant* (1879) 4 Ex D 219.
[14] See *Entores Ltd* v *Miles Far East Corporation* [1955] 2 All ER 493 for a discussion of instantaneous communication. Where technology allows instantaneous communication, a contract is concluded when acceptance is received, not when it's sent.

view that he or she may pay for something but never receive the products ordered. This is plain-old fashioned fraud and will be covered in the e-Crime section. From the point of view of the seller, the problem of repudiation is a real concern. At common law, the repudiation of a traditional signature may occur if the signature is a forgery; or, if the signature is a non-forgery, but was obtained through unconscionable conduct by a party to a transaction or fraud or unconscionable conduct by a third party to the transaction.[15] In the digital environment, 'it is submitted that the law should not in the electronic commerce environment alter this position as regards to the legal rights of parties to repudiate a digital signature'.[16]

Assuming that you can get beyond the writing requirement of an actual hand-made signature to bind an individual to an actual contract, other questions arise. Even though not all contracts concluded between a vendor and a consumer will require a written and signed document, other issues may give rise to situations where one party to an Internet transaction may have reasonable grounds to be uncertain about the other party's identity, and will be legally bound by the contract or the date of conclusion of the contract that is normally included in paper versions.

An electronic signature is 'a means of identifying a person by computer-generated code rather than a hand-written signature. This code, usually generated through the use of encryption keys, is attached to an electronic document as a means of signing the document.'[17] The Electronic Signatures Regulations 2002[18] which implements Directive 1999/93/EC of the European Parliament and of the Council on a Community framework for electronic signatures, defines an 'electronic signature' to mean 'data in electronic form which are attached to or logically associated with other electronic data and which serve as a method of authentication'. The use of digital signatures[19] and encryption[20] can alleviate the concerns highlighted above regarding the risks of repudiation and the requirement of writing. A digital signature fixes the identity of the contracting parties by removing doubts as to the authority of the parties contracting with each other. It also confirms the identity of the individual that has accepted the terms offered. Finally, a digital signature confirms the date the contract was formed confirming the exact time of formation. This is a function that cannot be performed by written documents.

Contract formation

The point at which the acceptance is communicated is also important for determining

---

[15] Adrian McCullagh and William Caelli, 'Non-Repudiation in the Digital Environment', available at: http://www.firstmonday.org/issues/issue5_8/mccullagh/.
[16] Ibid.
[17] Fraser Morel and Richard Jones, 'De-mystifying Electronic Signatures and Electronic Signatures Law from a European Union Perspective', World Data Protection Report, October 2002, BNA International Inc.
[18] The Electronic Signatures Regulations 2002 (SI 2002/318).
[19] A digital signature is a narrower subset of electronic signature. Although these terms are used interchangeably, a digital signature is a method of using encryption to certify the source and integrity of a particular electronic document. Electronic signature is the legal term of art.
[20] Encryption is the process of obscuring information to make it unreadable without special knowledge. The section on e-finance which follows hereafter covers this topic extensively.

when and where the contract is formed. In a face-to-face transaction, these points do not usually give rise to difficulty but where parties are dealing at a distance, as in e-contracts, the exact point at which the contract is concluded can be controversial. The exact point at which the contract is concluded is important because it establishes when a negotiating party's right to unilaterally withdraw is lost, which acceptance is first in time if there are competing acceptances for a limited number of contractual opportunities and it establishes where the contract is concluded which, in cross-border transactions, can help to determine which jurisdiction's law applies to the contract. See *Brinkibon Ltd* v *Stahag Stahl und Stahlwarenhandel GmbH* [1982] 1 All ER 293.

Similarly, in e-commerce there are specific rules as to how an order placed online is deemed accepted. These are set forth in the E-Commerce Directive as implemented by the Electronic Commerce (EC Directive) Regulations 2002 (SI 2002/2013). The E-Commerce Directive also makes provision for the principles to be applied by Member States to ensure that consumers who place online orders (namely make online acceptances) are protected.

Article 11(1) of the E-Commerce Directive defines these principles as:

• the service provider has to acknowledge the receipt of the recipient's order without undue delay and by electronic means (this does not apply where the contract was concluded exclusively through the exchange of e-mails); and

• the order and the acknowledgement of receipt are deemed to be received when the parties to whom they are addressed are able to access them.

Article 11(2) requires Member States to require 'the service provider makes available to the recipient of the service appropriate, effective and accessible technical means allowing him to identify and correct errors prior to the placing of the order'. Article 11(2) does not apply where the contract was made exclusively by exchange of e-mails.

As far as business-to-business transactions are concerned, parties are free to derogate from these provisions by agreement.[21] This approach has been criticised as failing to take into account the interests of SMEs[22] whose bargaining leverage is not always as strong as the law presumes it to be.

Web design contracts

Often a company will contract with a third party to design and update its website on a regular basis. This is especially true for SMEs that lack the capacity to employ a full-time website programmer and operator in-house. In these situations, it is essential that the SME enter into a written agreement that provides for the website designer to assign to the SME any rights in and to the copyright arising as a result of the creation and/or ongoing maintenance and updating of that same website. This is required because, in the absence of such an explicit assignment, the law states that the author

---

[21] Article 11(1)(2) of the E-Commerce Directive.
[22] Small to medium-sized enterprises.

of a work will be the first owner of any copyright which may subsist in it.[23] Thus, absent such an assignment, the website designer and not the SME would own the copyright to the website. However, where the website is being designed by a person who is an employee of the SME, the copyright in the website would be owned by the SME absent explicit agreement to the contrary.[24]

4.2 Taxation

On 26 November 1999 the Inland Revenue and HM Customs and Excise published 'Electronic Commerce: The UK's Taxation Agenda'.[25] The paper sets forth the taxation principles the UK will follow with respect to the Internet. In essence, the Government has emphasised that tax must not interfere with the growth of e-commerce and that tax policy should be neutral in its treatment of e-commerce as opposed to more traditional means of commerce. What this means is that the Government will not tax disproportionately transactions concluded over the Internet as opposed to through other means. In general, the Government has taken the position that it 'does not believe that it is necessary at this stage to make any major changes to existing tax legislation and regulations or to introduce new taxes'.[26]

4.3 Jurisdiction and the Internet

For the most part, we have been talking about e-commerce within the UK. However, we all know that more and more the Internet involves crossing borders. What are the legal implications of cross-border commercial transactions in the context of the Internet? Are there differences to note when entering into an e-contract with a business outside the European Union? To put some legal certainty in place, several pieces of legislation exist in the European Union to deal with jurisdictional disputes arising therein.

The Brussels Regulation (EC) 44/2001

Council Regulation (EC) No 44/2001 of 22 December 2000 on jurisdiction and the recognition and enforcement of judgments in civil and commercial matters[27] is the key regulation concerned herein. It replaces the Brussels Convention.[28] The Brussels Regulation was adopted with e-commerce in mind and it is an attempt to provide a framework usable for e-commerce. The rationale behind the Brussels Regulation is to achieve the European Community goal of a free market where goods, services, capitals and persons move freely from one Member State to another. Recital 1 of the Brussels Regulation states that to achieve such freedom, the measures relating to judicial cooperation in civil matters are necessary for the sound operation of the internal

---

[23] CDPA 1988, s11(1).
[24] Ibid.
[25] http://www.inlandrevenue.gov.uk/taxagenda/index.htm.
[26] Ibid.
[27] OJ L12 of 16.01.2001: see www.europa.eu.int/scadplus/leg/en/lvb/l33054.htm.
[28] Brussels Convention on Jurisdiction and Enforcement of Judgments in Civil and Commercial Matters, as amended by the Convention on the Accession of New Member States to that Convention, 27 September 1968.

market. The Brussels Regulation applies to all Member States except Denmark and applies to 'civil and commercial matters' only. Excluded from its scope are matters relating to: revenue, customs or administrative matters; status or legal capacity of natural persons; matrimonial matters, wills and successions; bankruptcy; social security; and arbitration.[29]

General jurisdiction

Article 2 sets out the principle of general jurisdiction – namely, that a person may be sued in whatever Member State he or she is domiciled in without regard to their citizenship. Article 59(1) states that to determine if a party is domiciled in the Member State whose courts are hearing the matter, the court shall apply its own internal law. Thus, in a matter before an English court, Sch 4 Civil Jurisdiction and Judgments Act 1982[30] would apply:

*   an individual is domiciled in the UK if he is resident in the UK and the nature and circumstance of such residence indicate that he has a substantial connection with the United Kingdom;

*   the substantial connection is presumed if has been resident in the UK for the last three months or more; and

*   an individual is a resident in a particular part of the UK if that place is where he is settled or has his usual place of abode.

Article 59(2) requires that if the individual is not domiciled in the forum state according to its law, the court of that state needs to decide if he is domiciled in another Member State using the law of such other Member State to determine this point. In the case of a company or other legal person, art 60(1) provides that such company or other legal person is domiciled at the place where it has a statutory seat or its central administration or principal place of business.

Special jurisdiction

In certain situations, the general jurisdiction rules are sometimes put aside. This will involve particular types of contracts the nature of which involve the disregard of the general jurisdiction rules. For instance, insurance matters (arts 8–14), consumer contracts (art 15), employment contracts (arts 18–21) are examples of such contracts. The starting point for the application of special jurisdiction is art 5.

Article 5 provides that a person domiciled in one Member State may be sued in another Member State in six different types of matters:

*   matters relating to contracts (excluding employment);

*   matters relating to maintenance;

*   matters relating to tort;

---

[29] Brussels Regulation, art 1.
[30] Civil Jurisdiction and Judgments Act 1982, ss41–46 et seq.

- a civil claim for damages or restitution following an infringement;
- the operations of a branch, agency or other establishment; and
- the payment of remuneration claimed in respect of the salvage of a cargo or freight.

The rules in art 5 do not render the rules based on domicile (art 2) inoperable. Rather, in those cases where the courts of a Member State have special jurisdiction, the claimant can choose to sue the defendant where he is domiciled or where the special jurisdiction arises.

Article 5(1) matters relating to contracts

Article 5(1) gives rise to special rules concerning contracts. First, a person domiciled in one Member State can be sued in another Member State other than the one in which he is domiciled. For instance, a contracting party may be sued in the courts for the place of performance of the obligation in question. This will apply mainly to disputes between professionals. If the jurisdiction issue is not dealt with contractually, art 5 of the Brussels Regulation would apply. Once again, the concept of what is a contract is an autonomous concept, namely, it is to be decided by reference to the Brussels Regulation and related matters and not by looking at national law concepts: see *SPRL Arcado* v *SA Havilland* [1988] ECR 1539. Article 5(1)(b) defines 'place of performance of the obligation' in question. For contracts involving the sale of goods, the place of performance is where the goods are delivered or should have been delivered. In the case of services, the place of performance is where the service was provided or supposed to have been provided. In the context of the Internet, there may be several jurisdictions to consider.

Article 5(1) matters relating to torts

According to art 5(1) the rule of jurisdiction with regards to tort is that a person domiciled in one Member State may be sued in the courts of the Member State where the harmful event occurred or may occur. For most torts, the correct jurisdiction is where the harmful event took place. In libel, it is usually the place of publication. With the Internet it is possible to have materials downloaded to several jurisdictions. If a person has a reputation in such jurisdictions there is a cause of action in each of them. This problem is explored fully in our discussion of Internet libel.

Articles 15–17 jurisdiction over consumer contract

To protect consumers some protective rules are put in place. Consumers when suing have a choice to bring proceedings in a place where the defendant is domiciled or where they are domiciled. This goes only one way, however, as proceedings against consumers may only be brought in the country where the consumer is domiciled. To benefit from the consumer protective rules, the following conditions must be fulfilled:

- a consumer contract must be involved;
- for the sale of goods on instalment credit terms; or

- for a loan repayable by instalments or for any other form of credit, made to finance the sale of goods; or

- in all other cases, if the contract has been concluded with a person who pursues commercial or professional activities in the Member State of the consumer's domicile or directs such activities to that Member State.[31]

A consumer contract is defined as one made by a person for a purpose outside its trade or profession; this definition is a concept to be interpreted autonomously.[32]

With regard to the Internet, the notion of directed activity can cause real problems. Websites, of course, are posted for the entire world to see. Yet, essentially, this means that a website may be sued in any country in the world where this website may be accessed. A potential problem with regards to defining the term 'directed' would appear to be the fact that whilst the Regulation introduces this concept in an effort to cater for the new e-commerce environment, there is in reality no legal definition of the term in the Brussels Regulation. Perhaps, one way to make sense of what 'directed' means is to look at the rationale behind the concept of active or passive websites:

> 'The concept of activities pursued in or directed towards a Member State is designed to make clear that point (3) applies to consumer contracts concluded via an interactive website accessible in the State of the consumer's domicile. The fact that a consumer simply had knowledge of a service or possibility of buying goods via a passive website accessible in his country of domicile will not trigger the protective jurisdiction.'[33]

In certain situations, the parties in advance can agree to decide which court will have jurisdiction to resolve a dispute between the parties. This can be done if such agreement is:

- in writing or can be evidenced in writing (this includes electronic communications);

- in a form that conforms with practices where the parties have established themselves; and

- in international trade or commerce, in a form which accords with a usage of which the parties are or ought to be aware of and that is regularly observed by parties to the same particular types of trades.[34]

However, for consumer contracts, the applicable provision is art 17 of the Brussels Regulation which strictly limits the options in terms of choosing a jurisdiction. Interestingly, contracts with consumers on the Internet that impose a jurisdiction on the consumer other than his or her actual domicile may, therefore, be contrary to the Brussels Regulation. For more on this point, see Wild, Weinstein and Riefa, *'Council Regulation (EC) 44/2001 and Internet Consumer Contracts: Some Thoughts on Article 15 and the Futility of Applying "In the Box" Conflict of Law Rules to the "Out of the Box" Borderless World', BILETA Conference 24–25 March 2004*: www.bileta.ac.uk.

---

[31] Brussels Regulation, art 15(1)(a), (b) and (c).
[32] Brussels Regulation, art 15(1)(c).
[33] 'Proposal for a Council Regulation (EC) on jurisdiction and the recognition and enforcement of judgments in civil and commercial matters (presented by the Commission)', COM (1999) 348 final 99/0154 (CNS).
[34] Brussels Regulation, art 23.

The European Commission has been urging the use of alternative dispute resolution mechanisms, eg, the use of mediation panels as opposed to litigation, etc, in the consumer area as a way to increase consumer confidence and allow cheaper and faster ways of resolving disputes. For instance, art 17 of the E-Commerce Directive requires that Member States shall avoid obstacles to the use of alternative dispute resolution mechanisms. In the online world, we have seen how organisations such as ICANN and WIPO have sponsored alternative dispute resolution mechanisms to resolve domain name disputes without the need for parties to go to court.

Finally, it should be noted that in a cross-border dispute it is necessary to determine not only which country's courts have jurisdiction, but also which law is to be applied to the resolution of the dispute. These two questions are distinct from each other: the fact that jurisdiction resides with one country does not necessarily mean that the law of that country is the applicable law, although it often will be. This issue, however, is complex and is beyond the subject area of this text. For more on this point, see Christine Riefa, '*Article 5 of the Rome Convention on the Law Applicable to Contractual Obligations of 19 June 1980 and Consumer E-contracts: The Need for Reform*', ICTL, Vol 13, No 1, 2004.

It is hoped that in this brief introduction to jurisdiction and choice of law that some sense for the complexity of this issue is obtained. Whilst in the Internet context, the general assumption is that the domicile of the consumer is the first place to look for where a dispute should be heard, in more complicated matters such as Internet libel or disputes between businesses, different rules will apply. Finally, note that choice of jurisdiction in which to hear the case does not mean automatically that that jurisdiction's law will apply. This is a separate, second step analysis, that must be undertaken apart from which court will hear the case.

e-Finance

5 Key Principles of e-Finance

An important function of electronic commerce sites is the handling of payments over the Internet. Most electronic commerce involves the exchange of some form of money for goods or services.

As will be noted in the next chapter, credit cards have dominated Internet payments since the dawn of e-commerce, primarily because they were already in wide circulation and as such have consumer confidence. This has been despite associated privacy and security concerns.[1] However, as the cost of using credit cards mounted coupled with the gradual availability of a wider range of electronic cash models, both consumers and merchants have begun to question the automatic use of credit cards in the Internet environment. Consequently, in recent years a number of payment systems are competing for widespread approval and eventual dominance.

---

[1] As security became a more dominant concern, credit card companies have started to charge higher fees for Internet enabled merchant accounts, the knock-on effect being that credit cards have become too expensive for many smaller purchases.

At present, four basic payment methods dominate both traditional and electronic business-to-consumer (B-2-C) commerce – (1) cash, (2) cheques, (3) credit cards, and (4) debit cards, which between them account for around 90 per cent of all consumer payments. A smaller but nevertheless growing percentage of consumer payments are made by electronic transfer. Credit cards though are by far the most popular form of consumer electronic payments online. Recent surveys, discussed in the next chapter, have found that more than 80 per cent of worldwide consumer Internet purchases are paid for with credit cards.

Another payment option is limited-use 'scrip', which is electronic cash issued (minted) usually by a private sector company rather than a central bank or a government. Most scrip cannot be exchanged for cash.[2] Instead it must be exchanged for goods or services by the company that initially issued the electronic cash. It is interesting to note at this point that early predictions of possible electronic payment methods pointed towards the adoption of scrip. Unfortunately, as will be noted in subsequent chapters, these predictions did not turn out to be accurate.

In practice, unless a merchant enjoys a monopoly situation within the market place, he needs to offer his customers a range of payment options that are safe, convenient, and widely accepted. Whilst in reality we are still many years, if not decades, away from a universally recognised and utilised electronic payments system on the Internet, there are already a wide range of experiments which pose questions with which the law must deal.

If one takes a closer look at this range of payment schemes, there is an obvious variety in terms of design, complexity and intended usage. This immediately goes some way towards distinguishing electronic money from traditional physical cash which by its very nature is a highly standardised product. The inevitable question is whether this means that electronic money may be classified as cash.

However, this is simply the tip of the iceberg. In order to appreciate fully the current and potential future implications of electronic money, it is worth examining the area on a case-by-case basis. This affords the opportunity to analyse each major payment system in this area and so progress towards an understanding of the way in which electronic money is evolving over time. Moreover, it is important to appreciate the fact that different sectors of the e-commerce environment will inevitably develop their own specific type of payment system (eg e-Bay and the PayPal system), thus generating 'pockets' of utilisation.[3]

Equally, as subsequent chapters will highlight, electronic money has undergone distinct stages of development; in essence key evolutionary stages. To start off with, many electronic money experiments were undertaken simply to prove that it could be done. Whilst many proved to be commercial failures, the systems demonstrated that electronic money was feasible. This was quickly followed by a range of payment

---

[2] Examples of scrip are the Beenz and Flooz experiments in the 1990s.
[3] For instance, we should expect to have electronic money systems which are much more applicable to B-2-B transactions while others are better for B-2-C or P-2-P transactions.

systems which recognised the necessity of attracting a large and loyal consumer base. As such, advertising, incentives[4] and niche marketing[5] were seen as essential components. The latest round of electronic money experiments focuses on the construction of highly sophisticated platforms for the creation and transfer of digital tokens that are sufficiently versatile that they may be used in a range of transactions.[6]

5.1 Is Electronic Money Cash?

The starting point for this discussion is to ascertain a definition of what constitutes legal tender in England and Wales. Section 2(1) Coinage Act 1971[7] refers to the following as legal tender:

'(i) Gold coins are legal tender of any amount.

(ii) Coins of cupro-nickel, silver or bronze are legal tender as follows:

– coins of cupro-nickel or silver denominations of more than ten pence are legal tender of payment of any amount not exceeding £10;

– coins of cupro-nickel or silver of denominations of not more than ten pence are legal tender for payment of any amount not exceeding £5;

– coins of bronze are legal tender for payment of any amount not exceeding 20 pence.

(iii) Coins may be made legal tender by proclamation of Her Majesty or 'called-in' by proclamation.

(iv) Bank notes are legal tender for payment of any amount (see also Currency and Bank Notes Act 1954, s1(1)(2)). Bank notes constitute choses in action, which are designated legal tender.'

Furthermore, s1(4) Currency and Bank Notes Act 1954[8] provides:

'That the holder of bank notes of any denominations shall be entitled, on demand made by him during office hours at the head office of the bank of England, to receive in exchange for the notes bank notes of such lower denominations, being bank notes which for the time being are legal tender in the UK or in England and Wales, as he may specify.'

Consequently, bank notes and coins are regarded as being legal tender and it is on this basis that they must be accepted by a merchant (creditor) in satisfaction of a consumer's (debtor's) payment obligation.[9] If this is compared with the electronic cash systems outlined above, then electronic cash that constitutes good title in the hands of whoever receives it may be said to share some of the qualities[10] of negotiable instruments with cash.[11]

---

[4] Most of which involved the company running at a loss for the first few years.
[5] For example, e-mail money for P-2-P transactions and coupon money in B-2-C commerce.
[6] It is also interesting to note that several of these systems involve partnerships with banks and financial houses.
[7] As amended by the Currency Act 1983. (Note that within the Eurozone euro banknotes are legal tender. See: Hans Weenink, 'The Legal Nature of Euro Banknotes', [2003] JIBLR 433. The UK is not part of the Eurozone.
[8] Section 1(3) of the Act states that: 'bank notes shall be payable only at the head office of the Bank of England, unless expressly made payable at some other place'.
[9] Section 1(3) Currency and Bank Notes Act 1954 states that bank notes shall be payable only at the head office of the Bank of England, unless expressly made payable at some other place.
[10] See: Akindemowo, 'The Fading Rustle, Chink and Jingle: Electronic Value and the Concept of Money', [1998] 21 UNSWLJ 466.
[11] See the rights of a holder in due course under s29 Bills of Exchange Act 1882.

However, it should be stressed that the acceptance of electronic cash in payment for goods and services is not due to the fact that it commands the status of legal tender as outlined above, but because a separate contractual promise[12] exists by the creditor to accept it. Nevertheless, between these parties, it is a true medium of exchange[13] and the prime function of money is to serve as a medium of exchange.

The prime function of money is to serve as a medium of exchange. However, money can also be regarded as a commodity in which case, money shall be treated as personal property rather than as currency. This may have serious consequences.

5.2 What is the Effect of Payment with Electronic Money?

Where a purchaser offers electronic money in satisfaction of his payment obligation, but the merchant ultimately does not receive value from the issuer,[14] the question needs to be posed as to whether recourse may be had to the purchaser for payment on the underlying contract.

In many respects, this depends on the legal significance of the tripartite relationship between the issuer, holder and merchant as well as on the construction of the agreements between the parties. One line of reasoning,[15] which is analogous to that in the case of credit cards, suggests that electronic money constitutes absolute payment for the goods and that the merchant must look only to the issuer for payment.[16] In *Re Charge Card Services*, the Court of Appeal held that there was a presumption of absolute discharge of the cardholder's liability to the vendor when payment is effected with a credit card.[17] The main basis for this inference is the fact that in most cases, the vendor does not have sufficient information about the cardholder (for example his address), to enable the vendor to pursue the cardholder directly for payment. Again, the existence of a peculiar accounting system under the scheme is such that the vendor can only look for payment from the card issuer.

With respect to electronic money, only merchants that have agreed with issuing banks and are equipped with special equipment and terminals can accept payment by that particular electronic money scheme. It could therefore be argued, by analogy with credit cards, that when the user of electronic money completes everything that he is required to do under the particular electronic money scheme to effect payment, then if the merchant ultimately fails to receive value, this is something that must be settled with the electronic money issuer. In other words, the merchant cannot thereafter turn to the user of the electronic money.

However, this is not as straightforward as it may initially appear. In circumstances where the electronic money scheme involves an accounting system or requires

---

[12] This is reliant on a series of agreements between the issuer of the electronic cash and various Internet merchants that it will be recognised and accepted in exchange for goods or services.
[13] Note that the status of a negotiable instrument can be acquired by mercantile usage.
[14] Whether due to the issuer's insolvency or because that payment was intercepted en route and as such was lost.
[15] *Re Charge Card Services* [1989] Ch 497 (CA); [1987] Ch 150 (QB).
[16] Ultimately, this may be in the capacity as an unsecured creditor if the issuer is insolvent.
[17] Refer to Chapter 6, p93 of this book.

verification and/or authorisation before payment is able to take place, it is more difficult to argue that the payment obligation is absolutely discharged. This is because under this type of system, the merchant has the opportunity to pass the cardholder's account details on to the electronic money issuer for verification and authorisation. Consequently, if the merchant chooses to retain these details, he is in a position to utilise this information to track down the holder if he ultimately remains unpaid.

Consequently, in the light of this, if one considers Mondex (see Chapter 7, p145 of this book), then it treats its smart cards as being equivalent to cash. As such, if it is lost or stolen, the value on the card is lost. Equally, this means that payment using the card will be treated as absolute in the same way as cash. By contrast, payment with a traditional cheque is only conditional in nature. In other words, payment takes place once the cheque has cleared and the creditor has received value.

Therefore, an electronic money scheme that involves a third party in order to discharge the user's indebtedness to the merchant may very well be regarded as conditional payment due to the risk that the third party may ultimately refuse to perform (ie authorise payment). However, whereas under the cheque example outlined above a bank undertakes no contractual obligation to the user that it would honour the cheque, many of the electronic cash schemes outlined above involve a direct promise from the issuer to the user that the merchant will be paid for transactions made with the use of the electronic cash and/or card.

At common law, payment lost in the post is generally treated as not discharging a debt obligation.[18] However, in circumstances where the contract stipulates a particular method of payment, that means is taken as meeting the obligation, once properly effected, whether or not it reaches the creditor.[19]

Also material is the purchaser's remedy against the merchant for undelivered or defective goods. This will be determined by the sale contract between the parties. It is unlikely that the purchaser's recourse will be against the issuer rather than the merchant.[20]

5.3 Foreign Currency

An additional issue arises as to the use of international electronic cash systems, or schemes originating in other countries such as the United States. If a foreign debt arises, the question must be posed as to how it may be discharged under English law.

The general rule is that a debt, which is expressed in the currency of a particular country, involves an obligation to pay the nominal amount of that debt in the legal tender at the time of payment of the country in whose currency the debt is expressed.[21] This obligation persists irrespective of any fluctuations, which may have occurred in

---

[18] *Luttges* v *Sherwood* (1895) 11 TLR 233.
[19] *Norman* v *Ricketts* (1886) 3 TLR 182.
[20] L Edgar, 'Payment Systems on the Net: the Issuer-Consumer Relationship', [1999] 1(6) EBL 911.
[21] Lex monetae.

the value of that currency in terms of sterling, or any other currency, between the time when the debt was incurred and the time of payment. This is known as the principle of nominalism.

Therefore, according to this principle, a foreign money obligation is payable in the legal tender of the lex monetac; an approach endorsed in the House of Lords in *Marrache v Ashton* [1943] AC 311. In that case, it was affirmed that in determining the proper discharge of a foreign currency obligation, no reference should be made to the law of the forum or the proper law of the obligation in question. Consequently, a debt that is expressed in a particular currency is payable by the tender of whatever constitutes valid legal tender under that state's law at the date of payment.

However, English law qualifies the principle of nominalism. This is through the introduction of the rule that a debtor is not always bound to tender payment in the foreign currency of the debt. Instead, he has an option to pay either in that foreign currency or in sterling, converted at the date of payment of the relevant obligation in question.[22] If the conversion rate used is appropriate, then it would be difficult to challenge such a tender in sterling: *Barclays Bank* v *Leven Brothers* [1977] QB 270.

In *Miliangos* v *Frank (Textiles) Ltd* [1976] AC 443, the House of Lords held that judgment could be ordered in a foreign currency. Prior to this case, it was a rule of English procedure that judgment could only be given in sterling by the courts. However, following this judgment, the approach to be adopted is that when faced with a debt, the claimant can choose either to receive a judgment in the relevant foreign currency or to have a sum designated in sterling, converted at the date when the court authorises enforcement of the judgment in sterling.[23]

Also of significance to this discussion is *Libyan Arab Foreign Bank* v *Banker's Trust Co* [1989] 1 QB 728. In this case, it was held that the law of the place where an account is kept governs the contract between a bank and its customer. Consequently, if a bank account were maintained in London, then the currency of payment, unless otherwise agreed by the parties, would be sterling. In other words, the proper law of the contract is at the heart of any enforcement of a foreign currency debt.

5.4 The Regulation of Electronic Money

There is currently no regulatory regime in the UK that specifically relates to the issuance of electronic money. Nevertheless, regulation is desirable due to the fact that it would create certainty and confidence in accepting payment by electronic money.[24]

Consequently, a key consideration of e-finance relates to the way in which electronic cash impacts upon existing statutory requirements (such as the Banking Act 1987,

---

[22] See: *Pymont Ltd* v *Schott* [1939] AC 145.
[23] The measure of a foreign currency payment obligation is measured in the currency of account whereas the denomination in which the payment is contractually required to be made is the currency of payment.
[24] For further discussion see: T Tether, 'Electronic Cash – The Regulatory Issues', [1997] 5 JIBFL, p202. (However, note that the discussion relating to the Financial Services Act 1986 needs to be read in the light of the Financial Services and Markets Act 2000.)

and the Bank Charter Act 1844), and whether or not control needs to be exercised over this growing section of the market. Given the fact that many of the examples of electronic cash discussed so far have been the product of private sector operations, it would appear counterproductive to try and limit its future growth and development to central banks. However, it should also be noted that many of the latest generation of electronic cash have attempted to form an alliance and/or partnership with existing banks, which in turn both simplifies[25] and complicates[26] the regulation of electronic cash.

The main objective of existing supervisory regulation in the field of banking is consumer protection.[27] Electronic money issuers, whether bank or non-bank institutions,[28] need to be solvent and to maintain a sufficient level of liquidity to enable them to meet the demands of their customers for repayment. Consequently, there is a requirement for issuers to maintain a minimum amount of their capital in available own funds. Ideally, issuers should comply with strict investment and monetary policies as is the case with banks so as to reduce their liquidity risk. Equally, issuing institutions need to comply with requirements aimed at preventing money laundering and tax evasion.[29]

5.5 Banking Act 1987

Initially, the question should be posed as to whether electronic cash, together with its issuance, constitutes a 'deposit-taking' business under s3 Banking Act 1987. The section provides that acceptance of a 'deposit in the course of carrying on … a business which for the purposes of the Act is a deposit-taking business' requires authorisation by the Bank of England. Sections 5 and 6 go on to define 'deposit'[30] and 'deposit-taking business'[31] respectively. Non-compliance and breach of some of the provisions is made a criminal offence.

As Tunkel and York[32] note, 'the question is whether a "mint" takes deposits of cash in exchange for the issue of "coins" to its customers. If so, it would need to apply to be an authorised institution.'[33] When applied to electronic money, the precise wording of ss5 and 6 become crucial to any analysis. On the one hand, it may be argued that money which is transferred to an electronic cash provider is a 'deposit' within

---

[25] In so much as the state will no longer be dealing with a purely private sector operation, with which there may be associated concerns as to liquidity.

[26] Existing banks and financial institutions are covered by the pieces of legislation which follow. However, little thought has been given to the way in which 'partnerships' are covered.

[27] Refer to Chapter 6 of this book.

[28] See various formats of electronic cash outlined above.

[29] For further discussion see: T C B Tether, 'Electronic Cash – The Regulatory Issues', [1997] 12 BJIB & FL 202; L Edgar, 'Payment on the Net – Regulating Digital Cash Issuers', [1999] 2(3) EBL; H S Obhi, 'Electronic Money – Does it Make the World Go Round?', [1999] 8 IT & Com LJ 29–32.

[30] Section 5(1)(a) defines a 'deposit' as a sum paid over to the deposit-taker on terms that it can be repaid to the depositor upon terms which the parties agree between them.

[31] Section 6(1) defines 'deposit-taking business' as one which finances the lending of money or certain other activities out of the deposits taken.

[32] D Tunkel & S York, 'e-Commerce: A Guide to the Law of Electronic Business', Butterworths, 2nd ed (2000).

[33] Ibid, at p383.

the meaning of s5. Equally, it may viewed as a consequence of this process that the provider will make use of the deposits lodged with it, thus coming within the wording of 'deposit-taking business'.

However, it has also been argued that the issuance of smart cards does not necessarily constitute deposit-taking because the customer buying the card from the bank is not making a 'deposit' and the issuer is not carrying out a 'deposit-taking business'. The statute defines the latter in terms which require the element of repayment of the deposit by the bank to the customer upon request. There is also the vital element that deposit-taking business must involve lending the deposit by way of credit business.[34] Usually, there is no 'repayment' of the purchase price of the electronic money or card. In many cases, it will not be possible to redeem the remainder of the value for cash.

5.6 The Bank Charter Act 1844

The first part of this chapter discussed the issue of electronic 'coins' and 'tokens' by electronic cash providers to their customers. This inevitably raises the question as to the applicability of the Bank Charter Act 1844, which restricts the issue of private bank notes.

Section 11 Bank Charter Act 1844 creates a monopoly in the Bank of England for the issue of private bank notes in England and Wales:

> 'It shall not be lawful for any Banker to draw, accept, make, issue, in England and Wales, any Bill of Exchange or Promissory Note or Engagement for the Payment of money payable to Bearer on Demand, or to borrow, owe, or take up, in England and Wales, any Sums of Money on the Bills or Notes of such Banker payable to Bearer on demand ...'

In this respect, one needs to query whether electronic money is comparable to a bill of exchange or promissory note and whether it involves an engagement for the payment of money as defined by this section. In order to address this, one needs to explore the definition of a bill of exchange and a promissory note under ss3(1) and 83(1) Bills of Exchange Act 1882 respectively:

> 'A bill of exchange is an unconditional order in writing, addressed by one person to another, signed by the person giving it, requiring the person to whom it is addressed to pay on demand or at a fixed or determinable future time a sum certain in money to or to the order of a specified person, or to bearer.'[35]

> 'A promissory note is an unconditional promise in writing made by one person to another signed by the maker, engaging to pay, on demand or at a fixed or determinable future time, a sum certain in money, to, or to the order of, a specified person or to bearer.'[36]

It is clear from the wording that both sections envisage documents to be in written

---

[34] Returning to the Mondex model, it is arguable that this does not fall within the scope of the Banking Act 1987 as it does not deal with the public directly. Rather, it utilises banks, which have already been authorised under the Act, to provide the product to their customers.
[35] Section 3(1) Bills of Exchange Act 1882.
[36] Section 83(1) Bills of Exchange Act 1882.

format with an accompanying signature.[37] As such, it is necessary to review the terms 'in writing' and 'signed' as defined in the Interpretation Act 1978. According to s5 of Sch 1 of the Act, it is assumed that: 'Writing includes typing, printing, lithography, photography and other modes of representing or reproducing words in a visible form'. Consequently, it may be argued that if the wording of this section is extended so as to include electronic printing, such as from a standard PC, then there is no reason why electronic cash is not covered by this provision.[38]

The remaining issue relates to the term 'signed'. The common law outlines the legal implications of a signature as:

'When a document containing contractual terms is signed, then, in the absence of fraud, or, I will add, misrepresentation, the party signing it is bound, and it is wholly immaterial whether he has read the document or not.'[39]

Equally, *Goodman* v *J Eban Ltd*[40] attempts to outline a general principle:

'The essential requirement of signing is the affixing, either by writing with a pen or pencil or by otherwise impressing on the document, one's name or "signature" so as to personally authenticate the document.'

Unfortunately, the term 'signed' is not defined in the Interpretation Act 1978 and case law on this issue has, until recently, been unclear. However, following the Electronic Communications Act 2000, the situation has been resolved. Section 7(1) states:

'(1) In any legal proceedings–

(a) an electronic signature incorporated into or logically associated with a particular electronic communication or particular electronic data, and

(b) the certification by any person of such a signature,

shall each be admissible in evidence in relation to any question as to the authenticity of the communication or data or as to the integrity of the communication or data.'[41]

---

[37] See: R Goode, 'Commercial Law', p483, 3rd ed, Penguin (2004) in which he states that 'Notwithstanding the broad interpretation of "writing" and "signature" to cover electronic messages and signatures, the general view is that the definition in s3 requires that a bill of exchange must be paper-based and the paper signed'. (See also: H Beale & L Griffiths, 'Electronic Commerce: Formal Requirements in Commercial Transactions', [2002] LMCLQ 467, at 483.)
[38] Implementation of the UNCITRAL Model Law would clarify any remaining doubts in this area as art 6 explicitly provides that electronic data messages have the same legal effect as paper-writings.
[39] Per Scrutton LJ, *L'Estrange* v *F Graucob Ltd* [1934] 2 KB 394, at 403.
[40] [1954] 1 All ER 763.
[41] Section 7 goes on to state the following:
'(2) For the purposes of this section an electronic signature is so much of anything in electronic form as –
(a) is incorporated into or otherwise logically associated with any electronic communication or electronic data; and
(b) purports to be so incorporated or associated for the purpose of being used in establishing the authenticity of the communication or data, the integrity of the communication or data, or both.
(3) For the purposes of this section an electronic signature incorporated into or associated with a particular electronic communication or particular electronic data is certified by any person if that person (whether before or after the making of the communication) has made a statement confirming that –
(a) the signature,
(b) a means of producing, communicating or verifying the signature, or
(c) a procedure applied to the signature,
is (either alone or in combination with other factors) a valid means of establishing the authenticity of the communication or data, the integrity of the communication or data, or both.'

Therefore, it is clear that an electronic signature[42] is intended to have the same legal effect as a written signature provided that the signature is verified by an accredited certification service provider.[43] However, despite the fact that both 'terms' may be applied to electronic cash, it remains unclear as to whether it satisfies the requirements of an 'unconditional order' or 'promise in writing' addressed by one person to another.

5.7 Encryption and Electronic Signatures

Before progressing with an analysis of the various regulatory regimes that may apply to electronic cash, it is perhaps worth taking a moment to look at the area of electronic signatures. In many respects, this links with the issue of encryption,[44] which is based on the concept of 'keys'.[45] In order to decipher a message, some form of 'key' is required. However, this key cannot be sent with the message itself, as if it were intercepted, the message could easily be read by a third party.

In 1976 a concept referred to as public key encryption was introduced, which largely resolved the problem outlined above.[46] The public key method allows a sender and a receiver to generate a shared, secret key over an insecure telecommunications line. This process uses an algorithm based on the sender's and receiver's public and private information. Therefore, whilst each set of keys[47] generated is related in the sense that they are derived from each other, they are still unique. The initial procedure is as follows.

* The sender determines a secret value, a.

---

[42] An electronic signature can be used to endorse an electronic document in a way that can be later validated for authenticity. A range of electronic authentication methods, of varying security and reliability, is available for individuals and institutions to use. (Whilst these are also referred to as 'digital signatures', the term 'electronic signature' is the preferred term used in Directive 1999/93/EC on a Community Framework for Electronic Signatures – see below.)

[43] It is obvious from the definition that it coincides with that contained in the EU Directive. Secondly, it might be observed that an electronic signature can be anything in electronic form which has some form of logical algorithm (mathematically or otherwise). However, the definition does not only look at the form of the signature, it also places emphasis on the intended function of the signature. It is therefore both a qualitative and functional definition. It refers to the intended function of the signature to prove authenticity or integrity or both.

[44] Encryption is defined as the transformation of data, via a cryptographic mathematical process, into a form that is unreadable by anyone who does not possess the appropriate secret key. The data, while in this unreadable form, is usually known as ciphertext.

[45] The key contains the binary code used to mathematically transform a message. Nowadays, most keys are based on the public key process (asymmetric cryptography).

[46] One point of interest is the Deep Crack experiment in 1999, whereby the Electronic Frontier Foundation built the first unclassified hardware (referred to as Deep Crack), for cracking messages encoded with DES. In January 1999, EFF together with Distributed.net (an international coalition of computer users), cracked a 56-bit DES encrypted message in less than one day. In fact it took them 22 hours and 15 minutes. Until that point the US Government had claimed that it was impossible for messages encrypted with DES to be broken, or if it was possible, that it would take a multi-million dollar network of computers several months to decrypt a single message. The Deep Crack system was built for a cost of $220,000 and when linked to Distributed.net, was able to test 245 billion keys per second.

[47] Section 14(3) Electronic Communications Act 2000 defines the term 'key' as:
'In this section "key", in relation to electronic data, means any code, password, algorithm, key or other data the use of which (with or without other keys):
(a) allows access to the electronic data; or
(b) facilitates the putting of the electronic data into an intelligible form ...'
and references in this section to depositing a key for electronic data with a person include references to doing anything that has the effect of making the key available to that person.

- A related value, A, is derived from *a*. A is then made public.

- The receiver determines a secret value, *b*.

- A related value, B, is derived from *b*. B is then made public.

- These public keys (A and B) are published to the world at large. They are usually placed in a directory kept with a Trusted Third Party[48] or sent by other means to the recipient.

Encryption in practice:

- party A then encrypts the message, first using his own private key[49] and then with party B's public key;

- the secret key is generated from (*a*,B) and (*b*,A) by an algorithm that makes it computationally infeasible to calculate the secret key from solely knowing the two public values, A and B;

- party B will then decrypt the message using party A's public key together with his own private key.

The Electronic Communications Act 2000[50] provides for the arrangements for registering cryptography service providers[51] and the legal recognition of electronic signatures[52] and the way in which they are created,[53] communicated and verified.[54] This was discussed earlier. However, of particular note here is s6 of the Act which defines 'cryptography support service':

> '(1) In this Part "cryptography support service" means any service which is provided to the senders or recipients of electronic communications, or to those storing electronic data, and is designed to facilitate the use of cryptographic techniques for the purpose of –

---

[48] See: G Jones, 'Trusted? Third? Parties', (2004) Hertfordshire Law Journal, 2(1), 62–66.
[49] This is the equivalent to party A signing the electronic document.
[50] The Act came into force on 25 May 2000.
[51] This is covered in Part I of the Act (ss1–6). In this regard, s1 of the Act states:
'(1) It shall be the duty of the Secretary of State to establish and maintain a register of approved providers of cryptography support services.
(2) The Secretary of State shall secure that the register contains particulars of every person who is for the time being approved under any arrangements in force under s2.
(3) The particulars that must be recorded in every entry in the register relating to an approved person are –
(a) the name and address of that person;
(b) the services in respect of which that person is approved; and
(c) the conditions of the approval.
(4) It shall be the duty of the Secretary of State to ensure that such arrangements are in force as he considers appropriate for –
(a) allowing members of the public to inspect the contents of the register; and
(b) securing that such publicity is given to any withdrawal or modification of an approval as will bring it to the attention of persons likely to be interested in it.'
[52] See: S Mason, 'Electronic Signatures: The Technical and Legal Ramifications' (1999) 10(5) Computers & Law 37.
[53] This is dealt with in Part II of the Act.
[54] It is also worth noting the fact that on 28 July 2000, the Regulation of Investigatory Powers Act 2000 received Royal Assent. The stated purpose of the Act is to ensure that the UK's law enforcement authorities and security agencies have sufficient powers to intercept communication taking place via the Internet and to discharge their responsibilities effectively. Subject to the provisions of the Act, service providers are under a legal obligation to provide access to transmissions and to disclose any protected (ie encrypted) electronic communication or data storage services in an intelligible form.

(a) securing that such communications or data can be accessed, or can be put into an intelligible form, only by certain persons; or

(b) securing that the authenticity or integrity of such communications or data is capable of being ascertained.

(2) References in this Part to the provision of a cryptography support service do not include references to the supply of, or of any right to use, computer software or computer hardware except where the supply is integral to the provision of cryptography support services not consisting in such a supply.'

Note that s6(2) means that approval of support services does not extend to the supply of, or any right to use, computer software or hardware, unless the supply is integral to the provision of the service.

Examples of such cryptography services[55] which require approval would include companies providing services 'certifying the public key of an individual, managing encryption keys, time-stamping electronic signatures, key storage, and the creation of directories of certificates'.[56]

The Electronic Signatures Directive[57] acknowledged the fact that e-commerce inevitably requires the use of 'electronic signatures' together with related services so as to permit the authentication of data used in the process of any transaction on the Internet.[58] The Directive makes a distinction between 'advanced electronic signatures'[59] (art 5(1)) and 'electronic signatures'[60] (art 5(2)) as follows:

'1. Member States shall ensure that advanced electronic signatures which are based on a qualified certificate[61] and which are created by a secure-signature-creation device:

(a) satisfy the legal requirements of a signature in relation to data in electronic form in the same manner as a hand-written signature satisfies those requirements in relation to paper-based data; and

---

[55] Just to confuse matters, these are frequently referred to as 'Trusted Third Parties'.
[56] D Tunkel and S York, 'e-Commerce: A Guide to the Law of Electronic Business', Butterworths, 2nd ed (2000), p59.
[57] Directive 1999/93/EC – the Electronic Signatures Directive.
[58] This Directive represents a slice of a larger plan to integrate electronic commerce into mainstream Internal Market rules. The European Community and its Member States are agreed that electronic signatures are vital to ensure confidence, security and efficiency in electronic communication and commerce. Central to this process is the role of providers of certification services (Trusted Third Parties). In other words, persons or bodies issuing certificates which would then be used to confirm the identity of a person signing electronically. The Directive is chiefly concerned with the 'regulation' of these entities as can be seen from its choice of legal base. The governance of e-commerce, as far as the EU is concerned, is largely to be shared between government and the private sector. This integrated approach of self-regulation and state regulation is reflected in the Directive. Paragraph 13 of the Preamble to the Directive, for instance, states that while Member States may decide how they wish to supervise compliance of the Directive by operators, there is room for private-sector-based supervision systems.
[59] Article 2(2) defines this as follows:
' "... advanced electronic signature" means an electronic signature which meets the following requirements:
(a) it is uniquely linked to the signatory;
(b) it is capable of identifying the signatory;
(c) it is created using means that the signatory can maintain under his sole control; and
(d) it is linked to the data to which it relates in such a manner that any subsequent change of the data is detectable.'
[60] Article 2(1) defines this as follows:
' "... electronic signature" means data in electronic form which are attached to or logically associated with other electronic data and which serve as a method of authentication.'
[61] Note that a 'qualified certificate' is provided by a certification-service-provider (Trusted Third Party) who fulfils the requirements laid down in Annex II to the Directive.

(b) are admissible as evidence in legal proceedings.

2. Member States shall ensure that an electronic signature is not denied legal effectiveness and admissibility as evidence in legal proceedings solely on the grounds that it is:

– in electronic form, or

– not based upon a qualified certificate, or

– not based upon a qualified certificate issued by an accredited certification-service-provider, or

– not created by a secure signature-creation device.'

As noted above, the Electronic Communications Act 2000 makes it clear that all types of electronic signatures, whether or not they are supported by 'approved' providers and irrespective of the jurisdiction where they were issued, will be legally admissible in court. Consequently, it will be left to the courts to decide, on a case-by-case basis, whether an electronic signature has been correctly generated and the weight that should be attached to it as against other evidence.[62]

5.8 Liability for Electronic Signatures and Certificates

The question should be posed as to the legal position between the sender and recipient in the case where one of their electronic signatures had been misappropriated and subsequently misused by a rogue party.

In general, the law on ostensible authority will apply. At common law, an English court will usually find that there is a duty of care between the parties, especially where the parties have habitually relied on each other's electronic signatures and encryption technologies in previous dealings. However, where there is no ostensible authority or assumption of responsibility, the loss will have to be borne by the person relying on that signature.[63]

However, in circumstances where a Trusted Third Party has certified that the signature in question was genuine and could be relied upon, then the principles in *Hedley Byrne* v *Heller* [1964] AC 465 might be utilised to assist the victim of the misuse of the electronic signature.

Finally, an electronic signature may also operate as a representation and as such may estop a party from denying liability under a document which carries his electronic signature.[64] A similar argument could be advanced in respect of the fraudulent use of secret test keys between banks.[65]

A different set of rules apply in the case of a consumer who has an electronic signature for use with a credit card (or for drawing money from an account that is in debit). The card issuer will not be able to rely on these principles to pass liability for

---

[62] For further discussion refer to: G Jones, 'Failings in the Treatment of Electronic Signatures', (2003) Hertfordshire Law Journal, 1(1), 101–106.
[63] See: *Brostoff* v *CKL* [1998] PNLR 635.
[64] *Greenwood* v *Martins Bank Ltd* [1933] AC 51.
[65] *Standard Bank London* v *The Bank of Tokyo Ltd* [1995] 2 Lloyd's Rep 169.

fraudulent use to the certificate holder because of the provisions of the Consumer Credit Act 1974 (ss83 and 84).[66]

EU Electronic Money Regulations Commission Recommendation Concerning Transactions by Electronic Payment Instruments and in Particular the Relationship Between Issuer and Holder (30 July 1997 (97/498/EC))

The aim of the Recommendation is to provide guidelines for EU Member States to follow when legislating in the area of rights and obligations of electronic money issuers and users.[67] As a recommendation, its implementation is intended to be only voluntary. It covers remote access payment instruments, such as payment cards, phone and home banking applications which allow access to the customer's account.[68]

The Recommendation covers the two kinds of electronic payment instruments:

*   reloadable electronic money instruments in the form of stored-value cards[69] (eg Mondex);[70] and

*   electronic tokens stored on network computer memory (eg Digicash's e-cash).[71]

As noted earlier in this chapter, a number of vital definitions are outlined in art 2 of the Recommendation. Paragraph (a) states that an 'electronic payment instrument' covers remote access payment instruments and electronic money instruments. Paragraph (b) defines 'remote access payment instruments' as those which enable a holder to access funds held on his or her account at a bank such as credit, debit, deferred debit or charge cards. However, the definition of 'electronic money instruments' in paragraph (c) is significant as it excludes credit and debit cards:

> '... a reloadable payment instrument other than a remote access payment instrument, whether a stored-value card or a computer memory, on which value units are stored electronically, enabling its holder to effect transactions of the kind specified in art 1(1).'

---

[66] These are discussed in greater depth in Chapter 6 of this book.

[67] The deadline for the implementation of the Recommendation by Member States was December 1998. It was not implemented in the UK because it was considered that the Banking Code contains provisions which cover similar grounds.

[68] Note that payment cards can be non-electronic as with credit and debit cards used in face-to-face and telephone sales.

[69] The requirements placed on issuers of remote access instruments are quite onerous. Article 6 states that the liability of a holder for losses incurred up to the time of notification of loss or theft is to be limited to EUR150; art 9 goes on to state that there is to be no liability on the holder for any loss incurred after notification of loss or theft has been made. Under art 8 the issuer is also required to keep proper records to enable transactions to be traced and errors rectified. Issuers will also be liable for non-execution or defective execution of the holder's transactions, provided that they have been initiated through authorised terminals. They are also liable for transactions not authorised by the holder; the extent of such liability is to be determined by the proper or applicable law of the contract.

[70] Due to the possible link to the holder's account in the former case, the need for consumer protection is deemed stronger for those kinds of electronic payments instruments.

[71] Requirements imposed on this type of issuer are much less onerous. Article 4(2) states that issuers need not offer the holder a statement of transactions beyond being able to verify the last five transactions and the outstanding balance stored. Under art 8(4) the issuer will be liable for loss of value or defective execution only where this is caused by a malfunction of the instrument or any authorised terminal or equipment; art 7(e) states that in the event of a dispute, it will be for the issuer to prove that a transaction was not affected by technical malfunctioning or other deficiencies.

Article 3 deals with the type of information that must be given to the holder of electronic money before and upon signing the contract regarding the terms and conditions of the contract:

'1. Upon signature of the contract or in any event in good time prior to delivering an electronic payment instrument, the issuer communicates to the holder the contractual terms and conditions (hereinafter referred to as "the terms") governing the issue and use of that electronic payment instrument. The terms indicate the law applicable to the contract ...

3. The terms include at least:

(a) a description of the electronic payment instrument, including where appropriate the technical requirements with respect to the holder's communication equipment authorised for use, and the way in which it can be used, including the financial limits applied, if any;

(b) a description of the holder's and issuer's respective obligations and liabilities; they include a description of the reasonable steps that the holder must take to keep safe the electronic payment instrument and the means (such as a personal identification number or other code) which enable it to be used;

(c) where applicable, the normal period within which the holder's account will be debited or credited, including the value date, or, where the holder has no account with the issuer, the normal period within which he/she will be invoiced;

(d) the types of any charges payable by the holder. In particular, this includes where applicable details of the following charges:

– the amount of any initial and annual fees,

– any commission fees and charges payable by the holder to the issuer for particular types of transactions,

– any interest rate, including the manner of its calculation, which may be applied;

(e) the period of time during which a given transaction can be contested by the holder and an indication of the redress and complaints procedures available to the holder and the method of gaining access to them ...'

Of particular note, art 3(2) states that the terms must be in clear comprehensible writing and in the official language of the Member State in which the electronic money instrument is offered. Furthermore, art 3(3)(a) states that the terms should include a description of the electronic money instrument, it's generation and technical operation.

It is obvious that the purpose of stipulating these details is to ensure that any potential user of the electronic money understands fully the extent of liabilities involved in using the instrument so as to enable him to make an informed decision on whether or not to use it.

Section III of the Recommendation goes on to deal with the obligations and liabilities of the parties involved. Articles 5 and 6 stipulate the holder's obligations and liabilities. Article 5 states:

'The holder:

(a) uses the electronic payment instrument in accordance with the terms governing the issuing and use of a payment instrument; in particular, the holder takes all reasonable steps to keep safe the electronic payment instrument and the means (such as a personal identification number or other code) which enable it to be used;

(b) notifies the issuer (or the entity specified by the latter) without delay after becoming aware of:

– the loss or theft of the electronic payment instrument or of the means which enable it to be used,

– the recording on his/her account of any unauthorized transaction,

– any error or other irregularity in the maintaining of that account by the issuer;

(c) does not record his personal identification number or other code in any easily recognisable form, in particular on the electronic payment instrument or on any item which he/she keeps or carries with the electronic payment instrument;

(d) does not countermand an order which he/she has given by means of his/her electronic payment instrument, except if the amount was not determined when the order was given.'

Therefore, the user is bound to use the electronic money in accordance with the terms governing its issue and to take reasonable care to keep it safe. Article 6 goes on to add detail to these terms:

'1. Up to the time of notification, the holder bears the loss sustained in consequence of the loss or theft of the electronic payment instrument up to a limit, which may not exceed ECU 150, except where he/she acted with extreme negligence, in contravention of relevant provisions under Art 5(a), (b) or (c), or fraudulently, in which case such a limit does not apply.

2. As soon as the holder has notified the issuer (or the entity specified by the latter) as required by Art 5(b), except where he/she acted fraudulently, he/she is not thereafter liable for the loss arising in consequence of the loss or theft of his/her electronic payment instrument.

3. By derogation from paras 1 and 2, the holder is not liable if the payment instrument has been used, without physical presentation or electronic identification (of the instrument itself). The use of a confidential code or any other similar proof of identity is not, by itself, sufficient to entail the holder's liability.'

Of key significance here is the fact that the holder must notify the issuer if the instrument is lost or stolen, or of any record of an unauthorised transaction, error or irregularity in maintaining the account. In much the same way that the Consumer Credit Act 1974 outlines the liability of the user prior to notification,[72] so too the Recommendation states that the holder may be liable for up to a maximum limit of ECU 150 for loss, theft or authorised misuse. However, once notice has been given, the holder's liability is eliminated, unless the issuer can prove 'extreme negligence' or fraud. There is also no liability on the part of the holder where the payment instrument has been used without presentation or electronic identification.

Similarities may also be drawn with paragraphs 12.9 and 12.10 of the Banking Code 2003, which contain similar provisions and that are applicable to cards issued by banks:

'12.9 If you act fraudulently, you will be responsible for all losses on your account. If you act without reasonable care, and this causes losses, you may be responsible for them. (This may apply if you do not follow s12.4.)

'12.10 Unless we can show that you have acted fraudulently or without reasonable care, your liability for the misuse of your card will be limited as follows:

•   If someone else uses your card before you tell us it has been lost or stolen or that someone else knows your PIN, the most you will have to pay is £50.

---

[72] See discussion of ss83 and 84 of the Consumer Credit Act 1974 in Chapter 6 of this book.

- If someone else uses your card details without your permission for a transaction where the cardholder does not need to be present, you will not have to pay anything.

- If your card is used before you have received it, you will not have to pay anything.'

However, several differences should be noted between the two documents. First of all, the Recommendation bases the unlimited liability of the holder in the case of loss or theft on the existence of 'extreme negligence'. By contrast, the Banking Code uses the term 'reasonable care'. The problem lies in the fact that English common law does not readily provide suitable definitions for the term 'extreme negligence' and as such it is difficult to state with confidence the points at which ordinary, extreme and gross negligence start and finish.[73] Secondly, the holder is not to countermand payment made with the instrument except if the amount was not determined when the order for payment was given. The aim is to reduce the incidence of the issuer or bank authorising payment which had in fact been countermanded by the holder.

Under art 7(1) of the Recommendation the issuer's obligation includes giving individual advance notice to holders of any alteration of the terms of issue so as to enable any user who wishes to withdraw from the arrangement to do so. There is also a prohibition on disclosing the holder's PIN or code to a third party and sending off unsolicited electronic money instruments, unless it is a replacement of an existing one.[74] In addition, the holder must be provided with the means of giving notice of loss or theft of the instrument or any unauthorised use. Article 8 goes on to outline the liabilities of the issuer:

'1. The issuer is liable, subject to art 5, art 6 and art 7(2)(a) and (e):

(a) for the non-execution or defective execution of the holder's transactions referred to in art 1(1), even if a transaction is initiated at devices/terminals or through equipment which are not under the issuer's direct or exclusive control, provided that the transaction is not initiated at devices/terminals or through equipment unauthorized for use by the issuer;

(b) for transactions not authorized by the holder, as well as for any error or irregularity attributable to the issuer in the maintaining of the holder's account …

4. The issuer is liable to the holder of an electronic money instrument for the lost amount of value stored on the instrument and for the defective execution of the holder's transactions, where the loss or defective execution is attributable to a malfunction of the instrument, of the device/terminal or any other equipment authorized for use, provided that the malfunction was not caused by the holder knowingly or in breach of art 3(3)(a).'

Of note is the fact that liability for loss caused by an aborted transaction rests on the issuer's shoulders, who in turn is liable for the non-execution or defective execution of the holder's transactions if it was adequately initiated at authorised devices/terminals or through equipment not under the issuer's direct or exclusive control. Provision is also made in art 8 with respect to the extent of liability and financial consequential loss involved.

---

[73] It cannot be assumed that the term 'gross negligence' is the same as 'extreme negligence'. The interpretation of the latter in the different jurisdictions may give rise to conflict, contrary to the primary objective of maintaining uniformity in the field.

[74] Article 7(2).

There is the question of whether the issuer will be liable for the use of the electronic payment instrument by a person named as a user under the agreement but who in fact is not the account holder. The issue will be determined by looking at the terms of the contract between the parties. It is unlikely that courts will hold the issuer liable for the fraudulent use of the instrument by a person who has the account holder's consent to use it. It may be that courts in the country will refer to the analogous situation of credit card holders and the treatment of a similar problem under the Consumer Credit Act 1974.[75]

On the whole it would appear that the Recommendation imposes a higher burden of liability upon issuers of remote access payment instruments. This is due to the fact that they must keep a record of the details of all transactions so as to enable errors to be traced and rectified.[76] By contrast, the obligations are relaxed with respect to the issue of electronic money which does not enable access to the holder's bank account. In this case, only the last five transactions need to be verifiable.[77] It is notable that the holder is liable if an electronic instrument in the form of a store-value card is lost or stolen. Like ordinary cash, they are lost to the holder's risk.[78]

Directive 2000/46/EC on the Taking-Up, Pursuit and Prudential Supervision of the Business of Electronic Money Institutions

Directive 2000/46/EC[79] is intended to complement the Recommendation outlined above by providing the regulatory framework for electronic payment institutions.[80] The Directive recognises the fact that the issue of electronic money has posed a series of new legal questions which were not considered at the time that existing legislation (which deals with traditional credit institutions like banks and building societies), was drafted. The Preamble sets out the objectives of the Directive for harmonising Member States' laws, regulations and administrative provisions relating to the prudential supervision of the business of electronic money institutions.

As a result of the Directive, electronic money institutions may be granted the 'European passport' (single licence) if they comply with the key principles set out in the First Banking Directive with regards mutual recognition of the licence,[81] prudential

---

[75] Refer to Chapter 6 of this book.

[76] Article 4(1).

[77] Article 4(2).

[78] This is mirrored by the Banking Code 2003, which states in para 12.12: 'You should treat your electronic purse like cash in a wallet. If you lose your electronic purse or it is stolen, you will lose any money in it, in just the same way as if you lost your wallet.' The Glossary to the Banking Code defines the term 'electronic purse' as follows: 'Any card, or function of a card, which contains real value in the form of electronic money which someone has paid for beforehand. Some cards can be reloaded with more money and can be used for a range of purposes.'

[79] Statutory Instrument 2002 No 682 – The Financial Services and Markets Act 2000 (Regulated Activities) (Amendment) Order 2002 implemented the Electronic Money Directive into UK law and came into force on 21 August 2002. For details of the consultation document relating to the implementation of the Electronic Money Directive see: http://www.hm-treasury.gov.uk/media/91F54/e_money.pdf.

[80] The Directive authorises non-bank institutions to issue electronic money provided that it is on a non-professional basis. It defines this new mode of payment neutrally as a surrogate for coins and banknotes which is stored on an electronic device (chip card or computer memory) and intended for making payments of limited amounts.

[81] Directive 77/780/EEC on the coordination of laws, regulations and administrative provisions relating to the taking up and pursuit of the business of credit institutions.

supervision[82] and with the principle of home Member State supervision.[83] In this regard, it should be noted that previous legislation had given the benefit of a 'single passport' enabling institutions free access to operate in other Member States. Consequently, the definition of 'credit institution' in Directive 77/780 was amended so as to enable electronic money institutions to share in the privilege of this common passport.[84]

The strength of this Directive lies in the fact that it recognises the unique nature of non-bank issuers and that this needs to be taken into account if a level playing field is to be achieved in terms of being able to compete with banks in the new business of issuing electronic money.

The Directive involves changes in the usual roles and inter-relationship between national central banks (eg the Bank of England) and traditional credit institutions. Consequently, in line with treating electronic money as real cash, the Preamble states:

'For the purposes of this Directive, electronic money can be considered an electronic surrogate for coins and banknotes, which is stored on an electronic device such as a chip card or computer memory and which is generally intended for the purpose of effecting electronic payments of limited amounts.'

Electronic money is then defined in art 1(3)(b)[85] as:

[82] Council Directive 89/646/EEC on the coordination of laws, regulations and administrative provisions relating to the taking up and pursuit of the business of credit institutions (repealed).

[83] Directive 2000/12/EC relating to the taking up and pursuit of the business of credit institutions. The purpose of the Directive is to consolidate the following Directives: (1) Directive 73/183/EEC on the abolition of restrictions on freedom of establishment and freedom to provide services in respect of self-employed activities of banks and other financial institutions (repealed); (2) Directive 77/780/EEC, as amended by Directive 89/646/EEC, on the coordination of the laws, regulations and administrative provisions relating to the taking up and pursuit of the business of credit institutions (both repealed); (3) Directive 89/299/EEC on the own funds of credit institutions (repealed); (4) Directive 89/646/EEC on the coordination of laws, regulations and administrative provisions relating to the taking up and pursuit of the business of credit institutions (repealed); (5) Directive 89/647/EEC on a solvency ratio for credit institutions (repealed); (6) Directive 92/30/EEC on the supervision of credit institutions on a consolidated basis (repealed); (7) Directive 92/121/EEC on the monitoring and control of large exposures of credit institutions (repealed). The Directive constitutes the essential instrument for achieving the single market from the point of view of both the freedom of establishment and the freedom to provide services in the field of credit institutions. The approach adopted is to achieve sufficient harmonisation to secure mutual recognition of authorisations and prudential supervision systems, making possible the granting of a single licence and application of the principle of home Member State prudential supervision.

[84] See: Statutory Instrument 2002, No 765, (The Electronic Money (Miscellaneous Amendments) Regulations 2002), s10 of which amends the Financial Services and Markets Act 2000 (EEA Passport Rights) Regulations 2001 as follows:
'(1) The Financial Services and Markets Act 2000 (EEA Passport Rights) Regulations 2001 are amended as follows.
(2) In reg 1(2) (interpretation), after the definition of "credit institution" insert – "electronic money institution" means an electronic money institution as defined in art 1 of Directive 2000/46/EC of the European Parliament and of the Council of 18 September 2000 on the taking up, pursuit of and prudential supervision of the business of electronic money institutions.'
(3) In para (3)(d) of reg 2 (establishment of branch: contents of consent notice), at the beginning insert "except where the firm is an electronic money institution".
(4) In para (4)(a)(ii) of that Regulation, after "credit institution" the first time it occurs insert "(other than an electronic money institution)".'

[85] As noted in the following Chapter of this book, electronic money is now defined by statute – Financial Services and Markets Act 2000 (Regulated Activities) Order 2001 (SI 2002/544), art 3(1), adopting art 1(3)(b) of the Directive. The definition is as follows:
'... monetary value as represented by a claim on the issuer which is:
(i) stored on an electronic device;
(ii) issued on receipt of funds;
(iii) accepted as means of payment by persons other than the issuer.'

'... "electronic money" shall mean monetary value as represented by a claim on the issuer which is:

(i) stored on an electronic device;

(ii) issued on receipt of funds of an amount not less in value than the monetary value issued;

(iii) accepted as means of payment by undertakings other than the issuer.'[86]

At first sight, the comparison of electronic money with physical cash may appear to detract from the statutory restriction against the issue of bank notes or coins by an institution other than the central bank. Indeed, the Directive goes on in art 1(4) to provide authority for credit institutions as defined thereunder to carry out the business of issuing electronic money:

'Member States shall prohibit persons or undertakings that are not credit institutions, as defined in art 1, point 1, first subparagraph of Directive 2000/12/EC, from carrying on the business of issuing electronic money.'

However, there would appear to be justification for less stringent supervisory and investment requirements than currently applied to banks. Under art 2(3):

'The receipt of funds within the meaning of art 1(3)(b)(ii) does not constitute a deposit or other repayable funds according to art 3 of Directive 2000/12/EC, if the funds received are immediately exchanged for electronic money.'

As such, the majority of electronic money instruments issued by the institution, on receipt of an equivalent amount in money, will not amount to deposit-taking. As noted above, one of the grounds for considering whether or not the supervisory provisions of the Banking Act 1987 should apply to electronic money institutions was the fact that issuing electronic money may involve 'deposit-taking'. Therefore, even though art 2(3) appears to provide some clarity on this question, it does not remove all grounds for possible doubt.

Article 1(3)(a) makes it clear that electronic money institutions, as used in the Directive, means an institution that 'issues means of payment in the form of electronic money' other than a credit institutions as defined in art 1(1)(a) of Directive 2000/12/EC.[87]

The prudential supervision stipulated by the electronic money institutions Directive applies only to non-bank issuers of electronic money, whereas the regime which applies to banks is found in the First and Second Banking Directives.[88] Furthermore, art 1(5) confines the scope of permissible business activities of the electronic money institutions as follows:

'The business activities of electronic money institutions other than the issuing of electronic money shall be restricted to:

---

[86] One early criticism of the draft Directive was the definition of 'electronic money' in terms of relating it specifically to monetary devises stored on chip card or computer memory. It was argued that a more technology-neutral definition would be preferable so as not to exclude possible development of other forms of electronic money. This was amended in the current definition under the Directive. Reference to specific forms of electronic money is now only made in the Preamble.

[87] 'Credit institution' shall mean an undertaking whose business is to receive deposits or other repayable funds from the public and to grant credits for its own account.

[88] First Banking Co-ordination Directive 77/780/EC; Second Banking Co-ordination Directive 89/646/EC.

(a) the provision of closely related financial and non-financial services such as the administering of electronic money by the performance of operational and other ancillary functions related to its issuance, and the issuing and administering of other means of payment but excluding the granting of any form of credit; and

(b) the storing of data on the electronic device on behalf of other undertakings or public institutions. Electronic money institutions shall not have any holdings in other undertakings except where these undertakings perform operational or other ancillary functions related to electronic money issued or distributed by the institution concerned.'

The exclusion of credit provision from the business of electronic money institutions removes another feature of traditional banking that had suggested the application of the Banking Act 1987.

If we consider the various forms of electronic money again, then several of the stored-value cards operate in such a way that the value must circulate between individuals until the whole value on the card is exhausted. In other words, there is no opportunity for the user to convert any remaining units back to physical cash.[89] However, the benefit of this type of system is that neither the user nor the merchant needs to defer to the issuer for authorisation and/or verification before each individual transaction is completed.

Turning back to the Directive, art 3 imports a different position in that the holder acquires the right to redeem the 'electronic money' at par value in coins and notes free of charge apart from what is strictly necessary to carry out the operation.[90] If one considers some of the more recent forms of electronic cash, then it is clear that the opportunity has been taken, in the light of the Directive, to stipulate the conditions of redemption in the terms of issue (ie in the contract). In many respects, this is common sense in so much as the user of a smart-card and/or electronic cash may find himself left with a remaining balance if he no longer wishes to use that institution's product.[91]

The main prudential supervisory provisions are contained in arts 4 and 5 of the Directive. Article 4 states:

'1. Electronic money institutions shall have an initial capital, as defined in art 34(2), subparas (1) and (2) of Directive 2000/12/EC, of not less than EUR one million. Notwithstanding paras 2 and 3, their own funds, as defined in Directive 2000/12/EC, shall not fall below that amount.

2. Electronic money institutions shall have at all times own funds which are equal to or above 2 per cent of the higher of the current amount or the average of the preceding six months' total amount of their financial liabilities related to outstanding electronic money.

---

[89] Mondex is structured in this way.
[90] Article 3 states:
'1. A bearer of electronic money may, during the period of validity, ask the issuer to redeem it at par value in coins and bank notes or by a transfer to an account free of charges other than those strictly necessary to carry out that operation.
2. The contract between the issuer and the bearer shall clearly state the conditions of redemption.
3. The contract may stipulate a minimum threshold for redemption. The threshold may not exceed EUR 10.'
[91] Equally, the holder of electronic money who is travelling in a different jurisdiction to his normal currency may wish to redeem the currency of the card at the end of his travels.

3. Where an electronic money institution has not completed a six months' period of business, including the day it starts up, it shall have own funds which are equal to or above 2 per cent of the higher of the current amount or the six months' target total amount of its financial liabilities related to outstanding electronic money. The six months' target total amount of the institution's financial liabilities related to outstanding electronic money shall be evidenced by its business plan subject to any adjustment to that plan having been required by the competent authorities.'

The most significant element of this is the requirement for any electronic money institution to have, at all times, funds which are at least equal to 2 per cent of the average of the past six months total amount of their financial liabilities related to outstanding electronic money.[92] This is in addition to the requirement that any institution must have a minimum initial capital of EUR one million.

Article 5 deals with limitations on investment. The most important aspect of art 5 is the requirement for any institution that issues electronic money to invest only in assets that attract a zero credit risk weighting and which are sufficiently liquid.[93] The purpose of this is quite clearly to ensure that such institutions will always have sufficient funds to honour requests for the redemption of funds made by their customers.[94] Furthermore, art 6 goes on to note that the specific requirements established under arts 4 and 5 must be verified at least twice each year by competent authorities in Member States.[95] Finally, the Directive declares that the standard for the management, administration and accounting procedures of electronic money institutions is that of soundness and prudence.[96]

5.9 The Principles of Payment

The law is not always clear on payment issues. Indeed, there is some conflict in the English authorities as to whether the resolution of disputes in this area is an issue of law or of banking practice. In practice, matters of banking practice influence the conclusions of the courts, leading to the fact that law and practice are intertwined.

Payment has been defined as 'the transfer of money or of a money fund, or performance of some other act tendered and accepted in discharge of a money obligation ... a gift or loan of money or an act offered and accepted in performance of

---

[92] It was intended that, in implementing the Directive, Member States would adjust these figures in order to reflect their particular circumstances (ie their national economy) and so treat those contained in the Directive as a guide. It is worth noting that the figures contained in art 4 are different to those initially proposed in the Draft Directive. The same can be said of art 8, which provides a waiver to small businesses. However, the question as to what might qualify for a waiver will be left up to the individual Member State to determine.

[93] Article 5(1)(a).

[94] If investment is not restricted to assets that permit sufficient liquidity, it may not be easy for consumers to redeem their electronic money for cash and huge losses would be incurred in the event that the issuer becomes bankrupt.

[95] Article 6 states:

'The competent authorities shall ensure that the calculations justifying compliance with arts 4 and 5 are made, not less than twice each year, either by electronic money institutions themselves, which shall communicate them, and any component data required, to the competent authorities, or by competent authorities, using data supplied by the electronic money institutions.'

[96] Article 7: 'Electronic money institutions shall have sound and prudent management, administrative and accounting procedures and adequate internal control mechanisms. These should respond to the financial and non-financial risks to which the institution is exposed including technical and procedural risks as well as risks connected to its cooperation with any undertaking performing operational or other ancillary functions related to its business activities.'

a money obligation'.[97] Consequently, 'any act accepted by the creditor in performance of a money obligation can constitute payment'.[98] It is characteristic of this definition of payment that some form of mutuality is required. In other words, the act of payment made by one individual must be acceptable to the other, otherwise there is no payment. In this regard, it should be noted that a party who has a money obligation would, in principle, be unable to coerce the creditor to accept payment.[99] This leads to an important point of law; the tender of payment is distinct from actual payment.[100]

Whilst the law of contract contains strict rules regarding the issue of when a tender of payment is acceptable, it nevertheless provides the parties with as much freedom as possible in relation to the form and method of payment.[101] In *TSB Bank of Scotland v Welwyn Hatfield DC*[102], Hobhouse J took the opportunity to make a distinction between the 'ministerial' or physical act of delivery of money and the payment of a debt:

> 'To discharge a debt there must have been an accepted payment of that debt, not a mere receipt by the creditor of the sum of money. The late Dr Francis Mann at p75 of the 'Legal Aspect of Money' [5th ed, 1992], says "No creditor is under any legal duty to accept any payment and no debtor can force any payment of any kind upon his creditor without the latter's consent express or implied, precedent or subsequent". All the debtor can do is make an unconditional tender of the relevant sum to the creditor; if the creditor accepts the sum the liability of the debtor is appropriately discharged or reduced; if the creditor refuses to accept the tender, the debtor may, provided that he remains ready and willing to pay the relevant sum and pays it into court if action is brought against him, raise the defence of tender to the creditor's claim in respect of the debt ... The physical or ministerial aspect of payment involves the delivery of money by one person to another. Where the two persons meet face to face and the debtor seeks to hand to the creditor legal tender the physical act of delivery (in the absence of some misrepresentation or mistake) will not be achieved without the concurrence of the debtor.'[103]

Mardorf Peach & Co Ltd v *Attica Sea Carriers Corporation of Liberica*[104] represents an example of a valid rejection of payment by the creditor. The case concerned a time charterparty under which the shipowners had the right to withdraw the vessel upon failure by the charterers to pay punctually into the shipowner's bank account. The last payment fell due on a Sunday, but the charterers made payment by bank transfer the next day, Monday. The shipowners' bank accepted this in the usual way without objection.[105] The court noted:

---

[97] RM Goode, 'Payment Obligations in Commercial and Financial Transactions (1983), p11.
[98] LS Sealy and RJA Hooley, 'Commercial Law: Text, Cases and Materials', Butterworths (2004), p684.
[99] *Charter Reinsurance Co Ltd* v *Fagan* [1997] AC 313 at 384.
[100] A creditor, who refuses a valid tender of payment and subsequently sues for the debt in question, could be defeated by the fact that there had been a valid tender before the action. However, it should be noted that a valid tender before action does not amount to payment for which some degree of acceptance is required. It is, however, sufficient to prevent liability for interest and costs arising. See: Civil Procedure Rules, r37(3).
[101] See: *The Laconia* [1977] AC 850; *The Brimnes* [1973] 1 WLR 386.
[102] [1993] 2 Bank LR 267.
[103] Ibid, at 271.
[104] [1977] AC 850, sub nom *The Laconia*.
[105] It was conceded by the charterers that payment should have been made on Friday which was the last business day but that since the bank accepted payment as the shipowners' agent, it was valid and they had waived their right to reject it.

'Looked at untechnically, the facts were that the money was sent to the bank, taken into the banking process or machinery, put in course of transmission to the owners, but rejected by the latter as soon as they were informed of its arrival and as soon as they were called upon, or able, to define their position. Put more technically, the bank, though agents of the owners, had a limited authority. It is not necessary to decide whether, in general, and in the absence of specific instructions, bankers in such institutions as these have authority to accept late payments – on this matter I regard *The Brimnes* [1975] QB 929 as a special case ... here it is clear that the bankers had no such authority and still less authority to make business decisions as to the continuance or otherwise of the charterparty but that per contra they had express instructions to refer the matter to the owners' agents.'

Consequently, the House of Lords held that the shipowners were entitled to reject the payment as their bank had only limited authority as agents to receive the payment and so had no power to accept a late tender on their behalf. It was said that the banker's act in crediting the owner's account was only ministerial and provisional and thus could be reversed.

5.10 Transfer of Funds

Whilst payment may be achieved by the physical delivery of legal tender (eg bank notes, coins, etc), this is both risky and expensive. As such, payment mechanisms and payment systems have evolved over time to facilitate the transfer of funds between parties in order to satisfy the payment obligation.[106] Professor Benjamin Geva has defined payment mechanisms and payment systems in the following way:

'Any machinery facilitating the transmission of money which bypasses the transportation of money and its physical delivery from the payor to the payee is a payment mechanism. A payment mechanism facilitating a standard method of payment through a banking system is frequently referred to as a payment system. Payment over a payment mechanism is initiated by payment instructions, given by the payor or under the payor's authority, and is often referred to as a transfer of funds.'[107]

Consequently, in practice, payment is usually made by the transfer of funds from one bank account to another (ie from the debtor to the creditor).[108] However, this is not quite as straightforward as it may first appear. If this method of payment is to amount to a discharge of the original debt, the creditor must consent[109] to receipt of funds in this way due to the fact that he is effectively substituting a claim against the debtor in favour of a claim against the bank. This is supported by *Tenax Steamship Co Ltd* v *Reinante Transoceanica Navigation SA*.[110] In this case, Brandon J held:

'I consider first the meaning of payment in cash ... In my view these words must be interpreted against the background of modern commercial practice. So interpreted it seems to me that they cannot mean only payment in dollar bills or other legal tender of the US. They must, as the shipowners contend, have a wider meaning, comprehending any commercially-recognised method

---

[106] It should be noted that payment does not necessarily involve the transfer of money. As will be noted later on in this chapter, the 'setting off' of an existing debt or barter could properly be deemed as 'payment'.

[107] B Geva, 'The Law of Electronic Funds Transfers', Matthew Bender, New York, looseleaf, s1.03[1].

[108] For further information see: M Donnelly, 'Electronic Funds Transfers: Obligations and Liabilities of Participating Institutions', (2003) C L Pract 10(2), 35–39.

[109] Consent may be either express or implied. For example, implied consent may be taken to arise from the fact that the creditor provides the debtor with his bank account details.

[110] [1972] 2 Lloyd's Rep 465, sub nom *The Brimnes*.

of transferring funds, the result of which is to give the transferee the unconditional right to the immediate use of the funds transferred. This would include both the direct and the indirect transfer methods used by Hambros as agents for the charterers in this case.'[111]

Brandon J's judgment that payment in cash meant any commercially recognised method of transferring funds which would provide the transferee with an unconditional right to the immediate use of the funds was approved in *A/S Awilco of Solo* v *Fulvia SpA di Navigazione of Cagliari*[112] with only a minor modification as to the wording to be used:

'[It] depends on the interpretation of the word "unconditional" in the context of the statement of principle by Mr Justice Brandon in *The Brimnes* ... If the word is understood in its narrow, legal sense as meaning that the transferee's right to the use of the funds transferred is neither subject to the fulfilment of a condition precedent nor defeasible on failure to fulfil a condition subsequent, I can see that the owners' right in this case to the use of the funds on 22 January could be described as unconditional. But Mr Justice Robert Goff obviously understood it in a much wider and more liberal sense as equivalent to unfettered or unrestricted ... The underlying concept is surely this, that when payment is made to a bank otherwise than literally in cash, ie in dollar bills or other legal tender (which no one expects), there is no "payment in cash" within the meaning of cl 5 unless what the creditor receives is the equivalent of cash, or as good as cash.'[113]

However, a great deal depends on the context and circumstances in which the payment obligation arises.

Payment is usually made by the transfer of funds from the bank account of the debtor to that of the creditor (ie the payer's account is debited and the payee's account is credited). Funds transfers are therefore credit and debit transfers.[114] However, it should be noted at this point that property rights are not transferred with a funds transfer, rather it leads to a readjustment of the separate property rights of the payer and payee.[115] This was explored in *R* v *Preddy*:[116]

---

[111] Ibid, at 476.

[112] [1981] 1 Lloyd's Rep 371, sub nom *The Chikuma*.

[113] Ibid, at 375.

[114] See: LS Sealy and RJA Hooley, 'Commercial Law: Text, Cases and Materials', Butterworths (2004), p690.

[115] A fund transfer does not involve any form of assignment, legal or equitable of property or debt the payer's bank owes to the payer. As noted by Cranston ('Principles of Banking Law', Oxford (1997): '... all that payment entails is at most messages, movements on accounts, and ultimately settlement between different banks ... In *Libyan Arab Bank* v *Bankers Trust Co* [1989] 1 QB 728, 750, Staughton J made the point in his description of an account transfer as follows: '... the process by which some other person or institution comes to owe money to the Libyan Bank [payer] or their nominee and the obligation of Bankers Trust [paying bank] is extinguished or reduced pro tanto. "Transfer" may be a somewhat misleading word, since the original obligation is not assigned (notwithstanding dicta in one American case, which speaks of assignment); a new obligation by a new debtor is created. Any account transfer must ultimately be achieved by means of two accounts held by different beneficiaries with the same institution. In a simple case the beneficiaries can be the immediate parties to the transfer. If Bankers Trust held an account with the A bank which was in credit to the extent of at least $13 million and the Libyan Bank also held an account at the A bank, it would require only book entries to achieve an account transfer. But still no property is actually transferred. The obligation of Bankers Trust is extinguished, and the obligation of A bank to Bankers Trust extinguished or reduced; the obligation to the Libyan Bank is increased by the like amount. On occasion a method of account transfer which is even simpler may be used. If X Ltd also held an account with Bankers Trust London, and the Libyan Bank desire to benefit X Ltd, they instruct Bankers Trust to transfer $13 million to the account of X Ltd. The obligation of Bankers Trust to the Libyan Bank is extinguished once they decide to comply with the instruction, and their obligation to X Ltd is increased by the like amount. That method of account transfer featured in *Momm & Others (T/A Delbrueck & Co)* v *Barclays Bank International Ltd* [1977] QB 790.'

[116] [1996] AC 815.

'I now turn to the first question which your Lordships have to consider, which is whether the debiting of a bank account and the corresponding crediting of another's bank account brought about by dishonest misrepresentation amount to the obtaining of property within s15 of the Act of 1968 ... The question remains whether the debiting of the lending institution's bank account, and the corresponding crediting of the bank account of the defendant or his solicitor, constitutes obtaining of that property. The difficulty in the way of that conclusion is simply that, when the bank account of the defendant (or his solicitor) is credited, he does not obtain the lending institution's chose in action. On the contrary that chose in action is extinguished or reduced pro tanto, and a chose in action is brought into existence representing a debt in an equivalent sum owed by a different bank to the defendant or his solicitor. In these circumstances, it is difficult to see how the defendant thereby obtained property belonging to another, ie to the lending institution ... For these reasons, I would answer the first question in the negative.'[117]

A division may be made between credit and debit transfers depending on the direction from which the instruction to the payer's bank is initiated. In a credit transfer, the payer 'pushes' funds from his account to that of the payee. The payer's bank receives an instruction to debit his account and causes a corresponding credit on the payee's account at the same or different bank to be made.[118]

By contrast, a debit transfer[119] involves a 'pull' of funds by the payee from the payer. It is an instruction by the payee to his bank to collect payment due to him from the payer's bank. When the payee's bank receives the instruction, credit is provisionally placed in the payee's account with the amount. The information is transmitted to the payer's bank and it debits his account with the amount if sufficient funds are available. Payment to the payee becomes final when the debit to the payer's account is irreversible.[120]

5.11 The Relationship Between Parties in Funds Transfer

A typical funds transfer transaction will involve at least four parties: (1) the payer; (2) the payee; (3) the payer's bank; and (4) the payee's bank. Where a foreign bank account is involved and a bank does not have a branch in that country, it will be necessary to appoint a correspondent bank there.

---

[117] Ibid, at 834.

[118] A common kind of credit transfer are the standing orders given by a customer to his bank to make instalment payment of fixed amounts for particular goods and services. The customer needs to complete the bank's pro forma standing order form by providing details of the payee's bank and account details, the frequency, duration and dates of payments and the specific amount due. The bank is under no obligation to make payment if there is insufficient funds in the account to cover the standing order on the due date.

[119] A major form of debit transfer is the direct debit, which enables companies providing household utilities such as gas, electricity and water to obtain payment of variable amounts periodically from consumers. The customer completes an instruction form to his bank to make direct debit payment. When signed and lodged by the payee to the payer's bank, it gives the bank mandate to debit the payer's account with the amount and to remit payment to the payee's bank. In most cases, only big companies and organisations (the payee is here more appropriately referred to as the originator) with strong financial standing are permitted to obtain direct debit payment from customers. This is because of the risk involved in that kind of transfer. The originator must be able to provide the banks with indemnity for any loss caused to them as a result of the direct debit transaction unless where it resulted from the fault of the bank. Transmission of direct debit instruction by the payee to his bank and between the banks involved in clearing can be done electronically as in the BACS system.

[120] For a discussion of direct debits, see: A Tettenborn, 'Pay Now, Sue Later – Direct Debits, Set-Off and Commercial Practice', (1997) 113 LQR 374.

A correspondent bank will also be nominated if either primary bank is not a member of the relevant clearing system. Therefore, apart from the bank customer relationship of debtor and creditor, in bank transfers, a principal-agent relationship exists between the payer and his bank and the payee and his bank. The bank acts as the customer's agent and a corresponding bank and his sub-agent.[121]

The bank has a duty in the course of usual banking operations to exercise reasonable skill and care. Thus a payer or payee in contractual relations with his bank can sue it for a breach of contract as well as negligence in the funds transfer operations. If no contract exists,[122] for instance when a bank accepts a bank giro credit form from a payer who holds no account with it, then it will be difficult to see the basis of a contractual liability.[123]

Usually, there will be no privity of contract between the payer or payee and the correspondent bank even though it might have been nominated directly by the payer or payee.

A bank will be held vicariously liable for the negligence of a correspondent to whom it delegated any aspect of the funds transfer transaction. However, in practice, banks tend to exclude liability for breach of duty by their correspondents. This is supported by the decision in *Calico Printers Association Ltd* v *Barclays Bank Ltd*.[124]

5.12 Associated Terminology

The first term that needs to be addressed is 'mandate'. Bankers use the term mandate to refer to the contract with their customers governing particular banking services. Once a mandate is binding on a bank, however, the bank must act or be in breach of contract. If the bank acts outside any authority so conferred, this will not be binding on the customer and the bank will be liable for any loss.[125] If the mandate is withdrawn, the bank must comply.

Second, banking networks are necessary to most payments. The correspondent banking system exists where banks need banks in other cities and countries to perform services on behalf of them and their customers, such as collecting bills of exchange (and occasionally cheques) and advising letters of credit. Additionally, banks constantly contract with one another in wholesale, over the counter (OTC) markets such as the interbank deposit market, the foreign exchange market and the OTC derivatives market. Banks also deal on formal exchange markets (such as the London International Financial Futures and options exchange or the Singapore International Monetary Exchange) either on behalf of customers or on their own account. Finally, banks act

---

[121] See: *Royal Products Ltd* v *Midland Bank Ltd* [1981] 2 Lloyd's Rep 194.
[122] Where a bank charges a non-customer fees to effect funds transfer, the existence of consideration may lead to a contract being inferred.
[123] A tortious claim for economic loss might lie, but may not be easy to establish.
[124] (1931) 36 Com Cas 71.
[125] See: *Patel* v *Standard Chartered Bank* [2001] Lloyd's Rep Bank 229. (A bank that pays out on a patently ambiguous mandate, without first seeking clarification from its customer, runs the risk of being unable to debit the customer's account.)

in syndicates or consortiums comprised a number of banks associated in carrying out some enterprise.

5.13 Clearing and Settlement

Payment effected through a payment system is commenced by the provision of payment by the originator to his bank. Where the payment is not undertaken 'in-house', then the originator's instructions will generate further instructions which will then pass between the originator's bank and the beneficiary's bank.[126] The process of exchanging payment instructions between participating banks is known as clearing. There are four major clearing systems[127] in the UK which are as follows:

1. Cheque Clearing System;[128]
2. Credit Clearing System;[129]
3. BACS; and [130]
4. CHAPS.[131]

All of these systems are multilateral net settlement systems with the settlement of balances across the participants' accounts held at the Bank of England at the end of each day, with the exception of NewCHAPS which is a realtime gross settlement system.

Consequently, where an 'inter-bank' transfer is involved, an inter-bank instruction

---

[126] Where the transfer of funds takes place between two accounts in the same bank, this will involve a simple internal accounting procedure whereby the originator's account is debited and the beneficary's bank account is credited.

[127] According to B Geva, 'The Clearing House Arrangement', (1991) 19 Can BLJ 138, the term 'clearing system' may be used in one of two senses. 'In its narrow sense, "clearing system" is a mechanism for the calculation of mutual positions within a group of participants (counterparties) with a view to facilitating the settlement of their mutual obligations on a net basis. In its broadest sense, the term further encompasses the settlement of the obligations, that is, the completion of payment discharging them.'

[128] This is used for the physical exchange of cheques and is operated by the Cheque and Credit Clearing Co Ltd.

[129] This is a paper-based credit transfer system used for the physical exchange of high-volume, low-value, credit collections such as bank giro credits.

[130] BACS provides a high-volume, low-value, bulk electronic clearing service for credit and debit transfers, including standing orders, direct debits, wages and salaries, pensions and other government benefits. BACS operates an automated electronic clearing system with a three-day clearing cycle. Each member having direct access to the system provides BACS with a tape or disk (input data) containing data relating to the payees' name, account details and amounts to be credited and when due. This is usually transmitted to BACS through a special telecommunication link. Upon receipt at the BACS head office in Edgware, Middlesex at the end of the first day, the input data is processed by BACS computers. This involves classifying the various debit and credit transfers into groups according to payees with accounts at the same bank (output data). There is an automatic self-balancing in the credit and debit instructions received at BACS. The output data is transmitted to the relevant member banks on the second day and upon receipt, the customers' accounts are credited or debited at the beginning of the third day. BACS then advises the Bank of England regarding settlement and adjustment of each bank's account accordingly. (For additional information see: Patick Nobbs, 'BACS Moves to Internet-Based Payments Infrastructure', (2004) Comps & Law 15(1), 18–19.)

[131] This is a dual currency system operated by the CHAPS Clearing Co Ltd. It is made up of an electronic sterling credit transfer system, called CHAPS sterling, and an electronic euro credit transfer system, called CHAPS euro. The system permits payments to be made both domestically between member banks in the UK and also between those members elsewhere in the EU through TARGET. (For additional information see: J Gordon, 'A CHAPS Payment is as Good as Cash – it is Official.', FRI 2004, Sep, 12–14; LC Ho, 'Bankers' duties to customers reaffirmed – CHAPS transfer and equitable set-off', JIBLR 2004, 19(11), 466–468.)

will pass from one bank to another.[132] Such instructions may pass directly between the originator's and beneficiary's banks or via a chain of banks. Each inter-bank instruction must be paid by the bank sending the instruction to the bank receiving it. The process whereby payment is made between the banks themselves of their obligations, as outlined above, is referred to as settlement.[133]

It should be noted that settlement may take place on either a gross or net basis.[134] With gross settlement, the sending and receiving banks settle each payment order on a individual basis without any regard to any other payment obligations arising between the two banks. By contrast, net settlement takes account of the mutual payment obligations of the two parties which are then set off against each other, with only the net balance being paid.[135]

A clearing system[136] is operated by the clearing house organisation and the banks which participate in this system, known as 'clearing banks', are members of the clearing house. Each member of the clearing system is bound by the rules of the clearing house through a multilateral contract.[137]

The sequence of banking operations involved in payment turns, in part, on whether there is a credit transfer or debit transfer. With a credit transfer, the payor instructs its bank to pay and the payor's bank responds by debiting the payor's account. With a debit sequence, the sequence begins with the payor authorising its bank to pay, but actual payment is initiated when the payee presents a debit instrument (such as a cheque) or a debit instruction (such as a direct debit) to the payor's bank.

5.14 Conditional and Unconditional Payments

Payment can be conditional or unconditional depending on whether furnishing the creditor with the means of payment involving the participation of a third party discharges the debtor's payment obligation. If it does, there is absolute or unconditional payment. However, if the creditor is entitled to pursue the debtor in the event that the means proves ineffective, it is only conditional.

Depending on the requirements in the contract, it is usually vital to distinguish conditional from unconditional payment. The provision of credit or instrument is sometimes referred to as 'conditional payment' in the sense that it is not absolute

---

[132] A 'correspondent payment' involves payment between banks in different jurisdictions. It can also involve payment between two banks in the same jurisdiction if payment is to be in foreign currency.

[133] For further discussion on this issue see: LS Sealy and RJA Hooley, 'Commercial Law: Text, Cases & Materials', (2003) 3rd ed, Butterworths, pp696–700.

[134] For further information see: R Goode, 'Commercial Law', (2004) 3rd ed, Penguin, pp473–475.

[135] Whereas 'gross settlement' takes place on a realtime basis, 'net settlement' is conducted on a periodic basis – either at the end of each day (same-day basis) or on the following day (next-day basis).

[136] For a discussion of the term 'Clearing System', see: B Geva, 'The Clearing House Arrangement', (1991) 19 Can BLJ 138, which states: 'In its narrowest sense, "clearing system" is a mechanism for the calculation of mutual positions within a group of participants (counterparties) with a view to facilitating the settlement of their mutual obligations on a net basis. In its broadest sense, the term further encompasses the settlement of the obligations, that is, the completion of payment discharging them.'

[137] This is based on the same principle as applied in *Clarke v Dunraven, The Satanita* [1897] AC 59.

payment. If the credit or instrument is dishonoured, the seller is not paid and the buyer is required to pay again.[138] Therefore, even the provision of a negotiable instrument or the procuring of the opening of a letter of credit is not effective as 'payment' in the strict sense of the term.

It is often said that payment by cheque or letter of credit provides only conditional payment whereas payment by credit card gives rise to absolute payment. However, it has been argued that by furnishing a letter of credit or cheque, the debtor makes no payment at all, even conditionally. By so doing, he simply complies with his promise to furnish the creditor with a means of payment. Until that means proves ineffective (such as by the dishonour of the cheque), no further payment can be enforced against the debtor.

As stated above, in the event of dishonour, the hitherto suspended liability to make payment on the underlying contract revives. Thereafter, the creditor can pursue the debtor for payment. Conversely, until the cheque or letter of credit is honoured, it cannot be said that payment has been made.

5.15 Revocation/Countermand

Countermand involves the obligation of a bank to comply with its customer's instructions to cancel a payment instruction. Notice of countermand must be clear and unambiguous[139] in nature. It must also be brought to the actual notice of the bank.[140]

5.16 Completion of Payment

This section deals with the completion of payment between the payor and the payee. The timing of completion is very important for a variety of reasons (tax, interest payments, originator revocation, and failure of the bank).[141]

This is the term used to describe the position between the banks themselves. It is relevant where they are making payment both on behalf of customers as well as on their own account. It is of particular relevance if there is a loss, for example, through the insolvency of one of the banks involved. If a payment has been completed, it may be said that the payor's bank cannot reverse a transfer to the bank which has subsequently become insolvent.[142]

In general, completion of payment via a funds transfer will be deemed to have taken place when the payee is given an unfettered, unrestricted right against his own

---

[138] See: *Alan (WJ) & Co v El Nasr Export Import* [1972] 2 QB 189.
[139] *Westminster Bank Ltd v Hilton* (1926) 136 LT 315.
[140] *Curtice v London City and Midland Bank Ltd* [1908] 1 KB 239.
[141] For a discussion of the timing of payment, see: J Vroegop, 'The Time of Payment in Paper-Based and Electronic Funds Transfer Systems', [1990] LMCLQ 64; B Geva, 'Payment into a Bank Account' [1990] 3 JIBL 108.
[142] Outside of insolvency, the notion of completion of payment has also been applied to whether the payor bank can stop a payment if it decides that there are insufficient funds, discovers that the payor will not reimburse it, or for other reasons such as a freeze order.

bank to the immediate use of the funds.[143] However, the precise moment at which point this takes place has been the subject of considerable debate. Perhaps the most persuasive argument is that it occurs when the payee's bank decides to make an unconditional credit to the payee's account, as outlined in the case of *Momm & Others (T/A Delbrueck & Co)* v *Barclays Bank International Ltd.*[144]

5.17 Mistaken and Void Payments

Mistaken payments occur for a variety of reasons. Clerical error within a bank may lead to payment being made twice, to payment taking place despite a countermand, or to money going into an incorrect account. In addition, there may be fraud, either by an officer of the bank or by a third party.

As such, the bank which has undertaken a mistaken payment has a number of possible legal claims. For the purposes of this text, we will focus on restitutionary claims; when property in the money has invariably passed to the recipient.

Money paid under mistake of fact is prima facie recoverable by the bank.[145] It does not matter that it was a careless mistake. However, the mistake must be as to a specific fact and not be a misprediction as to the nature of the transaction which would come into effect once payment was made (eg, a loan rather than the purchase of foreign exchange).[146] Note, however, that the mistake must be 'fundamental' which means that without the mistake the payment would not have been made.

Amongst the defences to an action for money paid under mistake are change of position, ministerial receipt, passing on, good consideration and estoppel. For example, a recipient providing good consideration has a defence to an action for mistaken payment. In the case of *B Liggett (Liverpool) Ltd* v *Barclays Bank Ltd* [1928] 1 KB 48, it was held that if, by paying, a bank had discharged genuine debts of its customer, it would be inequitable if it were not able to debit its customer's account, despite a lack of authority (eg as a result of a countermand, or an inadequate mandate). However, in *Crantrave Ltd (In Liquidation)* v *Lloyds Bank plc*,[147] the *Liggett* doctrine was discredited. Rather, the court held that without the authority of or ratification by its customer, a mistaken payment by a bank to a third party does not discharge any debt owed by the customer to the third party.

5.18 Payment Cards

The importance of payment cards for the discharge of retail payment obligations was noted at the very beginning of this chapter and will be pursued in the next chapter. Apart from credit cards to be covered later, there are a range of payment cards, as discussed below.

---

[143] *Tenax Steamship Co Ltd* v *Reinante Transoceanica Navigation SA* [1972] 2 Lloyd's Rep 465.
[144] [1977] QB 790.
[145] See: R Goode, 'Commercial Law', (2004) 3rd ed, Penguin, p563.
[146] The mistake may also be one of law.
[147] [2000] QB 917.

A debit card permits the customer to pay for goods and services at the point of sale (the so-called EFTPOS transaction).

A cheque guarantee card is used in conjunction with a cheque book and guarantees the payment of a cheque up to a specified amount.

An e-money card, can be used by the customer to pay for small value items and can be used independently of a bank account.

Of course, any one card may be multifunctional; an issue that will be discussed in the following chapters.

6 Payment Cards and the Internet

6.1   Types of Payment Card

6.2   Reasons for Using Credit Cards

6.3   Regulation of Credit Cards

6.4   Liability for Misuse

6.5   Credit Cards and Fraud

6.6   Terms and Conditions of Use

6.7   Section 75

6.8   Section 56

6.9   Differences Between ss56 and 75

6.10   The Consumer Credit Directive

6.11   Consumer Credit Act 1974: Applicability to the Internet

Payment cards have several features that make them an attractive and popular choice with both consumers and merchants. As will be noted later in this chapter, merchants receive fraud protection, whilst consumers obtain protection and limitation of liability under the terms of the Consumer Credit Act 1974. However, perhaps the greatest advantage of using payment cards is their universal acceptance, coupled with the convenience of leaving any currency conversion issues to the card issuer.

Equally, payment cards would appear to have few disadvantages for consumers and merchants. The major drawback is probably the associated transaction fees which can quickly accumulate for both groups; payment card service companies charge merchants per-transaction fees and monthly processing fees, which are in turn passed on to the consumer.

6.1 Types of Payment Card

Business people often use the term payment card as a general term to describe all types of plastic cards that consumers (and some businesses) use to make purchases. The main categories of payment cards are credit cards, debit cards and charge cards.

Credit cards

Credit cards are by far the most popular form of online payments for consumers, due to the fact that the vast majority of individuals already possess a credit card or are familiar with the way in which they work. Equally, credit cards are widely accepted by merchants around the world and provide assurances for both the consumer and the merchant. A consumer is also protected by an automatic 30-day period in which he can dispute an online credit card purchase. Finally, a user is free to choose whether to pay off the entire credit card balance or simply to pay a minimum amount each billing period, with interest being charged on any unpaid balance on a daily basis.

Payment is straightforward in that the process for an online purchase with a credit card is just as easy as in a brick-and-mortar store. Merchants that already accept credit cards in an offline store are able to accept them immediately for online payment due to the fact that they already have a merchant credit card account. Perhaps the only downside to the process is the fact that online purchases require an extra degree of security which is not required for offline purchases, as the cardholder is not physically present and as such cannot provide proof of identity as easily as when standing at a cash register.

Most credit cardholders can use their card to finance sale or supply transactions[1] and to obtain a cash advance.[2] The legal effect of a purchase transaction is the same as with a debit card but there are three differences:

1. the card may be issued by a credit card company rather than a bank;

2. some stores offer their own credit cards for use only in that store, hence there is only one contract that between the store and the cardholder;[3] and

3. where the cardholder obtains a cash advance from someone other than the card-issuer[4] there will be at least two contracts – the first between the cardholder and the card-issuer and the second between the card-issuer and the cash issuer.

A credit card has been defined as some document:

> 'The production of which to a relevant supplier will constitute payment for purchases and possibly enable the user to obtain cash, such that he renders himself liable to the issuer to reimburse him for all transactions entered into when using the card.'[5]

As will be noted later on in this chapter, certain elements of the Sale of Goods Act 1979, the Supply of Goods and Services Act 1982 and the Unfair Contractual Terms Act 1977 affect consumer protection and apply in general to credit card agreements. However, the legal framework and the liabilities of parties to credit card agreements is governed mainly by the provisions of the Consumer Credit Act 1974.

Debit cards

A debit card resembles a credit card but works in quite a different way. Instead of charging purchases against a credit line, a debit card removes the amount of the individual sale from the cardholder's bank account and transfers it to the seller's bank account. Debit cards are issued by the cardholder's bank and usually carry the name

---

[1] For instance, the purchaser buys goods with the credit card.
[2] Credit cards issued by banks for the purchase of goods and services from participating retailers are called 'three-party' cards.
[3] These are referred to as 'two-party' cards.
[4] For example, an individual makes a cash withdrawal on a Visa card from a Barclays ATM.
[5] Sally Jones.

of a major credit card issuer, such as Visa or MasterCard, by agreement between the issuing bank and the credit card issuer.

Charge cards

A charge card, such as one from American Express or Diner's Club, carries no spending limit, and the entire amount charged to the card is due at the end of the billing period.[6] As such, charge cards do not involve lines of credit and do not accumulate interest charges. The legal effects of charge card use are otherwise exactly the same as with credit cards.

In the United States, many retailers, such as department stores and the oil companies that own gas stations, issue their own charge cards.

Cheque cards

Cheque cards are issued by banks and building societies to their customers for use with cheques drawn by their customers.[7] This type of card is usually referred to as a 'cheque guarantee card', but this term is slightly misleading as the obligation assumed by the bank is not a secondary obligation dependent on default by the cardholder. Rather it is a separate and independent payment obligation as noted in *First Sport Ltd* v *Barclays Bank plc*.[8] Consequently, a cheque card involves two contracts. The first contract is between the card-issuer bank and the cardholder, which allows the bank to debit the cardholder's account with the amount of any cheque supported by the card. It also obliges the cardholder not to create an unauthorised overdraft and obliges the bank to honour any cheque supported by the card. The second, between the bank and the payee, obliges the bank to honour any cheque up to the limit stated on the card whether or not it creates an unauthorised overdraft on the cardholder's account.

Smart/digital cash cards

Banks have now started to develop smart cards (digital cash cards)[9] which come within

---

[6] The difference between a credit card and a charge card is that the latter facilitates payment rather than providing a credit facility.

[7] The standard conditions for use of a cheque card, which are set out in the Rules of the UK Domestic Cheque Guarantee Card Community, are that:
1. the cheque bears the name and code number;
2. the cheque is dated with the actual date of issue;
3. the cheque is signed before the expiry of the card in the presence of the payee by the person whose signature appears on the card;
4. the card number is written on the cheque by the payee; and
5. the card has not been altered or defaced.

[8] [1993] 3 All ER 789.

[9] Also known as 'electronic purses'.

the growing area of electronic cash systems.[10] These systems may be either in the form of a smart card system,[11] where electronic value is stored in a microchip, or software based where 'coins' are stored on an individual's computer. Whichever format is examined, there are a growing number of electronic cash systems in operation, several of which are examined in the following chapters.[12]

It is also worth noting an important question in relation to smart cards; whether or not this type of card falls within the definition of a 'credit-token' set out in s14(1) Consumer Credit Act 1974. It may be argued that it could very well be brought within the scope of s14(1)(b) of the Act, as it enables a cardholder to obtain goods or services from a supplier who is himself entitled to demand conversion of 'electronic cash' into traditional physical cash by the card issuer or merchant acquirer who admitted the supplier into the scheme. However, there are a number of commentators who disagree with this proposition on the basis that a 'digital cash card is a form of pre-payment card, whereby the cardholder pays for the card on issue. In no real sense is credit extended to him.'[13]

6.2 Reasons for Using Credit Cards

It may be wondered why the use of credit cards to make payment over the Internet[14] should be controversial or warrant examination. After all, the Internet is only an alternative medium for conveying the same credit card information, which could otherwise be communicated over the telephone or by the physical presentation of the card.

However, there are some features in the use of the credit card in Internet payment which are different and as such deserve special evaluation.

1.   The communication of credit card details over the Internet carries certain risks which are not attendant in the case of the physical or telephone conveying of card details.

---

[10] The question arises as to whether this type of payment card falls within the definition of a credit-token for the purposes of s14(1) Consumer Credit Act 1974. it may be argued that an electronic cash card falls within the scope of s14(1)(b) as it enables the holder to obtain goods or services from a supplier who is himself entitled to demand conversion of 'electronic cash' into real cash by the card-issuer or merchant acquirer who admitted the supplier into the scheme. However, see: LS Sealy and RJA Hooley, 'Commercial Law: Text, Cases and Materials', (2004) 3rd ed, Butterworths, p806, the authors submit that electronic cash will not fall within the scope of s14(1) for two reasons. (1) A ditigal cash card is a form of pre-payment card, whereby the cardholder pays for the card on issue, thus no credit is extended to him. (2) The words 'in return for payment to him by the individual' in s14(1)(b) implies that the card issuer undertakes to pay the supplier with a subsequent right to be reimbursed by the cardholder. However, if one looks at many electronic cash cards, the card issuer has usually already received payment from the cardholder in advance of the transaction.

[11] An ideal example of this is Mondex. For further discussion see: R Hooley, 'Payment in a Cashless Society', Ch 13 in BAK Rider (ed), 'The Realm of Company Law – A Collection of Papers in Honour of Professor Leonard Sealy', (1998), p245–252.

[12] For a basic discussion see: R Goode, 'Commercial Law', (2004) 3rd ed, Penguin, pp780–781.

[13] LS Sealy and RJA Hooley, 'Commercial Law: Text, Cases and Materials', (2004) 3rd ed, Butterworths, p806.

[14] Credit cards are by far the most popular form of consumer electronic payments online. Recent surveys have found that more than 80 per cent of worldwide consumer Internet purchases are paid for with credit cards. In the United States, the proportion is about 94 per cent.

2.   Internet transactions are more likely to involve parties in different jurisdictions.

At English law, a payment made by credit card (and charge card) is presumed to be absolute.[15] This means that once the cardholder has rendered payment and the supplier has accepted payment by way of a credit card, the supplier cannot subsequently pursue the cardholder for payment.[16] There is no reported decision in which this presumption has been displaced. In *Re Charge Card Services Ltd*, Millett J stated:

> 'On the use of the card, three separate contracts come into operation. First, there is the contract of supply between the supplier and the cardholder (either in his own right or as agent for the account holder); secondly, there is the contract between the supplier and the card-issuing company, which undertakes to honour the card by paying the supplier on presentation of the sales voucher; and, thirdly, there is the contract between the card-issuing company and the account holder by which the account holder undertakes to reimburse the card-issuing company for payments made or liabilities incurred by the card-issuing company to the supplier as a result of his or his cardholder's use of the card. There are thus three separate contracts and three separate parties, each being party to two of the three contracts but neither party nor privy to the third.'[17]

The question before the court in that case related specifically to charge cards and whether they effected absolute payment by the cardholder when used to purchase goods or services. In other words, the question was posed as to whether, if the card-issuer fails to pay the supplier and then becomes insolvent, the supplier can then claim payment from the cardholder. Millett J was of the view that the supplier could not do this as the circumstances in which a charge card was used were such that a conditional payment could not be inferred.

The basis for this inference was that in most instances the procedure for payment does not facilitate the disclosure, to the supplier, of the customer's address and details, which could enable the supplier to trace him at a later date.[18] Millett J also pointed to the fact that the method of payment with the charge card is advantageous to both the supplier and the customer. This is due to the fact that the supplier is entitled to payment from the card issuer on a totally different basis to which the card issuer is entitled to repayment from the cardholder (customer).[19] Consequently, if a supplier could then trace the cardholder and demand immediate payment, this would undermine the entire basis of the payment mechanism and as such significantly disadvantage the customer. Millett J summed this up as follows:

> 'The terms on which the supplier is entitled to payment from the card-issuing company are quite different from those on which the card-issuing company is entitled to payment from the customer; and both differ from those on which the supplier would be entitled to payment from the customer if he were subject to any residual liability not discharged by the use of the card. The card-issuing company is liable to pay the supplier very shortly after the receipt of the sales vouchers and claim form, but is entitled to deduct its commission; while the customer is liable to pay the full face value of the voucher, but is entitled to much longer credit. If the customer is liable to pay the

---

[15] For a definition of absolute payment refer to the previous chapter.
[16] *Re Charge Card Services Ltd* [1987] 1 Ch 150.
[17] Ibid, at 158.
[18] The fact that the supplier would ordinarily have difficulties in identifying the customer without the co-operation of the card issuer means that it could not be the intention of the procedure that the customer should be sought after if the means of payment failed.
[19] For a discussion of repayment see above.

supplier on the failure or default of the card-issuing company, it is on terms more onerous than either, for he must be liable to make immediate payment of the full face value of the voucher. It is difficult to find any justification for imputing to the customer an intention to undertake any such liability.'[20]

6.3 Regulation of Credit Cards

When looking at the regulation of credit cards, it should be noted that the consumer credit agreement between the cardholder and card issuer is regulated by the Consumer Credit Act 1974. By contrast, charge cards are not classified as credit arrangements and as such are not subject to the Consumer Credit Act 1974. The only circumstances in which a credit card agreement for a card issued in this jurisdiction will not be governed by the Consumer Credit Act 1974 are:

• where the debtor is a company, rather than an individual; or

• where the credit limit exceeds the statutory ceiling of £15,000.

Where the Act is applicable, it is relevant in three respects.

• Section 51 of the Act makes it an offence to supply an unsolicited credit-token. Therefore, the way in which the credit card was supplied by the issuer to the holder affects the enforceability of the credit agreement.[21]

• The Act imposes limits on the cardholder's liability for unauthorised use of the card by a third party.[22]

• The Act imposes liability on the card issuer for the supplier's breach of contract or misrepresentation in relation to goods or services paid for with the card.

It is important to note that the Act uses the term 'credit-token' and it is worth clarifying why this applies to credit cards. Section 14(1) of the Act defines the term 'credit-token' as follows:

'A credit-token is a card, check, voucher, coupon, stamp, form, booklet or other document or thing given to an individual by a person carrying on a consumer credit business, who undertakes:

(a) that on the production of it (whether or not some other action is also required) he will supply cash, goods and services (or any of them) on credit, or

(b) that where, on the production of it to a third party (whether or not any other action is also required), the third party supplies cash, goods and services (or any of them), he will pay the third party for them (whether or not deducting any discount or commission), in return for payment to him by the individual.'

Furthermore, s8(2) of the Act states:

'A consumer credit agreement is a personal credit agreement by which the creditor provides the debtor with credit not exceeding £25,000.'

---

[20] *Re Charge Card Services Ltd* [1987] 1 Ch 150, at 169.
[21] Section 66 of the Act excludes the cardholder from liability under a credit-token agreement for use of a credit-token unless the credit-token has been previously accepted by the cardholder. See also Part V of the Act.
[22] The cardholder is obliged to report as soon as possible loss or theft of the card or where the PIN might have been disclosed to a third party.

If one considers the wording used in s14(1)(a), it refers to two-party credit cards which are issued by a creditor who is also the supplier of the goods or services. An example of this would be an 'in-house' store card which enables customers to buy goods on credit and to subsequently pay the required amount on the due date upon receipt of monthly statements. Note that even though there are only two parties, this credit agreement is still a form of debtor-creditor agreement under s12(1)(a) of the Act. Equally, s14(1)(b) envisages credit cards which are issued by a creditor in situations where the supplier is a third party. This three-party situation involves a debtor, creditor and supplier, thus resulting in the debtor-creditor-supplier agreements referred to in s12(1)(b) or (c). In this regard, it is worth noting the wording of s12 of the Act, which states:

'A debtor-creditor-supplier agreement is a regulated consumer credit agreement being:

(a) a restricted-use credit agreement which falls within s11(1)(a), or

(b) a restricted-use credit agreement which falls within s11(1)(b) and is made by the creditor under pre-existing arrangements, or in contemplation of future arrangements, between himself and the supplier, or

(c) an unrestricted-use credit agreement which is made by the creditor under pre-existing arrangements between himself and a person (the "supplier") other than the debtor in the knowledge that the credit is to be used to finance a transaction between the debtor and the supplier.'[23]

The cardholder is prevented from stopping payment once the card has been used even if he has a dispute with the supplier regarding the contract. However, where a cardholder (1) asserts a 'like claim' against the card issuer to that raised against the supplier pursuant to s75 Consumer Credit Act 1974; or (2) argues that the issuer is liable for some other act or omission relating to the transaction by virtue of the deemed agency provision in s56 of that Act, then he may be able to raise a set-off against the sum outstanding on his statement and will have a counterclaim against the card issuer in which case such a term is unlikely to have much use.

6.4 Liability for Misuse

Section 84 Consumer Credit Act 1974 states that 'misuse' by an unauthorised person occurring between loss or the theft of a card and notification of its loss or theft being given to the issuer, will be borne by the cardholder. A limit is, however, set at £50.[24] Section 84(5) goes on to state that notice takes effect when received by the creditor.

---

[23] Section 11 of the Act states:
'(1) A restricted-use credit agreement is a regulated consumer credit agreement –
(a) to finance a transaction between the debtor and the creditor, whether forming part of that agreement or not, or
(b) to finance a transaction between the debtor and a person (the "supplier") other than the creditor, or
(c) to refinance any existing indebtedness of the debtor's, whether to the creditor or another person,
and "restricted-use credit" shall be construed accordingly.'
[24] Section 84(1) states:
'Section 83 does not prevent the debtor under a credit-token agreement from being made liable to the extent of £50 (or the credit limit if lower) for loss to the creditor arising from use of the credit-token by other persons during a period beginning when the credit-token ceases to be in the possession of any authorised person and ending when the credit-token is once more in the possession of an authorised person.'

However, where it is given orally and the agreement so requires, it shall be treated as not taking effect if not confirmed in writing within seven days. In other words, notice will be ineffective unless it is confirmed in writing. Once the card issuer has been notified, s84(3) states:

'Subsections (1) and (2) shall not apply to any use of the credit-token after the creditor has been given oral or written notice that it is lost or stolen, or is for any other reason liable to misuse.'

However, it is worth noting that where a person misuses a credit card and that person acquired possession of it with the cardholder's consent, the cardholder (debtor) has unlimited liability.[25] In this respect, it is worth noting *Bank of Montreal* v *Demakos*[26] in which the credit cardholder was held liable for the fraudulent misuse of the card by his son, who was made a secondary holder under the card agreement. The son had incurred a debt far beyond the agreed credit limit, having deposited forged cheques to the bank. Whilst this is a Canadian case, it is likely that an English court would reach a similar decision.

Conversely, s83(1) states that a debtor under a regulated consumer credit agreement shall not be liable to the creditor for any loss arising from use of the credit facility by another person not acting, or to be treated as acting, as the debtor's agent.[27] However, it is worth posing the question as to whether a person should be treated as an agent if he obtained custody of the card for the limited purposes of safe keeping only. In the light of the wording contained in s84(2), it seems that the bank would not find it difficult to establish the cardholder's liability in such circumstances.

6.5 Credit Cards and Fraud

As noted earlier, the main concern in the use of credit cards for Internet payments is security.[28] In the case of the credit card, the cardholder's personal details on the card itself are the principal security feature. However, when these details are communicated over the Internet, there is the potential for interception by third parties who could then use them for unauthorised and fraudulent payments.[29] When this is coupled with the

---

[25] Section 84(2).

[26] [1996] 31 OR 757.

[27] Most credit card agreements will make it clear that the cardholder will be liable for all such cases.

[28] Several companies provide payment processing services. For instance, InternetSecure provides secure payment card services and supports payments with Visa and MasterCard for Canadian and United States accounts. The company provides risk management and fraud detection and handles transactions from online merchants using existing, bank-approved payment card processing infrastructure, secure links, and firewall technology to ensure complete security. InternetSecure notifies the merchant of all approved orders and supplies authorisation codes to customers who purchase soft goods that are downloaded upon payment card approval. The company is also responsible for ensuring that all transactions that it processes for payment card companies are credited to the merchant's account. Another company is First Data, which provides merchant payment card processing services with the ICVERIFY, PCAuthorize, and WebAuthorize programmes. ICVERIFY is intended for small retailers that use Microsoft Windows electronic cash registers and point-of-sale terminal systems. PCAuthorize is intended for smaller online stores (unlike ICVERIFY, it does not require any point-of-sale hardware), and WebAuthorize is for large, enterprise-class merchant sites.

[29] In many respects, the risk is also different due to the fact that unlike traditional commerce, where there is the added requirement of applying the customer's signature to the sales slip (thus providing the merchant with the opportunity to compare the signature), this does not occur on the Internet.

use of open networks, which may quite easily be intercepted by a third party without the sender's knowledge, the problem is exacerbated.

This led some Internet merchants to pursue a policy of requiring their customers to contact them by telephone or mail so as to communicate their credit card details as opposed to accepting online orders.[30] Consequently, the website was merely used for advertising purposes. This approach, however, necessarily restricts a merchant's potential market and as such is unacceptable in an e-commerce environment.[31]

However, as noted in the previous chapter, the most effective way to prevent the interception of credit card details over the Internet is the use of encryption so that only the right person has the right key to decrypt the details.

Nevertheless, even with the use of encryption a great deal depends upon the complexity of the encryption technology employed. It will also require the use of a Trusted Third Party (TTP); but even so, the buying process depends on initial contact with the TTP.

6.6 Terms and Conditions of Use

To date, card issuers have not been particularly swift to amend their standard terms and conditions of use so as to take into account Internet transactions. The general attitude seems to be that the existing terms are adequate for e-commerce purposes.

As matters stand, a transaction completed on a 'card not present' basis (ie a remote transaction either by telephone or mail, which will also include Internet sales) will not entitle the merchant to a guarantee of payment from his bank. This may be contrasted to a 'face-to-face' transaction in which case, so long as the signature on the sales slip matches that on the card, the merchant is guaranteed payment by his bank.

Consequently, it would appear that merchants have an interest in ensuring that their Internet customers, who choose to use a credit card, are properly authorised so to do. If they are not, then the merchant will be exposed to a 'chargeback'.[32] In this regard, it should be noted that banks are free to set a zero floor limit for Internet transactions so as to encourage e-commerce.[33]

As far as the UK is concerned, the limits on the cardholder's liability for fraudulent use, as set out in the Consumer Credit Act 1974, will probably apply even though the cardholder ignores a contractual requirement to use encryption. Consequently, these

---

[30] In the case of telephone sales, it is possible to ascertain other personal characteristics of the buyer for security purposes. For example, the supplier is able to tell (under normal circumstances) the gender of the user and whether the card is being used by a minor.
[31] For the full implications of this see the latter part of this chapter.
[32] In other words, they will be forced to repay, to the bank, the amount charged to the card on the transaction.
[33] In arrangements between merchants and merchant acquirers.

provisions will apply to Internet payments using a credit card as long as they have been intercepted unlawfully by an unauthorised third party.[34]

As noted above, ss83 and 84 of the Act state that a card issuer is not entitled to impose liability on a cardholder for more than £50 for any misuse of the card by a third party.

6.7 Section 75

One of the more attractive provisions of the Consumer Credit Act 1974, at least as far as the consumer is concerned, is s75. Where the consumer obtains goods or services from one person (the merchant) and the credit to pay for them from another (the creditor), the latter can be liable for the merchant's default in two situations:

1.   where the creditor himself contracts with the customer to supply the customer with the goods or services (s56);

2.   where s75 applies.

It should be noted from the outset that s75 applies to debtor-creditor-supplier agreements other than those where the creditor himself contracts to supply the goods and services to the customer.[35]

Section 75(1) of the Act states that:

'If the debtor under a debtor-creditor-supplier agreement falling within s12(1)(b) or (c) has, in relation to a transaction financed by the agreement, any claim against the supplier in respect of a misrepresentation or breach of contract, he shall have a like claim against the creditor, who, with the supplier shall accordingly be jointly and severally liable to the debtor.'

Thus, if the customer has used a credit card to pay for goods and services and has a claim against the merchant, for instance for misrepresentation, he can also sue the credit card issuer.[36]

---

[34] It would seem arguable that credit cardholders would be even better placed under the Distance Selling Regulations than under the 1974 Act. The Directive's substantive provisions cover five main areas: provision of information about the contract and its terms (arts 4 and 5); the right of withdrawal from the contract (art 6); the time for performance by the supplier (art 7); payment by card (art 8); and inertia selling (art 9). Consequently, art 2 defines distance contracts in such a way which is clearly intended to include Internet contracts. Article 8 then provides that Member States are to ensure that appropriate measures exist to allow a consumer:
• to request cancellation of a payment where fraudulent use has been made of his payment card in connection with a distance contract; and
• to be re-credited with the sums paid in the event of such fraudulent use.
Consequently, the Regulations would seem to require that the consumer cardholder be exempted from any liability for a transaction paid by fraudulent use of his credit card. This would go beyond the £50 limit under the 1974 Act. Whilst UK banks and card issuers have never made it a practice to collect the £50 from cardholders, even though they are clearly entitled to do so, legally speaking, the card issuers will probably not be allowed to insert clauses in their contracts with consumers, which fall foul of the Regulations.

[35] See discussion of s12(1) above.

[36] For those of you who feel sorry for the creditor as a result of s75(1), you should consider the implications of s75(2), which states that:
'Subject to any agreement between them, the creditor shall be entitled to be indemnified by the supplier for loss suffered by the creditor in satisfying his liability under subs(1), including costs reasonably incurred by him in defending proceedings instituted by the debtor.'

Section 75(3) goes on to clarify the scope of s75(1):

'Subsection (1) does not apply to a claim:

(a) under a non-commercial agreement, or

(b) so far as the claim relates to any single item to which the supplier has attached a cash price not exceeding £100 or more than £30,000.'[37]

Consequently, it would appear that s75 provides the credit cardholder with a convenient means of making a claim. This is even more the case in terms of Internet purchases, where the supplier may very well be located in another jurisdiction, thus raising issues of private international law.[38]

The following sections will explore the scope of the protection given by s75 to the debtor which is determined by the following issues:

- the types of transaction to which the provisions apply;

- the relevant debtor and supplier envisaged by the provisions;

- the type of actions against which a 'like claim' may lie against the creditor.

Step 1 – the claim must be by a debtor against a creditor

The first step in any exploration of s75 necessitates the identification of the debtor who may be entitled to protection. It excludes claims by a person who is not a debtor, which is defined by s189 of the Act as an:

'Individual receiving credit under a consumer credit agreement or the person to whom his rights and duties under the agreement have passed by assignment or operation of law, and in relation to a prospective consumer credit agreement includes the prospective debtor.'

Consequently, it may be seen that hirers under credit hire agreements as well as corporate bodies are excluded from the protection of s75. In addition, another significant class of persons excluded from the provision is the authorised credit card user who is not designated as an account holder by the card agreement. Such a person, who may be the spouse or child of the account holder, is not a 'debtor' for the purposes of s75 and therefore has no claim against the creditor. It should be noted that in general, credit card companies prefer not to open a joint account where more than one person is interested in using the card. Rather, most companies will name only one of the parties in the agreement as the account holder even though a second card will be issued to the other user.[39]

It should also be noted that the protection of s75 applies only where a claim is made against the relevant supplier.[40] The supplier in question must be the person to whom payment for the goods or services was made using the card, as it is with this

---

[37] However, it should be noted that a claim may be made where a credit card is used to make part payment of less than £100 in respect of an item priced over £100.

[38] Refer to the later sections in this chapter for a full discussion of this point.

[39] This is a favourite amongst examiners.

[40] If one examines the term 'supplier', as outlined in ss11(1)(b) and 189(1), then it refers to the party, other than the debtor, to the transaction financed by the credit agreement.

person that the creditor has the requisite pre-existing arrangement that is contemplated by ss12 and 187 of the Act.[41]

Returning to the initial discussion, the creditor who is sued under s75 will take the benefit of defences or limitation of liability to which the supplier is entitled. He will also be entitled to the supplier's right of set-off as well as any other defences available to him in his own right.

However, it should be stressed that if the person to whom payment by credit card was made did not in fact supply the goods or service, but was merely the agent of the person who did, then the creditor cannot be held liable for breach of contract or misrepresentation by the provider of the goods or service. This is based on the simple fact that the creditor can only be held answerable for the supplier's fault under the supply contract.[42]

For example, where travel and accommodation is arranged through a travel agent who does not actually operate the flight or furnish the accommodation, then if payment is made by credit card to the travel agent and not directly to the airline or hotel there can be no s75 claim against the creditor for the services supplied by the airline or hotel.[43]

Step 2 – the agreement must be a debtor-creditor-supplier agreement within s12(b) or (c)

The implication of this is that s75 applies only to regulated agreements. As such, if the consumer credit agreement is either an 'exempt agreement' or an agreement which lies outside the scope of the Act (as with credit cards issued to a company), then the protection of s75 cannot be invoked.[44]

The circumstances in which a 'like claim' against the supplier can be brought against the creditor are strictly restricted to the situations under subsections (b) and (c) of s12. In essence, these are situations where the creditor and supplier are different persons.

An ideal example of this would be the use of store credit cards, which are issued specifically for use only within designated branches of a particular store. So long as the credit is advanced to the customer by a legal entity separate to that of the supplier (whether or not a subsidiary or sister company) s75 will apply. All that matters is that credit has been provided by a creditor to enable the debtor to purchase goods and services from a third party.

---

[41] According to Goode, it is necessary to identify the supplier because the liability of the creditor to the debtor under s75 is coterminous with the liability of the supplier to the debtor for misrepresentation or breach of contract.

[42] In other words, s75 attaches to the claim against a supplier to whom the credit card was produced by way of financing a supply transaction.

[43] However, in view of reg 15 of the Package Travel, Package Holiday and Package Tour Regulations 1992, SI 1992/3233, the liability of the creditor has been extended. It is now a party to the contract made with the consumer with a credit card where the travel agent sells or offers for sale a package put together by an organiser.

[44] Debtor–creditor agreements under s13 and consumer hire agreements under s15 are also not within the scope of s75 protection.

By contrast, typical examples of situations where the creditor is also the supplier of the goods are in hire purchase agreements, credit sales and conditional sales. In these instances, the arrangement is such that the finance house or creditor[45] initially buys the goods from the dealer and then sells it the debtor on credit terms. Due to the fact that the creditor is the legal supplier, there is a direct contractual relationship on the supply contract between the creditor and the debtor. Consequently, the debtor is able to enforce the rights acquired under the supply contract directly against the creditor. In addition, the creditor is in a contractual relationship with the dealer and can sue him directly for misrepresentation or breach of the contract of sale.[46]

If one looks at *Renton* v *Hendersons Garage (Nairm) Ltd*,[47] the case involved a conditional sale agreement between the defendant finance company and the issue focused on whether a claim could be brought against the creditor under s75. This court held that the section did not apply to conditional sales as they were restricted-use agreements, which fell under ss11(1)(a) and 12(a). The purpose of s75 was to extend the categories of creditors who might be liable to a debtor for breach of contract where the actual delinquent was a third party such as a dealer. Consequently, in the circumstances of a restricted-use credit agreement, where the creditor is the supplier, the right of action against creditors that s75 extends to debtors is already available.

In his text on consumer credit, Dobson outlines the rationale behind the interpretation of s75 as follows:

'In fact s75 does not apply to hire purchase, conditional sale and credit sale agreements. This is, after all, only common sense, since in these cases there are in the credit agreement itself terms relating to the delivery, description and quality of the goods; and if one of those terms is broken the creditor will in any case be liable for what is his own breach of contract. Where a finance company makes a hire purchase, conditional sale or credit sale agreement with the debtor, the finance company buys the goods from the dealer and contracts with the debtor to supply the goods to the debtor. Thus the finance company supplies the goods on credit terms to the debtor.'[48]

According to s187, s75 contemplates the existence of a 'pre-existing arrangement' or 'contemplated future arrangements' between the creditor and supplier:

'(1) A consumer credit agreement shall be treated as entered into under pre-existing arrangements between a creditor and a supplier if it is entered into in accordance with, or in furtherance of, arrangements previously made between persons mentioned in subs(4)(a), (b) or (c).

---

[45] Often referred to as the 'owner'.
[46] The significance of this is that in hire purchase, credit sale and conditional sale, there is no need for the protection afforded by s75 or a right of indemnity in favour of the debtor as he can sue the creditor directly. See: *Porter* v *General Guarantee Corp Ltd* [1982] RTP 384 in which s75 was applied to a hire purchase transaction. The plaintiff wanted to trade in his car with a second-hand vehicle sold by a dealer. He intended to use the vehicle as a taxi. He was told by the dealer's sales representative that the vehicle was in excellent condition and had just been serviced. He entered into a hire purchase agreement with the defendant and took delivery of the vehicle. He found that it had several defects that rendered it unsafe for use on public roads and unusable as a taxi. He brought an action against the defendant for breaches of the warranty of merchantability and unfitness arguing that these amounted to breach of a fundamental term of the contract. The defendant was held liable, but the court also said that s75 applied and so the defendant was entitled to be indemnified by the dealer for liability incurred as a result of his breach. This decision was given per incuriam. However, see *Renton* v *Hendersons Garage (Nairm) Ltd* [1994] CCLP 29.
[47] [1994] CCLP 29.
[48] P Dobson, 'Dobson: Sale of Goods and Consumer Credit', (1996) 8th ed, Sweet and Maxwell, p367.

(2) A consumer credit agreement shall be treated as entered into in contemplation of future arrangements between a creditor and a supplier if it is entered into in the expectation that arrangements will subsequently be made between persons mentioned in subs(4)(a), (b) or (c) for the supply of cash, goods and services (or any of them) to be financed by the consumer credit agreement.'

It has been argued, particularly by credit card issuers, that they should not be held liable where they have no merchant agreement[49] with the particular supplier whose breach is in question.

If this is examined in greater detail, then in the case of a typical four-party credit card arrangement, various card issuers are involved in the settlement system. This is because the network is such that sale vouchers presented by suppliers with whom a particular card issuer has no merchant agreement are received and processed by passing it to the 'merchant acquirer' who pays the supplier. The card issuer collects payment from the debtor and then settles the merchant acquirer. The merchant acquirer and card issuer each has an agreement with the supplier and debtor respectively but in many cases, the supplier receives payment by cards issued by a company with whom it has no direct agreement.

An ideal example of this is the Visa scheme, within which there are several merchant acquirers that recruit new suppliers into the scheme. However, Barclaycard argued at one point, that where the supplier was signed on by another merchant acquirer, then even though it could process sales vouchers presented by that supplier, it was not liable under s75 for its breach of contract or misrepresentation because of the absence of any 'pre-existing arrangement' between them. This has been rejected. Consequently, it is submitted that since all the suppliers and merchant acquirers belong to the Visa scheme and its operation enables them to carry on business by inter-settlement, they cannot deny the significant consequences of the arrangement with respect to s75 claims.[50]

Therefore, looking at the essential elements of the scheme, one of the main reasons that credit cards issued by different merchant acquirers are acceptable to the supplier is due to the fact that there is the possibility of inter-settlement under the scheme. As such, this may be taken to suffice as a form of 'pre-existing arrangement' for the purposes of the Consumer Credit Act 1974.

Step 3 – s75 applies to a right of action for breach of contract or misrepresentation

The debtor cannot sue the creditor if the supplier is in breach of any duty other than misrepresentation and breach of contract. Equally, the source of the wrong to be redressed by the section must be the supply of goods and services contract. Actions in tort or breach of statutory duty[51] must be maintained under s56 or directly against the supplier.

---

[49] Agreement to accept the credit card for payment.
[50] Due to pressure from the Office of Fair Trading, Barclaycard gave up the argument.
[51] For instance under the Consumer Protection Act 1987.

As with the discussion above, if the supplier is in breach of a contract, which is ancillary to the sale contract, such as a 'maintenance' or 'after sales' contract, the debtor cannot recover from the creditor by virtue of s75.

Step 4 – the claim against the creditor must be a 'like claim' in relation to that against the supplier

The debtor's claim against the supplier for breach of contract and misrepresentation are monetary and where he rescinds the contract for misrepresentation, he would have a restitutionary claim to recover the purchase price of the goods or that paid for the services.

The creditor is jointly and severally liable with the supplier on any of these kinds of claims. In addition, the creditor is bound to return monies paid for the goods or service on the supply contract.

The question has arisen though as to whether the debtor's right to rescind the supply contract affects the credit agreements. In other words, can he rescind the credit agreement by virtue of the fact that he can treat the supply agreement as repudiated? It would appear that the cases *United Dominions Trust Ltd* v *Taylor*[52] and *Forward Trust Ltd* v *Hornsby*[53] support this contention on the basis that both the supply and credit contracts are linked together. In *United Dominions Trust Ltd* v *Taylor*, the Sheriff Principal stated:

> 'A reading of the Act discloses that it has created a completely new system of classifications and remedies to take effect whenever consumer credit is associated with the contract of sale and hire. These statutory remedies have been superimposed on existing contractual remedies ... One of the innovations of the Act is to treat two or more contracts, which are economically part of one credit transaction as transactions, which are legally linked. Where these linked transactions contain two contracts the fate of each contract depends on the other, even where the parties to the contract are different. This approach leaves no room for the idea of privity of contract which is fundamental to the common law contract.'

However, it should be stressed that this decision has been criticised by several commentators. Guest[54] argues that the word 'claim' in s75 suggests monetary compensation and that 'a like claim' refers to a claim in relation to the supply agreement and as such not a claim to repudiate the credit agreement.

It is also argued that the ability to rescind the credit agreement is inconsistent with the joint and several liability of both parties, as the supplier is not a party under the credit agreement. It is thought that if the intention behind the wording of s75 was that both the supply and credit agreements should stand and fall together, this would have been more clearly expressed within the statute.[55]

The debtor's action against the creditor is not destroyed by the fact that he may be

---

[52] [1980] SLT (Sh Ct) 28.
[53] [1996] CCLR 18.
[54] Though it should be noted that Guest's view is now in the minority.
[55] Equally, there is no mention in the Crowther Committee Report that the debtor should have a remedy other than a monetary claim pursuant to the section.

in breach of the credit agreement or has exceeded the credit limit in entering the supply transaction (s75(4)):

> '(4) This section applies notwithstanding that the debtor, in entering into the transaction, exceeded the credit limit or otherwise contravened any term of the agreement.'

Under s75(5) the creditor could choose to settle the claim or proceed with an action joining the supplier as third party. Furthermore, s75(2) provides the creditor with a right of indemnity against the supplier for loss incurred in satisfying the debtor's claim:

> '(2) Subject to any agreement between them, the creditor shall be entitled to be indemnified by the supplier for loss suffered by the creditor in satisfying his liability under subs(1), including costs reasonably incurred by him in defending proceedings instituted by the debtor.'

Step 5 – exemptions

Section 75(3) provides for two exceptions. First of all, where the supply contract with respect to which the claim is made is a non-commercial agreement and secondly, claims with respect to any single item with a cash price of less than £100 or over £30,000.

It is significant that the monetary limits under the Act are based on the price paid by the debtor for the transaction that was financed with the credit card as opposed to the amount of the credit or loan advanced. Indeed, this is particularly relevant where a credit card is used to effect part payment for the goods;[56] the debtor is able to claim for the amount of the whole loss even though in excess of the credit advanced on the card.[57]

Determining whether a particular claim is excluded from s75 on the basis of these two exceptions may not be so easy where, for instance, items are priced as a set for over £100 but individually cost less than that.

Application of s75 to Internet transactions

It is still debatable whether s75 applies to credit card transactions that have a foreign element.[58] For instance, if a cardholder purchases goods whilst abroad with a credit card issued by his local bank and then upon his return to the UK either realises that the goods are defective or that the supplier had misrepresented certain facts, the question arises as to whether s75 applies. In terms of the subject matter of this book and the increase in e-commerce, the position of a person who buys goods on the Internet using a credit card is growing in importance.

Arguments have been made for and against the application of s75 to the case of a foreign supplier.[59] It is arguable that the wording of s75 is sufficiently wide to cover the

---

[56] See: LS Sealy and RJA Hooley, 'Commercial Law: Text, Cases and Materials' (2004) 3rd ed, Butterworths, p813.

[57] For instance if a debtor pays the £50 deposit on a holiday worth £500 using his credit card, he may not only claim the whole of £500 with respect to breach of contract or misrepresentation but any other consequential loss in excess of that amount. As claims for goods bought with credit cards for less than £100 are excluded, it seems that many low value consumer purchases are excluded. (The alternative for the consumer in such a case is to resort to s56 deemed agency provisions or to sue the supplier directly.)

[58] In other words, where there is a foreign supplier and the transaction may be subject to foreign law.

[59] See: G Stephenson, 'Credit, Debit and Cheque Cards', p142, 1993, and for a contrasting view see: Paget's Law of Banking, para 2.68, 12th ed, 2002.

case of goods being purchased abroad. However, as to whether s75 specifically contemplated the provision of credit to finance a supply agreement with a supplier who is abroad, it is arguable that it did not.[60] Otherwise, it would have made similar provision applying the sterling equivalent to cash price in foreign currency, as done elsewhere under s9(2). Nevertheless, common sense dictates that it is in precisely this type of transaction that a consumer requires more, not less, protection.

Other arguments used by credit card companies to resist the application of s75 to supply agreements entered into abroad include the absence of a pre-existing arrangement with the supplier as mentioned above. However, this argument is refuted on the ground that the section does not require the existence of an agreement. Rather, it is submitted that the arrangement in which the credit card companies carry on business is adequate arrangement for the purposes of the Act.[61]

If one takes a common sense approach to this issue, then it is apparent that it is impossible that a particular card issuer would have a merchant agreement with every conceivable supplier who accepts its card for payment under the present settlement system. Consequently, the objection by credit card issuers that a particular supplier was not recruited by the card issuer cannot be maintained, especially given the fact that a cardholder is unlikely to know that the particular supplier in question did not have an agreement with the creditor when he entered into the supply contracts. Therefore, unless the existing network had made this type of information available to cardholders, it is now very difficult for them to limit the use of cards to suppliers acquired by their card issuers.[62]

Whilst this is generally accepted as being the case, it has also been argued that an additional element is missing from the current arrangement in the Visa and/or Mastercard networks, due to the way in which the term 'pre-existing arrangement' is defined by the Act. Section 187(1) states that:

'A consumer credit agreement shall be treated as entered into under pre-existing arrangements between a creditor and a supplier if it is entered into in accordance with, or in furtherance of, arrangements previously made between persons mentioned in subs(4)(a), (b) or (c).'

Section 187(4) goes on to state that a 'pre-existing arrangement' relates to that made between:

---

[60] If one is pessimistic, then it would appear difficult for a local creditor to obtain the right of indemnity given by s75(2) against an overseas supplier. In such a case, the supply contract may be governed by a foreign law, except where the proper law of the contract is English law or an English court has jurisdiction. The creditor would then face the problem of establishing the supplier's rights and liabilities under foreign law or be forced to settle the debtor's claim at home. Given that the creditor is unlikely to have any agreement with the supplier, the link with the foreign supplier in the complex credit card settlement network is likely to be minimal for purposes of the rationale behind the connected lender liability.

[61] See: *Re British Basic Slag Ltd's Agreements* [1963] 2 All ER 807 at 814 and 819.

[62] It is worth noting at this point the distinction between a 'closed loop' system and that of an 'open loop' system. If the card issuer pays the merchants that accept the card directly, not using an intermediary, such as a bank or clearinghouse system, then this type of arrangement is referred to as a closed loop system. This is because no other institution is involved in the transaction. American Express and Discover Card are perfect examples of this. By contrast, an open loop system involves three or more parties. Systems which use either Visa or MasterCard are examples of open loop systems. Many banks issue both cards. Unlike American Express or Discover, neither Visa nor MasterCard issues cards directly to consumers.

'(4) The persons referred to in subsections (1) and (2) are –

(a) the creditor and the supplier;

(b) one of them and an associate of the others;

(c) an associate of one and an associate of the others.'

Section 184(3) applies the criteria of control for determining whether companies are associated:

'(3) A body corporate is an associate of another body corporate –

(a) if the same person is a controller of both, or a person is a controller of one and persons who are his associates, or he and persons who are his associates, are the controllers of the other; or

(b) if a group of two or more persons is a controller of each company, and the groups either consist of the same persons or could be regarded as consisting of the same persons by treating (in one or more cases) a member of either group as replaced by a person of whom he is an associate.'

Therefore, this would seem to suggest that even though a direct agreement is not explicitly required by s75, there should at least be some form of control of the supplier by the creditor.

However, this is not the prevailing view. Most commentators agree that s75 extends to foreign credit card transactions irrespective of the absence of any prior agreement or direct arrangement between a particular creditor and the supplier.[63] In 1994, the Office of Fair Trading reviewed the provision of s75 in separate reports and adopted a similar view.[64]

More recently, though, several credit card companies have tried to rely on the lack of a pre-existing arrangement argument to deny liability in actions brought by debtors under s75. However, as Sealy and Hooley reassuringly note: 'on 19 September 2002 three credit card companies gave the Office of Fair Trading assurances that they would honour valid claims under s75 for purchases abroad'.[65] It is hoped that this will finally put an end to this particular debate, though the specific question as to the application of s75 to the Internet remains an area of continued discussion.

Another strong argument for the application of s75 to overseas transactions is the EU Directive on Consumer Credit.[66] As will be noted later in this chapter, art 11 provides that a debtor shall have a right of action against the creditor for certain breaches of the supply contract.

To date, the Directive has not been implemented in the UK due to the fact that many feel that the Consumer Credit Act 1974 more than complies with its provisions. As such, it would seem that for the UK to provide consumers with the benefit of the protection under this Directive, s75 of the Act must necessarily be extended to supply transactions entered into by parties within the European Union.

---

[63] This is a more realistic view because of the broad perspective of the protection to consumers.
[64] (See Report No OFT 132 Connected Lender Liability, May 1995 and Report No OFT 097 Connected Lender Liability, March 1994.)
[65] LS Sealy and RJA Hooley, 'Commercial Law: Text, Cases and Materials', (2004) 3rd ed, Butterworths, p813.
[66] 87/102/EEC.

If this is the case, there is no logical reason why a claim under a transaction made outside the EU should not be equally protected, after all, it is those situations that are probably more deserving of protection. The debtor being farther away from the supplier would find it harder to trace the supplier and to enforce his rights.

However, when considering the Internet, there is the preliminary problem of ascertaining the jurisdiction and proper law of the sale of goods or supply of services contract. The Rome Convention on the Law Applicable to Contractual Obligations 1980 and Council Regulation 44/2001/EC[67] will apply to determine the proper law and jurisdiction respectively. In the absence of express contractual provisions on choice of law, the Rome Convention, in certain circumstances, will make the governing law the state where the consumer[68] has his habitual residence.[69] Likewise, under Regulation 44/2001, arts 15–17 provide that a consumer may in certain types of contract be sued only in the courts of his domicile. This includes contracts for credit to finance the sale of goods and thus appears to cover credit card agreements.

Finally, it is worth noting the effect of EC Distance Contracts Directive 97/7/EC on this debate. The Directive specifically contains provisions that have application to credit card Internet transactions. Article 8 states that appropriate measures shall be put in place to permit a consumer to request cancellation of a payment where fraudulent use has been made of his payment card in connection with a distance contract and be re-credited with the sums paid in the event of such fraudulent use. Article 12(2) goes on to stipulate that Member States shall take measures to ensure that the consumer does not lose the protection granted by the Directive by virtue of the choice of law of a non-member country as the law applicable to the contract if the latter has a close connection with the territory of one or more Member States.

Consequently, it may be argued that the effect of these provisions is to ensure that in credit card Internet transactions by a UK consumer, English law would presumably apply as the proper law of the sale contract in the absence of any express contractual stipulation and English courts would be given jurisdiction.

The Internet has exacerbated the issue of whether the Consumer Credit Act 1974 applies to transactions that have a foreign element by resolving the problem of merchant inaccessibility; enabling merchants to advertise and sell their products to consumers all over the world. Today, it does not really matter to a cardholder who purchases goods on the Internet where the merchant is physically resident.

Equally, behind this surge in use of the Internet, there is the consumer expectation that the legal framework should be the same whether the Internet seller is based abroad or in the UK. As such, it is arguable on a policy level that the protection of s75 should apply to all Internet transactions. It is also worth pointing out that despite a number

---

[67] See: C Wild, 'Textbook on Conflict of Laws' (2005) 3rd ed, Old Bailey Press.

[68] For further discussion on this point see: Wild, Weinstein and Reifa, 'Council Regulation (EC) 44/2001 and Internet Consumer Contracts: Some Thoughts on art 15 and the Futility of Applying In the Box Conflict of Law Rules to the Out of the Box Borderless World', IRLCT, (19)1, March 2005.

[69] Article 5.

of European initiatives, in many jurisdictions there is nothing that corresponds to the high level of protection offered to UK cardholders under the Act.[70] This will be explored further at the end of this chapter.

If it proves to be correct that the Consumer Credit Act 1974, and in particular s75, applies to Internet transactions, then it lies with credit card companies to take the initiative to avoid possible actions for the breach of contract or misrepresentation by foreign suppliers. This can be ensured through precaution in the criteria for recruiting and policing suppliers and ensuring that whatever loses are incurred in settling debtors' claims can be duly passed on to suppliers overseas.

Equally, in the light of s84 Consumer Credit Act 1974 and the Distance Contracts Directive, it may be hard to throw on the debtor the risk of unauthorised misuse of credit card details transmitted on the Internet.

6.8 Section 56

At common law, the supplier of goods financed by a credit or hire agreement between the creditor and debtor is not the agent of the creditor.

In hire purchase agreements, the dealer who supplies the goods usually acts as a conduit between the parties by introducing the buyer to the finance house. In many cases, he is in possession of the creditor's loan application forms and will usually help the buyer to complete and send it off to the finance house. If the credit is approved, he also receives the initial deposit on behalf of the creditor, who pays him a commission for all the trouble. However, this is not regarded as sufficient for the supplier to be considered an agent, unless the creditor holds him out as being one. For further discussion refer to the House of Lords' decision in *Branwhite* v *Worcester Works Finance Ltd*[71] which confirmed that the dealer is not normally the agent of the finance company.[72] However, note that the creditor may be estopped from asserting that the supplier had no authority to make representations on his behalf.[73]

Section 56 Consumer Credit Act 1974 reverses the common law position by providing that in a regulated agreement, certain antecedent negotiations falling under subs(1)(b) or (c) shall be deemed to be made by the supplier as an agent of the creditor as well as in his actual capacity. In this regard, s56(1) states that:

'In this Act "antecedent negotiations" means any negotiations with the debtor or hirer –

(a) conducted by the creditor or owner in relation to the making of any regulated agreement, or

(b) conducted by a credit-broker in relation to goods sold or proposed to be sold by the credit-broker to the creditor before forming the subject matter of a debtor-creditor-supplier agreement within s12(a), or

---

[70] Elsewhere recovery on claims against creditors is usually limited to the amount advanced on the credit.
[71] [1969] 1 AC 552.
[72] For further discussion see: P Dobson, 'Dobson: Sale of Goods and Consumer Credit', (1996) Sweet and Maxwell, pp324–325. In addition, see *Campbell Discount Co Ltd* v *Gall* [1961] 1 QB 431; *Woodchester Equipment (Leasing) Ltd* v *British Association Canned and Preserved Foods Importers and Distributors Ltd* [1995] CCLR 82.
[73] *Lease Management Services Ltd* v *Purnell Secretarial Services Ltd* [1994] CCLR 127.

(c) conducted by the supplier in relation to a transaction financed or proposed to be financed by a debtor-creditor-supplier agreement within s12(b) or (c),

and "negotiator" means the person by whom negotiations are so conducted with the debtor or hirer.'[74]

The key provision though is subs(2), which states:

'Negotiations with the debtor in a case falling within subs(1)(b) or (c) shall be deemed to be conducted by the negotiator in the capacity of agent of the creditor as well as in his actual capacity.'

This provision anticipates that the negotiations shall be deemed to have been contracted in the course and within the scope of the deemed agency. Therefore, it renders unnecessary issues as to whether or not the particular representation is within the scope of the agent's actual or apparent authority.

As s56(2) refers to 'antecedent negotiation', it is important to determine in a credit card context whether negotiations or dealings, prior to the conclusion of the supply contract, can be regarded as 'antecedent'. In this respect, s56(4) clarifies the fact that:

'For the purposes of this Act, antecedent negotiations shall be taken to begin when the negotiator and the debtor or hirer first enter into communication (including communication by advertisement), and to include any representations made by the negotiator to the debtor or hirer and any other dealings between them.'

In the light of this, there are a number of interpretations which may be placed on events. First of all, it would be unusual if the point at which the credit card agreement was signed is decisive in determining what is antecedent; so precluding all negotiations and dealings that follow it. Indeed, if this was the case, a number of potential acts and omissions, for which the s56 remedy could be used, would be excluded by this construction.

A more realistic and practical interpretation would appear to be that the provision applies to dealings and statements which post date the signing of the credit card agreement, but pre-date the particular supply agreement. Goode supports this construction on the ground that each fresh use of the credit card constitutes the creation of a new and binding extension of the credit agreement, to the extent of the drawing.[75] Consequently, the creditor's offer to lend money is regarded as a continuing offer accepted by the use of the card any time before it is revoked.[76]

According to s56(4), antecedent negotiations include representations, which are defined under s189(1) of the Act as including any condition or warranty, and any other statement or undertaking whether in writing or not.

It has been suggested that this includes pre-contractual and non-promissory

---

[74] Subsection (1)(b) relates to the hire purchase kind of situations where the supplier first sells the subject matter of the credit transaction to the creditor who in turn lets it under a hire purchase agreement to the debtor. Whereas, subs(1)(c) fits the typical credit card situation.

[75] R Goode, 'Commercial Law', (2004) 3rd ed, Penguin, pp780–781.

[76] However, it would appear that, in the light of the definition of 'antecedent negotiation' and 'negotiator' outlined above, the deemed agency under subs(2) arises only where a regulated agreement is actually concluded. Therefore, if the debtor eventually enters into a regulated consumer credit or consumer hire agreement with the creditor, there will be no action for anything said or done by the supplier pursuant to a deal which subsequently fell apart.

statements which never become a term of the contract as well as any statement which was not a promise at the time it was made which later becomes part of the contract.[77]

The significance of the provision is that the debtor can rescind or repudiate the credit agreement and recover damages from the creditor in respect of contractual statements; conditions, warranties or misrepresentations relating to the supply of goods and services. This is reinforced by s56(3) which reaffirms the importance of the deemed agency provisions by ensuring that creditors are unable to exclude it.[78]

Application of s56

Problems have arisen in the application of s56 where a debtor enters into a debtor-creditor-supplier agreement, for example with respect to a new car, having agreed with the supplier or credit-broker (the dealer) to trade-in his old vehicle. In these circumstances, the dealer will promise to buy the old vehicle and discharge, out of the purchase price, the balance outstanding under the credit agreement with respect to the old vehicle. If the dealer fails to fulfil this promise and goes insolvent, the issue arises as to whether the debtor can sue the creditor under s56(1)(b) or (c) on the credit agreement relating to the new car.

It is not disputed that the agreement to discharge the outstanding balance is a 'dealing' between the debtor and the car dealer. The issue arises as to whether it is with respect to the new car or the one traded-in. If the latter is the case, the creditor cannot be sued under s56. There are conflicting decisions.

In *United Dominions Trust* v *Whitfield*[79] the court held that the dealer's promise was inextricably related to the credit agreement for the new vehicle as to form an antecedent negotiation under s56. The facts were that the debtor obtained a first vehicle on a two-year hire purchase contract from UDT. Later, he approached a garage with a view to buying another car and the garage promised to take it in part-exchange for a second vehicle to be financed through FNS; and to pay off the debt to UDT. The debtor handed over the first vehicle to the garage, entered into the agreement with FNS and took possession of the second vehicle. The garage then failed to pay off UDT and went into liquidation. Consequently, the debtor had two debts but only one vehicle. He chose to pay off the sums due to FNS and stopped any further payments to UDT with notice to them outlining his reasons. UDT sued. He consented to judgment being entered against him not to be enforced pending his third party proceedings against the FNS under s56. The court found in his favour and it was held that they were liable for the dealer's breach in 'antecedent negotiations' with the debtor.

---

[77] This implication of 'representation' goes further than its ordinary meaning at common law where it is normally confined to positive statements.

[78] Section 56(3) states that:

'An agreement is void if, and to the extent that, it purports in relation to an actual or prospective regulated agreement –

(a) to provide that a person acting as, or on behalf of, a negotiator is to be treated as the agent of the debtor or hirer, or

(b) to relieve a person from liability for acts or omissions of any person acting as, or on behalf of, a negotiator.'

[79] [1987] CCLR 60.

In *Powell* v *Lloyd's Bowmaker Ltd*[80] the creditor was held not liable for the dealer's failure to pay off the outstanding debt owed on the credit agreement with respect to the old car; the rationale being that the dealer was not the agent of the finance house who financed the new vehicle either at common law or under s56(1)(b). It was stated that s56 makes the creditor agent of the supplier only with respect to the goods sold or proposed to be sold.[81]

6.9 Differences Between ss56 and 75

There are a number of ways in which the nature of the debtor's protection under s56 differs from that under s75 Consumer Credit Act 1974. First of all, s56 would appear to be somewhat wider in view of the fact that it is not subjected to monetary limits. Consequently, unlike s75, a debtor's claim with respect to items bought with a credit card for a cash price below £100 or above £30,000 will be brought within s56.

Section 56 will apply to non-commercial agreements and cover causes of action other than breach of contract and misrepresentation. Where the misrepresentation or breach of contract relates to the credit agreement, as opposed to the supply contract, the debtor will be able to rescind it under s56.[82]

According to s56(4), the deemed agency arises with respect to 'any other dealing' by the negotiator in the antecedent negotiations. As such, dealings with respect to ancillary contracts other than the supply contract appear to be covered unlike under s75 of the Act. In addition, under s56, the supplier remains liable notwithstanding the agency of the creditor and so could still be sued by the debtor. This is due to the fact that he makes the negotiations in his personal capacity as well.

Unlike s75, there is no provision under s56 that the creditor will be indemnified by the supplier for claims made by the debtor. It should be noted that no mention is made of the creditor being entitled to join the supplier in proceedings as a third party.[83]

6.10 The Consumer Credit Directive

The Lisbon European Council[84] set the objective for the European Union to become the most competitive and dynamic knowledge-based economy in the world by 2010, reflecting the overall objective of *e*Europe[85] to bring Europe online as fast as possible.[86]

---

[80] [1996] SLT (Sh Ct) 117.
[81] However, it should be noted that in *Forthright Finance Ltd* v *Ingate (Carlyle Finance Ltd, Third Party)* [1997] 4 All ER 99, the Court of Appeal rejected the above view in preference to the analysis in *Whitfield*.
[82] This means that the type of situation dealt with in *United Dominions Trust* v *Taylor* is unlikely to arise in the context of this provision.
[83] However, a creditor who satisfies the debtor's claims will be able to claim contribution from the supplier under the Civil Liability (Contribution) Act 1978.
[84] See: The Lisbon Strategy – Making Change Happen', COM(2002) 14.
[85] See: *e*Europe Benchmarking Report: *e*Europe 2002, COM(2002) 62 final, p3, which states: 'The assumption behind the 64 targets of *e*Europe was that they would have an impact on Internet penetration and eventually Internet use which are central objectives of *e*Europe'.
[86] There have been two previous reports assessing the progress of the *e*Europe strategy. See: Nice: The *e*Europe Update, COM(2000) 783, November 2000; Stockholm: Impacts and Priorities, COM (2001) 140, March 2001. (Both reports have described the various policy measures and assessed their impact.) Progress updates are currently published on the *e*Europe website: http://europa.eu.int/information_society/eeurope/benchmarking/index_en.htm.

In many respects, *e*Europe 2002[87] may be seen as having laid the foundations for this process by reshaping 'the regulatory environment for communications networks and services for e-commerce'.[88] *e*Europe 2005 is the latest Action Plan in the *e*Europe initiative and represents a change in focus. In drafting this latest Action Plan[89] the Barcelona European Council felt that it was necessary to follow *e*Europe 2002 with a strategy that focused on 'the widespread availability and use of broadband networks throughout the Union by 2005 ... and the security of networks and information, eGovernment, eLearning, eHealth and eBusiness'.[90] Consequently, *e*Europe 2005 aims to place users at the centre of its activities.[91]

However, the *e*Europe Benchmarking Report[92] has revealed a number of statistics which place a question mark against the European Union's success in encouraging its citizens to take full advantage of this e-commerce environment. Whilst Internet penetration in EU households increased significantly during 2000/2001 (18 per cent in March 2000, 28 per cent in October 2000, and 36 per cent in June 2001),[93] concern has been expressed at the possibility that penetration may now have levelled out at around 40 per cent of households.[94] Eurobarometre 56.0 would appear to support these findings in terms of consumer use of the Internet. The study revealed that cash still remains the preferred means of payment[95] for transactions conducted within individual Member States, closely followed by the use of cards.[96] Perhaps more significantly though, when assessing the relative success of the Commission's *e*Europe initiative, cash and cards continue to dominate the means of payment when reviewing payments conducted abroad. Furthermore, Eurobarometre 56.0 revealed that 56 per cent of EU consumers refuse to contemplate the use of 'electronic purses' whether to perform transactions at home or abroad.[97] In some respects it is hard to reconcile this particular figure with the findings of the *e*Europe Benchmarking Report which states that:

'*e*Europe has triggered a major industry-led smartcard initiative backed Euros 100,000,000 research funding. The market prospects for smart cards ... are positive.'

---

[87] The Fiera European Council endorsed the *e*Europe 2002 Action Plan in June 2000.

[88] *e*Europe 2005, Executive Summary, p1.

[89] The *e*Europe 2005 Action Plan succeeded the *e*Europe 2002 Action Plan endorsed by the Fiera European Council in June 2000.

[90] Barcelona European Council, Presidency Conclusions, paragraph 40, (http://ue.eu.int/en/Info/eurocouncil/index.htm).

[91] One example of this is the fact that on 14 January 2003, the European Council passed a Resolution regarding eAccessibility and the improvement of access for people with disabilities to the Knowledge Based Society. This followed an Opinion on the 14 November 2002 by the Committee of the Regions, which endorsed the main conclusions and recommendations presented in *e*Europe 2002. (For further discussion see: J Westwell, S Malloch and A Mansoor, 'EU Update', p142–145, Computer Law & Security Report, 19(2), 2003.)

[92] *e*Europe Benchmarking Report: eEurope 2002, COM(2002) 62 final.

[93] *e*Europe 2005, Executive Summary, p4.

[94] The report revealed that Internet penetration in businesses is far higher than the household rate. Data suggests that approximately 90 per cent of businesses (with ten or more employees) have Internet access. Over 60 per cent have a website.

[95] Rising from 42 per cent in 1997 to 47 per cent in 2001.

[96] The use of cards also rose from a figure of 30 per cent to 34 per cent.

[97] This trend appears to have remained relatively constant over time (1997: 56 per cent; 1999: 50 per cent; 2000: 60 per cent).

Nevertheless, both studies are in agreement when it comes to an analysis of purchases made online. Eurobarometre 56.0 states that 81 per cent of consumers have no experience with distance payment by telephone, proprietary computer systems or the Internet. The Benchmarking Report goes on to highlight the fact that:

> 'In October 2000, 31 per cent of EU Internet users had purchased online and this rose to 36 per cent by November 2001 ... However, only 4 per cent of users classified themselves as frequent purchasers and this is a major problem for e-commerce.'[98]

In light of these statistics, Eurobaromctre 56.0 concludes that:

> 'The trend is clear: as the opportunity for using such means has dramatically increased (56 per cent had had no opportunity in 1997),[99] the feelings of insecurity have increased significantly (the score was 10 per cent in 1997).[100] This picture is found in all Member States.'

In many respects, these figures would appear to suggest that there is still a considerable way to go before the objective of *e*Europe is realised. As Miller notes:

> 'Currently, business-to-consumer Internet transactions comprise only 20 per cent of European Union e-commerce. The principal reason for this lag is thought to be a lack of consumer confidence in shopping online.'[101]

However, it would be incorrect to suggest that this slow uptake has been due solely to risks associated with security[102] and/or privacy.[103] Consumer confidence is also dependent on concerns relating to payment mechanisms that may be used online. In this regard, the use of cards still remains the most important payment mechanism used in online purchases and Miller suggests the current lack of consumer confidence may be attributed to the concern:

> '... that merchants, having received payment, will not perform their side of the contract or perform it defectively, and consumers fear being left without a remedy or with a remedy that is difficult to enforce.'[104]

This concern is reflected in the data collected by the *e*Europe Benchmarking Report on the perceived disincentives for consumers to purchase online.

> 'Another factor is trust, how confident are consumers in being able to obtain redress in the event of an online dispute.'[105]

This is the key factor. Consumers are concerned with the level of protection that they

---

[98] *e*Europe Benchmarking Report: *e*Europe 2002, COM(2002) 62 final, p13.

[99] 22 per cent indicated an absence of opportunity in 2001.

[100] 25 per cent indicated that a sense of risk or danger was a reason for not using these means of payment in 2001.

[101] S Miller, 'Payment in an On-Line World', in L Edwards and C Waelde (eds), 'Law and the Internet', (2000) Hart Publishing, p57.

[102] The Commission has attempted to address such concerns through the e-Commerce Directive (Directive 2000/13/EC of the European Parliament and of the Council of 8 June 2000 on certain legal aspects of information society services, in particular electronic commerce, in the Internal Market), but progress is still slow. This has been supported by other initiatives including the electronic signature directive (Directive 1999/93/EC of the European Parliament and of the Council of 13 December 1999 on a Community framework for electronic signatures); see OJ L013, 19/01/2000, 12–20.

[103] For further discussion relating to the tension (potential conflict) between money laundering legislation and the Data Protection Act 1998, see: C Rees and K Brimsted, 'Charybdis or Scylla? Navigating a Course Between Money Laundering Law and Data Protection', (2003) Computer Law & Security Report, 19(1), p25.

[104] Ibid.

[105] *e*Europe Benchmarking Report: *e*Europe 2002, COM(2002) 62 final.

can expect to receive in the event that goods/services supplied by an online merchant prove to be unsatisfactory. As a point of interest, the Report goes on to note that: '[t]he relatively higher online consumption of the UK ... may benefit from greater familiarity using credit cards'. It will be noted later that the UK is regarded as having one of the most effective pieces of consumer credit legislation[106] within the EU. This may in turn account for the greater level of consumer confidence in the protection provided to them and as such the higher usage of cards on the Internet.

To date the Commission's response (which forms part of its overall '*e*Europe' initiative)[107] has been to take a series of measures, together with Member States, to improve e-commerce security focusing on 'awareness raising, technology support, regulation and international co-ordination'.[108] However, this forms only part of the solution to ensuring consumer confidence in the e-commerce environment.

Consumers require 'better and more harmonised consumer protection rules in the EU, in particular in relation to "new technologies" '.[109] As such, any proposal to revise the Consumer Credit Directive[110] must address this issue in order to enhance confidence in the online market. However, reform must also be considered alongside the objectives of *e*Europe 2005, which are to:

'... review and adopt legislation at national and European level; to ensure legislation does not unnecessarily hamper new services [and] to strengthen competition and interoperability.'[111]

It may be suggested that pursuit of a similar objective,[112] when the original Directive was passed, led to a number of the problems/concerns currently being experienced by the consumer credit market.

Whilst the original Consumer Credit Directive[113] was passed in 1987[114] it was based on a 1979 Commission proposal intended to establish a Community framework for consumer credit and in turn the creation of a common market in credit.[115] However, it was a product of its time in so much as it simply introduced minimum common rules on consumer protection through the approximation of the laws, regulations and

---

[106] In so much as it provides consumers with a greater level of protection than the minimum common rules set out in Directive 87/102/EEC.
[107] For further details on the Commission's '*e*Europe' initiative refer to the Action Plan and *e*Europe 2005.
[108] Security of payments: http://europa.eu.int/comm/comsumers/cons_int/e-commerce/secur_en.htm.
[109] Eurobarometer 56.0, 'Europeans & Financial Services', p1.
[110] 87/102/EEC.
[111] *e*Europe 2005, Executive Summary, p3.
[112] Directive 87/102/EEC was based on the approximation of the laws, which set to establish minimum common rules on consumer protection.
[113] 87/102/EEC.
[114] Deadline for implementation of the legislation: 1/1/1990. The European Commission Report of 11 May 1995 on the operation of Directive 87/102/EEC noted that the majority of the Member States had adopted stricter provisions than those laid down in the Directive for consumer protection. This was followed up by the European Commission Report of the 24 September 1997 on the operation of Directive 87/102/EEC and provided an overview of the comments made by Member States, the financial services industry and consumer organisations.
[115] See: Consumer Credit Rules for the 21st Century: http://europa.eu.int/rapid/start/cgi/guestin.ksh, in which it is stated that 'the provisions of the 1987 Consumer Directive (87/102/EEC) effectively go back to the "cash society" of the 1970s'.

administrative provisions of the Member States concerning consumer credit.[116] The Directive has been amended twice, initially in February 1990 by way of Council Directive 90/88/EEC[117] and then in February 1998 with the European Parliament and Council Directive 98/7/EC[118] but has nevertheless generated considerable criticism and dissatisfaction.

The most significant criticism of Directive 87/102/EEC has been that the market, which it was intended to regulate, has changed significantly since its introduction in the late 1980s, resulting in the fact that it 'seems out of step with these trends'.[119] Secondly, the general thrust of European Commission reports[120] on the operation of Directive 87/102/EEC has been that there is a real need to 'encourage the provision of consumer credit across national borders'.[121] This is supported by other aspects of these reports, which note that consumer groups have consistently expressed the view that there is a need for legislative measures to harmonise the area of consumer credit across the EU.[122] In 1997 a summary on the reactions and comments to the 1995 report[123] was produced which prompted the Commission to conclude that the Directive was 'no longer sufficiently in step with the situation of the consumer credit market and that it should therefore be revised'.[124] In order to address this marginal growth in the European frontier-free market in consumer credit, it was decided that the legal framework needed to be reviewed in order to allow consumers[125] to exploit fully this single market. In particular, it was noted that any revision of the Directive needed to rebalance the rights and obligations of both credit grantors and credit consumers, to ensure a high level of consumer protection and to adapt to the new credit techniques that had developed. As Internal Market Commissioner Frits Bolkestein noted:

'A new consumer credit directive has long been on the to-do list of actions for building the Internal Market in financial services and improving opportunities for e-commerce.'

On the 11 September 2002, the Commission adopted a proposal for a revised Consumer Credit Directive.[126] The aim is to:

'... promote the development of a more transparent, more effective market providing a high enough

---

[116] See: http://europa.eu.int/scadplus/leg/en/lvb/132021.htm. See also the recitals to Directive 87/102/EEC, OJ No L 42, 12/2/87, p48 et seq.

[117] Deadline for implementation of the legislation: 31/12/1992. European Commission Report of 12 April 1996 on the operation of Directive 90/88/EEC noted that the formula outlined in Annex II of the Directive had been adopted by all the Member States as the method of calculating the annual percentage rate of charge, except in Germany, France and Finland.

[118] Deadline for implementation of the legislation: 20/04/2000.

[119] Discussion paper for the amendment of Directive 87/102/EEC concerning consumer credit, p4.

[120] European Commission, Report on the Operation of Directive 87/102/EEC.

[121] Consumer Credit Directive: http://europa.eu.int/comm/consumers/cons_int/fina_serv/cons_directive/index_en.htm.

[122] Perhaps not surprisingly, the financial services industry favours the introduction of codes of conduct as opposed to further legislative measures.

[123] European Commission, summary report of reactions and comments.

[124] Communication from the Commission – Financial Services: Enhancing Consumer Confidence – Follow-up to the Green Paper on 'Financial Services: Meeting Consumer's Expectations'.

[125] As well as companies.

[126] See: Consumer Credit Rules for the 21st century: http://europa.eu.int/rapid/start/cgi/guestin.ksh.

degree of consumer protection so that the freedom of movement of credit can take place in better conditions for supply and demand.'[127]

In many respects this would appear to target the two main criticisms of Directive 87/102/EEC as well as the conclusions of Eurobaromter 56.0. However, if successful, this will be achieved at the expense of one of the original Directive's main objectives – that of minimum harmonisation.[128] As the proposal goes on to state:

'... the achievement of these objectives would involve contemplating moving on from minimum harmonisation to maximum and optimal harmonisation.'

Whilst it is hoped that this would guarantee a high level of consumer protection across the EU, it represents a significant change in approach to that originally adopted. If one refers back to the Commission's reports on the operation of Directive 87/102/EEC,[129] it may be noted that only consumer groups favoured legislative measures. Rather, the data reveals that Member States did not unanimously support Community-level harmonisation of provisions governing consumer credit. Equally, it may be argued that the objective of *e*Europe 2005 to 'ensure legislation does not unnecessarily hamper new services' does not sit easily alongside a Directive based on maximum harmonisation.

Given this potentially significant alteration to the area of consumer credit, the Committee has outlined six guidelines in accordance with which any revision of the Directive should take place.[130] These may be summarised as follows:

1. redefinition of the Directive's scope in order to adapt it to the new market situation in this area and better tracking of the demarcation line between consumer credit and real estate credit;

2. inclusion of new arrangements taking account not only of the creditors but also of credit intermediaries;

3. introduction of a structured information framework for the credit grantor in order to allow him to better appreciate the risks involved;

4. more comprehensive information for the consumer and any grantors;

5. more equitable sharing of responsibilities between the consumer and the professional;

6. improvement of the arrangements and practices for processing payment incidents by the professionals, both for the consumer and for the credit grantor.

If one returns to the issue of consumer confidence and concerns relating to the effectiveness of the Consumer Credit Directive in providing an effective framework for

---

[127] Summary Document, Discussion paper for the amendment of Directive 87/102/EEC concerning consumer credit, p2.
[128] For further discussion refer to: op cit, in footnote 109 above.
[129] See: The European Commission Report of 11 May 1995 on the operation of Directive 87/102/EEC, which was followed up by European Commission Report of the 24 September 1997 on the operation of Directive 87/102/EEC.
[130] Consumer Credit Rules for the 21st century: http://europa.eu.int/rapid/start/cgi/guestin.ksh.

redress, then the wording of art 11 of that Directive would appear to be unsatisfactory. During its initial proposal for a Directive 87/102/EEC, the Commission considered providing the consumer with the option of taking action directly against the lender without obliging them to first institute proceedings against the supplier of the goods/services.[131] However, the eventual wording was the result of a compromise.

Article 11 states that in certain circumstances the consumer can request payment from the lender if the complaint against the supplier is justified and the latter does not indemnify the consumer.[132] To date this has resulted in a wide variety of responses by the Member States. Whilst the Belgian response has been widely regarded as ineffective, the legislation in France,[133] Germany[134] and the UK[135] has gone far beyond the principle set out in art 11.[136]

The Commission's discussion paper goes on to note that if it is 'deemed appropriate to harmonise, it would be necessary to opt for a clearly defined system' as opposed to the approach set out in the current Directive that simply lays down only the foundations of regulation[137] and leaves considerable scope for Member States to go further.[138] 'The combined effect was a segmentation of the Internal Market into

---

[131] This approach is based on the notion that the signing of a contract of supply of goods/services is conditioned by the existence of a credit agreement. This generates a certain form of joint and several liability between the supplier of goods/services and the lender.

[132] Article 11 states that the consumer may seek redress against the grantor of credit when the following conditions are fulfilled.
• The consumer has entered into a credit agreement with a person other than the supplier of the goods or services purchased;
• the grantor of the credit and the supplier of the goods or services have a pre-existing agreement whereunder credit is made available exclusively by the former;
• the consumer obtains his or her credit pursuant to that pre-existing agreement;
• the goods or services covered by the credit agreement are not supplied or are not in conformity with the contract;
• the consumer has sought redress against the supplier but has failed to obtain satisfaction.

[133] France introduced the concept of 'linked credit' which provides for the situation in which the conclusion of the sale is subordinated to the party concerned obtaining a loan and vice versa. Under French law there is an obligation on the professional, seller of goods or provider of services, to specify in the contract of sale or supply that the payment of the price will be made by means of a credit even if the purchaser refuses the loan proposed to him by the seller and uses a credit from a body of his choice. There is also an obligation for the credit organisation to mention the commodity or service financed by the credit. The inter-dependence between these two agreements is fixed at two key moments – when they are signed and when they are performed.

[134] Germany introduced the notion of 'wirtschaftliche Einheit' (economic unit). A purchase agreement is a transaction linked to the credit agreement when the credit is used to finance the purchasing price and when the two agreements have to be considered as an economic unit. It may be assumed that there is an economic unit when the lender involves the seller in preparing or concluding a credit agreement. The purchase agreement can go ahead only if the consumer has not used the right to withdraw from his credit agreement. The contractual clause on withdrawal must refer to this right. Withdrawal remains valid even if the sum lent has not yet been paid back. The consumer can refuse repayment if he can invoke litigation which releases him from his obligations in relation to the seller.

[135] The UK maintained the formula set down in the Consumer Credit Act 1974 – that of 'joint and several liability'. See the discussion of s75 earlier in this chapter. It may be noted that where the lender is closely associated with the supplier of the goods/services in question, the damage must be borne by the lender and the supplier. The consumer must have the right to take action against one or the other or both in order to recover the amount of the damage suffered. However, this only applies to credit agreements mentioned in s12(b), (c) of the 1974 Act.

[136] The proposal does not permit Member States to go beyond the Directive and to keep or introduce a higher level of consumer protection.

[137] It contained a 'minimal clause' allowing Member States to go further than the rules of the Directive.

[138] As per France, Germany and the UK.

separate national markets and discrepancies in consumer protection.'[139] In other words, 'it has resulted in 15 different sets of rules' which affects the provision of cross-border credit.[140] Equally, it is noted that the Directive needs to be updated so as to 'ensure that the very specific consumer protection rules it lays down interface smoothly'[141] with the more widely applicable rules laid down by the directives on e-commerce[142] and distance selling of financial services. Finally, a number of Member States, including the UK, wish to modernise their consumer credit laws. (In this regard, the DTI published the third in its series of consultation documents[143] in December 2002 aimed at reforming the Consumer Credit Act 1974.)[144] It is felt that a new Commission proposal may anticipate and guide this process of modernisation.[145]

One area of potential concern to consumers based in the UK is that the new proposal will not permit Member States to go beyond the formula set down in the Directive. If this proves to be the case then s75 Consumer Credit Act (CCA) 1974 may very well be affected by such a requirement.[146] At present, under the CCA 1974 retailers and card issuers are jointly liable in the event of anything going wrong with transactions between £100 and £30,000. Under the Commission's proposal, the lender's liability would be restricted to apply only if the retailer is also acting as a credit intermediary. The obvious concern is that this will result in a weakening of the rights of UK-based consumers. However, if one takes a broader view of this proposed reform,

---

[139] See: Consumer Credit Rules for the 21st century: http://europa.eu.int/rapid/start/cgi/guestin.ksh.

[140] Questions and Answers on Consumer Credit, Memo/02/252.

[141] Ibid.

[142] For further discussion on the E-Commerce Directive (2000/31/EC) refer to: J Worthy, N Graham and R Finney, 'E-Commerce for Financial Services: Working With the New UK Rules', (2003) Computer Law & Security Report, 19(2), p121.

[143] For further discussion refer to: K Sanford and A Seager, 'Bringing the Consumer Credit Act into the Electronic Age', (2003), E-commerce Law and Policy, January, pp12–13.

[144] It aims to accomplish two things: (1) to remove any remaining obstacles to the recognition of electronically concluded contracts (by adopting a technology neutral approach); and (2) to bring the CCA 1974 in line with other legislation such as the Electronic Commerce Directive, the draft Consumer Credit Directive (see above) and the Distance Marketing of Consumer Financial Services Directive.

[145] See the recitals to Directive 87/102/EEC, OJ No L42, 12/2/87, p17. A number of key questions are posed in relation to the form that the new Directive should adopt.
• Is there a case for introducing a mechanism that would be based on one of the existing national systems?
• Should there be a pre-existing agreement between the supplier of goods and services and the lender?
• If principles of joint and several liability between the lender and the supplier are selected and if there are pre-existing agreements between them, should provision be made, as in the case in the UK legal system, for limits on the amounts covered by this mechanism or not?
• Is there a case for giving the consumer the right to take action directly against the lender when it is clear that the latter benefits from commercial advantages by operating with certain suppliers and has – commercial – means of action?
• Would it be appropriate or not in this respect for the consumer to first approach the supplier?

[146] This assumes that the Consumer Credit Act 1974 applies to the particular arrangement in question and depends on two factors. (1) The applicable law of a contract entered into by a UK consumer, on the Internet, will not necessarily be that of his own domestic law (eg English law). If the court of a Member State determines this issue, then the 1980 Rome Convention on the Law Applicable to Contractual Obligations will be applied. (For further discussion see: D Rowland and E Macdonald, 'Information Technology Law', (2000) 2nd ed, Cavendish Press, p170.) (2) There has also been considerable debate as to whether or not s75 of the CCA 1974 may be extended to the use of credit cards for Internet transactions. (See: Brindle and Cox (eds), 'Law of Bank Payments', (1999); P Robertson, 'Credit Cards and Internet Payment: Time for Another Look at s75 of the CCA 1974', (1999) Credit & Finance Law, 11(3), pp17–19).

then the approach of maximum harmonisation of consumer credit will ensure that a 'level playing field will be created within the EU'.[147] This can only be of benefit to consumers located in Member States and would appear to be an approach which they would welcome given the fact that Eurobarometer[148] revealed that 53 per cent of consumers consider consumer protection as a proper matter for full harmonisation throughout the EU.[149]

The Commission's proposal also introduces the notion of joint and several liability, though this is limited to instances where the retailer acts as a credit intermediary.[150] Whilst this represents a welcome development in terms of consumer protection across the EU, from the perspective of a UK consumer it may very well be seen as falling short of the protection currently afforded them by the CCA.[151] However, the Commission's proposal should be read in conjunction with its proposal on payment systems, which will include 'refund' mechanisms for non–cash means of payments including credit cards. It is anticipated that the interaction of these two directives will ensure an effective legal framework at the EU level.

If the overall objective of *e*Europe is to be achieved then the European Commission's measures to improve e-commerce security must be accompanied by reform of consumer protection. As both Eurobarometer 56.0 and the *e*Europe Benchmarking Report highlight, EU consumers do not currently have sufficient confidence in the Internal Market; a key reason being the absence of an appropriate level of common rules. The Commission's proposal appears to acknowledge the need for harmonisation and modernisation of this area, but the question remains as to whether the common rules that are finally introduced are adequate to encourage the greater use of online facilities by consumers.

---

[147] Directive 87/102/EEC was based on the approximation of the laws, which set to establish minimum common rules on consumer protection.

[148] Eurobarometer 56.0 (Question 16), December 2001.

[149] 19 per cent thought that harmonisation should only be partial, whilst 10 per cent felt that standards should not be harmonised at the EU level.

[150] An example of this would be where a car dealer provides finance for the purchase of a car via a brand related finance company.

[151] This may be linked in with the debate as to whether or not the CCA 1974 may be extended to cover the use of credit cards on the Internet. In the majority of Internet transactions the merchant acquirer (with whom the supplier has an agreement) is a different entity from the card-issuing bank. As such this will usually involve: (1) A supplier who has an agreement with a merchant acquirer in the same jurisdiction; and (2) a cardholder who is signed up with a card issuer in another jurisdiction. Whilst the CCA 1974 distinguishes between two-party and three-party credit agreements, it fails to explicitly address the now common four-party agreement. Consequently, banks have sought to take advantage of this apparent loophole. However, both the Office of Fair Trading and the DTI have expressed the view that credit card companies market their product specifically on the basis of its suitability for making payment when overseas (under the Visa and Access schemes). As such these companies cannot subsequently claim to be unconnected when it comes to the application of s75. (See: Report No OFT 132 Connected Lender Liability, May 1995; Report No OFT 097 Connected Lender Liability, March 1994.) Also see: S Miller, 'Payment in an On-Line World', in L Edwards and C Waelde (eds), 'Law and the Internet', (2000) Hart Publishing, pp58–62.

6.11 Consumer Credit Act 1974 – Applicability to the Internet

1. Does the CCA 1974 apply?

    - A credit card agreement is regulated by the CCA 1974.

    - What about cross-border provision of credit card services?

    - The CCA 1974 will apply in the following instances.

        - The proper law of the agreement is English law (see: arts 3 and 4 Rome Convention on the Law Applicable to Contractual Obligations 1980).

        - It should be noted that the English courts will always assume that another state's law is identical to that of England unless either one of the parties pleads an express case to the contrary. (This would involve the card-issuer locating an expert in the foreign law and introducing this evidence before the court.)

        - In a dispute, the jurisdiction of the English court is established (see: Regulation 44/2001/EC). Relates to the protection afforded to consumers under mandatory rules of the forum.

2. Does s75 apply to Internet transactions?

    - Section 75 applies where:

        - there is a 'debtor-creditor-supplier agreement';

        - it is 'made by the creditor under pre-existing arrangements ...'.

    - Are there 'pre-existing arrangements' between the card-issuer in England (bank), the cardholder and the supplier in France or Brazil?

        - The answer is 'no' if this requires a direct contractual arrangement between the bank and the supplier.

        - In the majority of Internet transactions the merchant acquirer (with whom the supplier has an agreement) is a different entity from the card-issuing bank. Will usually involve:

            - a supplier who has an agreement with a merchant acquirer in the same jurisdiction; and

            - a cardholder who is signed up with a card-issuer in another jurisdiction.

    - Whilst the CCA 1974 distinguishes between two-party and three-party credit agreements, it fails to explicitly address the now common four-party agreement.

        - Banks have sought to take advantage of this apparent loophole.

        - However, both the OFT and the DTI feel that credit card companies market their product specifically on the basis of its suitability for making payment when overseas (under the Visa and Access schemes).

- Consequently, they cannot then claim to be unconnected when it comes to the application of s75.

- Which argument is correct?

  - Section 187: an agreement is entered into under pre-existing arrangements if it is entered into in accordance with, or in the furtherance of, arrangements previously made between any of the following.

    - The creditor and the supplier.

    - One of them and an associate of the others.

    - An associate of one and an associate of the others.

    - Sections 189(1) and 184(1): whether or not companies are associates is defined in terms of common control.

    - The term arrangement suggests that something short of contractual relations between the parties will be sufficient.

    - However, it does suggest that this 'relationship' must be between the creditor and the supplier (or their respective associates).

    - The suggestion has been made to take a broader view of the commercial environment.

      - Goode argues that the network of contractual relationships taken as a whole constitutes an arrangement between the supplier and the creditor which is made by virtue of their membership of the Visa network.

    Jarrett v *Barclays Bank* [1997] 3 WLR 654.

    Re British Basic Slag Limited's Agreements [1963] 2 All ER 807.

    Report No OFT 132 Connected Lender Liability, May 1995.

    Report No OFT 097 Connected Lender Liability, March 1994.

3. Does the Internet make a difference?

   - It is arguable that the CCA 1974 did not envisage the provision of credit to finance a supply agreement with a supplier located in a different state.

   - The Internet simply multiplies the occasions when a given cardholder generates transactions involving overseas suppliers.

   - It may be suggested that the Internet will encourage the increased membership of suppliers in the Visa and Access networks across the world.

   - In terms of the cardholder (debtor), the physical location of the supplier does not really matter, simply the goods (and price of those goods) which the individual is searching for on his computer.

- For example, a programme or music file may be as easily downloaded from a supplier located in Brazil as it can from a supplier in England.

4. What about the Council Directive on Consumer Credit 87/102/EEC?

- Directive 87/102/EEC of 22 December 1986 dealt with the approximation of the laws, regulations and administrative provisions of the Member States concerning consumer credit.

- It was amended by the following measure: Council Directive 90/88/EEC of 22 February 1990 and European Parliament and Council Directive 98/7/EC of 16 February 1998.

- Article 11 provides that a debtor shall have a right of action against the creditor for certain breaches of the supply contract.

- It was not implemented in the UK as it was felt that the CCA 1974 complied with the Directive's provisions.

- Therefore, it may be argued that to provide consumers with the same protection as under the EU Directive, then s75 must be extended to supply transactions entered into by parties in the EU.

- Why should this be limited to the physical boundaries of the EU?

- On 11 September 2002 the European Commission adopted a proposal for a new Directive on consumer credit.

  - It was felt that the existing EU-wide rules had not kept pace with practice and only set minimum standards. (Being based on minimum harmonisation has resulted in 15 different sets of rules.)

  - The absence of common rules reduces cross-border transactions and leads to differences in consumer protection in Member States. (Cross-border lending is rare and there is little cross-border competition between credit companies.)

  - The new Directive will address these concerns by updating provisions to ensure that consumer protection rules interface smoothly with the more widely acceptable rules set down in the e-commerce and distance selling directives.

For further details refer to the 'Press Releases' section at: www.europa.eu.int.

5. What about the EC Distance Contracts Directive 97/7/EC?

- Article 8 provides that appropriate measures shall be put in place to permit a consumer to request cancellation of a payment where fraudulent use has been made of his payment card in connection with a distance contract and be re-credited with the sums paid in the event of such fraudulent use.

- Article 12(2) goes on to stipulate that Member States shall take measures to ensure that the consumer does not lose the protection granted by the Directive by virtue of the choice of law of a non-member country as the law applicable to the contract if the latter has a close connection with the territory of one or more Member States.

- It is argued that the effect of these provisions is that in credit card Intemet transactions by a UK buyer, English law would presumably apply as the proper law of the sale contract in the absence of the express contractual stipulation and English courts would be given jurisdiction.

6. What is the latest position in terms of the relevance of the CCA 1974?

- On 13 December 2002 the DTI published the third in its series of consultation documents aimed at reforming the CCA 1974.

- It aims to accomplish two things:

  - to remove any remaining obstacles to the recognition of electronically concluded contracts (by adopting a technology neutral approach); and

  - to bring the CCA 1974 in line with other legislation such as the Electronic Commerce Directive, the draft Consumer Credit Directive (see above) and the Distance Marketing of Consumer Financial Services Directive.

7 Electronic Cash and Smart Cards

As noted in the previous chapter, although credit cards are accepted as currently dominating online payments, it is simply a matter of time before some form, or forms, of electronic money become the accepted method of payment online. Indeed, Gartner Research estimates that electronic cash will be used in more than 60 per cent of all online transactions by 2009. Equally, as noted in the previous section, uncertainty still surrounds the security of credit card details online; consumers will readily adopt any alternative that can demonstrate the requisite anonymity and 'universal' acceptability amongst merchants.

7.1 What is Electronic Cash?

Electronic cash, also referred to as e-cash, digital cash and cybercash, is a general term that describes any system which enables value storage and exchange to take place and which is created and operated by a private entity (ie non-governmental entity).[1] The fact that it is 'electronic' means that the system does not use a physical medium (such as coins or paper documents).

Since electronic cash is issued by private entities, there is an obvious need for common standards among all issuers so as to enable one issuer's electronic cash to be

---

[1] See: G Levy and C Walker, 'Show Me the Money', (2001), E-commerce and Policy, May, pp13–14.

accepted by another issuer. In the age of e-commerce, this not only means within one state or even within an economic region (ie the European Union), but ideally on a global scale. Quite understandably, these common standards have not yet been met. We are still faced with a situation where each private entity follows its own standards and, as noted below, this has led to the failure of several promising electronic cash experiments during the 1990s. The goal must be for electronic cash to achieve universal acceptance.

If we once again consider the use of credit cards as a method of payment, then many merchants often impose a minimum purchase amount. This is for good reason. The bank fee could potentially amount to a significant proportion of the purchase price if consumers were permitted to use their credit cards for any type/size of transaction, thus reducing the merchant's profit margin. The same is true for Internet purchases. Small purchases, such as the purchase of a single MP3 file, are not profitable for merchants that accept payment only via the use of a credit card. Consequently, there is already a potentially significant market for the use of electronic cash, that of small purchases on the Internet (micropayments).

Electronic cash also has another potential advantage over credit cards. Children and teenagers, who are far more Internet aware than their parents, are eager to participate in the online market, and potentially represent a significant percentage of online buyers. However, they are too young to qualify for a credit card of their own. Aside from borrowing their parents' cards (a favourite question in any exam paper), how do they access this market? More importantly, how does the market access them? In theory, electronic cash provides the solution.

Equally, if one looks at the infrastructure utilised by electronic cash, the Internet, then it already exists. As such, the additional costs incurred by consumers or merchants, who wish to use electronic cash, are theoretically very low. In addition, the Internet is global in nature, providing the added advantage that the physical distance between consumer and merchant does not affect the overall cost. By contrast, the cost incurred when transferring traditional cash is proportional to the distance involved.

Electronic cash does have disadvantages though. True electronic cash is just like traditional cash in that it cannot be easily traced. Consequently, the problem of money laundering arises whereby criminals convert money that they have obtained illegally into cash that they can spend without having it identified as being the direct result of criminal activity. Equally, as will be noted later, electronic cash is potentially susceptible to forgery or double spending,[2] though it should be stressed that as time goes by, it is becoming far more difficult to forge electronic cash than it is to use a fraudulently obtained credit card number.

---

[2] The issue of double spending has been addressed from the very beginning of the electronic cash era. Cryptographic algorithms ensure the production of tamperproof electronic cash that can, if necessary, be traced back to its original owner. In essence, a two-part lock provides anonymous security for the user of electronic cash. However, it also acts as a signal when someone attempts to double spend. This double-lock procedure is generally hailed as protecting the anonymity of electronic cash users whilst at the same time providing a built-in safeguard to prevent tampering and/or double spending.

Finally, whilst electronic cash has, to date, been successful in some parts of the world, it has not yet become a global success story. If electronic cash is to become a popular alternative payment system then it requires widespread acceptance and the adoption of a restricted number of electronic cash standards. Customers do not want to be faced with the choice of either having:

• to deal with a wide range of different brands of electronic cash in order to be able to freely purchase goods from a majority of the merchants that accept electronic cash; or

• to deal with a smaller selection of electronic cash brands but at the expense of restricting the number of merchants from whom they can purchase goods.

7.2 A Legal Definition of Electronic Money

The European Commission issued a Recommendation on Electronic Payment Instruments (97/489/EC).[3] Whilst it is not legally binding it provides a code of good practice for institutions seeking to issue electronic or digital money.[4] Of particular interest at this stage is art 2, which states:

'For the purpose of this Recommendation, the following definitions apply:

(a) "electronic payment instrument" means an instrument enabling its holder to effect transactions of the kind specified in art 1(1). This covers both remote access payment instruments and electronic money instruments;

(b) "remote access payment instrument" means an instrument enabling a holder to access funds held on his/her account at an institution, whereby payment is allowed to be made to a payee and usually requiring a personal identification code and/or any other similar proof of identity. This includes in particular payment cards (whether credit, debit, deferred debit or charge cards) and phone- and home-banking applications;

(c) "electronic money instrument" means a reloadable payment instrument other than a remote access payment instrument, whether a stored-value card or a computer memory, on which value units are stored electronically, enabling its holder to effect transactions of the kind specified in art 1(1);

(d) "financial institution" means an institution as defined in art 4(1) of Council Regulation (EC) No 3604/93 ...'

Nevertheless, the Recommendation is supported by a legally binding Directive,[5] which establishes a regulatory framework to ensure that institutions issuing electronic money within the European Union meet certain basic requirements. Directive 2000/46/EC[6] defines electronic money in the following terms:[7]

' "Electronic money" shall mean monetary value as represented by a claim on the issuer which is:

---

[3] Commission Recommendation of 30 July 1997 concerning transactions by electronic payment instruments and in particular the relationship between issuer and holder (Text with EEA relevance) (97/489/EC).

[4] As discussed in a previous chapter, the Recommendation covers two classes of payment instruments: (1) electronic money instruments, and (2) remote access payment instruments.

[5] Directive 2000/46/EC of the European Parliament and of the Council of 18 September 2000 on the taking up, pursuit of and prudential supervision of the business of electronic money institutions.

[6] For further discussion see: J Chuah, 'The New EU Directives to Regulate Electronic Money Institutions – A Critique of the EU's Approach to Electronic Money', (2000) 8 JIBL.

[7] Article 1(3)(b).

(i) stored on an electronic device;

(ii) issued on receipt of funds of an amount not less in value than the monetary value issued;

(iii) accepted as means of payment by undertakings other than the issuer.'[8,9]

Generally, there are several possible types of electronic payment methods, which could be classified as electronic money. Within this chapter we will focus on the two main types – electronic cash and electronic cheques.[10]

7.3 The Evolution of Electronic Cash

Even though there have been many high profile failures in recent times, (predominantly as a result of the dot-com crash), the concept refuses to be ignored. Many believe that electronic cash is still finding its feet and that any scheme which manages to overcome the problem of establishing itself and then operating for sufficiently long to become a self-sustaining, profitable entity, has a successful future. Without doubt, recent schemes have undoubtedly learnt from the mistakes of their predecessors – the main one being that support from key players in the finance market is far more important than innovation.

This has led commentators such as Guttmann[11] to categorise electronic cash schemes into three generations. He suggests that the first generation, between 1994 to 1996, proved the technological feasibility of electronic cash, despite the fact that virtually all these schemes were commercial failures. The second generation, 1997 to 2000, was characterised by a far more focused approach, targeting specific segments of the e-commerce market, for instance as e-mail money for P2P transactions or as coupon money in B2C commerce. Guttmann goes on to state that the third, and current, generation focuses on the construction of online-payment platforms for the creation and transfer of digital tokens, which may then be used in a large variety of situations.

However, all such electronic cash schemes must address consumers' fears and provide them with confidence in the product. In other words, any successful scheme must deal with the key issues of privacy, security, acceptability, independence and convenience. Consumers wish to be reassured that electronic currency cannot be illegally copied, reused, or forged.

---

[8] The question may be posed as to whether there is a potential conflict between the European Union's approach to electronic money and the fact that electronic money lacks a number of the typical characteristics of cash. For example, (1) electronic cash is not legal tender, (2) the acceptance of electronic cash does not necessarily discharge a debt unconditionally, (3) spare amounts of traditional cash may be combined quite easily; this is not always the case with electronic money (one exception is the InternetCash system, which is discussed below), (4) the use of cash as legal tender is generally regulated by the state. However, this is not the case with electronic money, where the issuer will impose terms and conditions.

[9] It should be noted that electronic money is now defined by statute – Financial Services and Markets Act 2000 (Regulated Activities) Order 2001 (SI 2001/544), art 3(1), adopting art 1(3)(b) of the Directive. The definition is as follows:

'... monetary value as represented by a claim on the issuer which is:

(i) stored on an electronic device;

(ii) issued on receipt of funds;

(iii) accepted as means of payment by persons other than the issuer.'

[10] For more information on these developments see: www.netbill.com, and http://nii-server.isi.edu/info/NetCheque.

[11] R Guttmann, 'Cybercash: The Coming Era of Electronic Money', (2003) Palgrave MacMillan.

In this respect, electronic cash should only be capable of being spent once (this is not to say that it should not be capable of being reused in the future just as with traditional currency). Any merchant wants to be reassured that any electronic cash that he receives has not been double spent. Double spending arises when a consumer spends an electronic coin twice by submitting the same electronic currency to two different merchants within a short space of time. The risk is that by the time the electronic coin in question clears the bank for a second time, it is too late to prevent the fraudulent act.

Second, if electronic cash is to compete successfully with traditional currency, any system should provide for anonymity. Consumers should be able to use electronic cash without revealing their identities.[12] Third, independence and universal acceptance mean that electronic cash should be unrelated to any single network or storage device. If electronic cash depends on a particular proprietary storage mechanism designed to hold just one type of electronic cash then it is not free-floating currency in the traditional sense. Electronic cash should be capable of being passed between states, of being freely transferable and of being accepted in the merchant's country. Finally, electronic cash should, ideally, not require any special hardware or software. If it does, then questions as to convenience will be raised. Indeed, it is this final issue that plagued many of the first generation electronic schemes.

7.4 Online and Offline Storage

There are two widely accepted approaches to holding electronic cash – online and offline storage. With online storage, the consumer does not personally possess the electronic cash. Rather, an online bank is involved in all transfers of electronic cash and holds the consumers' cash accounts. Consequently, any online system requires merchants to contact the consumer's bank in order to receive payment for a purchase. Whilst the obvious benefit of this approach is that it aids in the prevention of fraud by confirming the validity of the consumer's cash, it reduces the level of anonymity available under such a system.

By contrast, offline storage may be described as the electronic equivalent of keeping cash in your pocket/wallet. The customer holds it and is free to spend it without the involvement of a third party in the transaction. As with traditional cash, this guarantees anonymity, but the cost for such privacy is the increased concern over fraudulent activity. Consequently, some form of hardware or software safeguard needs to be utilised so as to prevent multiple and/or fraudulent spending. It is generally felt that current encryption techniques are capable of keeping the risk of double spending to a minimum.

---

[12] However, if we return to the issue of fraud, then double spending cannot be effectively detected or prevented if electronic cash is completely anonymous. In effect, anonymous electronic cash would guarantee the fact that it could not be traced back to the person who spent it. One possible way to counter this problem would be to attach a serial number to the various forms of electronic cash, which in turn could be used, if necessary, to demonstrate an association between the cash and a particular consumer. However, the concept of serial numbers inevitably raises privacy issues, as merchants could use these serial numbers to track spending habits of consumers.

7.5 Electronic Cash in Practice

At its most basic level, the process may be described in a few simple steps. However, it must be stressed that each electronic cash system outlined later in this chapter has its own idiosyncrasies and as such you should familiarise yourself with the relevant system and associated process.

To gain access to electronic cash, a consumer is required to open an account with an electronic cash issuer, either a bank that issues electronic cash or a private entity such as PayPal,[13] and then provide proof of identity.[14] Once an account has been established, the consumer may then withdraw electronic cash by accessing the issuer's website and presenting proof of identity; this may involve a digital certificate or a combination of a credit card number and a verifiable bank account number. After the issuer verifies the consumer's identity, it gives the consumer a specific amount of electronic cash and deducts the same amount from the consumer's account, together with a token processing fee. The consumer can then store the electronic cash in an electronic wallet on his computer, or on a stored-value card.

The next part of this chapter is dedicated to a discussion of the various electronic cash systems that have been developed over the past 15 years, following which a discussion of the legal principles governing electronic cash will take place.

NetCheque

In the early 1990s Clifford Neuman headed a project, in association with the Pentagon's ARPA and the University of Southern California, to develop a software programme for the creation and exchange of electronic financial instruments which could be used to pay for goods and services over the Internet. The concept was straightforward, to extend the traditional cheque-clearing system to the Internet by setting up an online mechanism for fund transfers using cheques.

NetCheque was designed to work in much the same way as a conventional paper cheque whereby a payor would issue an electronic document, sign it electronically, have the signature authenticated by a third party and then send it to the payee who would endorse it with a signature. Once authenticated, the payee's endorsement would transform the document into an order to a bank computer for fund transfer. These NetCheque documents could be electronically exchanged between banks through electronic clearing-houses to settle accounts.

NetCheque was not a commercial success. The reason was, for once, not related to price as this was kept to a low user fee. Rather, the system relied on conventional

---

[13] See p134 of this book.
[14] See: S Annereau, 'Data Security Issues for Online Banking', (2002), E-commerce and Policy, September, pp14–16.

symmetric cryptography which, at that point in time, was gradually being replaced by more secure public-key encryption software.[15]

DigiCash

David Chaum was responsible for another early attempt at the establishment of an electronic cash system, which was based on the concept of digital coins. Chaum's goal was to develop an integrated online-payment platform using digital coins that would match traditional cash in terms of its main characteristics – convenience and anonymity.

When Chaum's company, DigiCash, launched its eCash system in 1994, it was at the forefront of technological development being the first electronic cash system to use public-key cryptography and digital signatures for security.[16] The system also incorporated another unique concept, that of 'blind-signatures' whereby a signature could be verified without identifying the signer. In theory, this promised a form of electronic cash that was as anonymous as traditional cash. In addition, eCash software enabled customers to recover their money in the event of a hard disk crash, thus addressing another significant consumer fear. Finally, eCash possessed another key feature (which is still proving to be successful today), that of bidirectionality. In other words, individuals were able to receive eCash from other users, thereby enabling peer-to-peer payments.

The target audience for the eCash software was the banking community, the idea being that they could integrate the software into their infrastructure, personalise the product and then offer their customers (consumers as well as business) the option of establishing an eCash account. Standard interfaces into the account applications of banks made the sign-up and funding processes of new eCash accounts easy and cheap. Consumers could fund eCash accounts online or offline with money from various sources. They could transfer funds between different bank accounts, use credit card payments, or even receive eCash deposits from other users. They would then simply connect to their bank's website and download digital coins from their eCash account directly onto their computer's hard disk. Once funded, the eCash account could be used immediately to conduct business with anyone equipped to receive the digital coins.

Unfortunately, despite this impressive array of features, progress on the promotion

---

[15] Since the NetCheque experiment in the early 1990s, a number of firms have attempted to design more effective e-check schemes utilising asymmetric public-key encryption software for security, and automated clearing-houses for the transfer of funds. These include: (1) eCheck.Net (a product of www.authorizenet.com); (2) the Electronic Check Service offerred by E-Commerce Exchange (www.ecx.com); and (3) the Electronic Check Systems by CyberSource (www.cybersource.com). In addition, the Financial Services Technology Consortium (www.fstc.com), a consortium of US financial institutions and US government agencies has launched the Electronic Check Project (www.eCheck.org). This has been designed to become the industry standard, with eChecks being accepted with existing checking accounts. In October 1999 the FSTC entered into a co-operation agreement with CommerceNet, a worldwide consortium of 500 e-commerce developers and end-users, which will assure the FSTC of a large user base for its system.

[16] Another key safety feature of the system meant that DigiCash permitted banks, customers and merchants to verify the authenticity of any eCash issued by a particular bank.

of eCash with banks was very slow. While a few banks[17] were signed up to launch its product, it proved difficult for DigiCash to persuade merchants and consumers to try the scheme.[18]

DigiCash folded in late 1998, the victim of a slow uptake of its product and resultant cash-flow problems.[19] Chaum sold his patents to a group of individuals who wished to continue with the scheme and who, in August 1999, established eCash Technologies.[20]

CyberCash

In 1995, CyberCash[21] introduced the first commercial electronic wallet and which provided the foundation for the launch of CyberCoins in 1996. The new software package enabled consumers to download an empty electronic wallet and to then fill it with between $20 and $100 from their bank account before shopping online. The digital coins contained in the wallet could then be spent at any website equipped to accept CyberCash payments.

At the point CyberCoins was launched, CyberCash had agreements with six US banks to offer electronic wallets to their customers. It had also managed to sign up 30 companies to offer the CyberCash facility to their customers. The problem faced by CyberCash was the slow expansion potential of such bank-mediated payment platforms. The expected profitability of the scheme was intended to come from transaction fees paid by banks, who would in turn charge their merchant clients a slightly higher fee so as to gain a profit margin themselves. However, this relied on being able to convince banks to deal with electronic wallets, which in turn relied on persuading merchants to adopt the concept of digital coins and finally on consumers to not only download wallets but to subsequently use them for Internet payments. Such a tripartite structure is inherently slow in terms of its growth, especially if the product offered is significantly different to anything that banks, merchants or consumers have hitherto been used to using.

In response to this slow uptake, CyberCash decided to market other online payment-processing services and software products. Whilst it continued to develop its electronic-wallet technology, it nevertheless shifted from its focus from its CyberCoin client-side wallet technology to a server-side service known as InstaBuy. In December 2000 CyberCash launched an updated version of its package CyberCash but for B2B transactions, which is now being built into the leading B2B platforms, such as Microsoft's CashRegister, Oracle's e-Business Suite and IBM's WebSphere Commerce

---

[17] These included Deutsche Bank 24, Bank Austria and Den Norske Bank.

[18] Neither side wanted to partake in this payment option without an adequate number of the other side having signed up already to do business with.

[19] Whilst a commercial failure, DigiCash nevertheless demonstrated that a complex yet efficient online-payment platform could be developed and operated. Indeed, DigiCash had managed to enter into agreements with six banks and over 100 merchants in Europe, Japan, Australia and the United States. More importantly, transactions totalling $32,000,000 had scored a 100 per cent success rate, with no security breaches reported.

[20] www.ecash.net.

[21] www.cybercash.com.

Suite. In addition, CyberCash has entered into partnership with YourAccounts.Com,[22] to integrate its CyberCash EFT package with their web-based electronic bill payment and presentment programme known as 'anywhere.B2B'. This has had the effect of shifting their market away from consumers and has narrowed the focus of CyberCash's digital wallet system to the automation of online purchasing rather than the actual process of spending CyberCoins.

InternetCash

InternetCash[23] is another system that provides electronic currency. Under this system customers need to purchase an InternetCash card from a high street store.[24] In much the same way as consumers purchase prepaid phone cards, these InternetCash cards come in denominations of $10, $20, $50 and $100. Consumers then go on to the Internet and activate their cards by entering a 20-digit activation code, which is located on the back of the card, and then choose a PIN, which subsequently serves as a password. Once activated, the customer can use the InternetCash card to pay for purchases at any website that accepts it. If the value of the goods or services exceeds the amount stored on any single card, the consumer is permitted to pay with up to 30 cards.[25]

Consumers are not charged,[26] as such, for the use of the system. Instead InternetCash deducts a transaction fee before remitting customer payments to merchants. In addition, the system avoids a number of concerns related to flexibility. As details relating to the electronic cash system are either stored in the consumer's head (the PIN code), or on a secure InternetCash server, customers are not limited to a single computer. Equally, given the nature of the system (ie a prepaid cash card), InternetCash provides a convenient payment system for teenagers and younger children who do not have access to credit cards. Indeed, this is one of the key points made on their website. Finally, the system aims to provide maximum security in the following ways.

- At no stage does a merchant see a customer's card number or PIN code. Consequently, customers may feel secure in the fact that their PIN remains secret. Equally, merchants are not faced with credit card-like requirements for the storage of data, or the fear of hackers and/or employee fraud.

- Every transaction is PIN-protected.

- Every payment is digitally signed. Therefore, there is no fear of double charging for consumers and merchants are not faced with the possibility of consumers claiming fraud.

---

[22] This is the e-commerce subsidiary of Output Technology Solutions.
[23] www.internetcash.com.
[24] They are also available from vending machines and ATM machines.
[25] More recent features of the system include the ability to transfer value from one card to another so that a consumer can consolidate the value of his cards, rather than paying with multiple cards. In addition, C2C commerce enables customers to transfer their balances to other customers' cards.
[26] Though they will be required to pay a small fee for C2C transactions – the payer will pay a small fee to transfer money to the recipient.

The system is quite straightforward. On a suitable website,[27] once goods have been purchased and placed in an online shopping basket, customers must choose the InternetCash payment option at the checkout. This will open a secure browser window hosted by InternetCash,[28] within which the customer enters his PIN code so as to use the card.[29] InternetCash's website creates a digital signature for the purchase.[30] Following verification of the payment information, the merchant then submits the payment request to InternetCash for processing. At that stage InternetCash will then verify that the customer has the right to use that account[31] after which it will transfer the appropriate amount to the merchant's account. The transaction's value is deducted automatically from the value of the consumer's card. Once the merchant receives confirmation that payment has successfully taken place, the merchant then sends the customer an order confirmation number indicating that the transaction has been completed.

NetCoin (Compaq/KCOM)

Compaq has also experimented with electronic cash. Its NetCoin electronic cash enables consumers to pay by the hour for access to video games as well as to download data such as clipart.

In parallel to this development, KDD Communications (KCOM) – an Internet subsidiary of Japan's largest global phone company[32] – has its own NetCoin electronic cash system which is distributed through NetCoin Centre. Consumers visit the NetCoin Centre, fill their electronic wallets with electronic cash and then shop online in much the same way as the Compaq system.

7.6 Electronic Money and the Use of E-mail

The high-water point of the e-commerce evolution, the so-called dot-com bubble between 1997–1998, provided an environment in which a range of new electronic cash schemes were encouraged to emerge. Guttmann refers to these as the 'second-generation experiments' and notes that they differed to previous schemes in three key ways.

- First of all, they all focused on niche Internet markets.

---

[27] InternetCash now appears as a standard payment option in the shopping packages of several commerce service providers, including Microsoft Site Server, IBM Net.Commerce, Intershop, and Mercantec SoftCart.

[28] This means that the customer does not enter his InternetCash number into the merchant's window. Rather, they use a Trusted Third Party (TTP) environment, in this case the Trusted Third Party is the InternetCash Corporation. The rationale for this is that (1) the InternetCash Corporation is responsible for InternetCash card payments, (2) the InternetCash Corporation servers already need to be 100 per cent available in order to process Internet payments, and (3) the InternetCash Corporation has put a considerable amount of effort into securing their environment.

[29] The use of a PIN code eliminates the potential problems associated with any customer who claims that he did not order the merchandise, use his card or otherwise wish to repudiate the transaction.

[30] The merchant only stores this encrypted digital signature from the customer and a payment authorisation number from InternetCash. Consequently, there is nothing in the merchant's database that could be of value to hackers or that presents a risk for customers.

[31] By checking the validity of the PIN code.

[32] Kokusai Denshin Denwa.

- Each one was established independently of the banking community and did not rely on this market for their diffusion.

- These schemes utilised e-mail as a means for the mobilization of fund transfers.[33]

Despite the mixed success of schemes such as NetCheque, DigiCash and CyberCash, a more refined form of electronic cash still had a potential user base with those who feel reluctant to use their credit cards on the Internet. In this respect, electronic cash is superior, in so much as the individual is required to only provide personal, sensitive information at the beginning when they register.[34] This is in contrast to the use of credit cards which requires personal details every time that a transaction is completed on the Internet (ie every time you purchase goods).

In many respects, it may be suggested that this approach towards electronic cash will prove an ideal model for the Internet micropayments that were discussed earlier in this chapter. For instance, the purchase of MP3 files, cinema tickets, goods from supermarkets, or even gift vouchers (see discussion relating to www.GiftCertificates.com below).

It has also been suggested by a variety of commentators that this approach has a 'viral' potential in terms of the way that demand may spread. An ideal example of this is the PayPal scheme discussed below. If an individual suddenly receives an e-mail, informing him that 'You've Got Cash', but is not currently registered with the scheme, then in order to access that money he will have to do so. Furthermore, he will probably have to supply an account number to arrange for the transfer of that cash into a more traditional format.[35] Since human nature dictates that, following initial suspicion regarding the validity of the electronic cash scheme, very few people would refuse the opportunity to receive the 'cash', consequently, there is the potential, once sufficient momentum has built up, for such a scheme to spread quite rapidly. In other words, the larger the customer base of the system, the greater the potential for the scheme to be spread amongst Internet users. However, this depends on the ability of the electronic cash scheme to survive long enough to benefit from this effect. The initial cost of establishing, marketing and servicing a scheme for a relatively small number of merchants and consumers is not only expensive but also extremely risky. Whilst a few schemes have succeeded (PayPal being an ideal example), far more have failed.

PayPal[36]

In November 1999, a company called Confinity introduced PayPal,[37] which has quickly

---

[33] Payments that utilised e-mail were essentially harnessing an existing and well-used infrastructure, thus reducing their start-up costs. A significant consideration when looking at the financial viability of any electronic cash system.

[34] Furthermore, for the more paranoid individual, there is the reassurance that such information may be stored outside the Internet environment, and consequently, away from the threat of hackers. Equally, with the more sophisticated schemes, such information need not be shown to the other party in the transaction.

[35] This is all outlined below in relation to the PayPal scheme.

[36] For additional information see: Andres Guadamuz Gonzalez, 'PayPal: the Legal Status of C2C Payment Systems', CLSR 2004, 20(4), 293–299.

[37] www.paypal.com.

become a popular electronic cash payment system providing payment processing services to both businesses and individuals.[38] In essence, PayPal attempts to eliminate the need to pay for online purchases by mailing cheques or using payment cards by allowing Internet consumers to send money instantly and securely to anyone with an e-mail address,[39] including an online merchant. In addition, PayPal transactions clear instantly so that the sender's account is reduced and the receiver's account is credited when the transaction occurs.[40] Consequently, anyone with a PayPal account is able to withdraw cash from their PayPal accounts at any time by requesting that PayPal send them a cheque or make a direct deposit to their checking accounts. Below is an illustration taken from the PayPal website outlining the way in which the system operates.

In order to make use of the system, an individual or business must first of all register for a PayPal account, which requires that you provide your name, address, e-mail address and credit-card or bank-account information.[41] There are three different ways to fund the account.

1. Charging the purchaser's credit card for any transactions (payments).

2. Debiting a checking account for any payments.

3. The purchaser sends a cheque to create a positive balance in his account at PayPal, and has any payments deducted from the account.

One of the advantages of PayPal is that there is no minimum amount that a PayPal

---

[38] As a money transfer system, PayPal was originally launched for C2C (customer-to-customer) transactions. However, the company behind this service recognised the obvious gap in the Internet micropayment market. As such, it introduced B2C transactions, by offering accounts for businesses. Consequently, PayPal has consolidated its position as a neutral intermediary offering low risk to both seller/receiver and buyer/sender of the money.

[39] PayPal is a convenient way for auction bidders to pay for their purchases, and sellers like it because it eliminates the risks of accepting other types of online payments.

[40] All recipients are instantly credited with the funds in their accounts for immediate use, as opposed to having to wait for the clearing of any electronic fund transfers which may take up to a week.

[41] This will depend on how you want funds transferred in and out of the account.

account must contain, nor is there any minimum transaction amount, making this service an ideal vehicle for Internet micropayments.[42] Whenever you want to pay someone out of your PayPal account, you provide all the relevant information on a standardised online form, including the recipient's name and e-mail address, the amount to be sent and the choice of payment mode.

Another feature of the system is the ability of customers to maintain funds in their accounts for later use.[43] Consequently, by enabling payees to keep their funds for subsequent purchases, the scheme generates an autonomous circuit of money, which operates parallel to the banking system.[44] This has two effects. First of all, this 'autonomy' makes PayPal money closer to a true form of cybercash, which is capable of circulating beyond the traditional bank-based route. Secondly, rather than relying for income on transaction fees or subscription fees, PayPal is able to earn a profit on the float,[45] which is money that is deposited in PayPal accounts and not used immediately.[46] Consequently, it is able to offer its service free of charge to individuals.[47] Therefore, individuals who use PayPal to send money to other individuals, called a peer-to-peer (P2P) transaction, pay no transaction fee. After two years in business though, PayPal began charging a transaction fee to businesses that used its system to collect payments.[48]

Merchants[49] must have PayPal accounts to accept PayPal payments, though a consumer can use PayPal to pay a seller for purchases even if the seller does not have a PayPal account. PayPal will automatically create an account and then send the recipient an e-mail notification[50] together with a link to this new account. To collect the cash, the seller or merchant that received the e-mail must register and provide PayPal with payment instructions. PayPal will then either send the merchant a cheque, or will deposit funds directly into the merchant's cheque account.

The clear advantage of PayPal as an electronic cash scheme is that it does not require any proprietary software, the system simply links into the existing network of e-mail and web clients. In order to allay the fears of potential clients as the security of the

---

[42] See the discussion above.
[43] Though it should be noted that this is the method by which PayPal finances its operations.
[44] In February 2002, the US state of Louisiana stated that it intended to classify PayPal as a bank so that it could treat its fund transfers within that state under the same regulatory framework as any other commercial bank.
[45] PayPal reinvests unused balances parked in customer accounts in an escrow account at Merrill Lynch for a return of about 1.25 per cent.
[46] For transactions between customers (P2P), no fee is charged for using PayPal. Instead, PayPal makes money on the float, which means that when money sits dormant in one of their accounts, they collecting interest on that money. By contrast, PayPal charges merchants and business accounts a 2.2 per cent discount rate plus 30 cents on the money. To put this into context, this rate is in most instances far better than that charged by merchant banks for accepting credit cards.
[47] Though it does not offer its customers any interest on unused balances in their accounts.
[48] In June 2000, and in response to initial problems surrounding income-generation (see discussion relating its use on eBay below), PayPal decided to introduce business and premier accounts which required recipients of credit card payments to pay 1.9 per cent plus 25 cents for each transaction. In October 2000 this fee was extended to all customers who received over $500 in credit card payments during a six-month period, irrespective of their account category. See: D Cave, 'Losing Faith in PayPal', Technology & Business, (www.salon.com) 23 February 2001.
[49] Here are some examples of US sites that currently accept PayPal: www.88-cellular.com; www.cellular-battery.com; www.sccards.com.
[50] Using the subject heading 'You've got cash!'.

PayPal system, Confinity not only placed a considerable emphasis on security protection[51] but also decided to impose an upper limit of $200 per transaction.[52]

However, the true success of PayPal lies in the fact that it managed to launch its system on a very large scale and managed to maintain a gradual expansion of its customer base over time. This was due to two main factors. First of all, PayPal managed to attract a significant number of venture capitalists from the very beginning together with support from Deutsche Bank, Nokia and Goldman Sachs. This provided the foundation for its launch. However, Confinity recognised the fact that the system could only make a profit if a sufficiently high volume of customers were integrated into it – only at that level would they have sufficient unused balances to make a profit.[53] This is where the second key factor came into play. The company decided to introduce a sign-up bonus of $10 together with a referral bonus for anyone who encouraged someone else to register. By February 2000, PayPal had managed to attract up to 190,000 customers, signing up 9,000 new accounts every day.[54] By October 2000, PayPal had nearly 4,000,000 customers, of which 300,000 were business accounts. Today PayPal has approximately 10,000,000 customers in 36 countries.

PayPal grew rapidly by providing an ideal go-between for buyers and sellers on auction sites such as eBay, Yahoo! Auctions, and Amazon Auctions.[55] Indeed, PayPal has remained as the preferred payment method in online auctions organized by eBay despite eBay's decision in May 1999 to purchase Billpoint.com,[56] so that it could offer customers its own e-mail payment service. Whilst Billpoint grew rapidly, PayPal nevertheless remained the most widely used system on eBay,[57] leading to the decision by eBay in October 2002 to purchase PayPal for $1.5 billion.[58]

The continued success of PayPal has demonstrated that e-mail may be utilised to provide a convenient, safe and efficient payment system, forming the basis for the growth of electronic cash in recent years.[59]

---

[51] To this end, Confinity decided to keep minimal levels of information relating to user account details. In addition, all transfers are routed through a secure server protected behind state-of-the-art firewalls. For further information see: J Sapsford, 'PayPal Sees Torrid Growth with Money-Sending Service', Wall Street Journal, 16 February 2000; R Crigely, 'I'll Gladly Pay You Tuesday: How PayPal has Already Won the Battle of the Internet Payment Systems', The Pulpit (www.pbs.org), 2000.

[52] Larger transfers were permitted, but only with preauthorisation.

[53] D Clark, 'PayPal Plans IPO, Despite Draught in Initial Offerings', Wall Street Journal, 1 October 2001.

[54] In March 2000 Confinity merged with X.com, one of its competitors. The result was an expansion of PayPal's services to include: (1) $100,000 in fraud protection per account, (2) increased maximum spending ceilings of up to $1,000, and (3) enhanced service packages for P2P accounts, including electronic billing and batch payments.

[55] However, one problem faced by PayPal was the large number of its customers who received payments via credit cards. This not only led to a very high cost for credit card processing but also meant that the company's revenue-generating capacity was limited due to the low level of funds left in its accounts for the float.

[56] A software specialist for P2P payments.

[57] At that stage in its development PayPal completed approximately 130,000 transactions per day averaging $50 and resulting in a daily volume of around $6 million.

[58] PayPal continues to offer payment services under its own name, but is operated as a division of eBay.

[59] This has led traditional banks to follow suit and create their own Internet payment sites. One example, which will be discussed later, is Citibank's c2it payments service.

c2it

PayPal's continued success has inspired others to adopt a similar approach, but at the same time to try and 'iron out' some of the glitches. In July 2000, Citibank[60] decided to pursue the idea of e-mail money and launched a P2P payments service called c2it.

The c2it scheme is designed so that people can send cash via e-mail to anyone with an e-mail address. Customers establish a c2it account for cash transfers funded out of a traditional account (ie credit card,[61] cheque or savings account). However, unlike the PayPal system, the c2it scheme involves a more demanding set of transaction fees. These consist of a minimum charge of $0.50 plus 1 per cent of the value being transferred, with a ceiling set at a maximum of 2.2 per cent of the transaction in question. In addition to this, cross-border transfers cost between $10 and $15. Whilst these fees are lower than credit card or wire transfer charges, individuals who form the small transfer market (consumer transactions and/or families transferring funds to one another) may consider other alternatives.[62]

Significantly, the c2it service is available to users holding accounts at other banks, taking advantage of the viral-marketing discussed above, namely that if a recipient does not have a c2it account, they will need to establish one in order to receive the cash. Citibank is hoping to encroach on the market shares currently enjoyed by other systems such as PayPal and Billpoint, due to its brand – namely that the scheme is associated with the largest US bank.[63]

As noted above, partnerships are key to the launch and continued success of any electronic cash system. In this respect, Citibank has managed to tie in large Internet companies, the main one being AOL (America Online) in July 2000.[64] Subsequently, in May 2001 Citibank entered into an agreement with Microsoft, which allows c2it to be utilised by users of Microsoft's Internet services.[65] At the same time, another agreement was finalised with AuctionWatch, which connected c2it to its online auction services. The ability to enter into such high profile and potentially far reaching agreements with Internet services/companies provides Citibank with a large user base for its c2it service and so ensure its leadership position in online-payments systems.

---

[60] America's largest bank.

[61] Under the c2it scheme accounts which are supported via a credit card can be used to make international transfers to over 30 countries. In essence, this provides c2it with the advantage of a very strong global presence.

[62] However, the fact that recipients are not subject to any form of charge/fee may prove of greater value to merchants who are subject to fees every time they receive payment via credit cards. It may be that such benefits may be passed back to consumers (in the form of lower prices), so as to encourage them to start to utilise this system.

[63] Being a bank is it subject to regulatory supervision as well as protected by deposit insurance, thus instilling greater confidence in consumers.

[64] For the European readership this may not appear that significant. However, if one looks at the US Internet market, then AOL is the predominant player – just look at any cinema poster or US based advert. The result was that the c2it service was immediately made available to around 30,000,000 AOL subscribers under the brand name AOL Quick Cash.

[65] This is under the brand name MSN. This agreement has meant that from the beginning, this payment service has been embedded in the MSN platform. Consequently, it may be automatically accessed from any MSN base. For further information see: P Beckett and R Buckman, 'Citigroup, Microsoft Sign Pact Allowing Online Money Transfers', Wall Street Journal, 13 April 2001.

7.7 The Development of Electronic Money for Niche Markets

Another category of electronic cash that arose during the late 1990s focused on the B2C segment of the e-commerce market. A number of Internet companies decided to follow the consumer loyalty approach evidenced in frequent-flier miles and to develop their own online currencies. For instance, in May 2000, American Airlines announced that its 38,000,000 frequent-flier members would not only be able to accumulate frequent-flier miles by buying goods and services on AOL, but would also be able to spend them there. In many respects, this has proved to be an ideal way to familiarise people with the concept of electronic cash, instilling spending power in the frequent flier miles themselves.[66]

Beenz and Flooz were two key players in the late 1990s, which pioneered the use of 'scrip'[67] that could be bought, traded, and exchanged for merchandise, or act as a discount on merchandise, at a number of Web retailers. However, as will be noted below, by August 2001, both companies had ceased to operate. Whilst the concept may be seen as a technological success, it proved to be a commercial failure, requiring consumers to learn new, unique techniques for making Web payments.

Flooz[68]

Flooz.com was launched in early 1999 and served as an online currency (scrip) which consumers could purchase and send via e-mail to other individuals.[69] Recipients of Flooz were then able to spend that money on participating websites (at the time there were 75 sites accepting Flooz).[70] In addition to this, all participating merchants could issue Flooz as a promotional tool and to reward consumers. Flooz.com also targeted companies, providing them with a method of rewarding employees for their performance, establishing a special website for its corporate customers in March 2000. Finally, Flooz.com entered into partnerships with four major online-rewards companies[71] so as to provide a means whereby consumers could convert electronic currency between the various forms[72] (though this was only a uni-directional process). More importantly though, Flooz.com benefitted from $43,500,000 in initial investment for the launch of its electronic cash system.

In an attempt to expand its user base, Flooz.com not only implemented an $8,000,000 advertising campaign, which at one time included Whoopi Goldberg, but

---

[66] In 2000, the FFS (Frequent Flyer Services) reported in *The Economist* that an estimated three trillion unused air miles were locked in the accounts of airline customers. If this is equated into monetary terms, then US airlines sell these miles for between one and three cents. Consequently, if these miles could be used online to purchase goods, then they could represent between $30 to $90 billion in spending power.

[67] For a definition of scrip see the chapter introducing e-finance.

[68] Flooz is an Arab word for money.

[69] Flooz was automatically convertible into dollars on a one-to-one basis. However, it may be suggested that since all Flooz balances were fully backed by equivalent sums of dollars, this electronic cash did not constitute an independent source of cash capable of adding to a state's money supply.

[70] These included Bames & Noble, J Crew, Dean & Deluca, Godiva Chocolatier, Martha Stewart and Tower Records.

[71] Beenz, FreeRide, MyPoints, and Netcentives.

[72] For instance, 200 Beenz could be converted into one Flooz.

also implemented a variety of new marketing strategies to deepen brand recognition. It's website was even one of the first to include a customer care centre, which boasted live help. However, as with PayPal above, Flooz.com relied on word of mouth and the viral spread of its product, whereby recipients of Flooz would subsequently open accounts with the company.

Flooz.com took off almost immediately. By February 2000, around 450,000 people had sent or received Flooz, with almost $5 million worth of Flooz certificates in circulation. The key appeared to be the fact that Flooz.com relied on fees paid by participating merchants to finance its scheme. All other aspects of the service were offered for free so as to maximise the system's attractiveness to as wide an audience as possible. However, ultimately this also led to its downfall during the dot-com crash of 2000/2001.[73] The final blow came in June 2001 amidst claims that a Russian gang had charged $300,000 of Flooz currency to stolen credit cards over a period of three months.[74] The credit card processor subsequently refused to pass any genuine revenue to Flooz.com until it was satisfied that it held sufficient reserves to cover any fraudulent orders. Inevitably, this drain on the system's cash flow led Flooz.com to close its website on 8 August 2001. By the end of August the company had filed for bankruptcy.

Beenz

Another payment system introduced in early 1999 took the form of coupon money made available to Internet consumers. This British company, Beenz.com, aimed to generate a global web currency that could challenge the dominance of credit card companies as an online payment method. Beenz.com offered its scrip for sale on its website;[75] the scrip was called Beenz, with the company's logo including a small kidney bean. However, Beenz.com regarded its currency as something more than electronic cash and encouraged consumers to earn Beenz by surfing the net, websites, or shopping online for goods.[76] Consumers could then spend their Beenz at any of 300 Internet websites that accepted this online currency,[77] and who in turn could give away Beenz as promotional incentives to reward their consumers.

Beenz.com benefitted from over $80,000,000 in venture capital, and was able to establish ten operational sites in North America, Europe and East Asia. Whilst each one

---

[73] By running at a loss in the early stages, Flooz.com never had sufficient cost controls in place with which it could have withstood much higher cash-burn rates once the Internet crash slowed down revenue growth.

[74] See: G Wearden, 'Flooz.com Collapse Linked to Massive Credit Card Fraud', Yahoo! Finance (uk.news.yahoo.com), 28 August 2001.

[75] Beenz could be purchased at a rate of 100 Beenz to a pound while merchants accepting Beenz for payment could exchange them back to Beenz.com at a rate of 200 Beenz to a pound. The difference between the two exchange rates represented the company's source of income.

[76] For further information see: T Weber, 'Someday, a Hill of Beenz Might be Worth a Lot', Wall Street Journal, 20 December 1999; S Miles, 'Flooz.com Says it is Seeking Merger, but Service Remains Offline for Now', Wall Street Journal, 10 August 2001; E Joyce, 'For Flooz, Time was Money, and Time Ran Out', internet.com (www.atnewyork.com), 30 August 2001.

[77] These merchants included, Barnes & Noble, Eddie Bauer, Martha Stewart, Garden.corn, Hammacher Schlemmer, Dell, Sharper Image, Borders and Wine.com.

of these sites focused predominantly on local/regional merchants, consumers could purchase goods from any of the 300 retailers that accepted Beenz.[78] By the middle of 2000, Beenz.com had more than 1,000,000 customers using their currency to purchase goods online.

However, the company was hit hard by the dot-com crash both directly and indirectly (many of its partners were dot-com start-ups) and in December 2000 the company was forced to downsize in an attempt to keep afloat. In addition, Beenz.com implemented two addition strategies.[79] Unfortunately, neither of the new strategies was able to save Beenz.com and the company was forced to close its site in August 2001.[80] As noted above, whilst both Flooz and Beenz were technologically sound concepts, they attempted to introduce a product that was too unique. In essence, they failed to meet the real needs of consumers.

GiftCertificates.com

GiftCertificates.com enables customers to purchase gift certificates from over 700 different merchants over the net. These gift certificates can then be sent to other individuals as gifts, who can then redeem the certificate either in the issuer's store or on its website. The system also provides SuperCertificates, which can be e-mailed as a gift to individuals who can then exchange them for gift certificates of their choice.

Electronic cash coupons for teenagers

In 1999 RocketCash, Cybermoola and iCanBuy.com, introduced coupon-money schemes aimed at teenagers. As discussed at the beginning of this chapter, whilst this section of society is probably the most familiar with the Internet, it is also limited by the fact that very few teenagers have access to credit cards. In this respect, coupon money attempted to overcome this problem by offering an alternative payment mechanism.

Accounts could be opened and subsequently loaded with electronic cash, by sending cheques through the post or by parents transferring funds[81] as gifts, into those accounts. In addition, just as with the Beenz scheme, promotional bonuses and gift certificates were used to encourage consumers to shop on their website.

Despite the initial success of these schemes, iCanBuy.com had a user-base of 350,000 young consumers by the middle of 2000, most of these sites disappeared as a

---

[78] Each of the sites converted Beenz into the respective national currency at exchange rates that would give Beenz the same value everywhere in cyberspace.

[79] The first was BeenzCodes which was a new reward. These unique codes could be issued to consumers offline at point of sale, in direct mailings and inside product packages which could be redeemed online for prizes. The second strategy involved entering into collaboration with Mondex to develop a Beenz-enabled smart card, which account holders could use to pay in Beenz at over 18 million locations where MasterCard was accepted.

[80] For further information see: S Junankar, 'Beenz.com Seeks Buyer', ZDNet (UK) (www.zdnet.co.uk), 30 March 2001; L Enos, 'E-commerce Currency Firm Scales Back', E-commerce Times (www.newsfactor.com), 20 December 2000.

[81] Through traditional credit card payments.

result of the dot-com crash of 2000/2001.[82] Cybermoola and iCanBuy.com were both forced to close down. All had to shut down when initial venture-capital support was withdrawn. The only one of these to survive the crash was RocketCash, which continues to operate.

eCash's Monneta

As noted above, following the failure of the CyberCoin experiment, eCash Technologies continued to build on the foundations laid by that scheme. After taking over Chaum's eCash experiment in late 1999, eCash Technologies expanded the scope of its schemes to cover eight banks, 300 merchants, and managed to establish 30,000 accounts by February 2000. Of particular note was its testing of the eCash P2P scheme in conjunction with Deutsche Bank 24, which was made available to a wide variety of peer-to-peer transactions.

During 2000, eCash Technologies continued to develop a variety of payments options which were then integrated into a single software package known as Monneta. Monneta included a range of options including (1) 'debit' payments deducted from an individual's cheque account, (2) a 'prepaid' option based on storing value in an eCash account, (3) a P2P feature enabling the transfer of funds between eCash accounts, and (4) a B2C application linking consumer and merchant accounts. By 2001, eCash Technologies had decided to work on a multi-currency eCash software product for cross-border transactions.

Perhaps one of the limitations of the Monneta system was that eCash Technologies indirectly interacted with merchants or consumers given the fact that it relied on banks for its application and scope for growth. In many respects, this may explain the reason why eCash found it difficult to gain a foothold in the US market to the same extent as in Germany.[83] As with many of the other systems examined in this chapter, eCash Technologies' product ultimately failed as a 'stand-alone' product and was the subject of a takeover on February 2002 by InfoSpace. The Monneta now forms part of a broader electronic-payments platform that is directly marketed to merchants, and the system is backed a company (InfoSpace) which has the resources and expertise to launch back such a product.[84]

7.8 The Evolution of 'Smart' Cards

As noted above, there are a number of electronic cash alternatives to traditional payment mechanisms. However, it is also worth looking at card based payment mechanisms, such as magnetic strip cards and smart cards. Both of these payment mechanisms are not being used solely for Internet applications; they are being marketed

---

[82] Once again, none of these companies was in a position of profitability by the time of the dot-com crash. Having invested in expensive infrastructure and promotion of their products, they were vulnerable to sceptics who suddenly doubted the future profitability of e-commerce.

[83] The lack of a bank partner such as Deutsche Bank may explain this.

[84] On a positive note, eCash Technologies proved that the technology exists for a fully integrated, global, safe and fast electronic cash system whose currency is almost as anonymous as hard cash.

and used as alternatives to carrying physical cash. In many respects, they have proved to be far more popular with consumers than the various types of electronic cash outlined above. In part this may be attributed to the public's 'love-affair' with plastic cards as a means of payment for retail purchases.[85]

7.9 Magnetic Strip Cards

A magnetic strip card is a plastic card that has some form of magnetically encoded strip or strips on its exterior. To date, over one billion magnetic strip cards have been issued worldwide and are used for applications such as bank debit cards, credit cards, telephone cards, employee identification cards, and cards for building and machine access privileges.

To the extent that they are used as 'electronic purses'[86] that allow the cardholder to use the card to purchase goods or services, these cards support a form of electronic commerce. For example, prepaid phone cards enable a consumer to buy units of time on a card at a pre-specified price.[87]

7.10 How Does a Magnetic Strip Card Work?

Magnetic strip cards generally have one magnetic strip on them that contains two or three tracks of information. Consequently, special magnetic strip card readers are necessary to both read and encode the cards. Equally, in line with concerns about privacy and the potential for fraudulent activity, the data that is encoded onto the card may be encrypted, making it difficult for potential thieves to decode or copy the information onto another card.

However, one of the main disadvantages of this type of card is that it is vulnerable due to the fact that the information is magnetically encoded and stored on the exterior of the card. This means that the data may be readily copied, forged, or altered. Therefore, whilst the data may be encrypted to enhance security the ability to exactly copy the encoded data and create a forged copy of the card is still a threat. Another major drawback is the fact that the magnetically stored data is physically vulnerable in as much as it may be damaged by placing the card too close to a magnet. In addition, over time the magnetic strip may gradually deteriorate and/or become scratched, rendering the card useless. Magnetic strip cards are typically one of three types.

1. Online strip cards which are used to read customer information from the strip. The information is then used to access information about the cardholder from a central computer. They are commonly used for debit cards, credit cards, and library cards, as well as for building access.

2. Offline strip cards which store information that can be interpreted by the card

---

[85] See: L Healy, 'Looking to a Smart Future', E-commerce Law and Policy, January 2002, pp8–9.
[86] Note the definition of 'electronic purse' in Chapter 5 of this book.
[87] This enables the customer to avoid feeding money into a pay phone or being charged an unknown amount to their phone bills.

reader and altered. An example of this would be a telephone card or travel card[88] that store the amount of units to the card. As the card is used, so the value is deducted by the reader and the updated amount encoded back to the card. The card reader re-writes data to the strip reflecting the transaction.[89]

3.   Smartcard hybrids, which represent a combination of magnetic strip technology with that of smart cards, so generating a hybrid model.

7.11 Smart Cards

The appearance of a smart card is very similar to that of a traditional credit card; the difference being that the smart card contains a microprocessor and a storage unit; an electronic microchip embedded in a small gold plate on the front of the card rather than a magnetic strip in the back like a conventional credit or debit card. As such smart cards are capable of storing at least 100 times more data than magnetic strip cards. Nevertheless, to date, they are predominantly used in Europe.[90]

Smart card technology attempts to overcome most of the limitations associated with magnetic strip cards but they are more expensive to issue.[91] Smart cards can be divided into two categories.

1.   Memory smart cards, which contain relatively less information and processing capabilities than their 'intelligent' siblings and are typically used to record a monetary or unit value that the cardholder can spend.

2.   'Intelligent' smart cards have the additional feature of being able to add and process a wider variety of information components than a memory smart card. They also have greater processing capabilities for programmed decision-making necessary for multiple application requirements.

How does a smart card work?

The term 'electronic purse' is used to refer to monetary value that is loaded onto the smart card's microprocessor and which can be used subsequently by consumers for purchases. However, as noted above, merchants accepting smart cards as a form of

---

[88] Refer to the discussion of Octopus and Oyster cards below.
[89] An example of a magnetic strip card with both online and offline functions is used by Lehigh University in the United States (though these are now becoming more popular with UK institutions). This involves a multi-purpose card designed to be more convenient for students, staff and the institution. The card contains two magnetic strips. The top strip is used for online access to account information. The card allows staff and authorised students after-hours access to certain buildings. The online feature allows the user to report the card missing and for the central database to be immediately updated to deny entry to the possessor of the card. Other services include checking out library books, purchasing food, purchasing goods from vending machines, and using on-campus laundry machines. Students can then 'top-up' their accounts throughout the semester. (It should be stressed that parents favoured this system because they could place money on their child's account and know the specific uses for which it could be spent.) The second strip is used for offline access to on-campus photocopying machines.
[90] Dataquest reported that 90 per cent of the smart cards shipped in 1995 went to Europe. Only 2 per cent went to North and South America combined. This balance is changing though, with North and South America combined now accounting for around 20 per cent of the market.
[91] See: R Abeyratne, 'Emerging Trends in Computer Law and the Use of the Smart Card in Civil Aviation', (1998), Communications Law 3(1), p16–19.

payment must have a smart card reader,[92] whereby the chip makes contact with electrical connectors that transfer data to and from the microprocessor.

As with magnetic strip cards, smart card technology may be used in either an on-line or offline mode. Offline smart card technology can be used in countries lacking a good or reliable telecommunications infrastructure, required for real-time authorisations, or in remote locations. An example of this is Visa's Chip Offline Pre-authorised Card.[93]

A typical example of the way in which a smart card operates would be as follows. The consumer loads money to the smart card by visiting a machine and by either putting in cash, credit card or checking account information he may load the amount desired directly onto the smart card.[94] The consumer is then free to use the smart card for any purchase at a location where the merchant accepts the smart card. At that stage the consumer will insert the smart card into the smart card reader, enter a valid password, and the amount of the purchase will be deducted from the balance on the card.

The smart card reader computes a running total of the sales amounts deducted from the customers. At the end of the day,[95] the merchant will insert his own smart card into the reader along with a valid password and is then able to download the amount of the sales that have been recorded since the last download. The smart card can then be taken to the bank for immediate cash payment.

Another option is for the merchant to use a networked personal computer and banking software. In this situation, the merchant will simply insert his smart card and transfer the amount on the smart card directly into a bank account. An example of the use of smart cards is the Citibank and Chase Manhattan Bank pilot project, which implemented smart cards for consumers on the upper West Side of Manhattan.

Another example of a store value card is the Mondex card[96] and was developed to provide a digital-cash system based on smart cards which could be filled up with cash and used for transactions via Mondex-enabled phones, computers and personal digital assistants.[97] The customer purchased the Mondex card[98] already credited with value prior to its use, though the customer had the option of reloading the card by accessing

---

[92] Most smart cards can be read directly from a reader placed in the PCMCIA slot, which is a standard feature of most modem laptops and personal computers.

[93] This is usually abbreviated to COPAC.

[94] Another variation is to download the money directly from a personal computer if the smart card issuer has software available for such downloads and the user has a smart card slot.

[95] Or at any time interval designated by the merchant.

[96] A pilot scheme was carried out in Swindon between 1995 and 1998 where the card was accepted for small payments ordinarily made with cash such as bus and train fares, car park tickets, and students' library photocopying.

[97] The great advantage of Mondex Electronic Cash system was that it did not need any central clearing authority because of the ability of its chips to authenticate, authorise and transfer payments (including direct card-to-card transfers). The elimination of any central clearing authority also promised to make digital-cash systems much cheaper, despite the high start-up costs involved in enabling access devices with Mondex compatibility.

[98] Mondex (www.mondex.com), a British software company launched in 1993 by two UK banks (National Westminster and Midland).

his bank account through the cash point machine[99] or telephone. When value on the card was spent with a participating retailer, the value of the goods or service was transferred from the customer's smart card to the retailer through his Mondex retail terminal. As with the above example, at the end of the working day, the retailer was able to download the value of all the Mondex payments as a lump sum into his bank account.[100]

However, the development of smart card technology first took off in Europe,[101] as opposed to the US,[102] and was pioneered by the French.[103] The large majority of French citizens were exposed to this technology at a relatively early stage due to the fact that many of France's public sector businesses began to promote the use of smart-card technology. An ideal example of this was France Telecom, which launched the first stored-value chipcard application known as telecarte.[104]

Most French citizens now use the 'carte bancaire' in lieu of traditional credit cards. In essence, this is a smart debit card[105] tied to a checking account, which has an overdraft facility, thus enabling the card to function in much the same way as a credit card.[106] These immensely popular bank cards are issued by a consortium of France's leading commercial banks.

Finally, Gemplus[107] is a French software company that was founded in 1988. This is one of the world's two[108] leading developers of smart card technology with worldwide demand for its many software applications.[109]

---

[99] The amount was debited to the customer's bank account in the normal way that cash withdrawn from the cash point machine is debited.
[100] If the retailer and customer had different banks, then each party settled with his banks and settlement between banks inter se which is the same as in the clearing of cheques.
[101] It should not really be surprising that smart card experiments proved so popular in Europe at a far quicker rate than in the US, especially in smaller European countries such as Holland, Denmark and Norway, where there are only a couple of banks controlling the entire domestic market. This oligopoly situation ensures that the coordination problem associated with launching local smart card experiments is considerably reduced. Once launched, these experiments have enjoyed success because individuals are less attached to traditional plastic money than in the US. As such, they are far more open-minded and willing to utilise new forms of smart cards. Given the relatively high telecommunication costs and incidences of credit card fraud in Europe, people have also been attracted by the dual promise of lower costs and added security offered by smart cards. Finally, as is the case in France, smart cards enjoy the active support of European governments, which in turn means that public sector enterprises have successfully pushed for widespread use of such cards by their clients.
[102] In the US there has been no comparable government support. Equally, the country has thousands of American banks which makes the launch of bank-sponsored smart card projects extremely difficult to coordinate. As a result, this coordination role has in essence been delegated to Visa and MasterCard which possessed the centralized payments systems. However, neither company was very aggressive in pushing the use of smart cards in the US for fear of (1) adverse reactions from consumers, and (2) the fact that smart cards could undermine their rather lucrative credit card market (which was deemed more profitable because of the high interest charges that could be charged on unpaid balances). (See: 'Visa and Better Business Bureau in Move to Build Consumer Confidence in Online Shopping', E-commerce and Policy, November 2000, News Analysis, p15.
[103] The French model was actively encouraged by the government.
[104] In addition, the French government and Social Security Agency issued a health insurance card.
[105] In essence, this is a hybrid model discussed above.
[106] Subject to settlement of outstanding debit balances at the end of each month.
[107] See: www.gemplus.com.
[108] The other one being Mondex, mentioned above.
[109] The company specializes in all aspects of smart card technology, especially security protection, e-commerce and wireless applications.

7.12 From Octopus to Oyster

In Hong Kong, the octopus card, which is a rechargeable contactless smart card used in an electronic payment system, has begun to dominate the way in which people live and travel. The system was originally launched in September 1997 as a fare collection system for city's transport network,[110] but has since evolved into an e-cash system for use in convenience stores, supermarkets, restaurants and parking garages. It has become one of the world's most successful electronic cash systems, with nine million Octopus cards circulating and over 80 service vendors.

The UK has adopted a similar smart card for use on the London Underground. Indeed, many Underground Stations display signs stating that their ticket vending machinery has been updated for use by Oyster Smartcards. However, there is growing dissatisfaction with the UK model, not least because it lacks a number of the characteristics that made the Octopus cards a success. It is believed that the Oyster card does not have a 'top up' capability and does not possess the same ease of registration.

The rationale behind the Octopus model is that it may be used to pay for goods/services for which a consumer would traditionally use either a debit or credit card. In terms of use on the transport system, the cardholder simply passes the card over a sensor on entry to the underground system and then again on exit. Once the 'sweeping process' is completed, the fair is automatically calculated and deducted from the consumer's account.[111] By contrast, the Oyster system is somewhat more traditional in that a consumer purchases the equivalent of travel fares for a pre-determined period, such as a monthly, and then uses that card to determine whether or not he is permitted to travel within a certain zone. This is due to the fact that the Oyster cards, unlike their far more complex cousin, the Octopus card, do not hold

---

[110] The Octopus card was created by the five main travel firms in Hong Kong (MTR, KCRC, KMB, City Bus and the Hong Kong & Yaumati Ferry Company) for the purpose of travel payment.
[111] Topping up Octopus cards is very straightforward. A customer simply uses one of the several thousand machines situated around Hong Kong, inserts his card followed by either cash or a credit/debit card and value is then transferred to the Octopus account.

any value in terms of electronic cash. Consequently, they truly are simply a travelcard; though as the Octopus system demonstrates, it is a scheme which could evolve over time into something more complex.

7.13 Advantages and Disadvantages

The main advantage of using a smart card over that of traditional cash is the fact that cash is vulnerable to theft. By contrast, smart cards with identification pictures and/or passwords make them less susceptible to theft as their reusability value is substantially lower. In addition, smart cards provide an electronic record of purchases and the ability to print out transaction data which can serve as business receipts.[112]

If one reviews credit cards, as noted in the previous chapter, they are vulnerable to fraudulent online or phone purchases if the card is stolen. Equally, many credit card merchants require a minimum purchase amount due to the commission fee required by the issuing credit card company.[113] Finally, in terms of smart cards providing an alternative to debit cards, one clear advantage of smart cards is their ability to be used in an offline environment.[114] Bank debit cards require that a good, reliable telecommunications infrastructure is in place.

Finally, when used with strong cryptosystems, smart cards can store the cardholder's digital signature very securely and provide strong authentication and repudiation.[115]

This is not to say that smart cards do not carry with them a number of concerns. People are concerned that smart cards may be getting too smart and storing too much personal data. An example is the Malaysian government which is in the process of implementing a single smart card that contains a wide range of information.[116] It should be noted that for every different application included on the card, these will give rise to difference legal implications, in particular data protection. Nevertheless, despite such privacy concerns, the future of smart cards appears to be one of the most positive.

7.14 Summary

It is frequently commented upon that the law continuously plays 'catch-up' with regards to mercantile practice; this especially true in the area of e-commerce. The area of e-finance and electronic cash is developing at a rapid pace. Indeed, it was only the severe implications of the dot-com crash that slowed the pace of growth and development in this area.

---

[112] This feature may be seen as both an advantage and disadvantage (it provides convenience to the business traveller but removes the anonymity of cash).

[113] By contrast, smart cards can be used for any size purchase.

[114] Debit cards are in far wider use in the US than in Europe, which in turn may account for the disparity between the use of smart card technology in Europe and the US.

[115] Smart card technology provides a mechanism for authentication and non-repudiation for Internet transactions. If the purchaser has either a personal computer or a telephone device with a smart card slot, then verification via smart cards is possible for Internet transactions.

[116] National identification code; driver's license (and possible driving history); immigration details; health details; electronic cash; bank account details; and credit card.

In the short-term banks responded to these private sector operations by developing their own online banking facilities. However, there is a growing recognition that consumers, who are now becoming more comfortable with the concept of 'electronic cash', are developing expectations which outstrip the current products offered by banks. In essence, consumers want an electronic equivalent to traditional physical cash. The willingness of banks to become involved in this area is highlighted by the growing number of partnerships between banks and private sector operations to co-develop the latest generation of electronic cash products.

e-Crime

8 e-Crime: Its Nature, Scale and Impact

8.1 What is e-Crime?

The answer to this question is not as straightforward as one might, at first, think. The search for a definition will unearth differing opinions. First and foremost, it must be pointed out that this area of law has become somewhat littered with labels for criminal activity. Any journey into the academic, governmental or business texts will most likely lead to encounters with the following terms:

- 'computer crime';
- 'computer-related crime';
- 'cybercrime';
- 'Internet crime';
- 'hi-tech crime';
- 'e-Crime'.

This author has chosen to use the last of these as an umbrella term. There are several reasons for this. Firstly, 'e-Crime' is a label which appears to have gained international recognition in recent years. Evidence of this can be found in the title of the National Hi-Tech Crime Unit's *e-Crime Congress* in England and Wales. This body is backed by the Home Office and held its third annual meeting in April 2005.[1] It welcomed 500 delegates from some 22 countries, including the USA, Australia, Canada and many European Union states. Secondly, I am adopting a broad definition of the term 'e-Crime'. This is not now unusual. For example, the New Zealand Police Force's definition of 'e-Crime' covers 'offences where a computer or other information and communication technology is the tool used to commit an offence, the target of an offence, or used as the storage device in an offence'.[2] The Australian Federal Police

---

[1] The Welsh conference took place in February 2005.
[2] See: http://www.police.govt.nz.

Force has adopted an almost identical definition[3] and, closer to home, EURIM (the independent, UK-based all-party Parliament and Industry European Information Society Group) continues to use the term to refer to 'any criminal activity that involves the use of computers or networks in its execution'.[4] Lastly, the UK government has also embraced this term, as evidenced by the Home Office's announcement, on 24 December 2004, that it will be forming an 'E-Crime Strategy', to be published in the forthcoming year.[5]

Historically, a distinction has been made between computer crime and cybercrime. In his book, '*Fighting Computer Crime: A New Framework for Protecting Information*',[6] the renowned American computer crime expert, Donn Parker, offered up the following definitions.

Computer crime	A crime in which the perpetrator uses special knowledge about computer technology.
Cybercrime	A crime in which the perpetrator uses special knowledge of cyberspace.

A more detailed categorisation can be gleaned from the work of the UK Audit Commission's work over the past two decades. As Steven Furnell points out: 'it is possible to draw a distinction between those crimes that are computer-assisted and those that are computer- focused':

Computer-assisted crimes	Cases in which the computer is used in a supporting capacity, but the underlying crime or offence either pre-dates the emergence of computers or could be committed without them.
Computer-focused crimes	Cases in which the category of crime has emerged as a direct result of computer technology and there is no direct parallel in other sectors.'[7]

Note that these categories are not mutually exclusive. Moreover, official sources continue to indicate that such categorisation may be less clear cut than it used to be. For example, the National Criminal Intelligence Service (NCIS) Report of 2003 (*UK Threat Assessment of Serious and Organised Crime*) stated that 'the range of crimes that can be committed, either through or with the support of hi-tech tools and techniques, is limited only by the imagination and capability of the criminals'.[8]

One might be tempted to think that the term 'e-Crime' simply describes the criminal use of computer technology. However, in order to truly understand what e-Crime is, one must look at the context within which it is said to exist. The amazing advances in Internet and web-based information and communications technologies

---

[3] See: http://www.afp.gov.au.
[4] See: http://www.eurim.org/briefings/BR34.htm.
[5] See: http://www.homeoffice.gov.ac.uk/crime/internetcrime/strategy.html.
[6] Wiley & Sons Inc, New York (1988).
[7] Furnell, S, Cybercrime: Vandalizing the Information Society (2002) Addison Wesley, p22.
[8] See: http://www.ncis.co.uk/ukta/2003/default.asp, para 8.1.

(ICTs) have transformed the world in which we live. These technologies have helped to create a truly global marketplace, characterised by a constant stream of information which flows through networks and websites. In the light of these facts, e-Crime can often take the form of 'computer-mediated activities which are either illegal or considered illicit by certain parties and which can be conducted through global electronic networks'.[9]

Thus, it can be seen that an e-criminal is not merely a villain who uses his computer for nefarious purposes; both he and his criminal activities are truly defined by the virtual landscape in which he operates. For example, a fraudster can steal money from thousands of victims in a number of countries without leaving the comfort of his home (or work) computer station. The global connectivity of the Internet allows him to become an international criminal. Instead of running into a bank, wearing a balaclava and carrying a gun, to commit armed robbery, he can (potentially) 'enter' a bank anywhere in the world and escape with millions of pounds – not in swag bags, but in a vastly swollen host bank account, into which he has transferred his ill-gotten gains. The technology dispenses with the need for physical presence, weaponry and a getaway vehicle. Alternatively, one could view the technology as providing him with a disguise (to replace the balaclava), a stealthy alternative to the gun (computer systems, unlike bank buildings, are open 24 hours a day), and a perfect means of escape (a sophisticated programme could wipe away not only the virtual foot/fingerprints of the e-criminal but the traces of the e-crime itself).

The aforementioned technological advances have fed criminality in several ways. Firstly, they have simply rendered certain crimes easier to commit; made the criminals' lives less stressful. An obvious example is the advent of e-mail, which has been a boon to drug dealers, paedophiles and other disreputable types when arranging their deals and liaisons.

Secondly, the technology has created new opportunities to commit so-called 'traditional' crimes. Some of these may have been crimes for a long time, such as blackmail,[10] or relatively recent additions to the list of criminal offences, such as harassment.[11] In particular, fraud has been greatly facilitated by the technological advances. For example, a spoof website can be created with relative ease; the prefix 'web' being doubly apt in this context, as the computer fraudster seeks to lure his victims to the site[12] to trap them with his scam. The proliferation of content-related crimes has also occurred through the technology, such as offences against intellectual property (eg criminal breaches of copyright) and the creation and/or dissemination of obscene material (eg 'pseudo-photographs'[13] concerned with child pornography).

---

[9] Definition of 'Cybercrime' given by Thomas, D and Loader, B, Cybercrime: Law Enforcement, Security and Surveillance in the Information Age (2003) Routledge, p3.
[10] Originating, in its modern form, from s3 Libel Act 1843.
[11] Originating from s40 Administration of Justice Act 1970, through s5(1) Public Order Act 1986, to the offences of criminal harassment contained within ss1 and 4 Protection from Harassment Act 1997.
[12] For example, via hypertext links from e-mails.
[13] An apparently indecent image of a child which is comprised of images which, individually, would not be classed as indecent. This is achieved by using computer technology to modify it – see s7(7) Protection of Children Act 1978 (as amended by s84 Criminal Justice and Public Order Act 1994).

Thirdly, the new technology (particularly the Internet) has not only vastly extended the criminal landscape but has provided new opportunities for criminal behaviour within it. These new e-criminal activities are often forms of attack upon the integrity of computer and communications systems. For example, an individual may seek to gain unauthorised access to a computer system ('hack' into it) for the purpose of damaging or disabling it or its contents, perhaps by releasing a computer virus into it.

The previous discussion of the definition of 'e-Crime' made reference to the three distinct roles which, broadly speaking, computers can play in criminal scenarios. It is now appropriate to look at these individually in more detail.

The computer as a criminal tool

E-criminals use computers as communications tools in cyberspace.[14] Crimes which previously were committed only in the physical, offline world can now be perpetrated online as well. These online facilities enable the e-criminal to communicate on a one-to-one basis with individuals and corporate bodies,[15] or on a one-to-many basis with a multitude of people across the globe. An example of the former is the sending of threatening e-mails to somebody. This would be viewed as a form of cyberviolence, specifically 'cyberstalking'. Victims of online harassment suffer a range of emotions, from mere annoyance through anxiety to considerable distress and beyond. It has been said that 'the real fear, however, is that offensive and threatening behaviour that originates online will escalate into "real-life" stalking'.[16]

An example of the multi-victim form of communication is the practice of 'phishing', a term that derives from the way in which e-criminals trawl the Internet for private data. This involves the sending out of junk e-mails (spamming) to random, unsuspecting victims. These people are thereby directed to spoof websites where they can be deceived into providing details of their bank accounts and passwords. The fraudsters then access the victims' accounts and transfer money into host accounts. In 2004, just such a scam was set up in the UK by a gang of fraudsters operating from Russia. Those who responded and logged on to the address in the 'Barclays Bank' e-mail, found a website which looked virtually identical to the bank's website. E-criminals have learnt how to hide additional letters and characters in the spoof websites' addresses, in order to disguise their real locations. Indeed, some of these phishing e-mails link to websites that differ by only one character from the genuine website. These scams are becoming much more prevalent. Evidence of this was recently provided by MessageLabs, a leading British e-mail security company which monitors online traffic, when it reported that the number of these suspect e-mails which it intercepted had increased from 279 in September 2003 to 337,350 in January 2004.

A hybrid example of how computers can be used to communicate with individuals

---

[14] The term 'cyberspace' was first used by Gibson, W, in his novel *Neuromancer* (1994) Harper Collins.

[15] Under the *Salomon* principle, a business which has been incorporated gains a legal personality that is separate and distinct from those who work or invest in it – *Salomon v Salomon and Co Ltd* [1897] AC 22 (House of Lords).

[16] Ellison and Akdeniz: Cyberstalking: The Regulation of Harassment on the Internet – Crim LR Special Edition: Crime, Criminal Justice and the Internet (Sweet & Maxwell) 1998, p31.

and, simultaneously, with a collective audience is provided by President Clinton's first online interview (with CNN), in February 2000. During the interview, the chat room became overloaded with users, causing it to crash. Consequently, users became disconnected and were forced to connect again. A computer security officer from New York grasped the opportunity to re-select a nickname under which to appear in the chat session. He did so before the typist entering the President's responses was able to log in again. This meant that he now had control over what the President appeared to be saying. One of several supposed contributions from the President which followed was: 'Personally, I would like to see more porn on the Internet'. Although this was not a case of hacking, the security concerns are obvious.

The use of chat rooms by paedophiles as a means of communicating with their intended victims has recently caught the attention of the legislature in the UK. Since these individuals can retain a degree of anonymity online, it is easy for them to pose as children in order to gain the confidence of their victims. This practice of 'grooming' has been criminalised. It is now an offence to arrange or facilitate the commission of a child sex offence (planned to take place in any part of the world).[17] Paedophiles can, of course, also make use of the Internet's file transfer facilities to distribute and receive child pornography. In 2002, 'Operation Ore' was launched in the UK by the National Crime Squad, acting as the central co-ordinating agency and working with police forces around the country. The investigation was prompted by the findings of the US Postal Service's investigation into Landslide Inc, in Fort Worth, Texas. This had been revealed as a multi-million dollar Internet company selling child pornography and images of child abuse through its website. Its customers came from all over the world, including more than 7,000 identified as being based in the UK. One of the tactics used in 'Operation Ore' to catch these individuals has been to set up spoof child pornography websites. These websites contained initial warnings (to be read by the paedophiles) about the viewing of the material on them, thereby giving officers enough time to confirm these peoples' Internet addresses in order, ultimately, to locate and arrest them.

The computer as a criminal target

The first, natural question to ask here is: why would a computer system be targeted? The answer is that it will become a target for one of three main reasons. The e-criminal will be seeking to attack the information contained in, or the services provided by, the computer system in order to compromise its confidentiality, availability or integrity. Such criminal ends are often sought by the means of gaining unauthorised access to the computer system/network in question. This activity is commonly referred to as 'hacking'.

Confidential information may be the quarry of the hunting hacker. Law enforcement agencies and military institutions store a wealth of highly sensitive information on a range of issues, individuals and groups. The e-criminal and his partners in crime may wish to tap into such sources in order to gain the upper hand, whether for the purpose

---

[17] Section 15 Sexual Offences Act 2003.

of more strategic planning of e-crimes or for successful flight from capture. For example, terrorist organisations may use hackers to gain crucial information about ongoing investigations into them or potential weaknesses in security planning which can be exploited by them. Equally, they could simply wish to know whether some counter-intelligence information which they released previously has been received and acted upon in the way that they had hoped for. In short, they can seek to stay at least one step ahead of those who are pursuing them. If the investigative net is closing in on them, they can hack for the purposes of determining where would be the safest haven to retreat to, in the light of communications between domestic and foreign intelligence agencies.

Naturally, hackers target commercial systems and networks as well. The criminal scheme here will usually be to 'steal' intellectual property or to obtain other information which will assist in further crimes, such as fraud.

Government information is well-guarded by the provisions of the Official Secrets Acts of 1911 and 1989. However, commercial information is not afforded similar protection. Misuse of such information is, in the main, a civil matter. The criminal law will only intervene in certain, restricted circumstances. Clearly, if information is stored on a floppy disk and that disk is taken, a prosecution for the basic offence of theft[18] will follow. This will not be problematic because all of the five elements of that crime will be present: property (the floppy disk) belong to another will have been appropriated dishonestly with an intention to permanently deprive the owner of it. The information contained within that disk will be highly relevant in determining the true commercial value of that property. Of course, the monetary value of a disk can rocket from a few pounds to millions of pounds when confidential information is placed onto it. Although the Theft Act 1968 declares that 'it is immaterial whether the appropriation [of the property] is made with a view to gain, or is made for the thief's own benefit',[19] the value of the property may be influential in other ways. For example, the true value of the disk may well affect the decision as to whether the accused will be tried summarily or on indictment, theft being an offence triable either way. If a mode of trial hearing takes place,[20] the magistrates will view the property's commercial value as one of the crucial factors in deciding whether to try the case themselves or to send it up to the Crown Court for trial by jury. Moreover, even if they do decide to hear the case themselves, and they convict the accused, they may still send the case to the Crown Court for the purposes of sentencing if they feel that their powers are lacking in respect of that particular decision.[21]

The criminal process is not so easy in other circumstances. Often, the crucial issue will be whether the confidential information, when separated from the physical object in which it is contained, can itself be 'stolen'. What if the floppy disk is not

---

[18] Section 1 Theft Act 1968.
[19] Section 1(2).
[20] It will if the accused has decided not to exercise his right to choose trial by jury.
[21] A maximum of £5,000 fine and/or six-month custodial sentence for a single offence – see ss31(1) and 32(1) Magistrates' Court Act 1980.

appropriated, but the information on it is simply copied to one of the e-criminal's own disks? Can a charge of theft follow? Naturally, the first question to be asked is how the Theft Act 1968 defines the term 'property'. The answer lies in s4(1), which states that ' "Property" includes money and all other property, real or personal, including things in action and other intangible property'. However, this does not provide a complete solution to the problem posed. The further, key question is whether the intellectual property will fall within that statutory definition: *Oxford* v *Moss*[22] suggests that it will not. While studying at Liverpool University, Moss covertly removed and copied an exam paper. He intended to return the original to its rightful place so that his activities would remain undetected and he would pass the forthcoming exam with flying colours. However, his scheme was discovered and the question arose as to whether he had committed a criminal offence. He could not be successfully prosecuted for theft of the original exam paper because one of the five elements of that crime was seen to be missing – he lacked an intention to permanently deprive the University of that exam paper. However, he was, instead, charged with theft of the confidential information within that paper. At trial, the Liverpool magistrates acquitted him on the basis that confidential information could not be regarded as 'property' for the purposes of the Theft Act 1968. The Crown appealed to the Divisional Court, but the magistrates' decision was upheld on the basis that, whilst the holder of the information (the University) might possess limited rights in it which could be enforced at civil law, the information itself was not property and was, therefore, incapable of being stolen. In short, it was not 'intangible property' within the meaning of s4 of the Act. This line of reasoning was then followed in *R* v *Absolom*.[23] Therein, the accused had obtained valuable trade secrets relating to oil exploration. This information was said to be worth between £50,000 and £100,000. He attempted to sell it to a rival oil company. At trial, he was found not guilty of theft on the basis that such information did not amount to 'property'.

It should be pointed out that there are other offences with which individuals may, instead, be charged in similar circumstances. For example, under the Copyright, Designs and Patents Act 1988, it is a criminal offence to make or deal with articles which one knows or has reason to believe is an infringing copy of a copyright work.[24] Equally, the counterfeiting of registered trademarks is the subject of criminal liability under the Trademarks Act 1994.[25] Also, as mentioned previously, the e-criminal will often have gained unauthorised access to the information in question and could, therefore, be charged with the offence of hacking.[26]

Notwithstanding this, the fact remains that there has been strident criticism from those who think that there remains a dangerous lacuna in the law. For example, Professor Glanville Williams' longstanding criticisms still hold true. In 1983, he stated that:

---

[22] (1978) 68 Cr App R 183.
[23] (1983) The Times 14 September.
[24] Section 107(1).
[25] Section 92.
[26] Section 1 Computer Misuse Act 1990.

'It is absurd and disgraceful that we should still be making do without any legislation specifically designed to discourage this modern form of commercial piracy. Abstracting or divulging an official secret is an offence under the Official Secrets Act 1911, ss1 and 2; but Leviathan is not so much concerned to protect the secret and immensely valuable know-how of its subjects.'[27]

It is not the case, however, that this issue has been left unconsidered. In 1988, the Law Commission agreed, in essence, with its Scottish counterpart on the matter of whether information could be the subject of theft. Both Commissions expressed the view that questions about the legal status of information and, specifically, whether certain forms of dealing in information should be criminalised, raised wide issues of policy that extended beyond the field of computer law. This, together with the aforementioned difficulties of applying the law of theft to information, led them both to recommend no change in this area of the law. The English Law Commission stated that:

'... the definition of property for the law of theft, and the argument as to whether it is possible to appropriate information belonging to another with the intention of permanently depriving the other of it, are problems which have general implications outside the region of computer misuse.'[28]

A year earlier, in its Working Paper on Conspiracy to Defraud,[29] the Commission had already hinted at the view that although information, particularly confidential information, will often be regarded as a valuable commodity, it should not be seen as 'property' in the terms required for the crime of theft. At the same time, it had briefly considered whether a new offence concerned with the dishonest acquisition of confidential information should be created, but declined to offer up an opinion on this matter, stating that it was beyond the remit of that particular Working Paper:

'The whole area of obtaining confidential information and invasion of privacy is a complex one involving many aspects of both civil and criminal law going far beyond the realms of fraud.'[30]

In 1997, the Law Commission turned its mind to the issue of misuse of trade secrets. Commercial espionage is a worrying problem which has been fuelled by information technology. As the Solicitor General put it:

'The modern sorts of commercial activity, and the modern methods by which dishonest activity may be effected, makes one constantly worried that the overhauled bus may not be able to cope.'[31]

The Commission stated that it would be a mistake for the criminal law to pretend that confidential information is, in the strict sense, 'property'. However, it did concede that 'there is no distinction in principle between the harm caused by such misuse and the harm caused by theft'.[32] Consequently, it went on to propose a new offence covering the use or disclosure of another's trade secret (where the owner did not consent to its use or disclosure).[33]

---

[27] Professor Glanville Williams: Textbook of Criminal Law (1983) 2nd Ed, Stevens and Sons Ltd, p739.
[28] Law Commission, Working Paper No 110 (1988), para 3.69.
[29] Law Commission, Working Paper No 104 (1987).
[30] Law Commission, Working Paper No 104 (1987), para 10.45.
[31] 'Commercial Fraud or Sharp Practice – Challenge for the Law', Denning Lecture, October 1997, quoted in Misuse of Trade Secrets: Law Commission Consultative Paper No 150 (1997).
[32] Misuse of Trade Secrets: Law Commission Consultative Paper No 150 (1997), para 3.60.
[33] Ibid, para 1.30. – see also Hull, 'Stealing Secrets: A Review of the Law Commission's Consultation Paper on the Misuse of Trade Secrets' [1998] Crim LR 246.

These problems concerning confidential information point towards a pervasive theme within the law on e-Crime which will be discussed in more depth later on in this book. For now, it must be pointed out that governments and legislatures are presented with a genuine dilemma when it comes to solving e-criminal problems. Should they create computer-specific legislation or, alternatively, seek to change the substantive criminal law to adapt to these new challenges? On the particular issue regarding the confidentiality of information, it has been said that:

> 'In many areas, the fact of a computer's involvement in conduct raises issues of practice rather than principle and, short of a fundamental reform of the criminal law to take account of the enhanced value and status of information, it might be argued that computer-related activities should be left within the structure of the general criminal law.'[34]

There are other reasons why an e-criminal may seek to gain access to confidential information. His criminal pursuits might involve the use of such information in different ways. Information about individuals which is of a private nature is collected and stored by various institutions. For example, an individual's medical records may reveal highly sensitive information which could be used by an e-criminal against them. Such a scheme could simply seek to humiliate the person by publicly disclosing details of their illness or condition. For example, someone who has contracted AIDS[35] may be profoundly embarrassed and distressed by the revelation of such personal details. Despite much research into this condition and real advances in its treatment, prejudicial views about those who suffer from it persist. The individual concerned may not only encounter discrimination in a social context but also in the workplace. There are obvious concerns that may enter the minds of employers, fellow employees and those with whom the individual comes into contact through their employment. By its very nature, AIDS is an illness which can lead to other illnesses and conditions; the immune system is attacked by the virus, thereby rendering the sufferer vulnerable to a number of further infections and diseases. Both the AIDS virus itself and these other illnesses can potentially be passed on to others. This information can feed the fears of others, particularly since there is still widespread ignorance of the true, inherent medical risks and the ways in which they can be guarded against. Thus, it can be seen that even if the e-criminal's motive for disclosing such information about someone was simply to embarrass them, there may be further ramifications for that person; they may become a social pariah in their community and could potentially loose their job.

The e-criminal's motives may be even more malevolent. He may be threatening to disclose private information about an individual unless they give him money or pay him off in some other way. In law, this type of extortion is called blackmail, an offence found in s21 Theft Act 1968. Therein, it is defined as the making of an unwarranted demand with menaces. Further examples of information sources which the e-criminal could hack into and exploit for such purposes include telephone customer records and consumer credit records.

---

[34] Lloyd, I, Information Technology Law (2004) 4th Ed, Oxford University Press, p322.
[35] Acquired Immune Deficiency Syndrome.

Personal information may also be used as a criminal disguise. A hacker could seek details of a person's life in order to impersonate them online or offline, in furtherance of other criminal activities. This has come to be known as 'identity theft', and is a growing concern,[36] as evidenced by the government's recent, controversial proposals to introduce identity cards to combat such activities. Banking institutions have not only introduced new technology in the fight against credit card fraud, but have also recently announced that from 1 January 2005 high street retailers, rather than the banks themselves, will be liable to compensate victims where the fraudulent transaction was effected through anything other than the new technological system (Chip and PIN).

However, in general, it is much more difficult to confirm the true identity of somebody who is operating online; cyberspace creates shadows which compliment disguises. For example, an e-criminal who is feeling weary from his underhand activities may wish to take a short break to relax and think up further scams. To save on travel expenses, he could hack into a system to steal someone else's credit card number and then stay online to book a ticket.

A real life example of how individuals can indulge in widespread hacking for the purposes of stealing such information occurred in 2000. An individual calling himself 'Curador' began hacking into small e-commercial sites. During the period from January to March of that year he penetrated nine sites, variously located in Britain, the USA, Canada, Japan and Thailand, stealing between 750 and 5,000 card numbers in each case. It was estimated that, in total, some 26,000 cards may have been compromised.[37] He also took steps to share his findings, setting up two websites upon which he listed the stolen card details. On these websites he proclaimed himself to be the 'the Saint of e-commerce'. He subsequently attempted to justify his actions by claiming that he wanted to draw the website providers' attention to their security vulnerabilities. It was later reported that Curador obtained the credit card details of Bill Gates and used them to send him a consignment of Viagra tablets. In early March 2000, he goaded his pursuers by stating that:

'Law enforcement couldn't hack their way out of a wet paper bag. They're people who get paid to do nothing. They never actually catch anybody.'[38]

A couple of weeks later, he and his accomplice were traced to a village in Wales.[39] He was an 18-year-old man who had previously worked as an e-commerce consultant, and had actually helped to set up the type of sites which he later hacked into. The FBI estimated that the losses associated with the various intrusions were in excess of

---

[36] It has recently been reported, on 3 March 2005, that 25 per cent of adults in the UK have had their identity stolen, or know someone who has fallen victim to ID fraud. The source of this figure was a Which? Magazine survey – see http://news.bbc.co.uk/go/pr/fr/-/1/hi/business/4311693.stm. Note also, the somewhat ironic case which was reported in the press, where a member of a gang of identity thieves posed as Ricky Gervais, the well-known comedian, to defraud his bank account of funds to buy £200,000 of gold bullion. Gervais had, of course, himself sprung to fame through playing the character of David Brent in the series entitled 'The Office' on BBC television – see *The Guardian*, Wednesday 2 March 2005, p7.

[37] 'Curador pleads guilty'- SecurityFocus News, 29 March 2001: see http:// www.securityfocus.com/news/182.

[38] 'Curador taunts police over site break-ins' – InternetNews report, 27 March 2000: see http://www.internetnews.com/ec-news/article.php/318381.

[39] In Welsh, the word 'curador' means 'custodian'.

$3 million. In March 2001, he pleaded guilty to two charges of obtaining services by deception (in relation to setting up the two Internet sites), and six charges of intentionally accessing sites containing the original card details. Tried under his real name, Raphael Gray, he was convicted and sentenced to a three-year community rehabilitation order, during which he would receive treatment for the mental condition from which he was found to be suffering. After the trial, he was reported as saying:

'I would do it all again, but another time I would choose to ensure that I acted legally.'[40]

Alternatively, a hacker may commit so-called 'theft of service' offences. For instance, after breaking into a telephone switching system, he could steal long-distance calling services. This form of evasion of liability by manipulation of telephone services is often labelled 'phone phreaking'. Again, the e-criminal may be compromising such systems in order to commit further, more ambitious crimes. It has been recognised that 'in some cases, hackers have used the resources of compromised systems to perform intensive computational tasks such as cracking encrypted passwords stolen from other sites'.[41] Equally, the hacker may simply be stepping across a number of networks and systems to disguise his identity and location, making it more difficult for his pursuers to track him. This practice has become known as 'weaving'.

Rather than trying to make services available to himself free of charge, the e-criminal may instead seek to render them unavailable to others. A classic form of this activity is the launch of a 'denial of service' attack (DoS).[42] A denial of service attack results when legitimate user access to a computer or network resource is intentionally blocked or degraded as a result of malicious action taken by another user. The software required to carry out DoS attacks is widely available on the Internet. The motives behind such an attack can range from simple mischief to commercial rivalry or, indeed, extortion. The form of attack can vary in terms of its sophistication. A common method is to 'mailbomb' the target system. This involves sending vast amounts of e-mails to a site in order to clog the mail server, perhaps causing it to crash. For example, in 2000 a 15-year-old high school student in Canada, calling himself 'Mafiaboy', was charged with 66 counts of 'mischief to data' under Canadian law after it was alleged that he launched a series of denial of service attacks upon popular Internet sites (including Amazon.com, eBay, and CNN). This was not viewed as a sophisticated crime, as evidenced by the comments of an investigating officer in the case:

'It is our estimation that Mafiaboy wasn't that good … He wasn't what we would call a genius … almost anyone with knowledge of a computer could have launched the attacks.'[43]

In more advanced forms of DoS attacks, often referred to as Distributed Denial of Services (DDOS) attacks, Internet viruses can be used to programme millions of computers around the world to log on to a website on a particular date, overwhelming the computer systems which power that site and causing it to shut down. This is

---

[40] 'Teen Hacker Escapes Jail Sentence' – BBC News Online, 6 July 2001.
[41] Yee Fen Lim, 'Cyberspace Law: Commentaries and Materials' (2002) Oxford University Press, p249.
[42] See Chapter 9, footnote 88, for details of the proposals to criminalise those who launch or seek to launch such attacks.
[43] Per Sgt Jean-Pierre Roy of the Royal Canadian Mounted Police – 'Teen Charged in DoS Hack Attack' – Tech TV News Report, 19 April 2000: see http://www.g4TV.com.

achieved through what have come to be known as 'bot net armies.' The criminals use viruses or spyware downloaded onto unprotected computers. This enables them to control a vast number of software robots around the globe. Once triggered, all of these computers simultaneously bombard the targeted system. A much-publicised example of this occurred in February 2004, when criminal gangs, believed to be operating from Russia and Taiwan, threatened to launch such attacks against several well-known betting websites in the lead up to the Grand National horse race at Aintree, Liverpool. A spokesperson for the National High-Tech Crime Unit put it in the following terms:

> 'It's good old-fashioned blackmail … Companies have paid up in the order of $40,000 (£27,000) to $50,000 at a time.'[44]

Soon after this event, in March 2004, a similar attack was launched against the betting company William Hill before the three-day Cheltenham horse racing festival. The perpetrator had already targeted a number of sites earlier on in the year concerned with betting on sporting events, including American football's annual championship final, the 'Super Bowl'. Following a previous attack which was, in essence, launched to give credence to the threat posed, the William Hill company received an e-mail demanding $10,000 (£5,520) to avoid a repeat attack. Police called it the age-old protection racket with a cyber twist. The Director of incident responses for Cable & Wireless (one of Britain's largest Internet Service Providers) confirmed that this type of crime wave was growing, stating that 'the level of intensity is higher than any we've seen before. They are increasing the force and frequency and sophistication in these attacks.'[45]

As can be seen from these real-life examples, the criminal rewards can be substantial. Betting is reckoned to be the most profitable online medium, apart from pornography. It has been estimated that the online betting industry could be worth $15 billion in western Europe alone by the end of 2005. Such rich pickings attract the gaze of the e-criminal classes.

Those who target computers or computers networks do so either to gain information from them or to cause damage to them. Usually, either the access sought and gained is unauthorised or the modification of the programmes or data is unauthorised. Sometimes, of course, the former precedes the latter. In other words, an e-criminal may first hack into a system in order to damage the data contained within it. A frequent means by which such damage can be done is the release of a virus into the system. It should be noted that this can, of course, be done without hacking. For example, a virus can by attached to an e-mail which, when opened, enters the recipient's computer system and then spreads within it in any number of ways, depending upon its nature. The following real-life examples illustrate the voracity of some viruses and the financial costs which they can leave in their wake.

The Melissa Virus

In March 1999, a 34-year-old American, David Smith, released a virus via e-mail

---

[44] The Times, 24 February 2004.
[45] Yahoo! News, 16 March 2004.

attachment to some of his friends' and colleagues' computers. When they opened up the attachment, a programme was triggered which replicated the e-mail and then sent it to the first 50 addresses in the global address book[46] of those users. It was estimated that the virus spread to more than a million computers worldwide. Although the virus did not seem to cause much damage to individual computers onto which it was downloaded, approximately $80 million of dollars worth of damage was caused by its disruption of networks around the globe. Smith was arrested in April 1999, a week after he had released the virus. At his trial in New Jersey, USA, in May of 2002, Smith was sentenced to 20 months in prison and fined $5,000. This apparently lenient sentence can, to some extent, be explained by the facts that Smith pleaded guilty to the charge in question and had been co-operative with the police in their investigation. He was also deemed to be remorseful about his actions, which he described as a 'colossal mistake'.

The Sobig F Virus

In August 2003, this virus brought many computer systems to a standstill within a few days by clogging up inboxes with the tens of millions of e-mails which it had generated. At its peak, the virus was estimated to be generating approximately 6 per cent of all e-mail sent worldwide (about one in every 17). The virus installed a programme which then downloaded a further, malicious programme.[47] This then acted as a secret server for routing unsolicited e-mails (spam).

The Sasser Worm

In May 2004, an 18-year-old student from Rotenburg in northern Germany was arrested and charged with various offences relating to the 'Sasser Worm'. This virus had caused huge disruption to businesses and organisations during that month. Among its corporate and organisational victims were British Airways, the Maritime and Coastguard Agency, Taiwan's national post office, government departments in Hong Kong and Australia's Railcorp train company. When arrested, Sven Jaschan confessed to being the author of the virus and faced trial on 5 July 2005 in Germany on charges of computer sabotage, data manipulation and disruption of public systems. A 'worm' is a virus which is self-replicating. Indeed, the Sasser Worm did not require a computer user to open a file in order for it to be activated; it was able to invade systems directly via the Internet. Jaschan is thought to have been responsible for approximately 70 per cent of all viruses received worldwide in the first six months of 2004.

So, it can be seen that individual computers, computer systems or networks can be targeted by e-criminals in various ways and for different reasons. Use of the Internet dramatically increases the number of potential victims, the size of criminal gains to be had, and the scale of damage which can be caused, together with its accompanying financial costs to those victims. A final, recent example displays several of these

---

[46] The users in question were all running the Microsoft 'Outlook' personal organiser programme.
[47] Often described as 'malware'.

characteristics and also shows how the alleged e-criminal may, in fact, have been the victim of others.

In March 2003, a 19-year-old man from Dorset, Aaron Caffrey, faced trial at Southwark Crown Court on a charge of unauthorised modification of computer programmes or data.[48] The prosecution alleged that Caffrey had hacked into the computer server at the Port of Houston, Texas, in what was believed to be the first electronic attack to disable part of a country's infrastructure. The court heard that the teenager's intended target was a female chatroom user, called Bookie, with whom he had argued online over remarks she made about the USA. Caffrey, who suffers from Asperger's syndrome,[49] became upset because he felt protective over his much-loved American girlfriend, her people and her country. The jury was told that Caffrey had allegedly written an 'attack script' and posted it on his website. The attack had to travel through various intermediary computer systems to gain strength before finally reaching its intended victim's personal computer. One of those intermediary servers was housed at the Port of Houston, which is one of the largest shipping ports in the world. This was a denial of service attack by nature; it had the effect of freezing the port's web service, which contained vital data for shipping, mooring companies and navigational support firms. An investigation by US authorities had traced the computer's Internet provider number to a computer at Caffrey's home address. However, in his defence, the accused claimed that an unidentified party had planted the instructions for the attack script without his knowledge. He said that, in the past, he had hacked into friends' websites legally, at their request, to test their server security, but was not and never had been a 'cracker'.[50] The jury acquitted him.

The computer as a criminal storage device

As we have seen, some may use their computers as criminal tools or weapons to attack other computers, systems and networks. Others may, instead, simply use them as a store of information relating to their criminal activities. A smuggler of cigarettes or alcohol may keep lists of customers and contacts on his personal computer (from which he may also communicate with them via e-mail). A drug dealer may do the same. A hacker may store on his computer items of pirated software, details of stolen passwords, lists of stolen credit card numbers or programmes containing viruses which he has written. Paedophiles often store a great number of image files on their computers. A much-publicised example of this arose in the case of Paul Gadd, also known as Gary Glitter, who was sentenced to four months' imprisonment and fined £9,000 in 1999, following conviction for the possession of indecent photographs of children.[51] His crime was detected when he put his computer in for repair to a company called PC World. Many thousands of such images were discovered on the hard disk and the company contacted the police.

---

[48] Under s3 Computer Misuse Act 1990.
[49] A form of autism.
[50] A term used by legal hackers for illegal hackers.
[51] Under s160 Criminal Justice Act 1988.

The detection of e-Crime will be considered in detail in the following chapter. For now, it must be pointed out that the advances in technology have not only helped the criminals but have also enabled law enforcement agencies, through forensic computer science, to gather and scrutinise information which may not have been available to them in previous times. For example, if a criminal believes that by simply deleting a computer file he is destroying it forever in the same way that he would a paper file when he throws it onto a fire, he would be wrong. Computer forensic experts can recover deleted data and reconstruct activities on the Internet. Furthermore, since personal computers can store millions of pages of information, the amount of material which can be scrutinised in one location is vastly increased.

8.2 Who are the e-Criminals?

There seems to be a popular myth which pervades public opinion on this matter. As Ian Lloyd pointed out some years ago:

'The stereotypical depiction of a computer hacker tends to be that of a male teenager in a greasy T-shirt and torn jeans who spends hours slumped over a terminal, eyes gazing fixedly at the green glow of the VDU monitor. Banks, military installations, universities, companies and financial institutions fall before his relentless onslaught. Nowhere is safe, no one can keep him out, no one knows the scale of the threat, the silent deadly menace stalks the networks. Very often, however … the reality is more prosaic.'[52]

As it continues to advance at pace, technology itself widens the class of e-criminals. The criminal landscape is expanding; the Internet makes international criminals out of local villains. In turn, the pool of potential victims deepens. The fraudster can lure millions of people to his spoof website and the political extremist can deliver a 'hate speech' to a global audience. Technology has not only provided new ways of committing old crimes but has brought with it new forms of criminal behaviour, such as hacking and the spreading of computer viruses. The degree of expertise required to commit e-crimes has often been mythically overestimated. For instance, the Internet has delivered a range of websites which contain either instructions on how to make the e-criminal tools, or the tools themselves, readymade. The UK's National Criminal Intelligence Service recently confirmed that such websites:

'… contain downloadable prepared viruses, worms and Trojans. These "point and click" attack tools have removed the need for detailed knowledge of code programming, and have allowed a new breed of much younger hackers, nicknamed "Script Kiddies", to develop. The development and proliferation of such tools in part explains the ever-increasing incidence of such attacks and the rising costs to business and public Internet users.'[53]

Thus, it can be seen that e-criminals differ in terms of age and expertise. They also, of course, have different criminal motives and ambitions. In the same report, the NCIS stated that:

'Some criminals are idle while others are energetic, some are stupid while others are clever. It should

---

[52] Lloyd, I, 'Information Technology Law' (2000), 3rd Ed, Butterworths, p200.
[53] NCIS Report (2003): UK Threat Assessment of Serious Organised Crime – see: http://www.ncis.co.uk/ukta/2003/default.asp.

not be surprising therefore that some stick to what they have always done and feel secure in doing and possibly enjoy, while others are constantly looking to branch out or simply cannot resist every opportunity to make a dishonest penny, in some instances progressing from one type of crime to another, but often simply diversifying into new areas.'[54]

In order to understand who the e-criminals are, one must be aware of the fact that cybercrime has brought with it a change in the way that criminals, law enforcement agencies and society as a whole view crime and criminal behaviour. Returning to a previous example, a criminal who uses a computer to defraud another person will be viewed in very much the same way as the 'traditional' fraudster; he could have achieved the same result by speaking to them on the telephone or personally meeting with them. However, if that same criminal begins to use the Internet or other web-based information and communication technologies (ICTs) as a means to perpetrate his fraudulent scheme, suddenly he gains the opportunity to defraud a vast number of people in any number of locations around the world, with no significant added expense to himself. As Thomas and Loader put it:

'... using e-mail or the WWW to defraud hundreds of thousands of people, the use of the Net to spread information inexpensively, anonymously, or in great numbers all change the fundamental nature of the crime being committed, not merely the means by which it is done.'[55]

E-criminals fall into different categories; their powers, plans and pursuits vary. It is appropriate to view them in their separate groups in order to gain a clearer picture of what drives them in their criminal activities.

'Incidental' e-criminals

This group is comprised of those individuals who use computer technology in a basic, incidental way. For example, the use of e-mail for the purposes of setting up a drug deal or other conspiratorial communications, perhaps with an attachment of details which are crucial to the plan. The crimes themselves may be viewed as serious but the use of the technology is, in essence, supportive and facilitative rather than truly instrumental.

Hackers

These individuals use ICTs to break into computer systems. Their purposes for doing so distinguish them from each other. Some hackers seek to gain illegal entry into systems in order to explore them, viewing the information which they hold, and reporting back to their peers about how they managed to 'break in'. They do not usually have an intention to cause damage to the system or the data contained within it, and the satisfaction and kudos gained from trespassing onto that system is the only reward which they seek. It should be noted, however, that the activity of hacking often leaves behind a vulnerability in the system which can then be exploited by others; a 'hole in the fence'.

---

[54] Ibid.
[55] Thomas, D and Loader, B, 'Cybercrime: Law Enforcement, Security and Surveillance in the Information Age', (2003) Routledge, p6.

There are, however, malicious hackers, sometimes referred to in hacking circles as 'crackers', who deliberately cause damage to systems or data. For example, once in, they might delete or erase files or publicise confidential information which they find. Such individuals may also be perpetrating fraud, spreading computer viruses or attempting to shut down websites or ISPs by launching denial of service attacks. Some individuals, often referred to as 'hackivists', enter websites in order to deface them in furtherance of their cause; cybervandals with an activist agenda.

The most legendary of computer hackers is a man called Kevin Mitnick. He was arrested by the FBI in 1995 after a year-long hunt for him. He was already a fugitive from justice, having vanished after violating the terms of his probation for a hacking conviction. For years, he had been hacking into systems, including those of some of the world's biggest computer firms and branches of the US government. However, he never sought to cause damage to the systems which he hacked into; he simply studied confidential information within them and then disappeared without trace. He was often in a position to steal millions of dollars, but never did. Eventually, he was caught because he tried to crack the network of a rival hacker who was, in fact, working with the police. Mitnick was sentenced to five years' imprisonment, including eight months in solitary confinement. This was an unprecedented punishment for hacking. Moreover, when he was released in early 2000, he was placed on probation, the main term of the order being that he was forbidden from using a telephone or computer or connecting to the Internet for three years. In an interview in December 2002, Mitnick was asked whether he would do it all again; he replied that he would not, but added:

> 'Do I actually feel sad, emotionally sad for doing it? No. Do I regret it? In a sense, for the trouble I caused people. But not for looking at stuff I shouldn't have looked at.'[56]

Mitnick, now aged 39, has turned from poacher to gamekeeper. He has written a book, entitled *The Art of Deception*, which presents itself as a manual to help companies defeat hackers. In it he states that, above all, the hacker's most lethal weapon is 'social engineering'; the ability to trick people into giving information that they shouldn't give, such as passwords and other peoples' credit card numbers.

Many people criticised the sentencing decision in his case, claiming that the punishment was out of all proportion to his crimes. However, as Oliver Burkeman (the journalist who interviewed him on this occasion) explained:

> '... the Internet was young, the fears it evoked still nebulous and, worst of all, Mitnick was making the FBI look stupid.'[57]

It would be inaccurate to class Mitnick as a malicious hacker; his main motives seem to have been curiosity and intellectual challenge. Indeed, when asked why he did it, he has often simply stated that he did it for fun. Even those hackers who do, in fact, cause damage to systems do not often harbour any real malice. Research into the psychology of virus writers suggests that perhaps their only consistent characteristic is 'a fundamental disconnect between virus writing and acknowledging the large-scale

---

[56] *The Guardian*, 13 December 2002.
[57] Ibid.

consequences of those actions'.[58] The same research has also shown that that the stereotypical image of the virus writer as a teenage boy with no social life, wreaking electronic havoc, is simply inaccurate. From her research, Sarah Gordon reports that most virus writers are typical for their age, are on good terms with friends and family, and are often contributors to their local community. She puts forward the opinion that many malicious hackers have a borderline criminal view of the world and do not share mainstream ethical norms. She says that 'their judgment processes might be different, as well as their perception of risk and reward'.[59]

Notwithstanding these comments, it should not be forgotten how potentially destructive and dangerous computer viruses can be. For example, the SoBig.F virus was so powerful and widespread that it actually had the effect of profoundly slowing up the Internet. Further examples include the Welchia or Nachi worm, which was blamed for halting Air Canada's check-in system, Maryland commuter trains and a US Naval network, and the Slammer virus, which crashed the computers at an Ohio nuclear plant in early 2003.

Information merchants and mercenaries[60]

As their titles suggest, these are traders in information. Their motive is usually greed, seeking payment from the highest bidder for the information which they have stolen. They may offer up for sale pirated software, personal identity information or corporate secrets. They can be 'freelance' or perhaps employed by a company to indulge in corporate espionage against its rivals. Companies have always jealously guarded their trade secrets. The classic example is Coca Cola plc, whose rivals may know the ingredients of its main product but still to this day do not know the precise details of the process by which they are blended together. One could hazard a guess that the two busiest sections of Microsoft plc are the security wing of its research and development unit and the litigation department. The activities of information merchants and mercenaries will often be similar to those of other e-criminals. For example, hacking will usually be the means to their criminal ends (eg transfer of monies, identity theft, computer software piracy).

Members of terrorist, extremist or other deviant groups

Such people make illegal use of ICTs for political, social or sexual reasons. Terrorists may simply use the technology to assist them in their planning of illegal activities, or for waging electronic war on their enemies. Extremist groups, such as those from the far right of the political spectrum, may use the technology to promote and publicise 'hate speech'. For example, neo-Nazi groups consistently voice their racist views online and incite violence against minority groups (eg foreign workers and asylum seekers).

---

[58] Per Sarah Gordon, a Florida-based researcher for the Symantec Antivirus Research Centre: BBC News, 5 November 2003.
[59] Ibid.
[60] A description used by Thomas, D and Loader, B, 'Cybercrime: Law Enforcement, Security and Surveillance in the Information Age', (2003) Routledge, p7.

Information warfare, such as 'holocaust denial', is a means by which they seek to justify their causes and to recruit new members to their movements. Far right groups have also shown a tendency towards anti-central government protest and the promotion of isolationist policies. Michael Whine points out that (other) noted commentators[61] had some years ago suggested that:

> '... a new virtual racism has evolved through the medium of the Internet, that the interpenetration of various nationalist movements is amplified within Cyberspace, and that it is possible for far right groups of markedly different types to establish common networks and ideological alliances, particularly around a shared common enemy.'[62]

Other groups which fall into this category include those that indulge in and promote sexually deviant behaviour. The Internet has greatly boosted the creation and dissemination of child pornographic material. It has also increased the number and breadth of 'paedophile rings', whilst simultaneously providing such individuals with further opportunities to locate and target potential victims; for example, by 'grooming' child victims in chatrooms.

8.3 Where Do the Threats Come From?

For many years, the accepted view was that 'by far the greatest threat to a computer system comes from within – that is from employees'.[63] It was supported by statistics gathered by a number of organisations, including the UK Audit Commission. For example, in 1994 the Commision conducted a survey which revealed that external perpetrators were only responsible for 15 per cent of reported incidents, with the remaining 85 per cent being split between different categories of insiders.

However, as Steven Furnell points out, 'with the increasing role of the Internet in recent years (which serves to make systems more visible to outsiders), the apparent trend has changed dramatically'.[64] In the light of the great advances in Internet and web-based ICTs, the e-criminal landscape looks significantly different from how it used to. Again, statistics support this assertion.

- The results of an Audit Commission Survey in 1998 revealed that the proportion of outside abusers had risen to 39 per cent.

- The 1999 CSI/FBI Computer Crime and Security Survey revealed that 39 per cent of incidents came from outside.

- The 2001 CSI/FBI Computer Crime and Security Survey revealed that 47 per cent of incidents came from outside.

- The 2002 CSI/FBI Computer Crime and Security Survey revealed that nearly two-thirds of attacks on the 503 respondents' computer systems came from outside.

---

[61] Back, L, Keith, M and Solomos, J (1996) 'Technology, Race and Neo-Fascism in a Digital Age: The New Modalities of Racist Culture', Patterns of Prejudice 30 (2), Institute for Jewish Policy Research (JPR), London.

[62] Whine, M, 'Far right extremists on the Internet,' 'Cybercrime: Law Enforcement, Security and Surveillance in the Information Age', (2003) Routledge, p235.

[63] Bainbridge, D, 'Introduction to Computer Law', (2000) 4th ed, Longman, p285.

[64] Furnell, S, 'Cybercrime: Vandalizing the Information Society', (2002) Addison Wesley, p25.

- The 2004 E-CrimeWatch Survey, conducted in the US by the Software Engineering Institute,[65] revealed that (where the sources were identified) respondents reported that 71 per cent of attacks came from outsiders and 29 per cent from insiders.[66]

It is appropriate to look in some detail at the most up-to-date e-Crime surveys that have been conducted in the UK. These are the National High-Tech Crime Unit's surveys of 2004 and 2005, each entitled *High-Tech Crime – The Impact on UK Business*.[67] The 2004 survey, which was published in February of that year, surveyed 201 medium and large-sized companies in the UK. It was designed to mirror the CSI/FBI survey to enable cross-comparisons.

On the specific issue of where the threats of e-Crime come from, the survey asked the respondents to clarify, where possible, whether particular types of e-criminal activity came from within their organisations or from an outside source. The responses were recorded and reported in the following way. (It should be noted that the respondents were asked to describe who had committed such acts. If more than one incident had occurred in the previous 12 months, respondents were asked to think of just the last incident, in order to make the information as accurate as possible.) The numbers in the 'Internal' 'Both', 'External' and 'Don't Know' columns are listed in terms of the percentage of each criminal activity from each source.

Type of Criminal Activity	Internal	Both	External	Don't Know
Virus attacks	4	9	77	10
Denial of service attacks	12	6	68	15
Corporate website spoofing attacks	0	0	96	4
Criminal use of Internet	62	10	7	21
Theft of data	48	8	16	28
Financial fraud	21	18	25	36
Unauthorised access, or penetration of, systems	22	0	56	22
Sabotage of, or damage to, data or networks	53	0	20	27
Unauthorised access to, or penetration of, websites	9	4	45	45

The NHCTU's reflections upon these figures were as follows:

---

[65] A federally funded research and development centre, sponsored by the US Department of Defense and operated by Carnegie Mellon University.
[66] See: http://www.cert.org/about/ecrime.html.
[67] See: http://www.nhtcu.org.

'Acts of sabotage and data theft were most often committed internally. In addition, over a third of recent incidents of financial fraud were either wholly or partially committed by employees. Employees, rather than outsiders, typically were responsible for criminal use of the Internet. This rather wide category was generally interpreted by respondents to mean inappropriate use or abuse of the Internet by staff.'[68]

The figures also show that a really significant proportion of the e-Crime threat continues to come from sources outside these organisations. Outsiders were, in particular, targeting systems and websites in order to release viruses, to hack, to spoof websites, and to deny services. The 2005 survey, published in April, surveyed 142 companies in the UK (each company having 100 or more employees). It reveals similar trends in the nature and sources of e-criminal activity during the year 2004. Of particular note is the fact that, even when virus attacks are excluded, the survey reveals that most computer security incidents originated externally. However, data theft, criminal use of the Internet, financial and telecom frauds were more likely to be committed by employees.

8.4 The Need for Security

The facts show that more people use the Internet everyday and that an increasing number of organisations rely upon the Internet and other networked systems to conduct their business. This, in turn, means that the potential number of individual or corporate victims of e-Crime continues to grow. In the light of these things, the growing need for security measures is an obvious adjunct to the pursuit of profit and e-communication as a whole. There are a number of reasons why IT security should play a central role in corporate (and personal) planning. Lack of attention to it provides further opportunities to e-criminals. E-mails, programmes or websites may be masquerading as something which they are not. The bona fide recipients and users of them can be tricked into giving personal information which can then be used for criminal ends. The disclosure of such information can, for example, lead to identity theft, credit card fraud or even blackmail. Some programmes can actually monitor the keystrokes of the end user to capture crucial information, such as passwords. Websites can be defaced or spoofed, and systems disabled by denial of service attacks. Last, but not least, comes the ever-present threat of virus infection.

There are various mechanisms which can be used by individuals or corporations as security measures to combat e-Crime; for example, data encryption. In the UK, the Audit Commission has continued to promote the issue of IT security. In its survey report of 1998,[69] it voiced concerns about the lack of basic control safeguards and effective monitoring within some of the respondent organisations. Quoting the maxim that 'prevention is better than cure', the Commission highlighted a number of ways in which organisations could better protect themselves against e-criminal attack. Firstly, that regular risk analysis should play a central role in any IT security policy. Secondly, that the development and implementation of secured and controlled environments should be supported by staff computer awareness training, focusing on risks and

---

[68] See: http://www.nhtcu.org/NOPSurvey.pdf.
[69] UK Audit Commission (1998): Ghost in the Machine – An Analysis of IT Fraud and Abuse.

precautions. Thirdly, that responsibility for security and developing secure access should be assigned to specific people (Computer Security Officers (CSOs)). Fourthly, that the necessary financial commitment to security aspects should be made; low budget policies produce high risks. And lastly, that an organisation's IT security policy must be rigorously implemented.

However, a rather worrying discovery made by the NHTCU's 2004 survey was that only 30 per cent of the 201 respondent companies had a policy in place that requires use of data encryption of their corporate e-mail communications (on the fixed corporate networks or on portable devices). In the light of this figure, it was reported that:

> 'Most companies (70 per cent) believe that sufficient resources are being invested to prevent computer-enabled crime. The financial services sector, in particular, believes that it is investing enough. To some extent, this echoes the relatively low impact that such crimes are perceived as having, but it is a contrast with the actual cost impact that such crimes are estimated to have.'[70]

The same percentage of the respondent companies in the 2005 survey believed that they were spending sufficient funds on e-Crime prevention. The majority of these companies have anti-virus measures and firewalls in place. More sophisticated technologies are generally limited to larger companies, and biometrics are rarely used. Of particular note is the response that 41 per cent of these companies have implemented data encryption for portable devices which attach to, or communicate with, their networks (eg laptops, notebooks, PDAs and mobile phones).

Information Technology security and e-Crime are inextricably linked. Any credible system will seek to preserve the holy trinity of IT security: confidentiality, integrity and availability. It is appropriate to look at these three tenets in more detail before assessing the scale of the e-Crime problem.

Clearly, a key characteristic of a piece of information can be its confidential nature. The consequences of that information falling into the wrong hands can be catastrophic. For example, the US Secretary of State, Donald Rumsfeld, paid a surprise visit to frontline troops in three locations (Mosul, Tikrit and Falluja) in Iraq. If enemy forces had become aware of that visit in advance or, more specifically, the details of the itinerary, a real risk of assassination would have arisen.

A system may house highly sensitive information about individuals themselves. For example, as the title of the organisation denotes, members of 'Alcoholics Anonymous' initially seek and then receive treatment for their addiction in confidence. Any revelation of their membership could bring with it serious consequences in their personal or professional lives. Alternatively, it may be the location of the individual that is secret. For example, a witness protection programme simply cannot operate without strict safeguards against the release of information relating to alternative identities given to its subjects and the situation of the 'safehouses' into which they are placed. A more prosaic example might be where an employee suffers from an illness or condition, the details of which they wish to be kept confidential in the workplace. Take the teacher who is dyslexic or the doctor who is receiving treatment for a form of cancer; each may

---

[70] See footnote 68 of this chapter.

share this information with their employer but ask for it to go no further. Equally, corporate bodies themselves may seek to 'hide' information which could indicate to their rivals that they may be struggling to hold their position in the market place; corporate spies will be hunting for this and other information. Of course, confidential information can also be used to corrupt or blackmail people.

The integrity of a system, and the data contained within it, is of upmost importance. People who use the system or have information about them stored on it must be confident that it is secure. As noted previously, malicious hackers may seek to gain entry to a system in order then to modify its programmes or data. The following case, referred to in the Audit Commission's 1994 survey,[71] demonstrates the potential dangers posed by a lack of integrity in systems and data. A nurse hacked into a computer system in order to make unauthorised modifications to the data within it. This person prescribed drugs for a patient which would have been potentially life-threatening to them, if taken. There were also some changes made to other patients' records. Thankfully, the drugs were not administered because the unauthorised modifications were discovered in time. The nurse was prosecuted under s3 Computer Misuse Act 1990.

It must be pointed out that the institution itself may face legal action as well. For example, the Data Protection Act 1998 contains criminal offences relating to the unauthorised obtaining or disclosure of personal data, procuring such disclosure, or the selling of such data.[72] One notable change that has beeen made is that the mens rea of these offences now includes knowledge or recklessness,[73] whereas previously it was simply comprised of either knowledge or belief. In short, an organisation can be prosecuted for failing to protect data that is stored in its system.

Systems and data must, of course, be accessible to authorised users. For example, a customer's credit rating is information which is crucial to a mortgagee's decision on whether to lend them money to purchase a property. Returning to medical issues, a patient's health records must be available to an anaesthetist before an operation, so that they can determine whether the patient is allergic to any particular drug; ignorance of such matters could lead to serious injury or, indeed, death in the operating theatre. Clearly, the data itself must be accurate but the system must be robust enough to withstand attacks upon it. In short, there must be proper safeguards against system failure; a successful denial of service attack upon a local health authority could lead to numerous catastrophes within a very short space of time.

The importance of IT security has long been recognised and continues to be a crucial element of the strategic thinking in the fight against e-Crime. Evidence of this can be found in explanatory notes to legislation, commissioned reports, and press releases from governments, legislatures and law enforcement agencies around the world. For example, in its draft Green Paper on Information Security, the European Commission stated the following:

---

[71] UK Audit Commission Survey (1994): Opportunity Makes a Thief.

[72] See s55.

[73] *Cunningham* recklessness is the only form of recklessness recognised by English criminal law since the House of Lords' decision in *R v Gemmell and Richards* [2003] UKHL 50.

'Individual, corporate and national wealth expresses itself increasingly in the form of information. The growth and performance of an estimated two out of three of the economy relies upon manufacturing or services heavily dependent on information technology, telecommunications and broadcasting, and therefore depends critically on the accuracy, security and trustworthiness of information. This is of as great importance and interest for individuals as for commerce, industry and public administrations. Correspondingly, the protection of information in all its aspects, here referred to as Information Security, has become a central policy issue and a major concern worldwide.'[74]

Lastly, the need for effective vetting of potential employees must also be recognised. Recently, the Financial Services Authority confirmed the existence of a growing trend. Individuals involved in organised crime are applying for jobs in the financial sector in order to commit fraud. Where this is not possible, existing employees are sometimes corrupted through bribery or placed under duress by these criminal gangs. The need for continued monitoring of the workforce is further illustrated by the fact that the latest personal organisers and mobile phones can be connected to computers in order to steal data, such as bank account details and corporate secrets. In the light of the FSA's recent survey of the security systems of 18 firms, including High Street banks, insurers, fund management firms and stockbrokers, the Chief Executive of the NCC group, Rob Cotton, stated that:

'Companies are focussing their spending on securing systems from external attack via sources such as the Internet and are not sufficiently aware of the threat posed by people with internal access.'[75]

8.5 What is the Scale of the e-Crime Problem?

The development and growth of ICTs has brought with it changes in criminal behaviour within the electronic arena. In the early days of the computer age, the technology simply provided further opportunities to commit pre-existing, 'traditional' crimes, such as theft and fraud offences. However, the technological advances soon began to spawn new forms of e-criminal activity. For example, it has been said of the Internet that:

'It has created an entirely new environment which has generated new opportunities for the development of novel forms of behaviour. These activities include the unauthorized appropriation of intellectual property such as visual imagery, software tools and music products. Such activities will also include the waging of information warfare via the illegal invasion of computer space and the destruction of materials within it. In each case, the activity is largely free of traditional and terrestrial constraint. As such, the behaviours tend to lie outside our existing experiences, and they demand both new forms of understanding and also responses.'[76]

Over the last decade there has been a significant increase in the number of reported cases of e-Crime. The UK Audit Commission has conducted surveys every three to four years on the reported incidents of computer crime and abuse. The resulting statistics bear testament to the trend. The following figures were released in the Commission's 1998 survey report.[77] Overall, 46 per cent of the 900 UK respondents to the survey reported some form of an incident.

---

[74] See: http://www.cordis.lu/infosec/src/info1.htm, para 1.
[75] See: http://news.bbc.co.uk/go/pr/fr/-/1/hi/business/4005355.stm, p2.
[76] Wall, D, 'Policing the Internet: Maintaining Order and Law on the Cyberbeat – the Internet, Law and Society' (Edited by Akdeniz, Walker and Wall), Pearson (2000), p156.
[77] UK Audit Commission (1998): Ghost in the Machine – An Analysis of IT Fraud and Abuse.

	Fraud	Viruses	Theft	Hacking	Other	Total
1984	60	–	17	–	–	77
1987	61	–	22	35	–	118
1990	73	54	27	26	–	180
1994	108	261	121	47	–	537
1998	67	247	88	56	52	510

The Commission then produced an update on IT abuse in 2001 via a survey that was based on the responses of 688 business organisations.[78] It was interesting to note that this survey revealed that, despite the increase in e-Crime overall, incidents of hacking had actually reduced in number – a similar trend started to emerge in US surveys at that time.[79]

The NHTCU's surveys of 2004 and 2005 have now provided us with fresh data to help assess the current scale of e-criminal activity.[80] In the 2004 survey, it was stated that 83 per cent of the 201 respondent companies had experienced at least one of the computer-based crimes that they were asked about. It was stated that 'predictably, the one type of computer-based crime mentioned by 77 per cent of those interviewed was an attack by a computer virus. All types and sizes of organisation reported this problem.'[81] The figures listed below show the percentage rates of computer-related crimes that were experienced by those organisations in 2003.

Type of Computer-Related Crime	Percentage Affected
Virus attacks	77 per cent
Denial of service attacks	17 per cent
Financial fraud	14 per cent
Criminal use of Internet	14 per cent
Theft of data	12 per cent
Corporate website spoofing attacks	12 per cent
Unauthorised access to, or penetration of, systems	9 per cent
Sabotage of, or damage to, data or networks	7 per cent
Spam attacks	3 per cent

---

[78] UK Audit Commission Update (2001): yourbusiness@risk: An Update on IT Abuse.
[79] See, for example, the CSI/FBI Survey (2001).
[80] See: http://www.nhtcu.org.
[81] Ibid.

The survey revealed that the larger organisations (with 5,000 plus employees) were generally much more likely than smaller companies to experience crime such as theft of data; sabotage of, or damage to, data or networks; or unauthorised access to, or misuse of, corporate websites or systems. Over a quarter of the financial services organisations reported some form of financial fraud, compared with 14 per cent of the organisations overall. Moreover, it seemed that the financial services organisations were much more likely to be victims of website spoofing. One third of them reported incidents of this e-Crime, compared with only 12 per cent of the sample as a whole. Another type of organisation which reported above-average incidence of financial fraud were the telecommunications companies. Also, not surprisingly, they were significantly more likely to be the victims of denial of service attacks.

Type of Computer-Related Crime	Average Number of Incidents per Org.
Virus attacks	255
Unauthorised access to, or penetration of, websites	185
Financial fraud	145
Criminal use of Internet	98
Corporate website spoofing attacks	10
Theft of data	6
Denial of service attacks	5
Sabotage of, or damage to, data or networks	3
Unauthorised access to, or penetration of, systems	1

The figures from the 2005 survey on the percentage rates of computer-related crimes are listed below (please note this year's survey has dropped two types of computer-related crime (spam attacks and corporate website spoofing), added two new types (website defacement and telecoms fraud) and expanded or re-named other types).

Type of Computer-Related Crime	Percentage Affected
Viruses, Worms or Trojans	83 per cent
Use of company systems for criminal or other illegitimate purposes	15 per cent
Denial of service	14 per cent
Unauthorised access to, or penetration of, systems	11 per cent
Theft of information or data	10 per cent
Financial fraud	9 per cent
Telecoms fraud	6 per cent
Sabotage of, or damage to, data or networks	4 per cent
Website defacement	2 per cent

The figures from the 2005 survey on the average number of incidents of each type of computer-related crime experienced per organisation in 2004 are listed below.

Type of Computer-Related Crime	Average Number of Incidents per Org.
Viruses, Worms or Trojans	2,686
Financial fraud	35
Use of company systems for criminal or other illegitimate purposes	8
Unauthorised access to, or penetration of, systems	6
Website defacement	3
Sabotage of, or damage to, data or networks	3
Denial of service	2
Theft of information or data	2
Telecoms fraud	2

The most notable aspect of these latest figures is the number of virus attacks which were launched against these organisations during the last year. On average, each of the respondent companies was subject to a virus attack seven times a day.

Across the Atlantic, the surveys recently conducted in the US reveal the same overall trend of an increase in e-criminal activity. The Software Engineering Institute's 2004 E-Crime Watch Survey,[82] which polled 476 Chief Security Officers (CSOs) and

---

[82] See: http://www.cert.org/about/ecrime.html.

senior security executives, reported that no less than 43 per cent of the respondents had seen an increase in e-Crimes and intrusions from the previous year.[83] Soon afterwards, the Computer Security Institute (CSI) and the US Federal Bureau of Investigation (FBI) reported the results of their 2004 survey (this survey has been conducted by these organisations annually for the last nine years).[84] It polls security experts in US corporations, government agencies, universities, financial and medical institutions about a wide range of security issues. The trend of a reduction in hacking incidents seems to have continued over the last three years. According to the 2004 survey, just 53 per cent of the 494 US computer security practitioners acknowledged the unauthorised use of a computer in their organisation within the previous 12 months; the smallest percentage recorded since 1999. It was also found that denial of service attacks were the most costly for organisations and that fewer organisations are reporting computer intrusions to law enforcement. New questions in the survey revealed that 15 per cent of respondents reported that wireless networks at their organisation had been abused and 10 per cent experienced the misuse of public Web applications. This survey also pointed towards an overall increase in the amount of e-Crime.

The link between levels of IT security and e-Crime becomes ever clearer. In May 2005, the publisher of CSO magazine, Bob Bragdon, made the following comments in the light of the findings from the 2004 E-Crime Watch Survey[85] which he had just released into the public domain:

'The increase in e-Crime over the past year again demonstrates the need for corporate, government and non-governmental organisations to develop coordinated efforts between their IT and security departments to maximize defence and minimise e-Crime impact. There is a lot of security spending going on, but not much planning. It's essential for chief security officers and information technology professionals to find the most manageable, responsive and cost effective way to stop e-Crime from occurring.'

8.6 What is the Impact of e-Crime?

E-criminal activity may impact upon individual and corporate victims in several ways. The most obvious loss will usually be financial. However, there are other potential consequences, including disruption of services, loss of data, personal anguish or embarrassment, and damage to corporate image. It must be recognised that financial loss is concomitant with most of these other consequences. For example, damage to corporate image will usually have a direct effect upon customer and trading relations, the ability to raise financial capital (in particular, it could effect the company's share price), and ultimately, therefore, the company's standing in the market place.

For these reasons, financial loss is often used as the primary indicator of the impact of e-Crime. In the US, the 2004 E-Crime Watch Survey[86] gave a snapshot of the sizeable financial impact that e-criminal activity can have. The 476 respondents to the survey reported that e-Crime cost their organisations, in total, $666 million. In the UK,

---

[83] Ibid.
[84] See: http://www.gocsi.com.
[85] See footnote 82 above.
[86] Ibid.

the NHTCU's 2004 survey told a similar story.[87] Before looking at the figures in more detail, it is important first to understand how the respondent organisations were asked to assess the financial impact of e-Crime upon them. The NHTCU invited them to take the following into matters into account:

*   the cost of service and support;

*   end-user down time;

*   reputational damage (including brand image, shareholder value and loss of clients).

Respondents were asked to provide cost estimates within ranges, based on the spread of responses in the CSI/FBI study in the US[88] and using experience of previous related studies by NOP World. The following figures show the estimated costs of computer-enabled crime across the 494 respondent organisations in 2003.

Type of Computer-Enabled Crime	Estimated Cost
Financial fraud	£121 million
Unauthorised access to, or penetration of, systems	£472,000
Sabotage of, or damage to, data or networks	£802,000
Unauthorised access to, or penetration of, websites	£949,000
Other crime	£8.1 million
Virus attacks	£27.8 million
Denial of service attacks	£1.3 million
Criminal use of Internet	£23 million
Theft of data	£6.6 million

It can be seen from these figures that there is real variation in the level of impact according to the type of crime. It is important to explain why the results are dominated by the figures for financial fraud; the answer comes from detailed analysis of the statistics. Nearly one-third of the 201 respondents were financial services organisations. Of these, three companies in particular reported that they had suffered large losses to this type of crime. The collective financial impact upon them was some £60 million.

The total financial impact of e-Crime across all of the respondent organisations was estimated at £195,153,500. This crudely translates into around £1 million per organisation. Clearly, with the aforementioned prevalence of financial fraud within only a small proportion of those organisations, that average figure is somewhat misleading when viewed on its own. The NHTCU recognised this, but pointed out that

---

[87] See footnote 80 above.
[88] See footnote 84 above.

'nevertheless, a sizeable number of organisations are seeing an impact in the tens of thousand of pounds'.[89]

The figures from the 2005 survey reveal a continued growth in the financial impact of high-tech crime. While malware (malicious programmes) caused the largest financial losses because of the sheer volume of attacks, financial fraud and denial of service attacks were much more costly per incident.

8.7 Conclusions

It can be seen that e-Crime poses difficult, complex questions for society as a whole and the criminal justice system, in particular. Governments and legislatures are charged with the demanding task of trying to legally shadow advancements in technology and the new forms of e-criminal activity which accompany them. The evidence from a number of surveys points towards a continuing trend: e-Crime is increasing every year.

It must be pointed out that the true scale of e-Crime is impossible to assess with any real accuracy. The reason for this is that so much e-criminal activity remains unreported. This is usually referred to as the 'dark figure' of e-Crime and there are some clear reasons for its existence. Firstly, the technology itself provides the more sophisticated e-criminals with the means to avoid detection. Secondly, many victims of e-Crime will not want to admit that they have fallen prey to the e-criminals. Companies are often loath to report e-criminal activity to the police because they fear that any resulting publicity will damage their corporate image. However, it is worth noting that the NHTCU's 2005 survey reveals that companies are becoming more concerned about the effect that security incidents might have on their ability to do business than any accompanying risks of damage to their reputations. In the truly global market place that has been created by ICTs, a company that is shown to be vulnerable in terms of IT security can quickly lose its market position and, possibly, suffer the fatal injury of insolvency. For example, a company such as Amazon.com relies completely upon its electronic mail order services in its business of selling books around the world. A well-publicised breach of IT security could lead to it losing millions of customers within a day, a striking irony being that the information and communications technology itself would spread the bad news extremely fast. Lastly, by its nature, e-criminal activity can create jurisdictional and extraditional problems.[90] Long gone are the days when the class of international criminals was small and exclusive. In the e-criminal world, anyone with a personal computer and a connection to the Internet can offend around the globe.

---

[89] See footnote 80 above.
[90] See Chapter 9 of this book.

9 The Detection and Prosecution of e-Crime

9.1 Introduction

9.2 Discovering the Identity and Location of e-criminals

9.3 Jurisdiction

9.4 The Task of Gathering Evidence

9.5 Computer Forensics

9.6 Presenting the Evidence in Court

9.7 The Investigators

9.8 International Cooperation and Harmonisation of e-criminal laws

9.9 The Council of Europe's Convention on Cybercrime

9.1 Introduction

A number of practical and legal problems may confront those who pursue suspected e-criminals. For example, if the alleged perpetrator is located in one country and the 'victim' in another, there may be real difficulty in trying to establish the identity of the wrongdoer and of obtaining enough evidence to support a conviction, together with complex jurisdictional issues.

The art and process of pursuit can be further complicated by other matters. For instance, the rapid pace of technological change can present the e-criminal with a head start. The law enforcement agencies require the technical expertise and the resources to react to such changes.[1] They also, of course, require the legislative bodies to create new law or to adapt the existing law to clear a path for the prosecution of these new e-criminal activities. It must also be noted that the sophisticated e-criminal will continue to search for technological ways to hide his identity, conceal his crimes, cover his tracks, or make good his escape.

Technological change does not only benefit the 'bad guys'. Information and communications technologies have provided law enforcement agencies with useful weapons in the fight against e-Crime. For example, the Internet has enabled online investigators to find offenders who leave their digital fingerprints in cyberspace. It has also given them some of the benefits which have been exploited by the criminals themselves, such as the ability to remain anonymous or to adopt alternative identities. The investigation, in 2002, into paedophile rings on the Internet, codenamed 'Operation Ore', used a number of investigative tactics to identify suspects. For

---

[1] A recent study, commissioned by the all party e-commerce lobby group, EURIM, has reported that there is a huge backlog of e-Crimes and a serious shortage of skills to deal with them – see 'Police need more e-Crime skills' at http://news.bbc.co.uk/go/pr/fr/-/1/hi/technology/3725305.stm.

example, spoof child pornography websites were set up and police officers used technological tracing tools to pinpoint the Internet addresses of individuals who visited those sites. Police officers also posed online as children in chatrooms to capture individuals who visited them to 'groom' victims into the world of paedophilia.[2]

As discussed previously,[3] the Internet has not only facilitated and created new opportunities for committing pre-existing, 'traditional' crimes. It has also spawned new forms of harmful behaviour. These present new challenges to the law enforcement agencies and to the criminal justice system as a whole because the traditional, physical boundaries do not restrain the perpetrators. Online offending and transborder data flow have, particularly in the last decade, forced changes in the strategies, policies and practicalities of policing. Dr David Wall places these new forms of harmful behaviour into four different categories.[4] Firstly, (cyber)obscenity, which he describes as the trading of obscene materials within cyberspace. Secondly, (cyber)trespass, which he explains is the unauthorised access to computer systems, into spaces where rights of ownership or title have already been established. Thirdly, (cyber)theft, which he says relates to a range of different types of acquisitive harm, including the fraudulent use of credit cards and (cyber)cash, the raiding of online bank accounts, and the appropriation of intellectual property (cyberpiracy). Lastly, he refers to cyberactivities, such as hate speech or cyberstalking, which have a violent impact upon individuals or groups; he labels these as forms of (cyber)violence.

Within these categories sit numerous types of activity. Whilst some of them may share characteristics with others, either within or across groups, most of them will significantly differ from each other. Consequently, they each pose individual investigatory challenges, and 'each type of cyberbehaviour requires a different strategic response towards it'.[5]

The Internet has transformed the criminal landscape. E-criminals can offend around the world in any number of ways with an impact which has never before been experienced by the unfortunate (or unwary) victims. The financial and other consequences of e-Crime for corporate victims were considered in particular detail in the previous chapter of this book. Here, it must be noted that individuals and groups can also suffer greatly at the hands of e-criminals. For example, acute embarrassment or even social ostracism may follow the publication of material relating to an individual on the Internet. Hate speech may cause great offence to many people and may also incite others to harm members of particular racial or political groups. Individuals may be defrauded or have their identity stolen so that they can be impersonated online.

The international nature of e-Crime inevitably leads to certain conflicts of law. The definitions of crimes, or their key elements, may vary across jurisdictional lines. The inconsistency of substantive laws may also be accompanied by differences between

---

[2] See Chapter 8, footnote 17.
[3] See Chapter 8.
[4] Wall, D, 'Policing the Internet: Maintaining Order and Law on the Cyberbeat – The Internet, Law and Society' (Edited by Akdeniz, Walker and Wall), Longman (2000), pp156–157.
[5] Ibid, p158.

investigative techniques, which are also governed by national, or local, law. Lastly, it must be remembered that societies hold differing views on what constitutes 'criminal' behaviour and on how 'serious' each form of it is.

9.2 Discovering the Identity and Location of E-criminals

An online communication can be the means to one or more criminal ends. It may be designed to wage a personal vendetta or incite violence towards a particular racial group. It may seek to trick people into revealing information about themselves which can then be used to defraud them or to steal their identity. It may be a weapon of damage or destruction, loaded with a computer virus, which will be fired at a system or network. It may simply be one of many which will be sent to flood a system, website or server in order to disrupt or deny service. The e-criminal is the source of this communication; he must be identified and found.

The investigative pursuit of the e-criminal can be a challenging journey. As the world of global communications expands, the ownership of its constituent parts becomes more diverse. Equally, the technologies which drive it continue to develop and increase in number. It has not gone unnoticed that these realities play into the hands of e-criminals. As Yee Fen Lim explains:

'The communications of a hacker or other criminal may pass through as many as a dozen (or more) different types of carriers, each with different technologies (eg local telephone companies, long-distance carriers, Internet service providers (ISPs), and wireless and satellite networks). The communication may also pass through carriers in a number of different countries, each in different time zones and subject to different legal systems. Indeed, each of these complications may exist within a single transmission. This phenomenon makes it more difficult (and sometimes impossible) to track criminals who are technologically savvy enough to hide their location and identity.'[6]

The very nature of the technological advances may pose further problems. For example, in the wireless and satellite communications sector, the fact that an e-criminal uses a cellular phone can both help and hinder the task of finding out who and where he is. There is no doubt that the technology can greatly assist officers in their investigation of crimes. For instance, it was reported in the press at the beginning of this year that Cambridgeshire police had found the body of the student, Sally Gleeson, who went missing on New Year's Eve.[7] A forensic scientist has been drafted in to trace through the mobile phone records of this woman in order to track her movements on the night in question and, more specifically, to determine her approximate location on the two occasions when she sent text messages to her friends asking for their help. However, when the criminal's mobile phone records are the subject of scrutiny, the findings may be misleading. He could manipulate the phone so that it sends out false information about his identity. Alternatively, if he has not done this, he may use different mobile phones at different times for different purposes. Indeed, even if he has not considered the possibility that his phone could be used to trace him, he may

---

[6] Yee Fen Lim, 'Cyberspace Law: Commentaries and Materials', Oxford University Press (2002), p265.
[7] *The Guardian*, 8 January 2005, p5.

regularly replace it[8] and this could render the task of gathering evidence more difficult. It must also be recognised that investigative techniques such as the forensic examination of cellular phone records and physical tracking through telephonic means may well come into conflict with the laws of privacy and be subject to legal challenge. Moreover, jurisdictional problems can arise where, for example, the investigations relate to communications on a satellite-based network where the earth-based gateways are located in another country. In such a situation, the information sought by the investigators, such as the content of the communications and the identities of the callers and the recipients, together with rules and procedures concerned with access to and seizure of it, will often be governed by that country's laws.

The more sophisticated the e-criminal, the more difficult he is to trace. Firstly, however, it must be noted that one advantage is shared between all e-criminals. It will often be the case that the best chance of tracing them arises when they are online. There are several reasons why this form of investigation is more complicated than it seems. In addition to the obvious time constraints, there are some key issues to be addressed if successful tracing is to occur. Firstly, the expertise must be available at the relevant time and in the appropriate location; e-criminals offend around the globe around the clock. Secondly, there must be practised procedures for timely communications between law enforcement officers and the staff of ISPs and other carriers.

Data preservation and retention is another key issue. The term 'traffic data' has been said to consist of 'any data processed for the purpose of the conveyance of a communication on an electronic communications network'.[9] Such data may be crucial to an e-criminal investigation. However, it is possible that the relevant ISP's system may not, in fact, generate such information. Even if it does, that information may either not be recorded by the system or may only be retained within it for a short period of time. The legal powers relating to the access and scrutiny of such data will be considered in more detail later on in this chapter. For now, it must be noted that in English law there is a general, statutory rule that 'personal data processed for any purpose or purposes shall not be kept for longer than is necessary for that purpose or purposes'.[10] The Regulation of Investigatory Powers Act 2000 did not impose a duty upon communication providers to retain communications data. However, it did empower senior police officers to require disclosure of it in the interests of the detection and prosecution of crime.[11] It must also be noted that, in the light of the 11 September disaster in New York, the Home Secretary was given the power to draw up a code of practice which specifies periods of time during which communications providers can be required to retain communications data.[12]

---

[8] In the UK, the average user replaces their mobile phone every 18 months. Fifteen million mobile phones are discarded in the UK each year – *The Guardian*, 8 January 2005, p12.
[9] Article 2(b) Communications Data Privacy Directive 2002/58/EC.
[10] The Fifth Data Protection Principle, as stated in Sch 1 Data Protection Act 1998.
[11] Section 22.
[12] Under s102 Anti-terrorism, Crime and Security Act 2001.

Yet the skilled e-criminal may not be unduly worried when he is actually online because he may be using a criminal disguise; identity theft and online impersonation are becoming more prevalent each year. He may even have the skills to hack into the system which stores the information relating to his activities; once in, he can delete that information, covering his tracks and retaining his anonymity.

9.3 Jurisdiction

Given that e-Crimes will often involve transborder data flow and be, in other respects, extraterritorial in their nature, some difficult jurisdictional issues may arise. National and international boundaries do not represent hurdles to e-criminals. The development of ICTs is fast delivering to the world's population the ability to transmit information and property with ease. The first, obvious advantage to the e-criminal element of that population is the real, and virtual, distance which can be placed between the perpetrators and the scene of their crimes; the remoteness from their victims. Take, for example, a typical fraud scam. The spoof website which seeks to lure the unsuspecting victims may be run by a computer server in Brazil. Thousands of people from around the world visit it every day. The e-criminal who created this cybertrap sits at home in Russia, gleefully harvesting the rewards of his master plan. Equally, if the scam is played out by means of e-mail, the message will often run through the communications networks of a number of countries in search of its victims.

Ironically, the e-criminal can be physically proximate to the victim but just as difficult to catch as if he were on the other side of the world. For instance, rather than daily shouting abuse at his neighbour over the garden fence, the cyberstalker will, remaining anonymous, insult and threaten him online. If he routes his e-mail communications through several countries on its way to the victim's personal computer nextdoor, the police's task of discovering who he is and where he is located will be made more difficult. In their pursuit of him, they must seek the co-operation and assistance of law enforcement agencies in those other countries. The human resources, levels of expertise, and technical and procedural mechanisms may vary significantly across those foreign agencies. This can either hinder or halt the investigation. Often, time is of the essence; the e-criminal is more effectively tracked when he is actually online.

The discovery of the e-criminal's location may simply mark the first significant step on the investigative trail. The evidence of his e-criminal activity may sit in a remote location, either because the perpetrator has stored it there himself or simply because this is an aspect of the networks he has been using. If the data is, in fact, found to be stored locally or nationally then the investigators may have little difficulty in obtaining and executing a search warrant. However, if this is not the situation, the legitimacy of such a warrant may be questioned in another jurisdiction. Furthermore, it must not be forgotten that in countries which have a federal structure, such as the US, the laws of states may be different in respect of the alleged e-criminal activity. The online behaviour in question may be criminal in one state but not in another where the investigative trail leads to. Alternatively, the laws of that other state may prohibit the transborder execution of a search warrant, requiring instead that the warrant be sought in the courts of the state (or district) where it is intended to be executed.

In 1989, the Law Commission proposed that the concept of joint jurisdiction be woven into the statutory fabric of the then forthcoming Computer Misuse Act 1990.[13] This recommendation was accepted and the territorial scope of the offences under the Act was duly addressed in ss4 and 5. In essence, any jurisdictional claim must be based upon proof of a 'significant link' with this country.[14] For the purposes of an offence under s1 of the Act,[15] a domestic court will establish jurisdiction if the accused was in this country when he caused the computer to perform the hacking function or, alternatively, if the computer to which he secured (or intended to secure) unauthorised access was in this country. For the purposes of an offence under s3 of the Act,[16] the 'significant link' with domestic jurisdiction will be established either where the accused was in this country when he did the act which caused the unauthorised modification of computer material, or where the unauthorised modification itself took place on a computer in this country. Thus, in essence, jurisdiction will be established when either the accused or the victim computer was located in England or Wales at the time of the alleged criminal activity.

The criteria for claiming jurisdiction in relation to a s2 offence[17] are somewhat more complex. The Act states that a domestic court may claim jurisdiction in any of the following circumstances.

• Where all aspects of the conduct take place in this country.

• Where the further offence referred to in s2 is intended to take place in this country. Note that here there is no need to establish the usual 'significant link' requirement for the unauthorised access component of the offence.[18]

• Where the 'significant link' requirement can be established[19] and the further, intended offence(s) will be committed (either wholly or in part) in another country (or countries), and such conduct would be an offence under the law in that other country (or countries).

The territorial scope of inchoate offences related to the offences in the Act is detailed in ss6 and 7.

Offences such as computer fraud or computer forgery, which are not attacking the integrity of systems but, instead, are using computer technology as a means to achieve specific criminal ends, are covered by Part 1 Criminal Justice Act 1993. Under s2(3), jurisdiction can be claimed in the light of a 'relevant event' occurring in England and

---

[13] See Law Commission Report No 186 (1989), para 4.2.
[14] Referring to the jurisdiction of England and Wales. Note that the Act applies to Scotland and Northern Ireland, as well: see s4(6).
[15] The basic hacking offence.
[16] The offence of unauthorised modification of computer programmes or data.
[17] The offence of hacking with intent to commit or facilitate the commission of further offences.
[18] See s4(3).
[19] See s5(2).

Wales. Under s2(1), a 'relevant event' is defined as 'any act or omission or other event (including any result of one or more acts or omissions), proof of which is required for conviction of the offence'.

The Council of Europe's Convention on Cybercrime[20] contains similar jurisdictional provisions. Therein, art 22 provides that a Member State will have jurisdiction in respect of offences committed within its territory (including ships and planes which are registered in that state), or in respect of offences committed by any of its nationals outside its territory where the conduct is criminal in the place where it is committed,[21] or in the event that the offence is committed outside the jurisdiction of any state.

Given the fact that e-criminal activity will often be international, the investigation of it will regularly involve liaison between, and the mutual assistance of, law enforcement agencies from different nations. This is facilitated by the Criminal (International Co-operation) Act 2003. In addition, the Convention on Cybercrime promotes general principles relating to 'international cooperation'.[22] Of course, even when the investigators have gathered sufficient evidence for a prosecution, jurisdiction may have to be claimed and, if the suspected e-criminal is abroad, a request for his extradition put before the courts. In order to succeed in an extradition procedure, the applicant must establish that the accused's actions amounted to a criminal offence of sufficient seriousness in both jurisdictions. This is sometimes referred to as the 'double criminality' principle. Under s2 Extradition Act 1989, the offence must be punishable by a minimum of 12 months' imprisonment.[23] This requirement is mirrored within the Council of Europe's Convention on Cybercrime.[24] Therein, art 24 states that extradition should be made available for any of the offences established under the Convention, as long as a custodial sentence of at least one year could be imposed in both of the relevant states.

R v *Governor of Brixton Prison and Another, ex parte Levin*[25] provides a good example of some of the jurisdictional and extraditional issues which can arise in e-criminal cases. The accused, a Russian national located in St Petersburg, used his skill as a computer programmer to gain unauthorised access to the computer of a bank located in the US and to divert funds from that bank's customer accounts to accounts controlled by his accomplice at another US bank. However, the scheme was discovered and the relevant accounts were frozen. At the request of the US government, the accused was arrested and detained in England.[26] At the committal hearing, the magistrate found that the US government had made out a prima facie case on 66 criminal charges, including theft, false accounting, forgery, unauthorised access to a computer and unauthorised modification of computer material. Consequently, he ordered that the accused be committed to custody to await extradition.

---

[20] See: http://conventions.coe.int/Treaty/en/Treaties/Html/185.htm.
[21] The 'double criminality principle'.
[22] See art 23.
[23] See also ss8(1) and 15 Computer Misuse Act 1990.
[24] See: http://conventions.coe.int/Treaty/en/Treaties/Html/185.htm.
[25] [1996] 4 All ER 350.
[26] In execution of a warrant under s1(3) Extradition Act 1989.

The accused applied for a writ of habeas corpus[27] on the principal ground that the records of the instructions and transfers contained in the computer printouts were hearsay evidence and, therefore, not admissible. His counsel also argued that one of the offences cited by the extradition applicant had not been committed, in the light of the decision in *R* v *Gold*.[28] In addition, the jurisdictional claim was challenged. Levin's counsel claimed that the criminal activity had occurred in Russia, not the US. Specifically, it was argued that the fraudulent transfers were instigated when Levin pressed the keys on his computer keyboard in St Petersburg and that, therefore, Russian law applied. In response, it was argued that the place where the changes to the data occurred was the Citibank computer in Parsipenny, US. This argument was accepted by the court, based on the reasoning that the effects upon the data at the US bank when Levin pressed his keyboard in Russia were instantaneous. Beldam LJ explained that:

> 'The applicant's keyboard was connected electronically with the Citibank computer in Parsipenny; as he pressed the keys, his actions, as he intended, recorded or stored information, for all practical purposes, simultaneously on the magnetic disc in the computer. That is where the instrument was created[29] and where the act constituting the offence was done.'[30]

The Divisional Court dismissed the application, confirming that the magistrate had rightly committed Levin to custody to await extradition to the US.

9.4 The Task of Gathering Evidence

By its very nature, electronic data is vulnerable; it can be destroyed, deleted or modified with ease. Given this, the task of gathering the evidence of e-crimes is more complex than it seems. The data must not only be retrieved, but must be preserved before and after such retrieval. The authenticity and cogency of that evidence must then be established through, for example, computer forensic science. It should be remembered that electronic evidence will often include both the details of the core criminal activity itself and informational records of communications. For example, if it is alleged that an individual has tried to blackmail a business rival with the threat of releasing a virus into their computer system but, when the rival refused to pay up, released the infection into the system anyway, there may be several types of electronic evidence to be gathered: the e-mail in which the threat was made, records of its source and destination and the time that it was sent and received; also, the virus itself and its infectious workings, and the means by which it was released into the computer system (eg evidence of hacking or, if the virus was contained within a document that had been attached to a further e-mail, evidence of that further communication).

---

[27] This Latin phrase roughly translates as 'you have the body'. It is a prerogative writ used to challenge the validity of a person's detention, either in official custody (eg when held pending deportation or, as here, extradition) or in private hands. It derives from the royal prerogative and was, therefore, originally obtained by petitioning the sovereign. Petitions are now made to the Divisional Court of the Queen's Bench Division of the High Court. If the petition is successful, and a writ is issued by the court, the detention is deemed to be prima facie unlawful and the custodian is ordered to appear and justify it; if they cannot, they will be ordered to release the detainee.
[28] [1988] 2 WLR 812 (HL).
[29] One of the elements of the particular crime being discussed (within the Forgery and Counterfeiting Act 1981).
[30] [1988] 2 WLR 812 (HL).

Naturally, if the alleged e-criminal activity has taken place in one physical location, the task of gathering the evidence of it is much easier. Take, for example, the case *Attorney-General's Reference (No 1 of 1991)*.[31] Therein, the accused went to visit his former employer, a wholesale locksmith, to purchase some articles from him. While temporarily alone in a room, he keyed commands into a computer, effecting a 70 per cent discount on the articles he was to purchase. The Court of Appeal confirmed his conviction, under s2(1) Computer Misuse Act 1990, for securing unauthorised access to a computer with intent to commit a further offence of false accounting. In this case the electronic evidence was easily retrieved and presented in court, particularly since the activity did not involve any inter-computer communication. However, the garnering process becomes less easy where, for example, the accused is suspected of hacking into a system from a remote location. In *R v Whiteley*,[32] the accused hacked into a computer network from his home computer for the purpose of altering data contained on disks within it, thereby causing computers either to fail or to be rendered inoperable for some time. He was a skilled e-criminal and the nature of his activities demanded similar skill in the collection of evidence against him. Once he had hacked into the system, he gave himself the status of Systems Manager. He then proceeded to delete and add files, change passwords and wipe out audit files which were recording his activities. He even deleted a special programme which had been inserted into the system to trap him. The Court of Appeal confirmed his conviction, under s1 Criminal Damage Act 1981,[33] for criminal damage to property.

The dramatic development of ICTs in recent years has prompted governments and legislatures to reassess the legal powers relating to the interception of electronic communications. In the UK, the Regulation of Investigatory Powers Act 2000[34] empowered the Secretary of State to authorise the interception of communications where he/she considers it to be necessary for any of the following reasons:[35]

- in the interests of national security;

- for the purpose of preventing or detecting serious crime;

- for the purpose of safeguarding the economic wellbeing of the UK; or

- for giving effect to international mutual assistance agreements in connection with the prevention or detection of serious crime.

The Act recognised the differences between voice and data traffic. In a report produced for the Home Office, the increasing diversity in the range of technologies being used for access to the Internet had been noted. It was also pointed out that 'a selected subscriber will utilise Internet services (eg a single e-mail account) using multiple

---

[31] [1992] 3 WLR 432.
[32] (1991) 93 Cr App Rep 25.
[33] Although, at the time of his appeal, the Computer Misuse Act 1990 was in force, he had been charged and tried on the basis of the law prior to it.
[34] Which replaced the Interception of Communications Act 1985.
[35] See s5.

access technologies'.[36] Moreover, the report referred to the number of anonymous communication services which subscribers could exploit to access Internet services, such as pre-pay mobile phones and Internet cafes. In the light of these facts, it was recommended that interception would be cheaper, more straightforward and more effective at the premises of the Internet Service Providers. Consequently, s12(1) of the Act provides that the Secretary of State may place obligations on, amongst others, ISPs to assist with interception warrants. Furthermore, under the Regulation of Investigatory Powers (Maintenance of Interception Capability) Order 2002,[37] the Secretary of State may require those companies which provide a telecommunications service to more than 10,000 customers to maintain a capability to intercept communications.

In addition to, or instead of, the actual interception of electronic communications, investigators may seek access to the data which flows from them. As previously noted, s12 Regulation of Investigatory Powers Act 2000 empowers a senior police officer to require a communications provider to disclose any communications data in its possession in the interests of the prevention and detection of crime. The term 'communications data' includes both traffic and location data but not, it seems, the content of any communication.[38] This can be a thorny issue and will be considered in more detail in the section on computer forensics below.

Encryption is another issue which has caught the legislative eye. It can be used by e-criminals to conceal their communications. They are attracted to it because even if the encrypted communication is intercepted, it cannot be understood unless, or until, it is deciphered. Cryptography support systems continue to be used and developed in the UK. Section 49 Regulation of Investigatory Powers Act 2000 provides for the imposition of disclosure requirements upon owners of encryption keys or any third parties who hold copies of them. Where an encrypted message has been lawfully intercepted, a person can only be required to disclose the cryptographic key (or a copy of the information in decrypted format) where there are reasonable grounds for believing:

- that a key to the protected information is in their possession;

- that the forced disclosure is necessary in the interests of national security, for the purpose of preventing or detecting crime, in the interests of the economic well-being of the UK, or for the purpose of ensuring that public authorities effectively exercise their statutory powers or properly perform their statutory duties;

- that such an imposition is proportionate to what is sought to be achieved by it; and

- that it is not otherwise reasonably practical to obtain possession of the encrypted information in an intelligible form.

---

[36] 'Technical and Cost Issues Associated with Interception of Communications at Certain Communication Service Providers' – see: http://www.homeoffice.gov.uk/oicd/techcost.pdf.
[37] SI 2002/1931.
[38] See the Home Office's Consultation Paper on a Code of Practice for Voluntary Retention of Communications Data, March 2003.

Any person who knowingly fails to comply with a disclosure notice which has been served upon them can receive a custodial sentence of up to two years and/or a fine.[39]

There continues a long-running debate concerning the tensions between the effective detection of crime and the protection of personal privacy. Indeed, it becomes more heated as ICTs develop at pace. The balance to be struck between these two important positions is simply one of the many legislative challenges of the electronic age.

The investigators of e-Crime will need to gain legal permission to access and seize potential evidence, so that it can then be scrutinised. The rules governing the granting, service and exercise of search warrants are found in the following statutes.

- Police and Criminal Evidence Act 1984.

- Computer Misuse Act 1990.[40]

- Copyright, Design and Patents Act 1988.[41]

Warrants will legitimise the seizure of anything which is reasonably considered to relate to the offence under investigation. Of course, during e-criminal investigations, much of the information which is of interest will be stored on computer hard, flash or floppy drives. Given this, there is often a real risk that crucial evidence could be modified or deleted by the suspect if the computer or software in question is left solely in his possession. However, the seizure of such items can conflict with human rights law.[42] Yet it should be noted that a police officer who is executing the warrant can 'require any information which is contained in a computer and accessible from the premises [referred to in the warrant] to be produced in a form in which it can be taken away and in which it is visible and legible'.[43] The requirement where the information in question is protected by encryption is that it be disclosed in an 'intelligible form'.[44] The process of 'imaging' is often used in e-criminal investigations; this is where an exact copy of a computer's hard drive(s) is taken away for forensic analysis.[45]

One last point concerns the search for and seizure of evidence related to the basic offence of hacking. In general, search warrants are not issued in respect of summary offences, but s14 Computer Misuse Act 1990 provides that one could be issued by a circuit judge where there are 'reasonable grounds for believing' that a s1 offence has occurred or may occur. The main reason for viewing this particular summary offence as exceptional to the general rule was explained by the Minister of State, who pointed out that the basic hacking offence:

> '... is not untypically committed in a private house, remote from the public gaze and with no one else present. I am not saying that this is a unique offence, but I cannot think of many others that are

---

[39] Section 53(5).
[40] In relation to the basic offence of hacking in s1.
[41] Where the suspicion is concerned with software piracy.
[42] See, for example, the US case *Steve Jackson Games Inc* v *United States Secret Service* 36 F 3d 457 (1994).
[43] Section 19(4) Police and Criminal Evidence Act 1984.
[44] Section 50(1) Regulation of Investigatory Powers Act 2000.
[45] See below on computer forensics.

committed in private houses to which the police have no access and that do not involve some other party other than the offender.'[46]

9.5 Computer Forensics

Computer forensics play a crucial role in the investigation of e-Crime. This science has been driven and shaped by several trends which have emerged through the history of computing. As Peter Sommer explains:

'The main trends have, in turn, spawned many lesser ones and all have interacted with, and reinforced, each other. They are: the growth in use and power of personal computers; the move in the design of corporate computer systems away from centralised monolithic mainframe towards a multiplicity of smaller but powerful machines which inter-work and inter-connect in a form usually called distributed processing; and the growth of networks, both private and, in the form of the Internet, globally public. All of these changes have had an impact not only on what computers can deliver to their owners but also in the types of evidence that may be found within them.'[47]

There are several common computer forensic techniques. The first, and most obvious, involves the seizure of the computer hardware. When this is done, legal rules and guidelines will govern the process. The computer itself should be photographed in situ, the cabling and any separate, external means of data storage (eg flash drives, zip or floppy disks) must be accurately labelled. Computers that are running at the time of the raid must be safely shut down, and the time at which this happens[48] must be separately logged. Lastly, an exact copy[49] must be made of every hard disk; this is called 'legal imaging'.

One of the reasons for imaging is to avoid contamination of the data stored in the computer. As Peter Sommer points out:

'... the very process of turning on a computer and/or seeking to copy its contents can alter the contents to such an extent that they become contaminated ... The [legal imaging] procedure should take place as soon as possible after a computer has been seized; subsequent examination is then carried out on the copies of the hard disk.'[50]

The computer is booted from the floppy drive with a minimal, simple operating system. That system has drivers which instruct the computer to recognise an external storage device. The image which is recorded on the external device is an exact replica of the computer's hard disk(s). However, one of the real benefits of the process is that it records not only those files which would usually be visible on the computer but also those parts of the disk(s) which hold other useful information, such as file names/sizes and date/time stamps. In addition, other revealing pieces of information can be recovered from this 'bit copy',[51] such as fragments of previously deleted files. Subsequently, a computer forensic expert could attempt to reconstruct such

---

[46] HC Official Report, SCC (Computer Misuses Bill), col 65, 28 March 1990.
[47] Sommer, P, 'Digital Footprints: Assessing Computer Evidence – Cyberspace Crime' (Edited by Wall, D S), Ashgate/Dartmouth (2003), p537.
[48] As recorded by the computer's internal clock.
[49] Note that usually, in fact, two copies are made, with one acting as a control.
[50] Sommer, P, 'Digital Footprints: Assessing Computer Evidence – Cyberspace Crime' (Edited by Wall, D S), Ashgate/Dartmouth (2003), p541.
[51] Sometimes also referred to as 'sector by sector copy'.

documents. Yet this is not the only way in which deleted files can be recovered. It may often be the case that such files can simply be 'undeleted'. Modern computer operating systems have built-in safety facilities to guard against accidental deletion. This means that although a file may have been marked for deletion, the contents of it will not disappear until the specific, spacial area which it occupied has been taken up by newer files.[52]

Clearly, such evidence-gathering operations can be more problematic where the investigation leads to corporate premises. In a large company there will usually be a lot of computers which are often extensively networked, either within specific localities of the organisation and/or across the company as a whole. The potential ramifications of seizing computer equipment in these circumstances are more serious and wide-ranging. Employees, customers and creditors may all be affected. Indeed, depending upon the nature and scale of seizure, the whole business could be stopped in its commercial tracks. In such a situation, the investigators may, instead, seek out somebody who works in that organisation (who is beyond suspicion) and who has sufficient technical knowledge of the computer system to help them with the 'imaging' process.

If, as is often the case in e-criminal investigations, some of the evidence is from the Internet, this could be stored either on the suspect's computer(s) or at remote sites. Consequently, differing forensic techniques may have to be used. In addition to the suspect's own computer, potential sources of the evidence would include the communications data records of his chosen ISP, data held at remote sites and, of course, the dialling data kept at the telephone company.[53]

Personal computers hold files which record Internet activity. Examples include files which log incoming and outgoing e-mail, subscriptions to newsgroups and, possibly, access to Internet Relay Chat (IRC) sessions.[54] In addition, computers 'cache' recently used data in case it needs to be reused again in the short term. This is a particularly useful process when used in relation to the Internet because the cache files store copies of websites as they are visited. These files are often retained for weeks or months afterwards. Consequently, time is saved because a webpage can be retrieved from the Internet browser cache file without the need to revisit the website itself. This, in turn, means that traffic on the Internet is reduced. The advantage given to investigators through this process is that 'some browsers and some specialist software can be used to view cache files and also associated "history" files which retain some date-and-time information. Thus, it is possible to determine what the users of a specific computer have been viewing and, to a limited extent and after careful interpretation, when.'[55]

---

[52] It must also be noted that useful information (eg evidence of the alteration/deletion of files or transmission of passwords) can be gleaned from 'swap files'. These are temporary files which are created on the hard disk of the computer when there is not enough random access memory (RAM) for a certain activity, such as where several programmes are running simultaneously.

[53] If he has a wireless connection, the ISP would hold the relevant data.

[54] It should be noted, however, that these types of files can be deleted by the user.

[55] Sommer, P, 'Digital Footprints: Assessing Computer Evidence – Cyberspace Crime' (Edited by Wall, D S), Ashgate/Dartmouth (2003), p545.

Another means by which e-criminal investigators can gather evidence is by eavesdropping on Internet traffic in transit; sometimes referred to as 'sniffing'. Firstly, it must be noted that this process is made difficult by the communications concept on which the Internet is based, called 'packet switching'. In simple terms, before they are sent off over the network, messages are broken up into pieces (packets) and then reassembled when they reach their destination. This concept has military origins,[56] being adopted by the Advanced Research Projects Agency (ARPA) within the US Department of Defence in the late 1960s as the basis for its own network (ARPANET). The obvious, military advantages which flowed from the concept were both secrecy and resilience of communications.[57]

In the light of this, it can be seen that Internet eavesdropping requires not only capture of the data, but reconstruction of it as well. The individual 'packets' contain information which reveals their origin, destination and content. Each of them is numbered to facilitate reassembly. As Peter Sommer explains, these technological realities can create genuine difficulties for the eavesdropping investigators:

'The practical problems are that at certain points along the path there will be vast amounts of regular Internet traffic to be sifted in order to find the material being sought and, in any event, it is basic to the design of the Internet that, even with the transmission of a simple e-mail message, constituent packets may use radically different routes, thus creating the possibility that not all of the relevant traffic has been captured.'[58]

This can often mean that unless the investigators are 'listening in' at a point in the network which is closely proximate to either the sender or receiver of the messages, the procedure may be fruitless.

Earlier in this chapter, the power given to senior police officers to force ISPs to disclose communications data for specified reasons was discussed.[59] It is appropriate to return to this issue here, in order to reveal some of the difficulties which have flowed from the interpretation of the term 'communications data' within s22 Regulation of Investigatory Powers Act (RIPA) 2000.[60] The Home Office has stated that:

'It is important to identify what communications data does include, but equally important to be clear about what it does not include. The term communications data does not include the content of any communication.'[61]

This distinction had also been made in the piece of legislation which RIPA 2000 replaced.[62] It means that the content of communications can only be used for investigative purposes; it is not admissible in court. This legal distinction is not readily found in other jurisdictions which are similar to that of the UK. A further, practical problem arises when it comes to Internet-based communications. In that digital world,

---

[56] The concept was devised by Paul Baran in 1964.
[57] It would be possible to route around points of failure.
[58] Sommer, P, 'Digital Footprints: Assessing Computer Evidence – Cyberspace Crime' (Edited by Wall, D S), Ashgate/Dartmouth (2003), p548.
[59] See footnote 11 above.
[60] The Regulation of Investigatory Powers Act 2000.
[61] The Home Office's Consultation Paper on a Code of Practice for Voluntary Retention of Communications Data, March 2003.
[62] Interception of Communications Act 1985.

often the technical means for collecting both forms of data, either 'communication' or 'content', are the same. This, in turn, means that separating the two from each other can sometimes be difficult. For example, some web-requests could fall into both categories.

9.6 Presenting the Evidence in Court

Even where the investigators are confident that they have uncovered enough evidence for a conviction, a final hurdle which the prosecuting authorities may encounter is the lack of understanding of IT within the courts system. Some real problems concerning practice and procedure in the courts and the police service for dealing with computer evidence were identified, in 2000, by the Computer Evidence Taskgroup.[63] It found that criminal courts are generally unfamiliar with the subject of computer evidence and regularly underestimate the technical complexity of cases that involve it. It was also reported that the mishandling of computer evidence 'quite frequently' leads to prosecutions having to be abandoned. It is perhaps for these reasons, together with those discussed above relating to the task of gathering evidence of e-crimes, that the following has been said:

> 'Most successful prosecutions rely on more than one stream of computer-derived evidence. What is needed is a multiplicity of independent streams of evidence, both computer and non-computer-derived, which corroborate each other. Any single stream may fail, either because of intrinsic inadequacy or because the courts find it too difficult to understand.'[64]

9.7 The Investigators

In the past, the UK police attracted criticism for what was seen as insufficient recruitment of officers with the requisite technical knowledge to effectively combat e-Crime. Such criticism continues.[65] However, in September 2000 the government announced that it was to establish a National Hi-Tech Crime Unit (NHTCU) at a cost of £25 million. This unit came into operation in April 2001. It was the first UK national law enforcement organisation tasked to combat serious and organised computer-based crime. The Unit describes itself as 'the linchpin in the UK's coordinated response to Cybercrime, working in partnership with other law enforcement agencies, business, industry and the IT world'.[66] It is a multi-agency unit, drawing skilled and experienced staff from the National Crime Squad, Her Majesty's Customs and Excise, the Military and the Intelligence Agencies. The Unit declares that its work 'is broadly divided into five key disciplines: tactical and technical support; crime reduction; intelligence operations; and digital evidence recovery.'[67] Since its launch, the NHTCU has been involved in a broad spectrum of computer-related

---

[63] 'BCS highlights court failings', The Computer Bulletin, British Computer Society, September 2000, p12.
[64] Sommer, P, 'Digital Footprints: Assessing Computer Evidence – Cyberspace Crime' (Edited by Wall, D S), Ashgate/Dartmouth (2003), p549.
[65] See footnote 1 above.
[66] See: http://www.nhtcu.org/NOPSurvey.pdf.
[67] Ibid.

crime investigations, including fraud, hacking, viruses and denial of service attacks, software piracy, online child abuse, extortion and drugs trafficking. Some of its recent successes are listed below.

• In May 2004, a gang of 'phishers' was exposed. It had posed online as a bank and e-mailed customers to lure their banking details from them. Computers, passports, chequebooks, bank cards and crack cocaine were seized during raids on several premises in London from which the gang was operating.

• In July 2004, following a joint operation with police in St Petersburg, members of a Russian gang were arrested and charged with offences relating to extortion and money laundering after they had threatened online bookmakers with denial of service attacks.

• In November 2004, a 35-year-old computer consultant, Ian Baldock, was jailed for four years after its was proven that he had downloaded more than 96,000 child pornographic images and movies.

• Last, but certainly not least, a recent NHTCU investigation, dubbed Operation Blossom, led to the successful prosecution of several individuals for conspiracy to defraud a Japanese bank, through its London offices, of £220 million.[68]

In December 2004, the government confirmed its intention to set up a new elite police body to combat organised crime, such as people-smuggling, drug-trafficking, fraud and money laundering. Part of its remit will be to crack down on the increasingly hi-tech methods which gangs use to carry out these crimes and to launder the proceeds from them. It will be called the Serious Organised Crime Agency (SOCA) and will be the result of a merger between the National Crime Squad, the National Criminal Intelligence Service and the investigative branches of the Customs and Immigration Service. Up to 5,000 agents will be employed by the new force, which is not likely to be operational until 2006.

Lastly, it has been reported in the press that the police are calling upon the government to set up a specialist unit, dubbed the 'Internet Safety Centre', to investigate Internet child pornography. This proposal appears in the light of recent Home Office figures which show that 2,234 people were charged with or cautioned for activities related to child pornography in 2003, compared with only 549 in 2001. The unit would be staffed by police officers, charity workers and computer experts. It would operate around the clock to investigate reports of suspicious images found on the Internet. However, there seem to be some funding problems which threaten to at least defer the establishment of such a unit. Stuart Hyde, from the Association of Chief Officers, is reported as saying: 'we're not expecting the government to suddenly put massive amounts of money into this'.[69]

---

[68] 'Latest Coup for High-Tech Crime Unit' – see: http://news.bbc.co.uk/go/pr/fr/-/1/hi/technology/4357307.stm.
[69] See 'Unit Needed to Tackle Net Porn' at: http://news.bbc.co.uk/go/pr/fr/-/1/hi/uk/4316511.stm.

9.8 International Cooperation and Harmonisation of E-criminal Laws

It used to be the case that criminal law was mainly driven and shaped by national interests alone; the policies, procedures and protective measures enshrined in the law of individual states were mostly home-grown. E-criminal activity has forced changes to this historical position.

Certainly, there remain longstanding cooperative relationships between countries when it comes to the investigation of crime, but problems can arise where the investigation extends to requests for searches of premises and seizure of items in another country. Moreover, the issue of extradition can be problematic where there is a marked legal disparity between the countries in question and, for example, the criminal activity which is being investigated is not covered under any bilateral agreement between them. In some situations, a country may refuse a request from a foreign law enforcement agency for legal permission to conduct a search and seizure operation within its borders, perhaps because equivalent powers would not be available to domestic investigators in the same circumstances. A lack of dual criminality[70] can also present an insurmountable hurdle when it comes to jurisdictional and extraditional issues, particularly where any mutual legal assistance treaty makes it a pre-requisite for cooperative measures.

In the light of these facts, the importance of a process of international harmonisation of substantive criminal laws and procedures cannot be overstated. It has been recognised that:

> 'Although bilateral cooperation is important in pursuing investigations concerning unlawful conduct involving the use of the Internet, multilateral efforts are a more effective way to develop international policy and cooperation in this area. The reason for this stems from the nature of the Internet itself. Because Internet access is available in over 200 countries, and because criminals can route their communications through any of these countries, law enforcement challenges must be addressed on as broad a basis as possible, because law enforcement assistance may be required from any Internet-connected country. That is, even if two countries were able to resolve all the high-tech crimes issues they faced, they would still (presumably) only be able to solve those crimes that involved their two countries. Multilateral fora allow many countries to seek solutions that will be compatible to the greatest extent with each country's domestic laws.'[71]

The Group of Eight (G-8) countries have been proactive for some time on this issue, forming a principled agenda and action plan nearly seven years ago. Following a meeting in Washington between the interior and justice ministers of Britain, Canada, France, Germany, Italy, Japan, Russia and the US, a set of initiatives were announced, all of which were aimed at combating e-Crime. The particular areas of focus were paedophilia, drug-trafficking, electronic fraud (eg money laundering and cyberpiracy) and industrial and state espionage. There was to be increased coordination in the training of law enforcement officers and prosecutors, further cooperation on the legal and procedural aspects of extradition, and a greater movement towards parity of computer forensics standards. Of particular note was the establishment of the 24/7

---

[70] Where the conduct which is under investigation is recognised as criminal behaviour under the laws in both the host and visiting states.
[71] Yee Fen Lim, 'Cyberspace Law: Commentaries and Materials', Oxford University Press (2002), pp274–275.

High-Tech Point-of-Contact Network, directly linking e-Crime experts from around the world with each other.

Within Europe, there have been a number initiatives launched in the last few years in the fight against e-Crime. They have come from both the European Union and the Council of Europe. These will now be considered in some detail.

In March 2000, the Lisbon European Council urged the main legislative bodies of the EU to implement a cohesive strategy towards e-Crime. In response, the European Commission released a Communication which contained a number of proposals. It was entitled: 'Creating a Safer Information Society by Improving the Security of Information Infrastructures and Combating Computer-related Crime',[72] and led to an analysis of the weaknesses in network security[73] and the recommendation of a coordinated approach to network and IT security.[74]

The Commission also recognised the need to harmonise the substantive criminal laws of the Member States within the EU.[75] The Commission's draft decision did not concern itself with so-called content-related or computer-related offences; it simply considered attacks against the integrity of systems. For example, arts 3–5 promoted the criminalisation of obtaining (or attempting to obtain) illegal access to information systems. The same was proposed in relation to illegal interference with information systems. Moreover, it was recommended that secondary participation in such criminal behaviour (instigating, aiding or abetting) should be rendered illegal as well. Article 6 proposed the setting of a minimum term of imprisonment (at least one year) in 'serious cases', described as being those which involve damage or economic benefit.

In addition, it was recommended that where 'aggravating circumstances' were shown to exist, the minimum term should rise to four years' imprisonment. 'Aggravating circumstances' were said to include: activities carried out within the framework of a criminal organisation; where substantial economic loss or physical harm or damage to critical infrastructure is caused; or where substantial proceeds result.[76] There was also a recommendation that 24/7 operational points of contact be established between national law enforcement agencies.[77]

9.9 The Council of Europe's Convention on Cybercrime[78]

The Council of Europe was founded in 1949. Its most significant achievement has been the creation, promotion and implementation of the European Convention on Human Rights (1953), which was adopted into English law via the Human Rights Act 1998.

---

[72] COM (2000) 890 final.
[73] 'Network and Information Security: A European Policy Approach' – see: http://europa.eu.int/information_society/eeurope/2002/news_library/new_documents/text_en.htm.
[74] Council Resolution of 6 December 2001: OJ 2002 C 43/02.
[75] See COM (2002) 173, para 1.6.
[76] Article 7(1).
[77] See art 12.
[78] See: http://conventions.coe.int/Treaty/en/Treaties/Html/185.htm.

Its headquarters are situated in Strasbourg, in north-eastern France, together with its judicial arm, the European Court of Human Rights.

The Council groups together 46 countries, 21 of which are from central or eastern Europe. It has granted 'observer status'[79] to some countries (eg Canada, US, South Africa and Japan). It is separate and distinct from the European Union. However, no country has ever become a member of the Council of Europe without having first become a member of the EU.

The draft text of the Convention was published in February 2000. An accompanying press release stated that:

'This legally-binding text aims to harmonise national legislation in this field, facilitate investigations and allow efficient levels of co-operation between the authorities of different states.'

It was opened for signature and ratification (including by non-Member States) on 23 November 2001. To come into force, it required five ratifications. This happened when, on 18 March 2004, Lithuania joined the other four countries which had previously ratified it (Albania, Bulgaria, Croatia and Estonia). Thus, the Convention has been in force since 1 July 2004. Some have welcomed it and others have doubted its potential efficacy:

'Convention supporters argue that it represents a significant step forward in tackling cybercrime because it commits signatories to prosecute computer-related crimes vigorously – which many countries fail to do currently. Council of Europe officials say that the Convention will end cybercriminals' "feeling of impunity".[80] They claim that by mandating sanctions and making cybercrimes extraditable offences, the Convention will improve deterrence and reduce the number of countries in which criminals can avoid prosecution ... Skeptics, however, point out that in order to serve as a deterrent, more states will have to sign the Convention and abide by its mandates. They note that the states that participated in the Convention's negotiations are not the "problem countries" in which cybercriminals operate relatively freely. Hackers frequently route cyberattacks through portals in Yemen and North Korea, neither of which are part of the Convention.'[81]

It must be noted that the Convention has received strong support from the Bush administration in the US. Particularly in the light of the 11 September disaster in New York, the President has been eager to construct and support measures that relate to cybercrime, cyberterrorism and cybersecurity. On the domestic front, he has persuaded Congress to pass several pieces of legislation to this end, such as the USA Patriot Act[82] and the Homeland Security Act.[83] Supporters of the European Convention on Cybercrime claim that a number of its provisions share the same ethos and policies of the US legislation; this may further explain why it has received a transatlantic seal of approval. The principal aims of the Convention are stated as:

'(1) Harmonising the domestic criminal substantive law elements of offences and connected provisions in the area of cybercrime; (2) providing for domestic criminal procedural law powers necessary for the investigation and prosecution of such offences, as well as other offences committed

---

[79] Non-membership, but consultative status.
[80] 'European cybercrime pact aims to set global benchmark,' AFP News, 22 November 2001.
[81] Archick, K, Congressional Research Service Report for Congress: Cybercrime: The Council of Europe Convention – Order Code RS21208.
[82] PL 107–56.
[83] PL 107–296.

by means of a computer system or evidence in relation to which is in electronic form; and (3) setting up a fast and effective regime of international co-operation.'[84]

The Convention categorises offences under the following Titles.

- Title One – offences against the confidentially, integrity and availability of computer data and systems (arts 2–6).

- Title Two – computer-related offences (arts 7–8).

- Title Three – content-related offences (art 9).

- Title Four – offences related to infringements of copyright and related rights (art 10).

Title One offences

Article 2

'Each party shall adopt such legislative and other measures as may be necessary to establish as criminal offences under its domestic law, when committed intentionally, the access to the whole or any part of a computer system without right. A party may require that the offence can be committed by infringing security measures, with the intent of obtaining computer data or other dishonest intent, or in relation to a computer system that is connected to another computer system.'

This article concerns itself with the criminalisation of certain forms of unauthorised access. It is recognised that 'the most effective means of preventing unauthorised access is … the introduction and development of effective security measures. However, a comprehensive response has to include also the threat and use of criminal law measures.'[85] The UK is, of course, already in compliance with this measure; such behaviour was rendered criminal by s1 Computer Misuse Act 1990. It should be noted that Parliament did not make the infringement of security measures a constituent element of that basic hacking offence.

Article 3

'Each party shall adopt such legislative and other measures as may be necessary to establish as criminal offences under its domestic law, when committed intentionally, the interception without right, made by technical means, of non-public transmissions of computer data to, or from or within a computer system, including electromagnetic emissions from a computer system carrying such computer data. A party may require that the offence be committed with dishonest intent, or in relation to a computer system that is connected to another computer system.'

This provision is aimed at protecting the right of privacy within data communications. It concerns itself with the criminalisation of the interception of communications between or within computer systems. It applies the right to privacy of correspondence[86] to all forms of electronic data transfer, whether by telephone, fax, e-mail or file transfer.

---

[84] Convention on Cybercrime (ETS No 185), Explanatory Report, p3 – see: http://conventions.coe.int/Treaty/en/Reports/HTML/185.htm.
[85] Ibid, p7.
[86] Enshrined in art 8 European Convention on Human Rights.

Article 4

'Each party shall adopt such legislative and other measures as may be necessary to establish as criminal offences under its domestic law, when committed intentionally, the damaging, deletion, deterioration, alteration or suppression of computer data without right.'

This provision is aimed at providing a similar level of protection against the intentional infliction of damage to computer data and programmes as is given to corporeal objects. It concerns itself with the criminalisation of the unauthorised deletion or amendment of data. An example of a UK domestic legislative measure that complies with it is the offence of unauthorised modification of computer material under s3 Computer Misuse Act (CMA) 1990.

Article 5

'Each party shall adopt such legislative and other measures as may be necessary to establish as criminal offences under its domestic law, when committed intentionally, the serious hindering without right of the functioning of a computer system by inputting, transmitting, damaging, deleting, deteriorating, altering or suppressing computer data.'

This provision criminalises the intentional hindering of the lawful use of computer systems, including telecommunications facilities, by using or influencing computer data. Note that the hindering must be 'serious', which involves the 'sending of data to a particular system in such a form, size or frequency that it has a significant, detrimental effect upon the ability of the owner or operator to use the system or to communicate with other systems (eg by means of denial of service attacks, malicious codes such as viruses that prevent or substantially slow the operation of the system, or programmes that send huge quantities of electronic mail to a recipient in order to block the communications functions of the system)'.[87]

At this point, it must be noted that legislative action in the UK on this matter seems to be on the horizon. On 10 March 2005, the All Party Internet Group (APIG) issued a press release, giving notice of a motion to move a Ten-Minute Rule Bill calling for amendments to the Computer Misuse Act 1990. One of the proposed amendments within that Bill[88] is to criminalise those who launch denial of service attacks. If enacted, the Bill will insert two new offences into the CMA 1990. One will be a basic offence of causing or intending to cause a denial of service attack. The other will target an aggravated form of such behaviour where, inter alia, the prosecution will be required to prove that the accused harboured an ulterior intent to commit or facilitate the commission of further offences.[89] The Bill was scheduled to be presented to Parliament on 5 April 2005. However, on that very day, the Prime Minister, Tony Blair, called for the General Election and Parliament was dissolved. Nevertheless, APIG remains hopeful and confident that the Bill will receive a parliamentary hearing within the next year, given the positive initial feedback that it has gained from various sources,

---

[87] Convention on Cybercrime (ETS No 185), Explanatory Report, p10.
[88] Computer Misuse Act 1990 (Amendment) Bill – see: http://www.apig.org.uk.
[89] See ss1(3) and 1(5) of the Bill, respectively. These would lead, if enacted, to the insertion of ss2A and 2B into the Computer Misuse Act 1990.

including the previous government. The Chairman of APIG, Mr Derek Wyatt MP, stated in the aforementioned press release that:

'The All Party Group was hoping that an MP would have picked this up as part of the Private Members' allocation for Bills, but sadly no one did, so it seemed sensible, given the work we undertook last year, to at least place on record what we think the Bill should look like, in the hope that the Government will come back to it after the General Election.'[90]

Article 6

'Production, sale procurement for use, import, distribution or otherwise making available of:

1. a device, including a computer programme, designed or adapted primarily for the purpose of committing any of the offences established in accordance with art 2;

2. a computer password, access code or similar data by which the whole or any part of a computer is capable of being accessed,

with intent that it be used for the purpose of committing any of the offences described above.'[91]

This provision concerns itself with the criminalisation of the production or supply of devices, passwords or codes which facilitate hacking (hacker tools).

Title Two offences

Articles 7–10 relate to 'ordinary' crimes which are frequently committed through the use of computer systems.

Article 7

'Each party shall adopt such legislative measures and other measures as may be necessary to establish as criminal offences under its domestic law, when committed intentionally and without right, the input, alteration, deletion, or suppression of computer data, resulting in inauthentic data with the intent that it be considered or acted upon for legal purposes as if it were authentic, regardless whether or not the data is directly readable and intelligible.'

This provision seeks to create a parallel offence to the forgery of tangible documents. It concerns itself with the criminalisation of computer forgery. In addition, it allows parties, when implementing the offence in their domestic law, to require in addition an intent to defraud, or similar dishonest intent, before criminal liability attaches.

Article 8

'Each party shall adopt such legislative and other measures as may be necessary to establish as criminal offences under its domestic law, when committed intentionally and without right, the causing of a loss of property to another person by:

1. any input, alteration, deletion or suppression of computer data;

2. any interference with the functioning of a computer system,

with fraudulent or dishonest intent of procuring, without right, an economic benefit for oneself or for another person.'

This provision concerns itself with the criminalisation of computer fraud.

---

[90] The General Election took place on 5 May 2005.

[91] Note that provision (1) therein is discretionary, but provision (2) is mandatory.

Title Three offences

Article 9

'Each party shall adopt such legislative and other measures as may be necessary to establish as criminal offences under its domestic law, when committed intentionally and without right, the following conduct:

1. producing child pornography for the purpose of its distribution through a computer system;

2. offering or making available child pornography through a computer system;

3. distributing or transmitting child pornography through a computer system;

4. procuring child pornography through a computer system for oneself or for another person;

5. possessing child pornography in a computer system or on a computer data storage medium.'

This provision seeks to strengthen protective measures for children, including their protection against sexual exploitation 'by modernising criminal law provisions to more effectively circumscribe the use of computer systems in the commission of sexual offences against children'.[92] It concerns itself with the criminalisation of the production or distribution of child pornography. A 'minor' is defined as a person under 18 years old, but a lower age limit of 16 years old may be set at the discretion of Member States.[93] The materials that are targeted are those which depict a minor, or someone who appears to be a minor, engaging in 'sexually explicit conduct'. This extends to 'realistic images'.[94] It is the production or distribution of such materials with the intent that they be transmitted over a computer system, or simple possession of them on a computer system or computer storage device (eg a disk or CD), which is criminalised.

Title Four offences

Article 10

'Each party shall adopt such legislative and other measures as may be necessary to establish as criminal offences under its domestic law the infringement of copyright, as defined under the law of that party ... where such acts are committed wilfully, on a commercial scale and by means of a computer system.'

The Council recognised that:

'... infringements of intellectual property rights, in particular of copyright, are among the most commonly committed offences on the Internet, which cause concern both to copyright holders and those who work professionally with computer networks. The reproduction and dissemination on the Internet of protected works, without the approval of the copyright holder, are extremely frequent ... The ease with which unauthorised copies may be made due to digital technology and the scale of reproduction and dissemination in the context of electronic networks made it necessary to include provisions on criminal law sanctions and enhance international cooperation in this field.'[95]

In the light of these facts, the provision concerns itself with the criminalisation of copyright infringement.

---

[92] Convention on Cybercrime (ETS No 185), Explanatory Report, p13.
[93] Article 9(3).
[94] Known and covered under English law as 'pseudo-photographs' – see s7(7) Protection of Children Act 1978 (as amended by s84 Criminal Justice and Public Order Act 1994).
[95] Convention on Cybercrime (ETS No 185), Explanatory Report, p14.

Article 11: aiding and abetting/attempts

The first part of this article is mandatory in nature; it requires Member States to criminalise the aiding or abetting of any of the offences contained in arts 2–10.

The second part of this article is discretionary in nature; it encourages Member States to criminalise attempts at committing any of the offences contained in arts 3, 5, 7, 8, 9(1)(a) and 9(1)(c).

Article 12: corporate liability

This article provides for the imposition of criminal liability upon corporate bodies where offences have been committed by a natural person for the benefit of the corporation, and that natural person holds a 'leading position' within it.

Article 13: sanctions

This article requires Member States to adopt 'effective, proportionate and dissuasive sanctions' as punishment of those convicted of the offences created in accordance with arts 2–11 (including the deprivation of liberty) and art 12 (including monetary sanctions).

Articles 16–21: the gathering of evidence of cybercrime

The Convention provides for the establishment of powers and procedures within Member States to help law enforcement agencies in this crucial task, providing for the following.

Article 16	Preservation of data orders (eg against ISPs) to guard against the destruction of evidence.
Article 17	Securing the retention of traffic data.
Article 18	Securing the production of data held on computer systems.
Article 19	Securing the supply by ISPs of information concerning their subscribers.
Article 20	The collection of real-time data (or requiring an ISP to do this and then to send it to the relevant law enforcement agency).
Article 21	Enabling the lawful interception of electronic communications.

Articles 22–24: jurisdictional and extraditional issues

Article 22 provides that a Member State will have jurisdiction in respect of offences committed within its territory (including ships and planes which are registered in that state), or in respect of offences committed by any of its nationals outside its territory where the conduct is criminal in the place where it is committed,[96] or in the event that the offence is committed outside the jurisdiction of any state.

---

[96] The 'double criminality principle'.

Article 23 promotes general principles relating to 'international cooperation'. The previously mentioned investigatory provisions and powers should be implemented on the basis of parity with domestic authorities whenever requested by a Member State.

Article 24 states that extradition should be made available for any of the offences established under the Convention, as long as a custodial sentence of at least one year could be imposed in both of the relevant states.

Conclusions

The opportunities for e-criminal offending are legion. Add to this the fact that many e-crimes are not reported and some simply remain undetected and the reality of the challenges faced by law enforcement officers and prosecutors begins to hit home. The technology itself can assist in the pursuit of the e-criminals and in proving to the court that they should be brought to justice. However, that same technology can enable the more skillful villains to stay at least one step ahead of their pursuers. For these reasons, it is essential that the ethos of international cooperation deepens and that the movement towards harmonisation of laws continues at pace. Lastly, the crucial element of IT security must be recognised and embraced by individuals and corporate bodies. This may not come cheap but, in the long run, prevention will be far less costly than cure.

10 Specific e-Crimes

10.1 Introduction

10.2 Computer Fraud

10.3 Piracy and Related Offences

10.4 The Law of Attempt

10.5 Hacking

10.6 The Limits of Authorised Access and the Use to Which it is Put

10.7 Aggravated Hacking – The Ulterior Intent Offence

10.8 Unauthorised Modification of Computer Programmes or Data

10.9 Computer and Internet Pornography

10.10 Cyberstalking and Online Harassment

10.1 Introduction

For the purposes of this book, a broad definition of 'e-Crime' has been adopted.[1] Under this umbrella term sits a range of criminal activities which are either assisted by computers/ICTs or focused upon them; the technology can provide the tool, target or storage device. This chapter will introduce the reader to some of the key forms of the increasing variety of illegal conduct to be found in the e-criminal world.

10.2 Computer Fraud

In general, fraudulent activity is simply facilitated by computers and ICTs rather than shaped by them. The criminal aim will usually be to dishonestly obtain property, credit or services, or to evade a debt or other liability. Often, the essence of the criminal activity will involve a deceit; a stratagem which has a long criminal pedigree, but which can be conducted on a much greater scale, against more victims and for vastly increased rewards, through the use of technology.

Defining 'computer fraud'

Computers and ICTs can play varying roles in fraudulent schemes. For example, a computer can be used to raid victims' bank accounts, perhaps after they have been tricked into providing their passwords and other banking details by means of a spoof website or deceptive e-mail. Here the computer technology is being used as a criminal tool and also provides the environment within which the crime takes place. If the e-fraudster has the skills, he can also use the technology to conceal his fraudulent

---

[1] See the start of Chapter 8 of this book.

208

activities, by inserting programmes to cover his tracks, or by impersonating someone else online after stealing their identity.

It should be noted that the computer can play each or all of these three roles (simultaneously) and that other e-criminal activity may be used to effect the fraudulent scheme. The potential criminal rewards for relatively little effort are illustrated by a scam which was recently being perpetrated on eBay, the Internet auction website.[2] Criminal gangs, thought to originate from Russia and Eastern Europe, were sending victims spam e-mails which, when opened, infected computers with key-logging software. This silently records every keystroke made by the victims and sends their online account log-in and password details back to the criminals, which enables them to fraudulently use the victims' accounts.

The Audit Commission's definition of the term 'computer fraud' has also been adopted by the Law Commission. This broad definition includes 'any fraudulent behaviour connected with computerisation by which someone intends to gain financial advantage'.[3] The Council of Europe has defined the term in the following way:

'... the input, alteration, erasure or suppression of computer data or computer programmes, or other interference with the course of data processing, that influences the result of data processing thereby causing economic or possessory loss of property of another person with the intent of procuring an unlawful economic gain for himself or another person.'[4]

Forms of computer fraud

Computer fraud can take several forms. The Audit Commission refers to the following three, distinguishing them in terms of what is done and when it occurs.

Input fraud

This is where the fraudster makes unauthorised alterations to data, or falsifies it, before or at the time of its entry into a computer. This is a relatively unsophisticated form of fraud; the only knowledge which is usually required is system-specific, such as awareness of the computer auditing procedures that are in place. A couple of case examples taken from Audit Commission surveys illustrate the ease with which input fraud can be perpetrated and stresses again the importance of regular, critical review of audit systems within organisations.

In one case,[5] a local authority officer submitted fictitious invoices by accessing colleagues' computer terminals at times when they had been left unattended. He stole £15,000, but his activities were detected during a routine budget monitoring process. He was sentenced to six months' imprisonment. The local authority reiterated to its staff the importance of logging off when leaving their computer terminals and system time-outs were introduced as a back up, together with more vigilant supervision. In

---

[2] Reported in *The Times*, 17 January 2005, p11.
[3] Audit Commission Survey (1987–1990), para 7.
[4] See: http://conventions.coe.int/Treaty/en/Treaties/Html/185.htm.
[5] Audit Commission Survey (2001), p13.

another case,[6] a local government wages clerk made false entries on times sheets which led to the overpayment of approximately 20 fellow employees. They were all parties to the crime and shared the proceeds between themselves, which amounted, in total, to £54,500.

Output fraud

This is where the fraudster manipulates the data at the point where it is outputted from the computer. Again, it is not usually sophisticated in nature and, in fact, occurs less frequently than input fraud. Sometimes both forms of fraud can be perpetrated, as illustrated by the following case example.[7] A bank manager falsified accounts to conceal the fact that he was embezzling funds; this was input fraud. However, he also suppressed computer-generated records which would have revealed his activities; this was output fraud.

Programme fraud

This is where the fraudster either creates or alters a programme for fraudulent ends. Consequently, it can be seen as a more sophisticated form of fraud which can be perpetrated in a variety of ways and is often difficult to detect. The fraudster may use a programme which generates false data, leading to monetary gain, such as in a case listed by the Audit Commission,[8] where software was written by two computer programmers and then added to an accounting programme. The programme was used for keeping stock of video films and recording the rental income from them. The software within the programme would generate false data when a special password was entered by certain storekeepers, thereby reducing their liability for VAT. Her Majesty's Customs and Excise was defrauded of £100,000. The two computer programmers were imprisoned for nine months and fined a total of £34,000.

A well-known form of programme fraud is 'Salami Fraud', so dubbed because it involves the perpetrator taking thin slices of money from a number of accounts and transferring them into a host account which he has set up. A real life example of this form of fraud was famously mimicked in film.[9] The actual crime was detected in Germany and involved the manipulation of a computer programme within a company's payroll department, in order to sweep up fractions of finances which would usually either be rounded up or simply ignored.

Fraud over the Internet

The most prevalent form of fraud over the Internet involves the use of another's credit card details during Internet transactions. These details, of course, have to be stolen first. There are several ways in which this can be done. Firstly, their transmission over the telecommunications network may be intercepted before it safely reaches its

---

[6] Audit Commission Survey (1984–87), cited as case 2.
[7] Audit Commission Survey (1981–87), cited as case 39.
[8] Audit Commission Survey (1984–87), cited as case 59.
[9] Superman III.

destination. Secondly, the e-criminal may hack into a computer system in order to obtain the relevant details.[10] Thirdly, the fraudster may impersonate a representative of a person's bank or credit card company on the telephone, or in an e-mail to them, in order to gain 'confirmation' of their credit card details. Fourthly, a spoof website may be set up to lure 'customers' to a new e-commercial opportunity, who then provide their credit card details in the genuine belief that they will receive goods or services in return for payment. Fifthly, e-criminals can actually create credit card numbers, if they have the programmes to do so. As Professor Ian Lloyd points out, 'computer programmes exist, and can be accessed over the Internet, which mimic the algorithms employed by credit card companies and so allow for the creation of genuine credit card numbers'.[11] And lastly, a link within the fraudster's website or his e-mail communications may secretly stable a 'trojan horse' programme which is released into the victim's computer in order to, for example, covertly record their keystrokes.

What is the scale of the computer fraud problem?

It has been suggested that the number of fraud cases that are detected and then prosecuted are 'just the tip of the iceberg'.[12] Any figures should be read in the light of the so-called 'dark figure' of e-Crime; the criminal activity that is either not detected or, though discovered, not reported. For example, a company may be loath to reveal itself as a victim of e-Crime for fear of damage to its reputation and any concomitant losses (eg of customers or trading partners).

In a report entitled 'Project Trawler' which was published in 1999, the National Criminal Investigation Service (NCIS) suggested that traditional methods of fraud 'have been given a new lease of life on the Internet'.[13] Some surveys, significant firstly because of the number of respondents involved,[14] have unearthed some worrying statistics. In 1999, it was estimated that the total losses in the UK to Internet fraud might range from £400 million to £5 billion.[15] In the US, the Internet Fraud Watch reported in February 2000 that:

> 'Consumers lost over $3.2 million to Internet fraud last year in incident reports to the National Consumer League's Internet Fraud Watch. A 38 per cent increase in Internet fraud complaints in 1999 coupled with an average consumer loss of as much as $580.'[16]

In the latest survey by the Audit Commission in the UK,[17] fraud was the fourth most common activity reported to the Commission. Again in the US, in 2002, the Internet Fraud Complaint Center (IFCC) Report, which was prepared by the National White Collar Crime Center and the FBI, revealed more than 48,000 cases of Internet fraud in which victims lost a total of $54 million.[18]

---

[10] For example, hacking into a retailer's computerised customer records.
[11] Lloyd, I, 'Information Technology Law', Oxford University Press (2004), 4th ed, p273.
[12] Bainbridge, D, 'Introduction to Computer Law', Longman (2004), 5th ed, p366.
[13] See: http://www.ncis.co.uk/contact.html.
[14] Over 10,000 consumers.
[15] Fraud Advisory Panel, established by the Institute of Chartered Accountants for England and Wales.
[16] See: http://www.fraud.org/internet/intstat.htm.
[17] See: yourbusiness@risk: An Update on IT Abuse, 2001.
[18] See: http://www.fraud.org/internet/instat.htm.

The National High-Tech Crime Unit's 2004 survey revealed that whilst computer fraud may not be the most prevalent form of e-criminal activity, in terms of its financial impact it can top the tables.[19] Therein, financial services companies reported themselves to be regular victims of fraud, as did telecommunications companies. The 2005 survey confirms that this particular trend continues. This comes as little surprise, given that information technology is crucial to the financial sector. As Professor Ian Lloyd points out, 85 per cent of all money transactions in the UK are handled by some form of Electronic Fund Transfer (EFT).[20] In the US, the 2004 E-Crime Watch Survey[21] and the Computer Security Institute (CSI) and the US Federal Bureau of Investigation (FBI) 2004 Survey[22] have reported some similar trends in computer fraud.

The use of spoof websites and e-mail to facilitate fraud is a consistent aspect of the reportage from these surveys. With regard to the particular types of computer fraud, auction fraud, non-delivery of goods and services, and credit card fraud seem to be by far the most prevalent. One form of Internet fraud which has received much press in recent times is 'identity theft', although the figures suggest that, as yet, this is a comparatively rare form of e-criminal activity. However, the Internet offers up an increasing number of opportunities for fraudsters: 'Pyramid schemes', spoof Internet banking services, companies which offer to repair customers' credit ratings, 'shell companies' which trade on securities markets, spurious products which are offered for sale to provide specific solutions to technological problems[23] and websites linked to telemarketing 'boiler rooms', all serve to deepen the pool of potential victims.

How does the law seek to combat computer fraud?

E-criminals will either be seeking a direct benefit from their fraudulent activity, typically money, or some indirect benefit by, for example, avoiding financial liability for their use of certain services. The term 'fraud' should be given a wider definition within this context; wider, that is, than the traditional meaning accorded to it in criminal law. The reason for this is that computer fraud can often involve the commission of crimes which do not usually fall within the category of 'fraud offences'.

It is important to note here that, at the time of writing this book, a new Fraud Bill has recently been presented to Parliament (in the House of Lords on 25 May 2005) which, if enacted, will radically reform the law relating to fraud. The key objective of the Bill is to modernise the existing statutory offences of deception which are used to tackle fraud (see details of these traditional, deception-based offences in the next section). It sets out provisions for a general offence of fraud, with three ways of committing it: by false representation, by failure to disclose information and by abuse of position. It also contains provisions for creating new offences of obtaining services dishonestly and of possessing, making and supplying articles for use in frauds. If

---

[19] National Hi-Tech Crime Unit Survey: High-Tech Crime 2004 – The Impact on UK Business – see: http://www.nhtcu.org/NOPSurvey.pdf.
[20] Lloyd, I, 'Information Technology Law', Oxford University Press (2004), 4th ed, p275.
[21] See: http://www.cert.org/about/ecrime.html.
[22] See: http://www.gocsi.com.
[23] Such as the 'Y2K' problem.

enacted, the Bill will repeal the deception offences in ss15, 15A, 16 and 20(2) Theft Act 1968 and ss1 and 2 Theft Act 1978. The Bill will, it seems, solve some of the real problems which currently exist in the law relating to these 'traditional' fraud offences (see the next section for details) and will assist the prosecution not only of serious and complex fraud (Serious Fraud Office prosecutions) but also of more routine cases brought by the Crown Prosecution Service and the Department of Trade and Industry.

One of the key problems of applying the current deception-based offences in computer fraud scenarios has been the legal fact that you cannot deceive a computer (see *DPP* v *Ray* in the next section). Although, in some such cases, the operational solution has been to rely upon the common law offence of conspiracy to defraud, it carries the fundamental limitation that it only applies when more than one person is involved (a criminal conspiracy stems from the meeting of at least two minds; it is that agreement which is the key element of the offence).

The new, general offence of fraud would not rely upon the concept of deception in any of its three forms. Fraud by false representation would use the concept of dishonesty, as currently defined in the law of theft. An example of the type of behaviour which would be covered by this new offence is where a person dishonestly misuses a credit card to pay for items. By tendering the card, he would be falsely representing that he has the authority to use it for that transaction. If he knows that he does not, or might not, have that authority, then he would be committing this new offence; it would be immaterial that the person (or computer) accepting the card for payment is 'deceived' by the representation. This new offence would also be committed by someone who engages in 'phishing' (sending e-mails to large groups of people which purport to come from a legitimate financial institution, such as an Internet bank). The sending of such e-mails implicitly makes a false representation which, in turn, fuels the request that the victims provide their credit card or bank account details; the phisher can then use this information for nefarious purposes (eg identity theft, fraud, etc).

The new offence of fraud by failing to disclose information would rely upon the concept of a legal duty of disclosure, so that, for example, a person could be successfully prosecuted for this offence where he intentionally fails to disclose information relating to a serious medical condition when applying for life insurance.

The new offence of fraud by abuse of position would use the concept of dishonesty in assessing whether the accused had taken criminal advantage of a privileged/responsible position. For example, the offence would cover the situation where someone is employed to care for an elderly or disabled person and has access to that person's bank account, but abuses their position by removing funds from it for their own personal use.

The new offence of obtaining services dishonestly would, for example, catch the individual who tenders an improperly obtained credit card to obtain services from the Internet; again, the concept of deception would not feature in this offence.

An example of the type of activity which would be criminalised by the new offence of possessing, making and supplying articles for use in frauds would be having, making or supplying computer programmes that can generate genuine credit card numbers, which can then be used to commit or facilitate fraud.

The Fraud Bill was presented to Parliament by the Attorney-General, Lord Goldsmith, who has stated that:

> '[It] will tighten existing legislation and create a new offence of fraud, in order to better protect the victims of fraud. This reform is needed to enable prosecutors to get to grips with the increasing abuse of technology, particularly in relation to fake credit cards and personal identity theft, which costs millions of pounds every year.'

At the time of writing, the Bill has only passed the first stage of its parliamentary journey (the First Reading). It may be some months before it is enacted (in its current or an amended form). For now, the current law relating to computer fraud must be examined in detail in the next section.

The traditional fraud offences

Most of these offences are found within ss15–20 Theft Act 1968 and ss1–2 Theft Act 1978. However, it must also be noted that the basic offence of theft[24] requires consideration here because, particularly in the light of the House of Lords' decision in *R v Gomez*,[25] in certain circumstances there can be an overlap between it and some fraud offences. Indeed, the Law Commission stated as far back as 1988 that: 'when a computer is manipulated in order dishonestly to obtain money or other property, a charge of theft or attempted theft will generally lie'.[26]

Obtaining property by deception – s15 Theft Act 1968

Section 15(1):

> 'A person who by any deception dishonestly obtains property belonging to another, with the intention of permanently depriving the other of it, shall on conviction on indictment be liable to imprisonment for a term not exceeding ten years.'

This is an offence which is triable either way. If tried on indictment, it carries a maximum sentence of ten years' imprisonment and/or a fine. The deception, which is clearly a key element of the offence, can be 'deliberate or reckless'; mere negligence will not suffice.[27] The concept of 'deception' has been clarified in case law. In *Re London and Global Finance Corporation Ltd*,[28] Buckley J defined it in the following way:

> 'To deceive is ... to induce a man to believe that a thing is true which is false, and which the person practising the deceit knows or believes to be false.'

The victim must, in fact, have been deceived. *Miller*[29] illustrates this point. Therein,

---

[24] Found in s1 Theft Act 1968.
[25] [1993] AC 442 (HL).
[26] Law Commission's Working Paper No 110 (1988), para 3.4.
[27] Section 15(4).
[28] [1903] 1 Ch 728.
[29] [1992] Crim LR 744.

the accused had pretended to be a licensed taxi driver and charged the victims an extortionate sum of money for their journey. The victims stated that by the time the journey had ended they realised that the accused was not a licensed taxi driver, but that they paid the money to him to avoid trouble. The accused argued, on the strength of their evidence, that at the time he obtained the money from them there was no deception at play. The Court of Appeal ruled that it was open for the jury to decide that the deception caused the obtaining; that the victims would not have got into the taxi and then later felt under pressure to pay the high price for the journey were it not for the original deception.

The apparent requirement that there must be some person who is deceived naturally raises a key question within the context of e-Crime: in the eyes of the law, can a computer be deceived? The answer was given by the House of Lords in *DPP* v *Ray*.[30] Having approved the aforementioned definition given to the concept of 'deception' in *Re London and Global Finance Corporation Ltd*, Lord Morris confirmed that:

> 'For a deception to take place there must be some person or persons who will have been deceived.'

Thus, it can be seen that any deception must be played upon a human mind; a computer cannot be deceived. This has profound implications for e-criminal cases. For example, in the following two scenarios, which are factually quite similar, the legal outcomes may be very dissimilar.

Scenario A
A bank employee gains permitted access to a bank's computer system and dishonestly instructs it to transfer money from one account into another. Here only the computer has been 'deceived' and so a s15 conviction will not be possible.

Scenario B
A bank employee sends a message to the computer of another bank employee, requesting confirmation of such a transfer. Here a person has been deceived and so a s15 conviction is still possible.

In fact, this legal lacuna has caused few problems in practice for two reasons. Firstly, since the decision of the House of Lords in *R* v *Gomez*,[31] many cases of obtaining property by deception could instead be charged as theft, under s1 of the same Act. And secondly, it is quite often the case that at some point during the criminal transaction a human mind will actually have been deceived (as in scenario B above).

Obtaining services by deception – s1 Theft Act 1978

Section 1(1):

> 'A person who by any deception dishonestly obtains services from another shall be guilty of an offence.'

---

[30] [1974] AC 370.
[31] [1993] AC 442 (HL).

Section 1(2):

> 'It is an obtaining of services where the other is induced to confer a benefit by doing some act, or causing or permitting some act to be done, on the understanding that the benefit has been or will be paid for.'

This is an offence which is triable either way. If tried on indictment, it carries a maximum sentence of five years' imprisonment and/or a fine. An example of the type of criminal behaviour which this offence is aimed at is the hiring of a car through deceptive means. It covers a wide range of services, including those relating to travel, the household, leisure and accommodation. However, it must be noted that the stated principle in *DPP* v *Ray*[32] still applies here because it is a deception-based offence. Indeed, the statutory wording of the offence reinforces that principle here by requiring the services to be deceptively obtained from 'another'. Finally, it must be noted that the statutory definition of 'services' is limited to those that are subject to payment.[33] Given this, the act of deceptively obtaining free services is a legal impossibility.

Evasion of liability by deception – s2 Theft Act 1978

Section 2(1):

> 'A person who by any deception –

> (a) dishonestly secures the remission of the whole or part of any existing liability to make a payment, whether his own liability or another's; or

> (b) with intent to make permanent default in whole or part on any existing liability to make payment, or with intent to let another do so, dishonestly induces the creditor or any person claiming payment on behalf of the creditor to wait for payment (whether or not the due date for payment is deferred) or to forgo payment; or

> (c) dishonestly obtains any exemption from or abatement of liability to make payment;

> he shall be guilty of an offence.'

This is an offence which is triable either way. If tried on indictment, it carries a maximum sentence of five years' imprisonment and/or a fine. An example of the type of criminal behaviour which this offence is aimed at is the giving of false information to a creditor as part of a request to be relieved from all or part of a debt liability. Again, the aforementioned principle from *DPP* v *Ray*[34] will apply here, presenting a potential obstacle to successful prosecution.

Obtaining a money transfer by deception – s15A Theft Act 1968

Section 15A(1):

> 'A person is guilty of an offence if by any deception he dishonestly obtains a money transfer for himself or another.'

This is an offence which is triable either way. If tried on indictment, it carries a maximum sentence of ten years' imprisonment and/or a fine. It should be noted that

---

[32] See footnote 30 above.
[33] See s1(2).
[34] See footnote 30 above.

the section declares that a 'money transfer' occurs when a debit is made to one account which results in a credit to another account.[35] The offence was created[36] in order to plug the loophole in the law which was highlighted by the House of Lords' decision in *R* v *Preddy*.[37] Therein, the defendants made several applications to borrow money in the form of mortgage loans from building societies. These applications contained various pieces of false information. Some of them were successful and the funds were electronically transferred from the lenders' bank accounts to the bank account of the solicitor who was acting on behalf of the defendants. The defendants had been convicted on several counts of either obtaining or attempting to obtain property by deception. Their appeal to the House of Lords was successful, resulting in their convictions being quashed. In order to fully understand the decision in this case, it is important first to consider the property rights which exist in a bank account. When someone's bank account is in credit, the legal relationship between the account holder and the bank is that of creditor and debtor, respectively. In other words, the credit balance, say £1,000, which is reported in paper and electronic bank statements does not refer to money sitting in the bank; instead, it points to a debt of £1,000 owed by the bank to the customer. Thus, the customer does not own the £1,000 which was paid into the bank, but he does own a form of intangible property[38] related to it. Specifically, he owns a chose in action, which is a legal right to sue the bank for that sum of money. The main reason why the Law Lords quashed the convictions of Preddy and his co-defendants was that when the transfer of funds was made from the lenders' bank accounts to the 'borrowers' account, each lender's right to sue their bank for the sum in question (their chose in action) was extinguished; it no longer existed at law. At the same time, a chose in action was legally born and given to the defendants against their bank in relation to the sums transferred into their account. Consequently, in the eyes of the law, the defendants had not received any 'property belonging to another' and could not, therefore, be considered guilty of obtaining such property by deception; in short, there was no property to obtain. A summary of the main points of their Lordships' decision follows.

The '*Preddy* problem'

* The House of Lords confirmed that an account in a bank or a building society is classed as a chose in action.

* A chose in action is a right that can be enforced by a legal action (eg a right to recover a debt).

* Their Lordships confirmed that where telegraphic or electronic fund transfers are made from one bank or building society account to another bank or building society account, the original chose in action is extinguished and is replaced by a new chose in action. In other words, when funds are transferred from A's account, his chose in action in respect of the money represented by the previous balance

---

[35] See s15A(2).
[36] The section was inserted via s1 Theft (Amendment) Act 1996.
[37] [1996] AC 815.
[38] Intangible property is 'property' for the purposes of the Theft Act 1968 – see ss4(1) and 34(1).

dies, and a new chose in action is born which belongs to B, the person into whose account the funds have been transferred.

- Consequently, since the borrower did not get the lender's chose in action, it was held that 'property belonging to another' had not been obtained.

In the light of that decision, anyone who engineered a fraudulent electronic transfer might have escaped conviction not only for obtaining property by deception but also, possibly, for theft,[39] on the basis that the property obtained (or appropriated) did not 'belong to another'.

Consequently, the offence of obtaining a money transfer by deception (under s15A) was duly created. Henceforth, in similar scenarios, a person could be convicted of this new crime where they had deceptively obtained a credit to their bank account resulting from a debit to another person's bank account. The offence not only covers the obtaining of loans but extends to situations where, for example, someone has been deceived into making a gift of money to the accused or somebody else, or perhaps where they have been deceived into buying goods or services from them. Remember, however, that the deception must have been played upon a human mind.[40]

You can't deceive a computer: the lacuna revisited
Before moving on to consider the other traditional offences which can be used in the fight against computer fraud, it is important to look again at the legal conundrum confirmed in *DPP* v *Ray*.[41] The problem of the lacuna has been considered by the Law Commission on two occasions. Firstly, in 1999 the Commission recommended that, rather than taking the approach of extending the concept of 'deception' to include machines, a new offence related to theft should be established; a general fraud offence.[42] In 2002, the Commission returned to this issue, then stating:

> 'We now believe that [the misuse of credit cards and other payment instruments] would be covered in a more convincing and less artificial way if the concept of deception were replaced by that of misrepresentation. Since the merchant who accepts the card in payment does not care whether the defendant has authority to use it, it is debatable whether the merchant can be said to be deceived. It is clear ... however, that by tendering the card the defendant is impliedly and falsely representing that he or she has authority to use it for the transaction in question. In our view that should suffice, even if the defendant knows that the representee is indifferent whether the representation is true. We have therefore concluded that this form of the new offence should be defined in terms of misrepresentation rather than deception.'[43]

It can be seen that this proposed new offence would shift the focus from the issue of whether the victim was, in fact, deceived to more detailed consideration of the

---

[39] Although, now it would be submitted that a charge of theft lies here; that is, appropriation of the lender's right to sue the bank for the amount of money transferred (ie theft of the chose in action) – see *R* v *Burke* [2000] Crim LR 413. See also the decision of the Court of Appeal in *R* v *Williams (Roy)* [2000] 1 Cr App R 2, where the transfer of funds was viewed as involving an appropriation of the victim's right as the owner of the credit balance to dispose of it.

[40] See, for example, the case *Holmes* v *Governor of Brixton Prison* (2004) The Times 28 October (DC).

[41] See footnote 30 above.

[42] Law Commission: Legislating the Criminal Code: Fraud and Deception (1999).

[43] Law Commission, Report No 276, Fraud (2002), para 7.16.

accused's wrongdoing. As Professor Clarkson points out: 'this approach would have the advantage that it would make no difference whether the misrepresentation was directed at a person or a machine'.[44] In fact, the government has now responded to these recommendations by introducing the Fraud Bill to Parliament on 25 May 2005: see the section in this Chapter entitled 'How does the law seek to combat computer fraud?' for detailed consideration of the new offences contained within the Bill.

The Council of Europe's Convention on Cybercrime has formulated an offence of fraud which avoids the concept of deception. It proclaims that:

'Each party shall adopt such legislative and other measures as may be necessary to establish as criminal offences under its domestic law, when committed intentionally and without right, the causing of a loss of property to another by (a) any input, alteration, deletion or suppression of computer data, or (b) any interference with the functioning of a computer system, with fraudulent or dishonest intent of procuring, without right, an economic benefit for oneself or another.'[45]

The basic offence of theft – s1(1) Theft Act 1968

Section 1(1):

'A person is guilty of theft if he dishonestly appropriates property belonging to another with the intention of permanently depriving the other of it.'

This is an offence which is triable either way. If tried on indictment, it carries a maximum sentence of seven years' imprisonment and/or a fine. In the light of the previous discussion on the lacuna in the law relating to deception-based offences, it might be thought that, in the absence of evidence supporting a charge of conspiracy or attempt, a person who simply 'deceives' a computer into transferring money to his bank account could not be not be successfully prosecuted. However, as David Bainbridge points out: 'the criminal law is not so easily defeated. Usually, the offence of theft will be committed, regardless of the interposition of a computer.'[46] The key elements of the offence are not usually difficult to establish in such cases, as shown below.

Appropriation

According to s3(1) of the Act: 'any assumption by a person of the rights of an owner amounts to appropriation, and this includes, where he has come by the property (innocently or not) without stealing it, any later assumption of a right to it by keeping or dealing with it as owner'. The interpretation of this concept, in case law, has afforded it an almost neutral, as opposed to pejorative, meaning. Specifically, the much-debated question of whether an act done with the consent of the owner of the property amounts to an appropriation of it was conclusively answered by the House of Lords in *R* v *Gomez*.[47] Their Lordships confirmed that the issue of consent was irrelevant to the concept of appropriation. Professor J C Smith declared that the effect of this decision was to create an extraordinarily wide offence. This led him to state that:

---

[44] Clarkson and Keating, 'Criminal Law: Text and Materials', Sweet & Maxwell, 5th ed, p819.
[45] Article 8 – see: http://conventions.coe.int/Treaty/en/Treaties/Html/185.htm.
[46] Bainbridge, D, 'Introduction to Computer Law', Longman (2004), 5th ed, p376.
[47] [1993] AC 442 (HL).

'Anyone doing anything whatever to property belonging to another, with or without his consent, appropriates it; and, if he does so dishonestly and with intent by that, or any subsequent act, permanently to deprive, he commits theft.'[48]

Cases such as *Burke*[49] and *R v Williams (Roy)*[50] have paved an alternative path for prosecution in cases where the deception-based offences would have presented problems.

Property

The definition of 'property' is also wide, covering 'money and all other property, real or personal, including things in action and other intangible property'.[51]

Belonging to another

Property is deemed to belong to another if that person has possession or control of it, or has a proprietary right or interest in it.[52] Given this, the definition accorded to the word 'owner' is wider than that in common parlance.

Dishonestly

You will not find the concept of 'dishonesty' explained within the Act, although it is (negatively) defined to some extent therein.[53] The test for dishonesty is found in case law, specifically in *R v Ghosh*.[54] It is a two-stage test, the first being an objective question and the second being a question compromised of both subjective and objective elements, as follows:

• was what was done dishonest according to the ordinary standards of reasonable and honest people; if so

• did the defendant himself realise that what he was doing was dishonest according to those standards?

If the jury (or magistrates) answer both questions in the affirmative, the appropriation will be deemed a dishonest one.

Intention to permanently deprive

The accused must intend that the owner of the property will be permanently deprived of it. Borrowing can equate to permanent deprivation where the property is returned after a very long time or, for example, where it is returned with no 'goodness' or value left in it.[55]

---

[48] Smith & Hogan: 'Criminal Law', Butterworths (2002), 10th ed, p518.
[49] See footnote 39 above.
[50] Ibid.
[51] Section 4(1).
[52] Section 5(1).
[53] See s4.
[54] [1982] 2 All ER 689.
[55] See the case of *Lloyd* [1985] 2 All ER 661.

Other offences under the Theft Act 1968

The Act contains several other offences which could potentially feature in computer fraud cases. For example, the offence of false accounting under s17, which can be a useful charge for several reasons. Firstly, it is not a requirement that the accused actually obtains any benefit from his actions; it is sufficient that he acted 'with a view to gain ... or with intent to cause loss'.[56] Secondly, it is not necessary to prove that anyone was deceived. And thirdly, 'this offence is committed at the time when the account is destroyed, defaced, concealed or falsified, or (once it has been falsified) when it is produced or used. Thus, it bites at an earlier time in the fraudster's activities and can be seen, in some instances, as an alternative to a charge of attempting one of the deception offences.'[57]

The offence of suppression of documents under s20 can potentially be used in cases where the accused's actions would be viewed as merely preparatory to other offences. Indeed, the Criminal Law Revision Committee expressed the opinion that this offence may provide 'the only way of dealing with a person who, for example, suppressed a public document as a first step towards committing a fraud but did not get so far as attempting to commit the fraud'.[58]

Company officers who publish (or concur in publishing) false statements with intent to deceive shareholders or creditors can be prosecuted under s19. The term 'officer' includes any director or company secretary and extends to a company auditor as well.[59]

Lastly, it should be noted that s32(1) confirms that one form of the offence of cheating has been retained at common law. This is the offence of cheating the Inland Revenue. An example might be where a person alters the computerised reports in their accounts system and submits an amended report in order to reduce their liability for VAT. It lends itself to the more serious cases of revenue fraud because it can result in a lengthy custodial sentence and/or a fine. For example, in *Mavji*,[60] the accused was imprisoned for six years and made criminally bankrupt in the sum of £690,000. Another of its advantages is that, again, there is no requirement that a person be deceived.

The common law offence of conspiracy to defraud

Necessarily, this offence cannot be committed by one person alone; a key element of all conspiracy offences is the presence of an agreement between two or more persons to pursue a criminal course of conduct. Here again, it is immaterial that no one is, in fact, deceived. This is evidenced in the comments of Viscount Dilhourne in *Scott* v *Metropolitan Police Commissioner*:[61]

---

[56] See s17(1).
[57] Phillips, Walsh and Dobson, 'Law Relating To Theft', Cavendish (2001), p236.
[58] Criminal Law Revision Committee, Eighth Report: Theft and Related Offences, 1966, Cmnd 2977, para 106.
[59] See the case of *Shacter* [1960] 2 QB 252.
[60] [1987] 2 All ER 758.
[61] [1975] AC 819.

'... to "defraud" ordinarily means ... to deprive a person dishonestly of something which is his or of something to which he is or would or might, but for the perpetration of the fraud, be entitled.'

The offence carries a maximum sentence of ten years' imprisonment and/or a fine.[62] In *Hollinshead*,[63] the Court of Appeal considered the rule that the contemplated fraud must be one which is to be perpetrated by one of the parties to the agreement in the course of carrying it out.[64] Their Lordships seemed to widen that rule to include cases where third parties effect the defrauding. In addition, it is not necessary to prove intent to defraud in the sense of intending to cause economic loss.

By its very nature, this offence can often give rise to jurisdictional issues. First, it must be noted that an agreement in England or Wales to carry out a fraud abroad is not indictable at common law. However, where the offence would otherwise be triable in this jurisdiction but for the fact that the fraud was intended to be effected abroad, s5(3) Criminal Justice Act 1993 provides some jurisdictional leeway. It enables the prosecution of any party to the agreement where they (or their agent) did anything in relation to the agreement before its formation, did or omitted anything in pursuance of the agreement once it is made, or became a party to that agreement, within this jurisdiction.

This offence stands alone, but it must also be remembered that a charge of statutory conspiracy to commit other offences (under s1 Criminal Law Act 1977) may also be possible on the same facts.[65] Indeed, it is important to note that a new section was inserted into the Criminal Law Act 1977[66] via s5 Criminal Justice (Terrorism and Conspiracy) Act 1998 to enable the prosecution of those who plan acts or events outside the United Kingdom. This provision is aimed at terrorists in this jurisdiction who conspire here to commit crimes abroad. The key requirement is 'double criminality'; that is, the agreed acts must amount to a criminal offence both in this country and in the country where they are to take place.

Conspiracy to defraud remains a useful, flexible offence which can assist prosecutors in e-Crime cases. For example, if the suspect has planned a fraudulent transfer of funds via computer technology but has not done an act which, in law, would be viewed as an attempt at a complete offence, he could be charged with this inchoate offence. Equally, it could provide an alternative route of prosecution where, for example, the individual could not be successfully prosecuted under the Computer Misuse Act 1990 because of a legal technicality.

---

[62] Section 12 Criminal Justice Act 1987.

[63] [1985] 1 All ER 850 at 857.

[64] This is a requirement for statutory conspiracy – see s1(1)(a) Criminal Law Act 1977.

[65] At one stage, the House of Lords took the view that conspiracies which centred around an agreement to commit a crime had to be dealt within under the Criminal Law Act 1977 (see *Ayres* [1984] AC 447). This position has now been changed by s12 Criminal Justice Act 1987, so that either offence can be charged in such cases.

[66] Section 1A.

10.3 Piracy and Related Offences

Copyright infringement – s107 of the Copyright, Designs and Patents Act 1988

It used to be the case that copyright infringement was only an offence at criminal law when done in the course of business. This has now been extended to situations where people infringe copyright 'otherwise than in the course of a business, to such an extent as to affect prejudicially the owner of the copyright'.[67]

This is an offence which is triable either way. If tried on indictment, it carries a maximum sentence of ten years' imprisonment and/or a fine. It is aimed at the making of, or dealing with, infringing articles. It can be used, for example, to combat computer software piracy. For the purposes of establishing mens rea, it is sufficient for the prosecution to prove that the accused either knew or had reason to believe that the article in question was an infringing copy of a copyright work.[68] The test to be applied for these purposes is an objective one: whether the reasonable man, having the defendant's knowledge of the facts, would have believed that the copy was an infringing copy.[69]

Forgery – s1 Forgery and Counterfeiting Act 1981

Section 1:

> 'A person is guilty of forgery if he makes a false instrument, with the intention that he or another shall use it to induce somebody to accept it as genuine, and by reason of so accepting it to do or not to do some act to his own or any other person's prejudice.'

This offence has not been successfully used in some spheres of e-criminal activity,[70] but remains a potent weapon in situations where, for example, individuals are alleged to have made copies of computer software and then sold them as originals. The statutory definition of a 'false instrument' includes 'any disc, tape, sound track or other device on or in which information is recorded or stored by mechanical, electronic or other means'.[71] The offence carries with it a maximum sentence of ten years' imprisonment and/or a fine.

False trade descriptions – s1 Trade Descriptions Act 1968

This offence is concerned with the application of false trade descriptions to goods or the supplying or offering for sale of goods which have a false trade description. The statutory definition of a 'trade description' includes an indication of who manufactured or produced the goods in question.[72] So, for example, anyone who makes, sells or offers for sale pirated copies of computer software which are presented in a way that

---

[67] Section 107(1)(e).
[68] Ibid.
[69] Confirmed by the Court of Appeal in *LA Gear Inc* v *Hi-Tec Sports plc* [1992] FSR 121.
[70] See, for example, the case of *Gold* [1988] 1 AC 1063.
[71] Section 8(1)(d).
[72] Section 2(1)(i).

indicates, directly or indirectly, that they are original can be prosecuted for this offence. It is an offence triable either way. If tried on indictment, it carries a maximum sentence of two years' imprisonment and/or a fine. Prosecutions are usually conducted by trading standards officers.

Unauthorised use of trademarks – s92 Trademarks Act 1994

This is an offence triable either way. If tried on indictment, it carries a maximum sentence of ten years' imprisonment and/or a fine. It is aimed at individuals who, without permission of the trademark holder, place signs on goods or their packing which are identical to (or are likely to be mistaken for) registered trademarks. Equally, the sale, hire or simple possession of such goods is a criminal offence. Liability is strict here, unless the defendant can prove, on a balance of probabilities, that he reasonably believed that the use of the sign in the manner in which it was used was not an infringement of the registered trademark.[73] In the case of *Johnstone*,[74] the appellant argued that the reversal of the burden of proof on this matter was an infringement of his right to a fair trial, as enshrined in art 6 of the European Convention on Human Rights. The Law Lords rejected his appeal. He was sentenced to six months' imprisonment[75] for selling bootleg music recordings.

10.4 The Law of Attempt

Attempts under s1 Criminal Attempts Act 1981

Section 1(1):

> 'If, with intent to commit an offence to which this section applies, a person does an act which is more than merely preparatory to the commission of the offence, he is guilty of attempting to commit that offence.'

This inchoate offence can sometimes be used as a weapon in the fight against e-Crime. However, first it must be noted that a person cannot be found guilty of attempting a summary offence,[76] of attempting to conspire,[77] or of attempting to aid, abet, counsel or procure the commission of an offence.[78]

How then could this offence be used to combat computer fraud? Take, for example, the suspected fraudster who has not managed to fully execute his criminal plan. His uncompleted fraud could be viewed as attempted theft. If he is charged with this offence, a key issue will be whether he went past the stage of preparing to steal, to a point where, in law, he is deemed to have attempted theft. The section dictates that he must have done an act which was 'more than merely preparatory to the commission

---

[73] Section 92(5).
[74] [2003] UKHL 28.
[75] There was also a confiscation order of £130,000.
[76] A summary offence is one which can only be tried in the magistrates' court – s1(4) Criminal Attempts Act 1981 refers to indictable offences only (in this statutory context, the phrase 'indictable offence' connotes an offence triable either way or on indictment).
[77] Section 1(4)(a).
[78] Section 1(4)(b).

of the offence'. The task of determining whether an act is more than merely preparatory has been considered through a long line of case law. In *Eagleton*,[79] the 'Rubicon Test' was created, which Lord Diplock later understood to mean that only acts immediately connected with an offence could be viewed as attempts to commit it. He explained that 'the offender must have crossed the Rubicon and burnt his boats'.[80] In *Osborn*,[81] Rowlatt J considered that the accused must have actually started committing the offence or, as he put it, been 'on the job'. A similar approach was advocated by Lord Lane in *Gullefer*,[82] when he stipulated that an attempt begins 'when the defendant embarks upon the crime proper'. This particular phrase seems to have been adopted and applied in cases since then.[83]

David Bainbridge gives a good example of how difficult this issue can be within the context of computer fraud:

> 'Consider the case of an employee of a bank who decides, on his own, to transfer money to his own account from a customer's account. First, he switches on a computer terminal. Second, he enters the appropriate password to gain access. Then, he enters the instruction at the keyboard which causes the funds to be transferred. Finally, he draws the money out of the account. The problems arise when the bank employee fails to complete the offence of theft of the money for one reason or another. At what stage in the course of the events described do his actions become more than merely preparatory? A reasonable member of a jury might conclude that the offence of attempting to steal is not made out until the third act has been carried out – that is, the entry of instructions which cause the computer system to transfer the money to the employee's account.'[84]

Clearly then, the task of distinguishing a mere act of preparation from an attempt in computer fraud cases can be a testing one. However, it should be noted that this challenge will only have to be faced on rare occasions. The reason for this is that s2 Computer Misuse Act 1990 introduced an offence which caters for this scenario and others like it. Specifically, the offence is comprised of hacking with intent to commit certain further offences (such as theft). Once the prosecution has established that hacking occurred, as it often will have in computer fraud cases, they must simply prove that the accused intended to commit one of the further offences. This offence can be seen as preparatory by nature but is, of course, legally complete when both of these elements are shown to have existed; it is only thoughts, not actions, which must be proven in relation to the further offence(s).

10.5 Hacking

To begin with, a warning. The term 'hacking' is sometimes inaccurately defined, even within legal textbooks. In order to truly understand this activity and the law which renders it criminal, it is important to grasp the precise, legal meaning of the term. A 'hacker' is someone who seeks to gain unauthorized access to computer programmes

---

[79] (1855) Dears CC 376.
[80] *DPP* v *Stonehouse* [1978] AC 55 at 68.
[81] (1919) 84 JP 63.
[82] [1990] 3 All ER 882.
[83] See the following cases: *Jones* (1990) 91 Cr App Rep 351; *Campbell* (1991) 93 Cr App Rep 350; *Attorney-General's Reference (No 1 of 1992)* (1993) 96 Cr App Rep 298; *Tosti* [1997] Crim LR 746; *Toothill* [1998] Crim LR 876.
[84] Bainbridge, D, 'Introduction to Computer Law', Longman (2004), 5th ed, pp375–376.

or data. It is crucial to note that a person who tries, but fails to gain such access is still a 'hacker' in the eyes of the criminal law. He is not preparing to hack, attempting to hack, or unsuccessfully hacking; he has hacked. In other words, there is no requirement within the criminal offence of hacking that the accused actually gains the unauthorized access which he seeks.[85] The clear advantage of this is that it sidesteps the potential hurdles within the law of attempt.[86] Professor J C Smith gave a succinct summary of the legal threshold in metaphorical terms:

'... it is enough that he [the accused] is out fishing without a licence. Indeed, it is enough that he sets out to fish without a licence.'[87]

Hacking can pose a threat to the security and integrity of computer systems and networks. It is often the means by which people pursue further criminal ends, such as fraud, theft, blackmail, computer virus infection, or commercial piracy. Even where the hacker's only motive is curiosity or the inherent intellectual challenge of the process, their activities may leave behind a vulnerability within the system which can then be exploited by 'malicious hackers'.[88] Furthermore, where a hacker has not, in fact, secured access to a system, he may still have weakened or 'damaged' it in his attempts to do so. It can be seen from this that the rationale behind the criminalisation of hacking is comprised of both the need to prevent various forms of criminal behaviour and to combat the dangers, costs and inconveniences which can flow from hacking activities.

Before considering the two criminal offences of hacking in detail, it is worth analysing the legal concerns which led to their enactment. In 1987, the Scottish Law Commission recommended that hacking should be criminalised only where there was intent to commit further acts, such as the alteration or erasure of data.[89] In 1989, the English Law Commission recommended that hacking should be a criminal offence in the absence of such further intent.[90] In the interim, the House of Lords' decision in the case of *Gold*[91] had highlighted the need for legislative action. Therein, the two defendants, who were journalists, discovered by means of a 'dishonest trick'[92] a password which allowed them to gain unauthorised access to British Telecom's Prestel network. This password gave them widespread, unbilled access to the system and they made extensive use of it. Their activities eventually roused suspicions and they were arrested. The first, key question was with which offence they should be charged, if any. Given the fact that no deception had been played upon a human mind, a charge

---

[85] Although, in practice, if he has actually obtained such access this will assist the prosecution in proving that the accused had the requisite mens rea for the offence.

[86] See the previous section of this chapter. Note also the general rule that it is legally impossible to attempt a summary offence (see s1(4) Criminal Attempts Act 1981); the basic offence of hacking (under s1 Computer Misuse Act 1990) is a summary offence.

[87] Smith & Hogan: 'Criminal Law', Butterworths (2001), 10th ed, p726.

[88] Sometimes referred to as 'crackers'.

[89] Sc Law Com No 106 (1987).

[90] Law Com No 186 (1989).

[91] [1988] 1 AC 1063.

[92] Albeit, a relatively unsophisticated one. They surreptitiously noted and memorised a BT engineer's password as he entered it when demonstrating the Prestel system at a computer exhibition. This is often referred to as 'shoulder surfing'.

under s15 Theft Act 1968 was not pursued.[93] However, they were prosecuted for forgery under s1 Forgery and Counterfeiting Act 1981. The essence of this offence is the making of a 'false instrument' with the intention of inducing somebody to accept it as genuine. The two defendants were convicted. However, they launched a successful appeal. Their main ground of appeal was that they had not created a 'false instrument'. The prosecution argued that the password details were such an instrument. Both the Court of Appeal and the House of Lords disagreed with this assertion.

Before considering the reasons why the appellate court quashed Gold's conviction, it is important to understand the logistics of the electronic process which took place within the Prestel system when the password details were entered. Once entered, the details were momentarily held in the system while the validity of the password was checked by it. When the password corresponded with an authorised user, the system allowed access and the password information was then deleted from the control area's memory. The following reasons were given for allowing the appeal against conviction.

1. The statute itself defines an 'instrument' as including 'any disc, tape, sound track or other device on or in which information is recorded or stored by mechanical, electronic or other means'.[94] The appellate courts cited and applied one of the general presumptions of statutory interpretation. They considered that any alleged 'instrument' should be construed eiusdem generis with the specific items which are mentioned in the statutory definition. In other words, any such 'device' must be of a similar type or nature to them. The problem for the prosecution here was that the devices specifically mentioned in the statute were physical objects: discs, tapes and soundtracks. Since the password details took the form of electronic signals, they were not considered to be a 'false instrument'; they lacked the requisite physicality.

2. The prosecution argued that if the password details could not be regarded as a 'false instrument', then the user segment of the Prestel system could. This submission was rejected on the grounds that the Act dictates that the 'instrument' must be one 'on or in which information is recorded or stored by mechanical, electronic or other means'. Given that the log-in process took less than a second, no such recording or storage had taken place. In the Court of Appeal, Lord Lane CJ had opined that the Act did not seek 'to deal with information that is held for a moment whilst automatic checking takes place and then is expunged. That process is not one to which the words "recorded or stored" can properly be applied, suggesting as they do a degree of continuance.'[95] The House of Lords agreed with his view.

3. Even if the password details had been held to be an 'instrument', they were not a false instrument. The password details were themselves genuine; they did not purport to be something which they were not. Any falsity was inherent in the appellants' use of them.

---

[93] See footnote 30 above.
[94] Section 8(1).
[95] [1987] 3 WLR 803 at 809.

Lord Lane CJ declared that 'the Procrustean attempt to force these facts into the language of an Act not designed to fit them produced grave difficulties for both judge and jury which we would not wish to see repeated. The appellants' conduct amounted, in essence ... to dishonestly obtaining access to the relevant Prestel data bank by a trick. That is not a criminal offence. If it is thought desirable to do so, that is a matter for the legislature rather than the courts.'[96]

This decision further strengthened the case for statutory intervention. It came in the form of the Computer Misuse Act 1990, which created three new offences.

Section 1	Intentionally seeking to secure unauthorised access to programmes or data held on computer.
Section 2	Intentionally seeking such access with intent to commit or facilitate the commission of further offences.
Section 3	Intentionally causing an unauthorised modification of the contents of a computer.

The lack of definition of the terms 'computer', 'data' and 'programme' within the Act is, of course, deliberate. The Law Commission was of the opinion that any such definitions would soon become outdated given the rapid pace of technological change. The courts have adopted a broad interpretative approach. For example, cash registers[97] and cable TV access boxes[98] have been classed as 'computers' for the purposes of this piece of legislation.

The basic hacking offence

Previously, an act concerned with seeking unauthorised access to data held on a computer did not, in the absence of further conduct, attract criminal liability. Section 1 of the CMA 1990 now ensures that it does not attract such liability:

'1(1) A person is guilty of an offence if –

(a) he causes a computer to perform any function with intent to secure access to any programme or data held in any computer;

(b) the access he intends to secure is unauthorised; and

(c) he knows at the time when he causes the computer to perform the function that that is the case.'

This is a summary offence which carries a maximum sentence of six months' imprisonment and/or a fine.[99] It is far-reaching in nature, as confirmed by Professor J C Smith when he explained that:

---

[96] [1987] 3 WLR 803 at 809–810.
[97] *Attorney-General's Reference (No 1 of 1991)* [1992] 3 WLR 432.
[98] *Maxwell-King* [2001] 2 Cr App Rep (S) 136 (CA).
[99] Note that, as a summary offence, in the eyes of the law it cannot be attempted – see s1(4) Criminal Attempts Act 1981. However, see also footnote 192 of this chapter for proposals to change the status of this offence to one which is triable either way. If such reform takes place, the basic hacking offence could then be attempted, in the eyes of the law.

'The idea, in effect, is to close the door in the hacker's face. The offence is committed though the hacker has no sinister purpose and is no more than a nosey-parker.'[100]

Before looking at this offence in detail, it must be noted that the Computer Misuse Act 1990 (Amendment) Bill, which was due to be presented to Parliament under the Ten-Minute Rule of 5 April 2005 (but wasn't because Parliament was dissolved on that day in preparation for the General Election), proposes that this basic hacking offence be re-categorised as an offence triable either way with a maximum sentence, following conviction on indictment, of two years' imprisonment and/or a fine.[101] The offence in s1 CMA 1990 can be broken down into its constituent parts, as follows.

Causing a computer to perform a function

It is not enough that the accused simply touches the computer or, for example, starts reading material which he finds already displayed on its monitor. He must interact with the computer. In other words, it 'must be made to "respond" in some way by performing a function'.[102] Given this, simply switching on the computer would be 'causing it to perform a function', although, on its own, it would not point towards the presence of the requisite mens rea.

With intent to secure unauthorised access

The prosecution does not have to prove that the accused targeted any particular computer, programme or piece of data.[103] Equally, it need not be shown that he used one computer to seek unauthorised access to another. This was confirmed by the Court of Appeal in *Attorney-General's Reference (No 1 of 1991)* when it declared that there were 'no grounds whatsoever for implying or importing the word "other" between "any" and "computer", or excepting the computer which is actually used by the offender from the phrase "any computer" '.[104] To hold otherwise would allow 'insiders' to slip the statutory net.

The accused must have intended to secure unauthorised access. The pervasive rules on 'intention' apply here as elsewhere in English criminal law; either direct or oblique[105] intention will suffice. It is important to consider the meaning of 'access' within the Act; the intent must be aimed at an unauthorised form of it. Section 17(2) sets the goalposts. Therein, it is stated that a person secures access to any programme or data held in a computer where, by causing the computer to perform any function, they:

* alter or erase the programme or data;

* copy or move it to any storage medium other than that in which it is held or to a different location in the storage medium in which it is held;

[100] Smith & Hogan: 'Criminal Law', Butterworths (2002), 10th ed, p726.
[101] Computer Misuse Act 1990 (Amendment) Bill – see: http://www.apig.org.uk. Then see, in particular, s1(3) of the Bill.
[102] Wasik, M, 'Hacking, Viruses and Fraud – The Internet, Law and Society', (Edited by Akdeniz, Walker and Wall) Longman (2000), p275.
[103] Section 1(2).
[104] [1992] 3 WLR 432 at 437.
[105] If inferred, after application of the *Nedrick* test, as amended in *Woollin* [1999] AC 82.

- use it; or

- have it output from the computer in which it is held (whether by having it displayed or in any other manner).

The next, natural question is: when is access unauthorised? The answer is found in s17(5). Therein, we are told that access of any kind by any person to any programme or data held in a computer is unauthorised if:

'(a) he is not himself entitled to control access of the kind in question to the programme or data; and

(b) he does not have the consent to access of the kind in question to the programme or data from any person who is so entitled.'

Where the alleged hacker is an 'outsider', a lack of authority will often be easily established. However, this task may be more testing where the alleged hacking is not remote. This is where credible, in-house IT policies can oil the wheels of prosecution. If, for example, it can be shown that the accused was confronted with a pop-up warning about the restrictions of access, he will struggle to convince the court that he was unaware of the line which he crossed, or attempted to cross. The Law Commission recommended that such boundaries should be clearly marked out, in whichever ways are reasonably practicable, and that only those who deliberately and disobediently step over them should be prosecuted, as distinct from those who simply acted carelessly, stupidly or inattentively.[106]

Knowing that the access is unauthorised

As previously stated, the offence is made out if the accused acts with an intention to secure unauthorised access, regardless of whether he succeeds; but he must also know, at the time, that the access he is seeking is unauthorised. In other words, the access which he seeks must, in fact, be unauthorised, and he must be aware of this. The legal definition of 'knowledge' extends to wilful blindness. Judicial confirmation of this can be found in *Westminster City Council* v *Croyalgrange Ltd*, in which it was declared that:

'It is always open to the tribunal of fact, when knowledge on the part of the defendant is required to be proved, to base a finding of knowledge on evidence that the defendant had deliberately shut his eyes to the obvious or refrained from enquiry because he suspected the truth but did not want to have his suspicion confirmed.'[107]

10.6 The Limits of Authorised Access and the Use to Which it is Put

What of the person who uses their authorised access for an unauthorised purpose? This is not a reference to the office worker who uses his work terminal to word process a private letter. Indeed, the Law Commission gave this as an example of the kind of conduct which should not attract criminal liability. However, *DPP* v *Bignell*[108] provided

---

[106] See Computer Misuse, Law Com No 186 (1989), para 3.36.
[107] [1986] 2 All ER 353 at 359, per Lord Bridge of Harwich.
[108] [1998] 1 Cr App Rep 1.

the Divisional Court with an opportunity to consider a more profound misuse of authorised access. On six occasions, a husband and wife, who were both officers in the metropolitan police, instructed police computer operators to extract information for them from the Police National Computer. This information was sought by them for private, unofficial purposes; namely, to confirm that Mrs Bignell's ex-husband was the registered owner of a number of cars. They were convicted of hacking under s1 of the Act, but they appealed successfully to the Crown Court. Therein, it was ruled that their use of the computer, even though it was for private purposes, did not fall within the definition of 'unauthorised access' provided by s17(5) of the Act. The Director of Public Prosecutions then appealed by way of case stated to the Divisional Court, contending that access to the Police National Computer had been limited to access for police purposes only and that the intentional securing of access with knowledge that it exceeded such limits of authorisation was an offence. The appeal was dismissed on the ground that such activity fell outside the boundaries of the Computer Misuse Act 1990. The court was of the opinion that this section of the Act was enacted to criminalise the 'hacking' of computer systems, not to protect the integrity of programmes or data. Astill J distinguished the activity of 'breaking into computers' from the misuse of data, stating that the former was covered by this Act and the latter was not. Indeed, reference was made to the decision in *Brown*,[109] in which it was held that information is not 'used' merely by being retrieved from a database, casting doubt on whether the activities of Mr and Mrs Bignell could even have attracted liability under the Data Protection Act 1984. So, the Divisional Court ruled that these two police officers were not hackers, on the grounds that they did, in fact, have authority to access that kind of information from the computer system and it mattered not that they sought access for an unauthorised purpose. In short, the court focused its attention on the level of access which was authorised, not the use to which that access was put.

This decision provokes strong criticism. Surely the key issue here was the true nature and extent of the authority given to people like the Bignells? The Divisional Court seemed adamant that the Bignells had authority to access the data in question, but that is debatable. Authorisation involves the giving of permission. That permission relates not only to the area of conduct but to the conduct itself within it. For example, when the key issue of trespassory entry is considered in a case of burglary, the alleged permission to enter is scrutinised in a realistic way. As Scrutton LJ put it in *The Calgarth*[110]:

'When you invite a person into your house to use the staircase, you do not invite him to slide down the banisters.'

Similar reasoning can be found in Professor J C Smith's report on the *Bignell* case. He stated that:

'If I give you permission to enter my study for the purposes of reading my books, your entering to drink my sherry would surely be unauthorised "access" to the room as well as to the sherry.'[111]

---

109 [1996] 1 All ER 545.
110 [1927] P 93 at 110.
111 [1998] Crim LR 54.

Surely the fact that someone is 'entering' for an undisclosed purpose will vitiate the permission given to them where that person recognises or deliberately ignores the strong possibility that this goes beyond their authority? In such circumstances, is it unreasonable to expect that person to clarify the terms of their authority? Surely not.

This is not to say that an individual who merely wonders whether, in fact, he may be overstepping the mark should attract liability. As Professor Smith put it, 'the fact that is crosses [his] mind that he might possibly be exceeding his authority would not suffice for knowledge'. But where someone has real doubts as to the extent of his authorisation and could, if they chose to, readily ascertain the limits of it, this should surely be classed as wilful blindness and, consequently, knowledge per se.[112]

Two years on, in *R v Bow Street Magistrates' Court, ex parte Allison*,[113] the House of Lords were given the opportunity to reconsider the Bignell decision. The appeal before their Lordships was against the Divisional Court's rejection of an application for judicial review of the Bow Street stipendiary magistrate's decision to refuse extradition. The case was concerned with the activities of an employee of the American Express credit card company, Jean Ojomo, and her alleged conspiracy with Mr Allison. The US government claimed that Ojomo had obtained unauthorised access to customer accounts in order to defraud the company of a large sum of money. It further claimed that this was part of a conspiracy involving several people, including Allison.

At the request of the US government, Allison had been arrested in England upon a provisional warrant issued under the Extradition Act 1989. That warrant alleged, inter alia, that Allison had conspired with Ojomo, within the jurisdiction of the United States, to secure unauthorised access to the company's computer system with intent to commit theft and forgery. The Divisional Court had ruled that s1 Computer Misuse Act 1990 was directed at external hackers and did not apply to misuse of information by a person, such as Ojomo, who was entitled to control the computer and access data of the relevant kind. Accordingly, since in its opinion no such offence had been committed by Ojomo, Allison could not be held to have conspired to it.

The House of Lords disagreed. Their Lordships held that, on its true construction, s1 of the Act was not concerned with authority to access kinds of data, but rather with authority to access the actual data involved. They confirmed that the section was designed to combat all forms of unauthorised access, whether by insiders or outsiders. In delivering the leading judgment, Lord Hobhouse stated that strong support for their decision could be found in the interpretation section of the Act. He declared that s17(5) has a plain meaning, subsidiary to the other provisions of the Act, and that:

'It simply identifies the two ways in which authority may be acquired – by being oneself the person entitled to authorise and by being a person who has been authorised by a person entitled to authorise. It also makes clear that the authority must relate not simply to the data or programme but also to the actual kind of access secured. Similarly, it is plain that it is not using the word "control" in a physical sense of the ability to operate or manipulate the computer and that it is not derogating from the requirement that for access to be authorised it must be authorised to the relevant data or relevant

---

[112] See footnote 107 above.
[113] [1999] 4 All ER 1.

programme or part of a programme. It does not introduce any concept that authority to access one piece of data should be treated as authority to access other pieces of data "of the same kind", notwithstanding that the relevant person did not in fact have authority to access that piece of data. These plain words leave no room for any suggestion that the relevant person may say: "Yes, I know that I was not authorised to access that data but I was authorised to access other data of the same kind".'

This decision did clarify a couple of issues. Firstly, it confirmed that where authority to access is given, it can be limited to specific types of programmes or data. In the case itself, Jean Ojomo had been authorised to access only those customer accounts which were assigned to her, but she had accessed various other accounts without any authorisation. Secondly, there is no conceptual presumption that authority to access one piece of data extends to other pieces of data of the same kind.

Nevertheless, certain issues remained somewhat opaque. Although their Lordships considered that the decision in *Bignell* was 'probably right', their stated reasons for this opinion are not wholly convincing. Lord Hobhouse said that a 'possible view of the facts' was that the role of the defendants had merely been to request another (the computer operator) to obtain information by using the computer. He pointed out that the computer operator's authority permitted him to access the data for the purpose of responding to requests made to him in proper form by police officers. Thus, it was argued, no unauthorised access had been secured. However, it is submitted that this view can be challenged in the light of the doctrine of innocent agency. First, it is important to note that academic opinion is split on this issue.[114] Surely, in the Bignells' case, any focus upon the computer operator was implicitly misplaced; he was blissfully unaware of the real reason behind the Bignells' request. The fact that he lacked mens rea means that he should not have been viewed as a participant in the crime at all; he was an innocent agent. In such cases, 'the principal is the participant in the crime whose act is the most immediate cause of the innocent agent's act'.[115] The Bignells fitted this description.

Furthermore, if the authority to access could be restricted to specific programmes or data, why couldn't equivalent limitations be placed upon circumstances? The person who was entitled to control access to that data was the Police Commissioner, 'who exercised such control and, through employee manuals, specified that access was for police purposes only'.[116] The Bignells' authority to view the data was, in reality, limited to circumstances where they were pursuing police matters. Certainly, the decision in *Allison* seems to support the convictions (in earlier, unreported cases) of individuals who had accessed the material themselves. For example, in *Bonnett*,[117] a police officer had accessed information from the Police National Computer to discover who owned

---

[114] Professor Martin Wasik holds the view that the doctrine of innocent agency has no place here (see Wasik, M, 'Hacking, Viruses and Fraud – The Internet, Law and Society' (Edited by Akdeniz, Walker and Wall), Longman (2000), p277), whereas Dr Ian Walden is clearly of the opinion that the use of the doctrine in these circumstances would be unproblematic (see Walden, I, 'Computer Crime – Computer Law' (Edited by Reed and Angel), Oxford University Press, (2003) 5th ed, pp307–308).

[115] Smith & Hogan: 'Criminal Law', Butterworths (2002) 10th ed, p142.

[116] Walden, I, 'Computer Crime – Computer Law' (Edited by Reed and Angel), Oxford University Press (2003) 5th ed, p307.

[117] Unreported, Newcastle under Lyme Magistrates' Court, 3 November 1995.

a particular car. He did this because he wanted to make an offer to buy the registration number of the car (which was BON1T). However, the conviction of *Farquharson*[118] and the like, who asked another to access the data in question, must surely be questioned in the light of their Lordships' reasoning in *Allison*.

Lord Hobhouse agreed with the Divisional Court's view that the Bignells could have been prosecuted under the Data Protection Act 1984. He also referred to the Law Commission's view that 'it would be undesirable for a hacking offence to extend to an authorised user who is using the computer for an unauthorised purpose'.[119] However, it is submitted that there was a false distinction made here between the Bignells' authority to access the data and the purpose for which they did it. That purpose breached one of the conditions of the permission given to them by the Commissioner. In short, they had exceeded their authority.

10.7 Aggravated Hacking – The Ulterior Intent Offence

The Law Commission held the opinion that the rules within the law of attempt[120] might be difficult to apply within the context of computer-related activities.[121] One of the examples which the Commission used to illustrate its concerns on this matter was where a hacker might pursue a 'scatter gun' approach to the task of discovering a password in order to fraudulently transfer money out of a bank account. The Commission thought that his actions of transmitting many combinations of 'passwords' in the hope that one of them will match the real one would not, on their own, be considered to be 'more than merely preparatory'[122] to the commission of the offence of theft and, therefore, not criminal attempts to commit that crime.

The creation of an ulterior intent offence has gone a long way to meeting these concerns. This is because the offence bites at an earlier stage. As discussed above, the basic offence of hacking is committed when the accused causes a computer to perform a function with an intention to secure what he knows to be unauthorised access to the system itself or the programmes and data held within it. For him to be successfully prosecuted for the more serious, aggravated form of hacking, the only additional element for the prosecution to prove is his intent to commit (or facilitate the commission of) one of a range of offences. In short, to show that he was hacking with further criminal intent. It is generally accepted that this s2 offence 'provides an alternative and, perhaps, better route to conviction where other offences are intended by the hacker'.[123]

In the Act itself, this offence is described as 'unauthorised access with intent to commit or facilitate the commission of further offences'.[124] It can be viewed either as a

---

[118] Unreported, Croydon Magistrates' Court, 9 December 1993.
[119] Law Commission's Working Paper No 110, Computer Misuse, para 6.24 (iv).
[120] See footnotes 79–83 above.
[121] Law Com No 186 (1989), paras 3.52–3.53.
[122] See s1 Criminal Attempts Act 1981.
[123] Bainbridge, D, 'Introduction to Computer Law', (2004) 5th ed, Longman, p388.
[124] See the marginal note by s2.

preliminary offence or as an aggravated form of hacking. It is triable either way and, if tried on indictment, carries a maximum sentence of five years' imprisonment and/or a fine:[125]

'2(1) A person is guilty of an offence under this section if he commits an offence under s1 above ("the unauthorised access offence") with intent –

(a) to commit an offence to which this section applies; or

(b) to facilitate the commission of such an offence (whether by himself or by any other person).'

The further offence which the accused intends to commit, or to facilitate the commission of, must meet the criteria laid down by s2(2). Therein, it is stated that the offence must either be one for which the sentence is fixed by law (eg murder),[126] or one for which the maximum sentence is not less than five years' imprisonment (this would include theft, blackmail and most fraud offences).

If, of course, the further offence is actually committed then the accused will most likely be charged with that offence. At the other end of the spectrum, it must be remembered that since this is an indictable offence a person can be prosecuted for attempting to commit it.[127] However, the main advantage of this s2 offence is that it provides a means of prosecuting those individuals who fall short of completing the further offence, and liability may be justified on the grounds that it is their state of mind (an intention to commit or facilitate the further offence) which is strongly indicative of their culpability.

In the light of s2(2), it can be seen that there is a broad range of further offences which can be the focus of the accused's ulterior intent. For example, in the *Allison* case,[128] one of the allegations against him was that he conspired to hack with intent to commit both theft and forgery. In *R v Governor of Brixton Prison and Another, ex parte Levin*,[129] the accused was convicted of hacking with intent to commit both forgery and false accounting.

It matters not that the further offence is to be carried out by someone other than the accused. Section 2(1)(b) makes it clears that an intention to facilitate the commission of a further offence will suffice. Of course, the accused may be facilitating his own commission of the further offence, but the subsection also expressly covers the situation where he is helping someone else to offend. An example comes from *Delaware*.[130] The accused worked for Barclays Bank in Poole, Dorset. He was approached by an old schoolfriend who asked him to repay a favour by disclosing the details of certain bank accounts to him. These were then passed on to two other people who used them for fraudulent purposes. This case is also illustrative of the fact that it is immaterial whether the further offence is to be committed at the time of the hack or on some

---

[125] Section 2(5).
[126] See footnote 180 below.
[127] Unlike the basic offence of hacking in s1, which cannot, in the eyes of the law, be attempted because it is a summary offence – see footnotes 99 and 101 above.
[128] See footnote 113 above.
[129] See Chapter 9, footnote 25.
[130] [2003] EWCA Crim 424.

future occasion.[131] A classic scenario would be where confidential information about someone is hacked and then, at a later date, used to blackmail them. Blackmail is an offence under s21 Theft Act 1968. It is comprised of the making of an unwarranted demand with menaces. Such a demand must be made with a view to gain or an intention to cause loss. The word 'menaces' within this context does not simply connote threats of violence but extends to 'any action detrimental to or unpleasant to the person addressed'.[132] Take, for example, the situation where a patient's medical records have been hacked into to make the discovery that they have AIDS.[133] The disclosure of such information could have profound personal, social and professional ramifications for the patient and, consequently, would be a potent threat.

Section 2(4) states that 'a person may be guilty of an offence under this section even though the facts are such that the commission of the further offence is impossible'. The legislature has taken the same approach to the issue of impossibility here as it did to statutory conspiracy[134] and the law of attempt.[135] In short, the factual impossibility of the further offence would not hinder a prosecution for hacking with intent to commit or facilitate it. Taking the previous example, if the hacker mistakenly believes that the AIDS victim is still alive when, in fact, they died two days before the hack, the argument that it is impossible to blackmail a dead person will be deemed immaterial in those circumstances. The accused will have hacked with intent whilst making a mistake of fact; this will not avail him. He can be compared with the person who tries to pick a pocket which, in fact, turns out to be empty.

How precise does the charge have to be in relation to the further offence? The following guidance was given by Beldam LJ in *Re Levin*:

> 'In our view, it is not necessary to do more than specify the type of offence which the accused had in mind so as to bring it within the requirements of s2(2).'[136]

A similar approach can be found in the law relating to accessorial liability.[137] Indeed, it must not be forgotten that those who aid, abet, counsel or procure hackers in their commission of offences under either s1 or 2 of the 1990 Act can also face prosecution.[138] For example, someone who intends to assist a hacker by disclosing a password to him would be viewed as that hacker's accomplice.

Lastly, it is important to note that if the prosecution have not convinced the magistrates or the jury that the accused, when hacking, harboured an ulterior intent, they can still find him guilty of the basic hacking offence (under s1) if the facts would support it and the time limits have been met.[139]

---

[131] See s2(3).
[132] Per Lord Wright in *Thorne* v *Motor Trade Association* [1937] 3 All ER 167.
[133] Acquired Immune Deficiency Syndrome.
[134] See s1(1)(b) Criminal Law Act 1977.
[135] See ss1(2) and (3) Criminal Attempts Act 1981.
[136] [1997] QB 65 at 78.
[137] See *Bainbridge* [1959] 3 All ER 200.
[138] See s44 Magistrates' Courts Act 1980 and s8 Accessories and Abettors Act 1861.
[139] See ss12(1), 11(2) and 11(3) Computer Misuse Act 1990.

The jurisdictional issues of hacking

Hackers will often be international e-criminals. Given this, the Computer Misuse Act 1990 had to address the matter of jurisdiction to guard against the possibility that such people might avoid prosecution by exploiting the international nature of their crimes to their own legal advantage. Section 4 of the Act lays down the simple requirement that a 'significant link' be established with the home country[140] in order to claim domestic jurisdiction. What then constitutes a 'significant link'? When a s1 offence is charged, the answer to this question is found in ss5(2)(a) and (b). Therein, it is stated that either of the following is a significant link with domestic jurisdiction:

• that the accused was in the home country (England and Wales, Scotland or Northern Ireland, as appropriate); or

• that any computer containing a programme or data to which the accused secured or intended to secure unauthorised access by doing that act was in the home country concerned at the time.

In short, jurisdiction will be established if, at the time of the offence, either the hacker was in the home country or the computer which he was hacking into was. If the accused is charged with a s2 offence, there is a further jurisdictional requirement in certain circumstances. If the accused operates from within any of the home countries, intending to commit or facilitate the commission of a further offence in a different country, those intended actions must involve the commission of an offence under that other country's law.[141] This is known as the principle of double criminality.

The jurisdictional net is also cast widely when it comes to alleged conspirators. Section 1A Criminal Law Act 1977[142] governs this issue. Its provisions can be summarised as follows.

A charge of statutory conspiracy can be brought where:

1. the agreed course of conduct would, at some stage, involve an act by one or more of the parties, or the happening of an event, intended to take place in a country or territory outside the UK – s1A(2);

2. that act or event would be an offence under the law in that other country or territory – s1A(3);

3. a party to the agreement (or his agent) did any one of the following (s1A(3)):

   a) did anything in England and Wales in relation to the agreement before its formation;

   b) became a party to the agreement in England and Wales;

   c) did or omitted anything in England and Wales in pursuance of the agreement.

---

[140] England and Wales, Scotland or Northern Ireland.
[141] See ss4(4) and 8(1).
[142] As inserted by s5 Criminal Justice (Terrorism and Conspiracy) Act 1998.

Other offences which can be used to target hacking

These may be considered where, for example, the alleged hacker was unaware that the access which he sought or gained was unauthorised – a key element of the offences within the Computer Misuse Act 1990.

Section 13 Theft Act 1968

Whilst confidential information will not come within the definition of 'property' for the purposes of theft,[143] the Theft Act 1968 does contain the offence of dishonestly abstracting electricity under s13, as follows:

> 'A person who dishonestly uses without due authority, or dishonestly causes to be wasted or diverted, any electricity shall on conviction on indictment be liable to imprisonment for a term not exceeding five years.'

A small, but definite amount of electricity will be abstracted during hacking activity, through the process of the host computer retrieving the information sought by the hacker from its store and then transmitting it to the hacker's computer terminal. The *Ghosh* test will be used to determine whether such abstraction was dishonest or not.[144]

Section 1 Regulation of Investigatory Powers Act 2000

Under this section, it is an offence to intentionally (and without lawful excuse) intercept any communication in the course of its transmission via a public communications system. The offence takes the form of modifying or interfering with the telecommunications system or its operation, or monitoring transmissions on it. It can be seen as an offence which targets the interception of transmissions. However, since hackers usually initiate transmissions, they will not normally fall within the boundaries of this offence. In the light of this fact, it has been said that 'this offence … applies only to the situation where the hacker is "eavesdropping"; that is, listening in for interesting communications to intercept'.[145]

Section 127 Communications Act 2003[146]

This section criminalises the improper use of a public electronic communications network. It covers five forms of activity. Firstly, the sending of grossly offensive, indecent, obscene or menacing messages (or other matter). Secondly, the causing of any such message (or other matter) to be sent. Thirdly, the sending of a message which one knows to be false for the purpose of causing annoyance, inconvenience or needless anxiety to another. Fourthly, the causing of such a message to be sent. And lastly, persistently making use of a public electronic communications network for the purpose of causing annoyance, inconvenience or needless anxiety to another. The hacker who threatens to release a computer virus into an e-commercial company's system unless he

---

[143] See the discussion of the case of *Oxford v Moss* in Chapter 8 at footnote 22.
[144] See footnote 54 above.
[145] Bainbridge, D, 'Introduction to Computer Law', (2004) 5th ed, Longman, p392.
[146] The offence under s43 Telecommunications Act 1984 of improper use of a public telecommunication has been replaced by this offence under s127 Communications Act (CA) 2003 (s43 was repealed by Sch 19 of the CA 2003).

is paid off would, for example, fall within s127(1)(a) of this Act; his blackmailing e-mail would be viewed as a 'menacing message'.

Data Protection Act 1998

The act of copying personal data from a computer system may render a hacker liable for the offence of processing personal data without having notified the Commissioner, under s21(1) of the Act. Other relevant offences under the Act include obtaining or disclosing personal data or procuring its disclosure to another person, under ss55(1) and (3).

10.8 Unauthorised Modification of Computer Programmes or Data

Introduction

Information is intangible property and, as such, cannot be 'damaged' in the traditional, legal sense of that word.[147] Although one could argue that 'damage' itself is intangible because it is simply a concept, the law has taken it to mean 'some physical harm, impairment or deterioration which can usually be perceived by the senses'.[148] Given this, any alleged damage or destruction of property can only be the subject of a charge under the Criminal Damage Act 1971 if the property in question is/was tangible. This poses legal problems where, for example, someone deletes, alters or in some other way modifies the contents of a computer. In such a case, there will be no perceptible physical damage to the computer. Moreover, the particular information which is deleted or changed will be viewed as intangible property.

Does this mean that before the Computer Misuse Act 1990 came into force such people could not be successfully prosecuted under the Criminal Damage Act 1971? In a word, no. However, successful prosecution could only be achieved in certain kinds of cases (dependent upon their facts) and through a combination of meticulous charging and intricate legal reasoning. For example, in *Cox* v *Riley*,[149] the accused was found guilty of criminal damage where he had erased the programme from a plastic circuit card which was used to operate a computerised saw for cutting programmed designs. Defence counsel argued that the only 'damage' done was to the electronic impulses which made up the computer programme and that since the programme was intangible property such 'damage' did not fall within the Act. The court dismissed this apparently strong argument by pointing out that the accused was not charged with damaging the programme but with damaging the plastic card in which it was housed. It was held that the card itself had been damaged by the deletion of the programme because that action had impaired its value or usefulness[150] which required 'time and effort of a more than minimal nature'[151] to replace it.[152] Such reasoning is

---

[147] See s10(1) Criminal Damage Act 1971.
[148] Smith & Hogan: 'Criminal Law', (2002) 10th ed, Butterworths, p698.
[149] (1986) 83 Cr App R 54.
[150] Although the saw could still be operated manually, in practice, it was significantly less effective.
[151] (1986) 83 Cr App Rep 54 at 55.
[152] One could possibly argue along similar lines if the card was reprogrammed rather than replaced.

difficult to fault since, despite the fact that the card had suffered no physical damage and had not been rendered useless, it 'was temporarily unable to perform the function it was designed to perform'.[153]

The legal tensions which were illustrated in this case (and others) caught the eye of the Law Commission which was, at the time, preparing its final report on the issue of computer misuse. It stated that:

'That the practical meaning of "damage" has caused practical as well as theoretical problems following the decision in *Cox* v *Riley* is evidenced by the experience of the police and prosecuting authorities who have informed us that, although convictions have been obtained in serious cases of unauthorised access to data or programmes, there is recurrent (and understandable) difficulty in explaining to judges, magistrates and juries how the facts fit in with the present law of criminal damage.'[154]

Rather than simply recommending that the Criminal Damage Act (CDA) 1971 be amended to include interference with computer programmes or data, the Law Commission considered that the best way forward was to tackle the problem directly by creating a new computer-specific offence. This recommendation was accepted and the result is the offence in s3(1) Computer Misuse Act (CMA) 1990, which will be considered in detail below. The Commission put forward two main reasons for the creation of this new offence. Firstly, it would avoid the potential uncertainties within the law which might flow from 'the theoretical difficulties posed by applying the concept of damage to intangible property such as data and programmes'.[155] And secondly, that since criminal damage is a basic intent offence, and can therefore be committed recklessly,[156] it is not the appropriate one to aim at this type of behaviour; the Commission thought that the new offence should target only those with specific intent. It is important to note that s3(6) CMA 1990 was specifically drafted in a way which seeks to avoid any overlap between itself and the CDA 1971. The Commission thought it wise to clarify the relationship between the new offence under s3 and the offence of criminal damage under the CDA 1971, as follows:

'For the purposes of the Criminal Damage Act 1971, a modification of the contents of a computer shall not be regarded as damaging any computer or computer storage medium unless its effect on that computer or computer storage medium impairs its physical condition.'

The Computer Misuse Act 1990 was duly created and brought into force. However, the case of *Whiteley*[157] was to cast doubt upon whether there would be clear water between the new Act and the CDA 1971. This case was actually tried after the CMA 1990 had come into force, but Whiteley had been charged under the Criminal Damage Act 1971 before the arrival of the new legislation. The decision of the Court of Appeal fuelled the debate as to whether the CDA 1971 could or would continue to be used in cases of alleged interference with computer programmes or data. Whiteley hacked into an academic computer system in order to delete, amend and add files. He had

[153] Smith & Hogan: Criminal Law (2002) 10th ed, Butterworths, p731.
[154] Law Com No 186 (1989), para 2.31.
[155] Law Com No 186 (1989), para 3.62.
[156] See *R* v *Gemmel and Richards* [2003] UKHL 50.
[157] (1991) 93 Cr App R 25.

considerable computing skills, evidenced by the fact that he detected and then deleted a programme which had been launched to track and trap him. Defence counsel argued that his activities had not resulted in any damage to tangible property, as required under the CDA 1971. It was submitted that the computer discs themselves had not been damaged and that his activities only affected the information stored on them, which was intangible property and, consequently, that his conduct fell beyond the reach of the Act. The Court of Appeal disagreed. Lord Lane CJ and his colleagues took the view that the computer discs had, in fact, been damaged because their usefulness had been impaired. He explained that:

> 'What the Act requires to be proved is that tangible property has been damaged, not necessarily that the damage itself is tangible. There can be no doubt that the magnetic particles upon the metal discs were a part of the discs and if the appellant was proved to have intentionally and without lawful excuse altered the particles in such a way as to cause an impairment of the value or usefulness of the disc to the owner, there would be damage within the meaning of s1 [of the CDA 1971].'[158]

Clearly, the Court of Appeal did not consider the intangibility of the damage to be an insurmountable hurdle here. Since the temporary impairment of property suffices as 'damage' under the Act,[159] the essential question was whether tangible property had been so damaged. The facts showed that Whiteley's activities had, on occasion, caused computer systems to crash. Thus, through tampering with the computer's control mechanisms (the programmes on the discs), he had rendered it temporarily inoperable, thereby criminally damaging it. Again, such reasoning is difficult to fault.

Lord Lane CJ grasped the opportunity to peer over at the newly-arrived offence of unauthorised modification of computer material in s3 Computer Misuse Act 1990 and stated that in future 'no doubt it will be used as the basis of criminal prosecution in the case of computer misuse'. Notwithstanding these words of his and those of the legislature in s3(6) CMA 1990, there are several reasons for arguing that the decision in this case should leave the door open to prosecution under the Criminal Damage Act 1971 in some cases. Firstly, the difference between the potential penalties which can be imposed under each Act. A conviction under s1 CDA 1971 carries a maximum sentence of ten years' imprisonment and/or a fine,[160] whereas one under s3 CMA 1990 carries a maximum sentence of five years' imprisonment and/or a fine.[161] The Law Commission declared that it would not be right to expose such offenders to the potentially higher penalties under the CDA 1971.[162] This view must surely be challenged. The financial and temporal costs to the owner of the property which flow from the activities of people like Whiteley can be very high indeed. Ironically, when arguing the case for criminalising hackers without first having to prove that they actually secured their intended access, the Law Commission itself cited a case in which the restoration of a computer system, following a hack, required 10,000 hours of skilled staff time. Professor J C Smith found it strange that a person 'whose

---

[158] Ibid, p28.
[159] See footnote 148 above.
[160] See s4(2) Criminal Damage Act 1971.
[161] See s3(7) Computer Misuse Act 1990.
[162] Law Com No 186, para 3.78.

electronic vandalism required 10,000 hours of skilled work to repair, ... should be liable to five years' imprisonment under the 1990 Act, whereas if he had used a hammer to cause the same loss (or even a penny's worth) he would be liable to ten years under the 1971 Act'.[163]

Secondly, the new offence is one of specific intent whilst the criminal damage offence is one of basic intent. Given this, if the prosecution cannot prove that the accused's state of mind went beyond recklessness, he could not be convicted of the new offence.[164] Furthermore, in the light of s3(6) CMA 1990, it seems also that he could not be convicted of criminal damage unless the effect of his activities upon the computer or computer storage medium was the impairment of its 'physical condition'. However, surely prosecutors could cite the decision in *Whiteley* in support of a submission that the deletion or alteration of data held within a computer disk does impair that disc's physical condition? If such a submission were rejected, this would confirm that the legal net which is cast from those two pieces of legislation has a sizeable hole in it, through which the reckless hacker can escape. That hacker's victim would feel justifiably aggrieved at the apparent lack of protection given to him by the law. As Professor J C Smith points out, the victim may be more than a little bemused to hear that the law's response to his plight could be: 'Well, there's nothing wrong with the computer. It looks exactly the same as it did yesterday. There's only one slight difference. It doesn't work.'[165]

Lastly, it must be noted that the new offence is aimed at the unauthorised modification of the 'contents of a computer' only.[166] Given this, any data or programmes which are stored within devices outside the computer[167] are not protected by this Act. Professor I J Lloyd gives a good example of a scenario in which this restriction may force the prosecution to look towards the Criminal Damage Act 1971 for the appropriate charge:

'... two individuals secure unauthorised access to an office containing a computer and a box of computer disks. Both individuals carry a magnet. One uses this to corrupt the contents of the computer's hard disk; the other produces a similar effect on the contents of the box of disks. We can assume further that the box of disks represents a "back-up copy" of the material held on the computer. In this situation, one person will be guilty of an offence under the Computer Misuse Act 1990 and the other will not. Given the nature and purpose of the legislation, this may be a justifiable situation. The question will be whether the second party might be prosecuted under the Criminal Damage Act 1971.'

Here again, the prosecution could submit that, in the light of the decision in *Whiteley*, the intangible nature of the damage caused by the magnet is no bar to successful

---

[163] Smith & Hogan: Criminal Law (2002) 10th ed, Butterworths, p732.
[164] It seems likely that the Law Commission's view was somewhat influenced by the fact that at that time the *Caldwell* test for recklessness was dominant in cases of criminal damage. However, this form of (inadvertent) recklessness no longer exists in English law – see *Gemmell and Richards* [2003] UKHL 50 (HL).
[165] Smith & Hogan: Criminal Law (2002) 10th Ed, Butterworths, p732.
[166] See s3(1)(a) Computer Misuse Act 1990.
[167] Such as floppy disks or zip disks or flash drives.

prosecution under the CDA 1971, and that the physical condition of the back-up discs in the box has been impaired.[168]

The s3 offence itself

This offence is aimed at computer saboteurs. It is triable either way and carries a maximum sentence of five years' imprisonment and/or a fine.[169] The jurisdictional rules relating to this offence are similar to those connected to the basic offence of hacking in s1.[170] The offence is laid out in s3(1), as follows:

'Section 3(1):

A person is guilty of an offence if –

(a) he does an act which causes an unauthorised modification of the contents of any computer; and

(b) at the time when he does the act he has the requisite intent and the requisite knowledge.'

From this it can be gleaned that the offence is comprised of four main elements, which will now be considered in detail.

The prosecution must first establish that a modification of the contents of a computer has taken place. Here, to 'modify' is to alter or erase any programme or data, or to add to its contents. Furthermore, any act which contributes towards causing such a modification is viewed as causing it.[171] In other words, contributing to a modification is modifying per se.

Next, it must be shown that the modification was, in fact, unauthorised. The concept of 'authority' which is used within the hacking offences in ss1 and 2 is continued here. Specifically, a modification is unauthorised if the person who causes it is not himself entitled to determine whether it should be made and he does not have the consent of someone who is so entitled.[172] In short, it is modifying without right or permission.

Once it has been established that the accused caused an unauthorised modification of computer material, the prosecution must turn to the mens rea of the offence. The task here is to prove that he had the requisite intent[173] and the requisite knowledge. The accused must have intended to cause both the modification itself and its consequence(s). The statute lists the forbidden consequences; the accused must have intended that at least one of them would flow from his modifying activities.[174] They are:[175]

• the impairment of the operation of a computer;

---

[168] Note also that it could, in addition, be argued that requirements laid down in s3(6) only apply where such storage devices are held within a computer system.
[169] Section 3(7).
[170] See s5(3).
[171] Section 17(7).
[172] Section 17(8).
[173] Again, this would include willful blindness.
[174] The Law Commission had recommended that 'the offence should not punish unauthorised modifications which improve, or are neutral in their effect' – Law Com No 186, para 3.72.
[175] See s3(2).

- the prevention or hindrance of access to any programme or data held in a computer;

- the impairment of the operation of any such programme;

- the impairment of the reliability of any such data.

It must also be proven that the accused knew that the modification which he intended to cause was unauthorised.[176]

The s3 offence at work

The first point to note is that this offence is one of specific intent (as are the hacking offences in ss1 and 2 of the Act). Yet the accused's intentions need not be directed at any particular computer, programme or piece of data. Moreover, it is immaterial whether he intends the modification or its effects to be permanent or temporary.[177]

A simple form of modification would involve the deletion of programmes or data. For example, a disgruntled worker might delete files on the day that he leaves the computer owner's employ. Equally, an 'outsider' might hack into a computer system to cause an unauthorised modification; such an individual could potentially attract liability under ss1, 2 or 3 of the Act. For example, in *R v Bow Street Magistrates' Court, ex parte Allison*,[178] the defendant was extradited for the offences of hacking with intent and unauthorised modification (under ss2 and 3, respectively).

The accused may have modified the programme or data in question by altering it. An alarming example of such activity is provided by the case of *Rymer*.[179] The accused, a nurse working in a hospital, secured unauthorised access to the computer system by using the personal identification number of one of the doctors, having memorised it on a previous occasion. The nurse made alterations to patients' drug doses and treatment records and was duly convicted of the s3 offence.[180] Alternatively, the accused's motive for altering data may be to cover up his criminal activities. In *Singha*,[181] the accused was a doctor who had been charged with manslaughter after one of his patients died from an asthma attack. He had prescribed for them a beta-blocker drug which was shown to have been causally significant to the death. Although a charge was not brought under s3, it surely could have been. The only potential hurdle might have been the issue of whether his modifications were unauthorised, given that he had the authority to access and alter patients' records. However, it could have been strongly submitted that his authority to modify was limited to legal purposes only. He was, instead, charged with the offence of perverting the course of justice.

---

[176] Section 3(4).

[177] Section 3(5).

[178] [1999] 4 All ER 1.

[179] *The Times*, 21 December 1993.

[180] Note that this is clearly a means by which someone could seriously injure or kill another. In a sense, the computer can be used as a murder weapon. It should be remembered that the s2 offence of aggravated hacking requires, inter alia, an ulterior intent to be proven and that a requisite intent could be aimed at certain non-fatal offences (eg inflicting GBH) and those offences for which the sentence is fixed by law (eg murder).

[181] [1995] Crim LR 68.

One of the requisite intentions referred to in s3(2) is the impairment of the reliability of data. The most obvious way of affecting the reliability of data is by altering it. However, the act of deleting data can render the surrounding or connecting data unreliable as well. Moreover, adding to data can also undermine it. This was confirmed by Mr Justice Wright in *Re Yarimaka*,[182] when he distinguished the sending of a legitimate e-mail from the sending of a bogus e-mail. The latter, he said, would contravene s3 because it involved a pretence that the password holder is the author when he is not, and that 'such an addition is plainly unauthorised, as defined by s17(8); intent to modify the contents of the computer as defined in s3(2) is self-evident and, by doing so, the reliability of the data in the computer is impaired within the meaning of s3(2)(c)'. Clearly then, if the data sent is inaccurate or untrue it will impair the reliability of the data to which it is added.

This offence is particularly aimed at individuals who intentionally introduce viruses into computer systems. In such cases, the accused will have added to the contents of a programme or data and will, consequently, have 'modified' for the purposes of the Act.[183] The classic means by which such viruses are introduced is e-mail attachments. However, it must be noted that the delivery of a virus via a floppy disk, zip disk or flash drive would attract liability as well. Take, for example, the scenario where the accused brings a floppy disk to work with him, having first placed a malicious programme onto it at home. By releasing that programme into his employer's computer system he will be modifying the material within it by adding to it. Once it has been established that he has done this without authority, his intentions will be legally scrutinised. The nature of the malicious programme will provide cogent evidence of what his intentions were. The virus itself may be designed to cause the system to slow down or crash, or to hinder access to certain programmes, or to destroy data. All of these functions would point towards requisite intents.

The fact that the accused did not himself introduce the virus into the system would not allow him to escape liability. For example, if he passes the infected floppy disk to an innocent (or reckless) colleague who then places it into the computer, the actions of the accused will still be deemed to have contributed to causing the modification, and that is sufficient.[184] Indeed, if that same floppy disk is then passed on to other people, the accused will continue to attract liability because his intent need not be directed at any particular computer, programme or piece of data, nor at any particular modification or kind of modification.[185]

There are many strains of computer viruses. Some can be truly malicious and destructive, causing international havoc with concomitant financial costs. Recent examples include the Melissa and Sobig.F viruses.[186] The s3 offence has been flexible enough in stretching to cover new forms of viruses as they have emerged. For example,

---

[182] [2002] EWHC 589.
[183] Section 17(7)(b).
[184] Section 17(7).
[185] Section 3(3).
[186] See Chapter 8, footnotes 46 and 47.

a 'worm' is a self-replicating programme which eats up spare capacity within computers. The offence caters for such viruses because, in adding additional data to the contents of computer files which, in turn, often hinders or prevents access to them or simply slows the operation of the system, they meet the criteria laid down in the section.[187] The same can be said of 'logic bombs,' which are malicious programmes that are primed to start operating at some point in the future; the trigger can be a specific date or event.[188]

In recent years, the courts seem to have hardened their attitude towards computer saboteurs. The following two cases illustrate the shift in sentencing policy. The case of *Pile*[189] delivered the first successful prosecution of a computer virus writer for a s3 offence. Using the pseudonym of 'The Black Baron,' the accused published programmes on the Internet which harboured computer viruses. He also released a programme which made those viruses difficult to detect. When downloaded from the Internet, the programmes released the viruses into the unsuspecting victims' computer systems. During a police interview, the accused explained that his main motivation was to 'create a British virus which would match the worst of those from overseas'. The estimated financial cost of his activities was £500,000. He pleaded guilty to ten offences in total (five under s1 and five under s3). He was sentenced to 18 months' imprisonment. Six years later, in the case of *Lindesay*,[190] a freelance software designer made some unauthorised modifications to the contents of some websites. These websites were owned by clients of his former employer and he gained access to them using his own Internet account. He also sent e-mails to the customers of one of these companies, a supermarket, announcing that it was going to raise prices. At trial, the motive for his actions was revealed: revenge. He had been employed on a short-term contract but was dismissed by his former employer on the grounds that his work was unsatisfactory. When he left the company, there was also a dispute about money which he claimed the company owed him. One month later, after having consumed a few alcoholic drinks and, as he claimed, acting on impulse, he made the aforementioned modifications. The financial cost of his actions was estimated at £9,000. He pleaded guilty to three charges under s3. The trial judge took into account several points which featured in his plea of mitigation, including his co-operation with the police, his character references, and his remorsefulness. Notwithstanding this, he was sentenced to nine months' imprisonment. He appealed against his sentence, but the Court of Appeal agreed with the imposition of a custodial sentence and did not consider it to be excessively lengthy.

One final point to note is that real doubt remains as to whether this s3 offence can be used to successfully prosecute people who launch 'denial of service attacks'. Such attacks often involve the flooding of e-commercial websites, causing them to crash and preventing genuine customers from visiting them for a period of time. The victims of these attacks can certainly argue that their computer systems are 'modified' each

---

[187] See ss17(7)(b) and 3(2).
[188] See, for example, the case of *Thompson* [1984] 3 All ER 565.
[189] (1995) *The Times* 16 November.
[190] [2001] EWCA Crim 1720.

time they receive a communication over the Internet. The difficulty comes in trying to establish that such modifications were unauthorised, given the open invitations to visit such websites. However, art 5 of the European Convention on Cybercrime[191] may soon prompt legislative action to fill this apparent lacuna. It states that:

'Each party shall adopt such legislative and other measures as may be necessary to establish as criminal offences under its domestic law, when committed intentionally, the serious hindering without right of the functioning of a computer system by inputting, transmitting, damaging, deleting, deteriorating, altering or suppressing computer data.'

This provision criminalises the intentional hindering of the lawful use of computer systems, including telecommunications facilities, by using or influencing computer data. Note that the hindering must be 'serious', which involves the 'sending of data to a particular system in such a form, size or frequency that it has a significant detrimental effect upon the ability of the owner or operator to use the system or to communicate with other systems'. This clearly encompasses denial of service attacks. It is important to note that in the UK there has already been an attempt to bring in legislation aimed at denial of service attacks. The Earl of Northesk introduced the Computer Misuse Act (Amendment) Bill 2002 to the House of Lords, but it did not complete its Parliamentary journey.

However, legislative action in the UK on this matter now seems to be on the horizon. On 10 March 2005, the All Party Internet Group (APIG) issued a press release, giving notice of a motion to move a Ten-Minute Rule Bill calling for amendments to the Computer Misuse Act 2005. In fact, this never occured because parliament was dissolved in preparation for the General Election on the very day that the motion was scheduled to be moved. One of the proposed amendments within that Bill[192] is to criminalise those who launch denial of service attacks. If enacted, the Bill will insert two new offences into the CMA 1990. One will be a basic offence of causing or intending to cause a denial of service attack. The other will target an aggravated form of such behaviour where, inter alia, the prosecution will be required to prove that the accused harboured an ulterior intent to commit or facilitate the commission of further offences.[193] The Chairman of APIG, Mr Derek Wyatt MP, stated in the aforementioned press release that:

'The All Party Group was hoping that an MP would have picked this up as part of the Private Members' allocation for Bills, but sadly no-one did, so it seemed sensible, given the work we undertook last year, to at least place on record what we think the Bill should look like, in the hope that the Government will come back to it after the General Election.'[194]

10.9 Computer and Internet Pornography

Introduction

It has been estimated that the pornography industry contributes at least $20 billion

---

[191] See: http://conventions.coe.int/Treaty/en/Treaties/Html/185.htm.
[192] Computer Misuse Act 1990 (Amendment) Bill – see: http://www.apig.org.uk.
[193] See ss1(3) and 1(5) of the Bill, respectively. These would lead, if enacted, to the insertion of ss2A and 2B into the CMA 1990.
[194] The General Election took place on 5 May 2005.

per annum to the global economy.[195] The debate concerning the existence and scope of pornographic material which is available on the Internet continues. That debate has led to the pursuance of a number of initiatives by national governments,[196] international organisations[197] and the Internet-based business community.[198] There is a lot of material on the Internet which is classed as 'obscene' or 'pornographic' and the criminal law has a role to play in the fight against its creation and distribution. It is certainly true that Internet pornography can pose real challenges to the law, but it is equally true to say that English law is fairly well equipped with offences to target this form of e-criminal activity. Some of the legal difficulties stem from pervasive themes of Internet crime, such as jurisdictional issues. Others are more specific to e-pornography itself, being as it is a content-related form of criminal activity.

The legal response to computer pornography

First and foremost, it is important to note that 'a distinction needs to be made between general pornographic material and specific sub-categories of pornographic material, such as child pornography, which has been the focus of law enforcement activity'.[199]

Obscene Publications Act (OPA) 1959

Those who publish obscene material run the risk of being prosecuted under this Act for an offence which is triable either way and carries a maximum sentence of three years' imprisonment and/or a fine. The offence is committed by any person who, whether for gain or not, publishes an obscene article or who has an obscene article for publication for gain (whether gain to himself or another).[200] This begs the question: when is an article viewed as being 'obscene' in the eyes of the law? The answer is provided in s1 of the Act:

> 'For the purposes of this Act an article shall be deemed to be obscene if its effect or (where the article comprises two or more distinct items) the effect of any of its items is, if taken as a whole, such as to tend to deprave or corrupt persons who are likely, having regard to all relevant circumstances, to read, see or hear the matter contained or embodied in it.'

It is important to note that Internet Service Providers (ISPs) can be classed as publishers; they are by no means immune from prosecution. This was made clear in a governmental statement released by the DTI some years ago:

> 'Primary responsibility for illegal material on the Internet would clearly lie with the individual or entity posting it. Under UK law, however, an Internet service provider (ISP) which has been made aware of the illegal material (or activity) and has failed to take reasonable steps to remove the material could also be liable to prosecution as an accessory to a crime.'[201]

---

[195] See 'Cashing in on Porn Boom,' BBC News, 5 July 2001.
[196] See: http://www.dti.gov.uk/iwreview.
[197] See, for example, the European Commission's 'Action Plan on Promoting Safe Use of the Internet' (1999) – see: http://158.169.50.95:10080/iap/decision/en.html.
[198] Internet Watch Foundation – see: http://www.internetwatch.org.uk.
[199] Walden, I, 'Computer Crime – Computer Law' (Edited by Reed and Angel), (2003) 5th ed, OUP, p300.
[200] Section 2.
[201] DTI, Net Benefit: The Electronic Commerce Agenda for the UK (DTI/Pub 3619, London, October 1998).

Indeed, the then Parliamentary Under-Secretary of State for the Home Office Department, Kate Hoey, stated that:

'In general, Internet Service Providers in the UK are not required to vet the material which their customers store and transmit. They do, however, acquire responsibilities once they become aware of material which is illegal.'[202]

However, the Internet Watch Foundation[203] has been very active in trying to prevent prosecutions of ISPs by regularly reporting instances of potentially illegal material to them so that they can act swiftly to remove it. It should also be noted that the EU's Electronic Commerce Directive states that ISPs should not be made liable where they didn't initiate the transmission, select the receiver of it and select or modify the information contained within it.[204]

A broad meaning is given to the word 'article' under the OPA 1959. Section 1(2) states that it includes 'any description of article containing or embodying matter to be read or looked at or both, any sound record, and any film or other record of a picture or pictures'. It has been said that 'there is no reason to doubt that [this definition] will include a magnetic disk or other form of electronic storage media'.[205]

The definition of the term 'publication' is also wide. Section 1(3) confirms that a person publishes an article when they do any of the following with it:

- distribute it;
- circulate it;
- sell it (or offer it for sale);
- let it on hire (or offer it for let on hire);
- give it;
- lend it;
- show it;
- play it;
- project it;
- (where the matter is data that is stored electronically) transmit it.

The decision in *Perrin*[206] is authority for the fact that the uploading or downloading of obscene material from a website amounts to publication of it. The accused had set up a webpage and placed onto it images of coprophilia, people covered in faeces, and men engaged in felatio. One of the grounds of appeal against conviction was that a key defence argument had been wrongly dismissed by the trial judge. This argument was that the only relevant publication of the material was to the police officer who

---

[202] House of Commons European Scrutiny Committee, Child Pornography on the Internet (1998–9 HC 34–ii, para 12.3).
[203] See: http://www.internetwatch.org.uk.
[204] Directive 2000/31/EC.
[205] Bainbridge, D, 'Introduction to Computer Law', (2004) 5th ed, Longman, p413.
[206] [2002] EWCA Crim 747.

accessed it and then recorded it on video tape. Defence counsel had submitted that it was wrong to determine whether the material was 'obscene' by referring to others who might access it. The Court of Appeal disagreed and declared that the test for obscenity in such cases would be:

'First, whether any person or persons were likely to see the article, and if so, whether the effect of the article, taken as a whole, was such as to tend to deprave and corrupt the person or persons who were likely, having regard to all relevant circumstances, to see the matter contained or embodied on it.'

Video Recordings Act 1984

This piece of legislation was brought in to target so-called 'video nasties'. It created the offence of supplying video recordings without a classification certificate. The case of *Meechie v Multi-Media Marketing*[207] illustrates some of the perennial difficulties of legally shadowing the advancements in technology. The court was presented with the task of applying this legislation to a multi-media product. The defendant company established something called 'The Interactive Girls Club'. One of the products made available to members of that club was a short computer game, the successful completion of which would lead to a display of erotic images. The company had not sought a classification certificate for this product. It was prosecuted for the supply[208] and possession with a view to supply[209] of these recordings.

The magistrates dismissed the charges on two grounds. Firstly, that visual images which are produced electronically by the use of information on any disc or magnetic tape must be shown as a 'moving picture'[210] and this series of images did not meet that criterion. They were considered too brief and disjointed and were simply likened to a set of still images. And secondly, that the product was considered to be a video game and, therefore, exempt from the classification requirements under the Act.[211]

The Divisional Court reversed this decision. It was of the opinion that the set of images could be regarded as a 'moving picture', despite their brevity. Furthermore, it declared that, in the eyes of the law, the set of images could be viewed separately from the game and that, consequently, they were not exempted from the provisions of the Act. It must be questioned whether such distinctions could be as easily made in future cases which involve more sophisticated multi-media products. The increasing degree of integration of text, sound and graphics in such products will place legal strains on the reasoning in this case when applied elsewhere.

Child pornography

This has been an area of particular concern to the public at large, the legislature and law enforcement agencies. The use of computer networks by paedophiles is not a new

[207] (1995) 94 LGR 474.
[208] Section 9.
[209] Section 10.
[210] Section 1(a) and (b).
[211] See s2.

phenomenon.[212] Child pornography is viewed as a serious crime for three main reasons. Firstly, 'in most cases, [it] is a permanent record of the sexual abuse of an actual child'.[213] Secondly, 'in most cases, [it] is a form of sexual abuse and exploitation in which depiction of children engaging in sexually explicit conduct poses a serious threat to the physical and mental health, safety and wellbeing of children'.[214] And lastly, in the light of research, it is now generally accepted that the risk of paedophiles acting upon their sexual desires and impulses is significantly increased by them viewing such material.

The practice of 'grooming' has also caught the legislative eye. This is where paedophiles enter Internet chatrooms and pose as children with the intention of luring victims into meeting them. It is now an offence to arrange or facilitate the commission of a child sex offence (planned to take place in any part of the world).[215] It is important now to consider how the law targets those individuals who create and distribute the pornographic material which feeds such behaviour. First and foremost, it must be noted that 'in the vast majority of cases, the fact that images or text are recorded and transmitted on digital media rather than on paper or video will not affect the determination of whether contents are obscene or pornographic'.[216] Moreover, other than jurisdictional problems, the use of the Internet to distribute child pornography does not usually, in itself, present legal obstacles to successful prosecution. However, some problems have been encountered in trying to apply relatively old legislation to newer, e-criminal activity.

Protection of Children Act (PCA) 1978

Section 1 of this Act makes it an offence to take or permit to be taken any indecent photograph of a child or to distribute or show such a photograph or to have it in one's possession with a view to distributing or showing it.[217] It is an offence which is triable either way and it carries a maximum sentence of three years' imprisonment and/or a fine.[218] It is worth noting that this offence meets the requirements laid down in art 9 of the European Convention on Cybercrime, so that no further domestic legislation is, as yet, called for.

The case of *Fellows*[219] highlighted a potential lacuna in the law which required urgent judicial and legislative attention. The accused was a computer specialist employed by Birmingham University. He covertly used one of the University's Internet-linked computers to compile an extensive database of explicit pornographic pictures featuring

---

[212] See Attorney-General's Commission on Pornography, Final Report (US Government Printing Office, Washington DC, 1986), p629.
[213] Akdeniz, Y, 'Child Pornography – The Internet, Law and Society' (Edited by Akdeniz, Walker and Wall), Pearson (2000), p232.
[214] Ibid.
[215] Section 15 Sexual Offences Act 2003.
[216] Lloyd, I, 'Information Technology Law', (2004) 4th ed, OUP, p337.
[217] Note that it is also an offence to publish or cause to be published any advertisement likely to be understood as conveying that the advertiser distributes or shows such indecent photographs, or intends to do so – s1(1)(d).
[218] Section 6(1).
[219] (1997) 1 Cr App R 244.

children as young as three. He made this pornographic material available over the Internet. It was argued on appeal that the images stored on computer disc were not 'photographs' and, consequently, fell outside the ambit of the Act. The Court of Appeal pointed to the fact that s7(2) speaks also of copies of photographs. Given this, there was no difficulty in finding that the images on the hard disk were covered by the Act, particularly since the statute did not state that the copies themselves had to be photographs. Fellows' appeal was duly dismissed and he was jailed for three years.

The legislature moved to further secure the legal position in such cases by placing a subsection into the Act via the Criminal Justice and Public Order Act (CJPOA) 1994.[220] Section 7(4)(b) now states that references to the word 'photograph' within the PCA 1978 include 'data stored on a computer disc or by other electronic means which is capable of conversion to a photograph'.

The CJPOA 1994 was also used to plug another potential loophole. This concerned so-called 'pseudo-photographs'. Such an item has been described as 'what appears to be an indecent image of a child [which] is made up of a collage of images, modified by the use of computer painting packages, none of the elements of which is indecent in itself'.[221] Section 7(7) of the PCA 1978 now confirms that these are considered to be legally akin to photographs:

'If the impression created by a pseudo-photograph is that the person shown is a child, the pseudo-photograph shall be treated for all purposes of this Act as showing a child, and so shall a pseudo-photograph where the predominant image conveyed is that the person shown is a child, notwithstanding that some of the physical characteristics shown are those of an adult.'

The Act also extends to copies of pseudo-photographs[222] and, in the light of section 7(4)(b), to data stored on a computer disc or other electronic means which is capable of conversion into a pseudo-photograph.[223]

Before looking at some case law to see how the statute has performed in practice, it is important to note the two defences listed in s1(4). The first involves a plea that the accused had a legitimate reason for distributing or showing or possessing the photographs. The second involves a plea that the accused had not himself seen the photographs and did not know, nor had any cause to suspect, them to be indecent. This latter defence could be readily available to someone who, for instance, had typed a word or phrase into an Internet search engine, clicked on one of the web addresses presented to him, but then quickly exited the website on discovering that it contained indecent material. If, unknown to him, a copy of the page has been saved to his computer's cache memory and is then subsequently discovered, he could plead his innocence on these grounds. It is also a defence which could potentially be used by ISPs.

So, the three main offences under the PCA 1978 involve the creation, distribution

---

[220] See s84(4).
[221] Lloyd, I, 'Information Technology Law', (2004) 4th ed, OUP, p337.
[222] Section 7(9)(a).
[223] Section 7(9)(b).

or possession (with a view to distribute or show) of indecent photographs (or pseudo-photographs).

Perhaps the most publicized conviction for a possession offence was that of Paul Gadd (also known as Gary Glitter).[224] Thousands of indecent images of children were discovered on the accused's hard drive by a computer technician who was repairing it. Gadd was sentenced to four months' imprisonment.

The previously discussed case of *Fellows*[225] is an example of a successful prosecution for both possession and distribution offences. Therein, Owen J. stated that 'the [pornographic] pictures could fuel the fantasy of those with perverted attitudes towards the young, and they might incite sexual abuse on innocent children'. Other examples include the cases of *McLeish*[226] and *Fitchie*.[227] In *McLeish*, a Roman Catholic priest pleaded guilty to 12 charges of indecent assault against boys as young as ten and also admitted possessing indecent photographs with intent to distribute them, actually distributing them and being involved in the importation of pornographic video films of children. His activities were discovered and reported to the UK police by law enforcement officers in Germany as part of an investigation entitled 'Operation Modem'. In *Fitchie*, the accused pleaded guilty to distributing indecent images of children over the Internet and to a charge of indecent assault against an 11-year-old boy which was featured in one of those films.

The case law involving the application of the PCA 1978 to the making of indecent images of children has not been so straightforward. In *Bowden*,[228] the accused had downloaded indecent images of young boys from the Internet and had also printed out some of them. He was convicted of nine possession offences but appealed his conviction for 12 making offences. Defence counsel submitted that he had not 'made' the images merely by downloading them or printing them out. The Court of Appeal disagreed. The reason given for dismissing the appeal was that the Act was not only concerned with the original creation of images, but also their proliferation and that, consequently, to download or to print such images was to create new material. It is submitted that this reasoning can be questioned in two ways. Firstly, surely a more accurate description of what the accused did was copying, rather than making or creating, the images? And secondly, it is debatable whether Parliament's intention was to render the actions of downloading or copying images from the Internet a making offence, in addition to them being a possession offence or a (potential) distribution offence. It is worth noting that the Court of Appeal did not feel the need to refer to Parliamentary materials for assistance in their interpretation of the statute on this particular matter.

The decision in *Bowden* was confirmed in the case of *Atkins and Goodland* v *DPP*.[229]

[224] *The Times*, 13 November 1999.
[225] (1997) 1 Cr App R 244.
[226] Stokes, P, 'Six years for priest who broadcast abuse of boys to Internet paedophiles,' *The Daily Telegraph*, 13 November 1996.
[227] Fleet, M, 'Pornographer is trapped by paedophile,' *The Daily Telegraph*, 26 July 1997.
[228] [2000] 2 All ER 418.
[229] [2000] 1 WLR 1427.

Therein, the Court of Appeal reiterated that downloading or printing images from the Internet falls with the definition of 'making' them, but stipulated that this must have been done with knowledge. The two accused appealed successfully on the ground that they had not possessed the requisite knowledge. Defence counsel called expert evidence to convince the court that most users of computers are unaware of the cache memory facility within their machines and that, in fact, the appellants were unaware of it.

The legal position on this issue moved on in the case of *Smith and Jayson*.[230] Therein, the Court of Appeal declared that the actions of opening e-mail attachments or downloading images from webpages could constitute 'making' indecent images for the purposes of the statute, if done intentionally and with knowledge that the image was or was likely to be indecent. Interestingly, the court also stated that there was no additional requirement for the prosecution to prove that the accused intended to store the images. Now, it seems, technical ignorance of the existence and workings of the cache memory facility of a computer will not be a viable defence.

Section 160 Criminal Justice Act 1988[231]

It is important to note that mere possession of an indecent photograph (or pseudo-photograph) of a child is an offence. It is an offence triable either way which carries a maximum sentence of five years' imprisonment and/or a fine. There is no requirement here of proving that the accused intends to distribute or show the indecent image which he has in his possession.[232] The section includes three possible defences. The first two are the same as those found in s1(4) PCA 1978.[233] The third involves a plea that the photograph or pseudo-photograph was sent to the defendant without prior request by him or on his behalf and that he did not keep it for an unreasonable time.[234]

Section 127 Communications Act (CA) 2003

Lastly, it is important to note that the sending of indecent images could constitute the offence of improper use of a public electronic communications network.[235] Given that the section refers to 'messages', it could be argued that pornographic images fall outside the ambit of this offence. However, it could be argued in reply that 'a picture is just another way of conveying a message'[236] and can, therefore, meet this legislative criterion.

---

[230] [2002] EWCA Crim 683.

[231] As amended by s84(4) Criminal Justice and Public Order Act 1994.

[232] Contrast s1(1) Protection of Children Act 1978.

[233] See the previous section of this chapter on the PCA 1978.

[234] Section 160(2)(c).

[235] The offence under s43 Telecommunications Act 1984 of improper use of a public telecommunication has been replaced by this offence under s127 CA 2003 (s43 TA 1984 was repealed by Sch 19 CA 2003).

[236] Bainbridge, D, 'Introduction to Computer Law', (2004) 5th ed, Longman, p393.

10.10 Cyberstalking and Online Harassment

Introduction

Within a legal context, the term 'stalking' refers to 'persistent threatening behaviour by one person against another'.[237] The term 'cyberstalking' has been used to refer to 'the use of the Internet, e-mail, or other electronic communications devices to stalk another person'.[238] As a form of threatening or harassing behaviour, stalking is characterised by common themes, whether conducted online or offline. The majority of stalkers are men and the majority of their victims are women. Stalking is, essentially, about control. Perpetrators of this crime usually seek to profoundly affect the lives of their victims by repeatedly following them, telephoning them, writing to them, damaging their property or impersonating them with a view to bringing them trouble or exposing them to ridicule and embarrassment. In most cases, the stalker is a former lover of the victim.

However, cyberstalking has a number of aspects which differentiate it from offline stalking. Firstly, there are, of course, no geographical constraints in cyberspace. Secondly, if the stalker's modus operandi is the impersonation of his victim, this is often more easily pursued online.[239] Thirdly, the Internet and other ICTs continue to present more means of stalking. And lastly, the online environment may boost his bravado and criminal ambitions; the stalker need not physically confront his victim and his threats or insults may, consequently, be more menacing, disturbing and hurtful.

By its very nature, cyberspace delivers the advantage of anonymity to the stalker if he has the skills to exploit this facility. This means that:

'Unbeknownst to the target, the perpetrator could be in another state, around the corner, or in the next cubicle at work. The perpetrator could be a former friend or lover, a total stranger met in a chat room, or simply a teenager playing a practical joke. The inability to identify the source of the harassment or threats could be particularly ominous to a cyberstalking victim, and the veil of anonymity might encourage the perpetrator to continue these acts. In addition, some perpetrators, armed with the knowledge that their identity is unknown, might be more willing to pursue the victim at home or work, and the Internet can provide substantial information to this end. Numerous websites will provide personal information, including unlisted telephone numbers and detailed directions to a home or office. For a fee, other websites promise to provide social security numbers, financial data, and other personal information.'[240]

A stalker's efforts to remain anonymous online make it more difficult for law enforcement agencies to confirm his identity, confront him and (possibly) arrest him before matters escalate further. It has been said that 'the real fear … is that offensive and threatening behaviour that originates online will escalate into "real-life" stalking'.[241]

Cyberstalking and online harassment can take several forms, including the following:

---

[237] Oxford Dictionary of Law (2002) 5th ed, Oxford University Press, p474.
[238] Yee Fen Lim, 'Cyberspace Law: Commentaries and Materials', (2002) Oxford University Press, p292.
[239] For example, by impersonating his victim in a chatroom.
[240] Yee Fen Lim, 'Cyberspace Law: Commentaries and Materials', (2002) Oxford University Press, p294.
[241] Ellison, L, and Akdeniz, Y, 'Cyberstalking: The Regulation of Harassment on the Internet, Criminal Law Review Special Edition: Crime, Criminal Justice and the Internet', (1998) Sweet & Maxwell, p31.

- sending threatening, abusive or obscene e-mails;

- spamming (sending large numbers of junk e-mail messages);

- sending computer viruses (either in e-mail attachments or via hacking);

- impersonating the victim online (for example, to provoke angry responses in chatrooms, perhaps thereby initiating online harassment by third parties).

Victims of online harassment suffer a range of emotions from mere annoyance through anxiety to considerable distress and beyond. This can lead to psychological injury. How then does the law seek to protect people from such harm?

It has been said that 'in contrast to the situation ... in the United States, existing United Kingdom laws are sufficiently flexible to encompass online stalking and e-mail harassment'.[242]

Communications Act 2003

Section 127:

'(1) A person is guilty of an offence if he –

(a) sends by means of a public electronic communications network, a message or other matter that is grossly offensive or of an indecent, obscene or menacing character; or

(b) causes any such message or matter to be sent.

(2) A person is guilty of an offence if, for the purpose of causing annoyance, inconvenience or needless anxiety to another, he –

(a) sends by means of a public electronic communications network, a message that he knows to be false,

(b) causes such a message to be sent; or

(c) persistently makes use of a public electronic communications network.'

This is a summary offence which carries a maximum sentence of six months' imprisonment and/or a fine.[243] It targets those who send certain types of messages over a public telecommunications system. It can be gleaned from the wording of the section that there are essentially three forms of this offence. Firstly, the sending of a message which is grossly offensive, indecent, obscene or menacing. Secondly, the sending of a false message, knowing it to be false, for one of three purposes: to cause annoyance, inconvenience or anxiety to the recipient. And lastly, the persistent use of a network for one of the three aforementioned purposes.

Malicious Communications Act 1988

Section 1:

'(1) Any person who sends to another person –

---

[242] Ibid, p34.
[243] The offence under s43 Telecommunications Act 1984 of improper use of a public telecommunication has been replaced by this offence under s127 CA 2003 (s43 TA 1984 was repealed by Sch 19 CA 2003).

(a) a letter, electronic communication or article of any description which conveys –

(i) a message which is indecent or grossly offensive;

(ii) a threat; or

(iii) information which is false and known to be false or believed to be false by the sender; or

(b) any article or electronic communication which is, in whole or part, of an indecent or grossly offensive nature,

is guilty of an offence if his purpose, or one of his purposes, in sending it is that it should, so far as falling within paragraph (a) or (b) above, cause distress or anxiety to the recipient or to any other person to whom he intends that it or its contents or nature should be communicated.'

This is a summary offence which carries a maximum sentence of six months' imprisonment and/or a fine. It is in many ways similar to the offence under s127 Communications Act 2003. However, there are some notable differences. Firstly, this offence requires an indecent or grossly offensive message to be sent for a purpose, whereas s127 CA 2003 does not. Secondly, here there are two forbidden purposes, whereas under the CA 2003 there are three. Thirdly, those forbidden purposes are significantly different; for this offence, the purpose of the action must have been to cause distress or anxiety, whereas under the CA 2003 the purpose must have been to cause annoyance, inconvenience or needless anxiety. And lastly, there is a possible defence laid out in the section for this offence.[244] This defence relates only to the situation where the accused has sent a communication which conveys a threat.[245] It is that the threat was used to reinforce a demand made by the accused on reasonable grounds and he reasonably believed that the use of the threat was a proper means of reinforcing the demand.[246]

The recent, well-publicised conviction of Christopher Pierson[247] gives an example of how this offence can be used to combat hoax e-mailing. Pierson, a 40-year-old man from Lincolnshire, sent 35 e-mails to the relatives of people who were holidaying in Asia at the time when the tsunami struck,[248] informing them that their loved ones had perished in the disaster. The e-mails looked as if they were official messages from the Foreign and Commonwealth Office; they were not and the statements made in them were untrue. Pearson had set up a bogus e-mail account and then accessed these peoples' e-mail addresses from the Sky News website, where they had been posted in a bid for information. He pleaded guilty to one charge of public nuisance and one charge under s1 Malicious Communications Act 1988. His plea in mitigation made reference to his psychological response to the stillbirth of his first child in 1991, the fact that his uncle had died only a few days before he sent these e-mails, and the strain placed upon him by his responsibilities of care for his diabetic son, his mother (who was suffering from breast cancer), his father (who had previously suffered a heart attack) and his Aunt (who was suffering from Alzheimer's disease). Sentencing him to

---

[244] No defences are referred to in s127 Communications Act 2003.
[245] See s1(1)(a)(ii).
[246] See s1(2)(a) and (b).
[247] See: http://news.bbc.co.uk/go/pr/fr/-/1/hi/england/lincolnshire/4201775.stm.
[248] 26 December 2004.

six months' imprisonment, the Bow Street magistrates stated that Pearson had put these people through 'emotional hell'. Furthermore, it had not escaped their notice that Pearson's actions revealed elements of planning which ran counter to his claim that this was a 'moment of madness' on his part.[249]

Protection from Harassment Act 1997

The Act provides a combination of civil and criminal measures. It was created in response to media clamour for more effective laws against stalking. There had also been important developments in the criminal law concerning the problem of stalking. In the case of *Ireland*,[250] the House of Lords had held that the making of silent phone calls which resulted in the victims suffering anxiety and depressive disorders could amount to assault occasioning actual bodily harm.[251]

There are two criminal offences contained within the Act; one is a summary offence and the other is an indictable offence.

The s2 offence – criminal harassment

Section 1:

'(1) A person must not pursue a course of conduct –

(a) which amounts to harassment of another, and

(b) which he knows or ought to know amounts to harassment of another.'

Section 2:

'(1) A person who pursues a course of conduct in breach of s1 is guilty of an offence.'

This is a summary offence which carries a maximum sentence of six months' imprisonment and/or a fine.[252] It targets people who pursue a course of conduct which they either know or ought to know amounts to harassment of another person. That 'course of conduct' must involve conduct on at least two occasions.[253] If the magistrates are not convinced that the accused actually knew his actions amounted to harassment of his victim, they must determine whether he ought to have known this. Section 1(2) provides the objective test to be applied in such circumstances: the accused will be deemed to have had constructive knowledge 'if a reasonable person in possession of the same information would think the course of conduct amounted to harassment of the other'. Section 7(4) confirms that 'conduct' includes speech, and the term 'harassing' is given a broad definition in s7(2), where it is said to 'include alarming the person or causing the person distress'. It is important to note the presence of the word 'include' in this (partial) definition. It is still possible to harass someone without alarming or distressing them.[254]

---

[249] Note also that Scotland Yard was forced to set up an incident room and spent ten days trying to contact those families and friends affected, at a cost of £10,000.

[250] [1998] AC 147.

[251] See also the case of *Burstow* which was heard on the same day by the same court and is reported alongside *Ireland*.

[252] Section 2(2).

[253] Section 7(3).

[254] See, for example, the case of *DPP v Ramsdale* [2001] EWHC Admin 106.

The case of *Kelly* v *DPP*[255] provides a useful example of how the offence works. The accused had previously been in a relationship with the victim. After being released from prison, he made three abusive and threatening telephone calls to the victim's mobile phone. All three of these calls were made within a period of five minutes around 3am. The victim did not answer the calls, which were recorded by the voicemail facility on her phone. She listened to them all later, one after the other, without a pause. In respect of these calls, the accused was charged with a s2 offence. The magistrates found as fact that the three calls were distinct and separate, but that the victim had been put in fear on just one occasion. They found the accused guilty and gave him a custodial sentence. His appeal was based upon two grounds. Firstly, that his actions did not amount to a 'course of conduct'. And secondly, that the offence was not committed unless the victim had suffered alarm or distress on more than one occasion. His appeal was dismissed. The Divisional Court held that that a 'course of conduct' could occur within a five-minute period, and that, on a s2 charge, it was sufficient that by virtue of the course of conduct that the victim was alarmed and that it is not necessary for them to have been alarmed on each, or on more than one, occasion. It was said that the purpose of the offence was to criminalise conduct which might not be alarming if committed once but which became alarming by virtue of being repeated.

A 'course of conduct' may fail to be established where the incidents are temporally distant. For example, in *Lau* v *DPP*[256] the fact that four months had elapsed between one incident, when the defendant slapped the victim, and another, when he had threatened her new boyfriend, precluded the finding of a 'course of conduct'. In *Hills*,[257] where the defendant had been violent towards his partner on two occasions six months apart, the fact that they had reconciled their differences and lived together in the interim period meant that the two incidents were not sufficiently connected to amount to a 'course of conduct'.

It can be seen from s7(2) that there is more of a focus upon the effect of the accused's behaviour than the behaviour itself. This victim-centred approach can only be applauded; their feelings are of paramount importance. If the particular victim is alarmed or distressed, it matters not that most people would not have reacted in the same way.[258] However, this begs the question whether the characteristics of the accused can be attributed to the reasonable person for the purpose of determining whether the accused ought to have known that his conduct amounted to harassment of the victim. The answers, it seems, is no. In *Colohan*,[259] the accused was a schizophrenic who had sent a number of abusive and threatening letters to a member of Parliament. He was convicted of a s2 offence but appealed on two grounds. Firstly, he argued that the trial judge had wrongly directed the jury; it was submitted that the jurors should have been told to consider what a reasonable person suffering from schizophrenia would have known. And secondly, he argued that his actions were reasonable when

---

[255] [2003] Crim LR 43 (DC). See also the decision in *Wass* v *DPP*, CO/1101/00, 11 May 2000 (QBD).
[256] [2000] Crim LR 586 (CA).
[257] [2001] Crim LR 318 (CA).
[258] See, for example, the case of *King* v *DPP* (20 June, 2000, unreported).
[259] [2001] 2 FLR 757.

viewed in the light of his illness and that, consequently, he had a viable defence under s1(3)(c).[260] Mr Justice Hughes explained the reasons for dismissing the appeal in the following way:

> 'We agree accordingly with the judge that, except insofar as it requires the jury to consider the information actually in the possession of this defendant, s1(2) requires the jury to answer the question whether he ought to have known that what he was doing amounts to harassment by the objective test of what a reasonable person would think. Its words, we are satisfied, are abundantly clear. As to s1(3)(c), that, we are satisfied, poses even more clearly an objective test, namely whether the conduct is, in the judgment of the jury, reasonable. There is no warrant for attaching to the word "reasonable", or via the words "particular circumstances", the standards or characteristics of the defendant himself.'

Harassment by e-mail is considered to be a serious matter. The decision in the case of *Norman*[261] bears testament to this. Therein, the accused had sent a large number of e-mails to a Jewish radio broadcaster, many of which containing anti-semitic remarks and some in which threats of future violence were made to the victim. The accused was convicted of racially aggravated harassment[262] and sentenced to 18 months' imprisonment. He appealed on two grounds. Firstly, that the broadcaster was known to have a controversial style on air and should not, therefore, be viewed as a vulnerable person. Secondly, that consideration should have been given to the fact that the threats were made online and not face-to-face. In dismissing his appeal, the Court of Appeal focused on what it saw as two aggravating factors present in the case: the accused had sent these many e-mails over a long period of time and their often racially abusive and threatening content was not to be viewed lightly. The court did, however, reduce his sentence by one third, taking into account his previous good character and the fact that he had apologised to the victim.

The s4 offence – putting people in fear of violence

Section 4:

> '(1) A person whose course of conduct causes another to fear, on at least two occasions, that violence will be used against him is guilty of an offence if he knows or ought to know that his course of conduct will cause the other so to fear on each of those two occasions.'

Again, this offence is centred around the victim's reaction to the behaviour in question and the same kind of objective test is used for the purposes of establishing constructive knowledge.[263] However, there is no requirement that the prosecution prove the victim was harassed. What must be shown is that the course of conduct pursued by the accused caused the victim to fear, on at least two occasions, that violence would be used against them. That fear must be specific, not general,[264] and must be for oneself and not, for example, for family members. In *Courti v DPP*,[265] X and Y lived together in Y's flat. The accused lived in a flat nearby. On two occasions, the accused threatened

---

[260] See the discussion of defences under s1(3) on the next page.
[261] [2003] EWCA Crim 3878.
[262] Under s28 Crime and Disorder Act 1998.
[263] See s4(2).
[264] See the case of *Henley* [2000] Crim LR 582.
[265] [2002] Crim LR 131.

violence towards either X or both of them. On the first occasion, the accused was abusive to both of them and threatened to stab X. Y was not frightened for her own safety, but was for the safety of X. On the second occasion, when the accused threatened violence to both of them, X was concerned not for his own safety but for the safety of Y, since X feared that the accused might force his way into Y's flat. The accused was convicted. On appeal, his conviction was quashed. It was held that the offence requires that, on at least two occasions, the victim fears that violence will be used against themselves. It is not sufficient that the accused causes the victim to fear violence against another person or vice versa.

Sections 1(3) and 4(3) provide possible defences to people who are charged with either a s2 or a s4 offence in the following circumstances:

- that the course of conduct was pursued for the purpose of preventing and detecting crime; or

- that it was pursued under any enactment or rule of law or to comply with any condition or requirement imposed by any person under any enactment.[266]

A further defence which is peculiar to the s2 offence is that in the particular circumstances the pursuit of the course of conduct was reasonable.[267] A further defence which is peculiar to the s4 offence is that the pursuit of the course of conduct was reasonable for the protection of himself (the defendant) or another, or for the protection of his or another's property.[268] In relation to any of these potential defences, the burden of proof lies with the accused but the standard of proof is set 'on the balance of probabilities'.[269] It is important to note that if the jury finds the accused not guilty of the s4 offence, they are empowered to find him guilty of an offence under s2, if the evidence supports such a finding.[270] The Act also gives the courts the power to impose restraining orders on those convicted of either offence.[271] Breach of a restraining order, being unlawful conduct, can never be regarded as reasonable[272] and carries a potential sentence of up to five years' imprisonment.[273]

---

[266] See ss1(3)(a) and (b), and ss4(3)(a) and (b), respectively.
[267] See s1(3)(c).
[268] See s4(3)(c).
[269] The usual standard of proof in civil law.
[270] Section 3(5).
[271] See s5.
[272] See the case of *R v DPP, ex parte Moseley and Others*, Judgment of 23 June 1999 (unreported).
[273] Section 5(5).

Index

New Editions of Textbooks

Only £15.95   Due 2005

Textbooks cover the fundamental rudiments of each subject area succinctly and clearly. Topics are broken down into logical chapters, and the Textbooks not only deliver a thorough grounding in the vital principles, cases and legislation, but also encourage the discussion and analysis of moot points.

Administrative Law	**Equity and Trusts**
1 85836 485 X	1 85836 598 8
Commercial Law	**Evidence**
1 85836 592 9	1 85836 599 6
Company Law	**Family Law**
1 85836 487 6	1 85836 600 3
Constitutional Law	**Jurisprudence: Philosophy of Law**
1 85836 489 2	1 85836 601 1
Conflict of Laws	**Land: The Law of Real Property**
1 85836 488 4	1 85836 602 X
Criminal Law	**Law of International Trade**
1 85836 594 5	1 85836 603 8
Criminology	**Law of the European Union**
1 85836 595 3	1 85836 604 6
Employment Law	**Obligations: Contract Law**
1 85836 596 1	1 85836 605 4
English & European Legal Systems	**Obligations: The Law of Tort**
1 85836 597 X	1 85836 606 2

Public International Law
1 85836 607 0

For further information or to place an order, please contact:

Customer Services
Old Bailey Press at Holborn College
Woolwich Road, Charlton
London, SE7 8LN
Telephone: 020 8317 6039
Fax: 020 8317 6004
Website: www.oldbaileypress.co.uk
E-Mail: customerservices@oldbaileypress.co.uk

Old Bailey Press

The Old Bailey Press Integrated Student Law Library is tailor-made to help you at every stage of your studies, from the preliminaries of each subject through to the final examination. The series of Textbooks, Revision WorkBooks, 150 Leading Cases and Cracknell's Statutes are interrelated to provide you with a comprehensive set of study materials.

You can buy Old Bailey Press books from your University Bookshop, your local Bookshop, directly using this form, or you can order a free catalogue of our titles from the address shown overleaf.

The following subjects each have a Textbook, 150 Leading Cases, Revision WorkBook and Cracknell's Statutes unless otherwise stated.

Administrative Law
Commercial Law
Company Law
Conflict of Laws
Constitutional Law
Conveyancing (Textbook and 150 Leading Cases)
Criminal Law
Criminology (Textbook and Sourcebook)
Employment Law (Textbook and Cracknell's Statutes)
English and European Legal Systems
Equity and Trusts
Evidence
Family Law
Jurisprudence: The Philosophy of Law (Textbook, Sourcebook and Revision WorkBook)
Land: The Law of Real Property
Law of International Trade
Law of the European Union
Legal Skills and System (Textbook)
Obligations: Contract Law
Obligations: The Law of Tort
Public International Law
Revenue Law (Textbook, Revision WorkBook and Cracknell's Statutes)
Succession (Textbook, Revision WorkBook and Cracknell's Statutes)

Mail order prices:	
Textbook	£15.95
150 Leading Cases	£12.95
Revision WorkBook	£10.95
Cracknell's Statutes	£11.95
Suggested Solutions 1999–2000	£6.95
Suggested Solutions 2000–2001	£6.95
Suggested Solutions 2001–2002	£6.95
101 Questions and Answers	£7.95
Law Update 2004	£10.95
Law Update 2005	£10.95

Please note details and prices are subject to alteration.

To complete your order, please fill in the form below:

Module	Books required	Quantity	Price	Cost
		Postage		
		TOTAL		

For the UK and Europe, add £4.95 for the first book ordered, then add £1.00 for each subsequent book ordered for postage and packing.

For the rest of the world, add 50% for airmail.

ORDERING

By telephone to Customer Services at 020 8317 6039, with your credit card to hand.

By fax to 020 8317 6004 (giving your credit card details).

Website: www.oldbaileypress.co.uk

E-Mail: customerservices@oldbaileypress.co.uk

By post to: Customer Services, Old Bailey Press at Holborn College, Woolwich Road, Charlton, London, SE7 8LN.

When ordering by post, please enclose full payment by cheque or banker's draft, or complete the credit card details below. You may also order a free catalogue of our complete range of titles from this address.

We aim to despatch your books within 3 working days of receiving your order. All parts of the form must be completed.

Name

Address

Postcode

E-Mail

Telephone

Total value of order, including postage: £

I enclose a cheque/banker's draft for the above sum, or

charge my ☐ Access/Mastercard ☐ Visa ☐ American Express

Cardholder: ....

Card number

☐☐☐☐ ☐☐☐☐ ☐☐☐☐ ☐☐☐☐

Expiry date ☐☐☐☐

Signature: ....Date: ....